D0592150

ACCOUNTING FOR SUCCESS

A History of Price Waterhouse in America 1890–1990

David Grayson Allen
Kathleen McDermott

HARVARD BUSINESS SCHOOL PRESS
Boston, Massachusetts

Printed in the United States of America
97 96 95 94 93 5 4 3 2 1

Unless otherwise noted, all photographs and exhibits were furnished by Price Waterhouse.

The paper used in this publication meets the requirements of the American National Standard for Permanence of Paper for Printed Library Materials Z39.49-1984.

Library of Congress Cataloging-in-Publication Data

Allen, David Grayson, 1943–
Accounting for success : a history of Price Waterhouse in America, 1890–1990 / David Grayson Allen, Kathleen McDermott.
p. cm.
Includes bibliographical references and index.
ISBN 0-87584-328-X
1. Price Waterhouse (Firm)—History. 2. Accounting—United States—History. I. McDermott, Kathleen. II. Title.
HF5616.U7P752 1993
338.7′61657′0973—dc20
92-15492
CIP

CONTENTS

PART II: REGULATED EQUILIBRIUM

PART III: CHALLENGE AND REDIRECTION

List of Exhibits

Preface

I

This book was originally conceived to help celebrate, in 1990, the one hundredth anniversary of Price Waterhouse (PW) in America. In 1987, during Joseph E. Connor's tenure as senior partner, the firm commissioned The Winthrop Group, Inc., to write its history. Because of the comprehensive research, the lengthy writing process, and the publication timetable, the process concluded during Shaun F. O'Malley's term five years later.

When the project began, this study was seen as a companion and sequel to Chester W. DeMond's *Price, Waterhouse & Co. in America* (1951). A partner in the firm, DeMond had produced a charming but internally focused history. As our research proceeded, it became clear that certain themes and issues central to PW's development since World War II had originated earlier. Accordingly, PW and the authors abandoned the plan to produce a book that would be, in effect, a companion volume to DeMond and decided to cover the entire history of the firm. In keeping with PW's original intent, and recognizing the value of the DeMond work, we lay greater stress on modern times, especially the period since World War II.

In writing this history, the authors have had full access to retired and current PW partners. Since this is the story of a partnership, the viewpoints, opinions, and recollections of these individuals are given a central place in the text. We have also examined the minutes of the firm's leadership committees and the partners' files kept in the Office of the

Firm Secretary. Other material has been gathered from a variety of sources, including the National Information Center, the New York practice office Records Center, National Human Resources, the National Administrative Center in Tampa, Florida, the archives of the British firm, and the retired partners themselves.

During the project, we met periodically with an advisory committee consisting of current and retired PW partners and a noted expert in business history. We are grateful for the advice, comments, and suggestions from this group, which included Albert H. Cohen, Burnell H. DeVos, Jr., Richard D. Fitzgerald, Roger G. Marcellin, committee chair Robert G. Nichols, and Harvard Business School professor Richard H.K. Vietor.

A note about authorship: when this project was conceived, David Grayson Allen acted as project director and co-author on early chapter drafts. Co-author Kathleen McDermott then assumed responsibility for expanding and completing the manuscript and subsequently revised the entire text. Davis Dyer served as general editor for the manuscript.

II

This scholarly history of a major accounting firm is unique to the American accounting profession, as befits PW, which is unique among the big firms. PW's long history as the pre-eminent firm has given it unrivaled opportunities and challenges. One important task of this history, then, has been to describe the firm's special place in the profession and in the business world, and to identify the business opportunities and problems attendant on being the profession's leader.

PW's long tenure at the pinnacle of the profession has intrigued many commentators. Beginning in 1930, and continuing today, observers have pointed to the air of mystery that surrounds the firm. Unlike the "blue chip" public companies that it audits, PW has long held its financial and operating information close to the vest. We hoped that a careful business history of this firm, while perhaps dispelling some myths, might also yield important insights about the challenges faced by a decentralized partnership and about the competitive and operational pressures it has experienced over the past four decades.

This book is about the growth of a professional institution, a partnership that has endured and flourished for one hundred years. It is a success story, describing how a small entity grew to dominate its profession and today is generally considered the most prestigious of the large firms. This is also a book about management and policy formation within a leading firm, identifying the changing processes through which practice strategies and organizational structures were developed. Finally, this is a history of the growth of an industry, viewed through the window that PW provides.

The world in which the partnership originated was very different from that of the 1990s, and there was nothing inevitable about PW's rise to leadership in the profession. In 1890, the British firm of PW established an agency in New York. Its sole function in its first year was to investigate the accounts of American breweries for British investors. At the time, Britain was the world's foremost economic power, and its investment in the United States was at an all-time high. All the agency's work came through referrals from the British firm. A single transplanted Englishman ran the American outpost, with temporary help supplied by the parent firm. The new entity operated in an undeveloped, unregulated environment, for although England had legislation starting in the 1840s defining the role of accountants, no corresponding laws existed in the United States. All American accounting firms at the time were small, and professional standards or generally accepted accounting principles as we know them today did not exist. Communication both nationally and internationally was relatively slow, and the fastest mode of transatlantic travel was by steamship.

Both PW and the profession have changed enormously since the firm's early days. The American partnership now numbers more than 900, in more than 100 offices, with 12,000 staff members. This firm, which is now the largest in the global PW organization, leads all other PW firms in developing referral work for multinationals outside its territory and has clients throughout American industry. At present, no dominant international economic power exists, and there are many countries that have adopted a global focus and competitive strategy. In the 1990s, capital is again flowing to Europe and to the Pacific Rim countries. The accounting profession, too, has been transformed into a global industry. The multinational accounting firm is a major business force that seems likely to grow still larger, perhaps through mergers, in the years ahead. Big Six practice is regulated and entrenched, making it difficult for newer or smaller firms to enter the market or to compete. In addition, the big firms' global focus, necessary to serve multinational corporations properly, and their reliance on instantaneous communication and computer technology place them squarely in the forefront of change in the 1990s.

PW's first century divides readily into three fairly distinct periods. The first embraces the years from 1890 to the late 1920s and the establishment and Americanization of the practice. The second, from the early 1930s to the early 1970s, encompasses the firm's period of dominance in a regulated environment as auditors to America's largest and most powerful corporations. The third era carries us to the present time, a period of global challenges and quickening competition.

During the first phase, many of PW's enduring and distinctive characteristics were established. The gradual Americanization of the firm, its decentralized structure, dispersed offices, autonomous partners, leading reputation, and generalist orientation were all in place by the early 1930s. The securities laws enacted in 1933 and 1934 mandated periodic financial reports of listed companies and marked the start of PW's long period of unrivaled professional leadership. The audit, which became the centerpiece of the firm's practice, assumed a new importance as the basis for the financial statements that led to greater investor confidence. George O. May's key role in the regulatory process and his extraordinary force of personality and intellect gave the firm an unmatched visibility, as well as an enduring reputation for integrity and probity. Also during these years, PW's roster of *Fortune* 500 audit clients—for many years more than twice that of its nearest competitor—brought a luster to the firm.

With the onset of the oil crisis and the beginning of American adjustment to the international economy in the early 1970s, PW along with the rest of American business embarked on a troubled and tumultuous period. Global challenge, heightened competition among the large firms, the growth of nonaudit services, a long series of congressional investigations, and a dramatic rise in litigation directed at accountants were among the most important changes characterizing the modern period.

Cutting across PW's century are six principal themes. The first is the central role of the partner. A study of a manufacturing company might highlight key products or markets. Price Waterhouse, in contrast, must give center stage to its people, for it is a partnership engaged in providing a professional service. The firm has been highly selective in its partnership admissions process and, as a result, its partners have always believed that they are "in a class by themselves." More than one partner told us of his first partnership meeting, when he surveyed with awe the tremendous talent assembled in one room. Out of this collective self-image grew a mutual respect and collegiality. Clearly, throughout its history, the firm has benefited from the frank and generous spirit growing out of these institutional values.

Though some aspects of the partnership endure, others appear to be yielding to modern imperatives. For example, PW traditionally governed itself under an unusually decentralized organizational structure and gave its few and far-flung partners a wide latitude. Today, the partnership is still relatively small compared to other accounting firms, and the "professionally autonomous partner" remains close to the core of the firm's strategic thinking. Since the early 1980s, however, a growing emphasis on specialization has begun to dislodge the traditional "generalist" orientation of firm partners. Similarly, a distrust, even disdain, for marketing has been transformed into a partnershipwide belief in the importance of identifying new service areas and developing new clients. Finally, a move away from the firm's geographical organizational structure toward another centered around services is a clear departure from most of PW's history.

A second theme running through this history is the significant role that the law has played in shaping the profession's rights and responsibilities. Government regulation, for example, furnished enormous opportunities for the profession in the audit and tax fields. Yet the law has also, more recently, provided a serious constraint in the form of liability suits brought against accountants. These suits underscore the inherent tensions of the professional role, for in their audit work accountants must serve both their clients and the public interest.

A third theme, the changing nature of accountants' services, can be traced in a circular fashion. The Securities Exchange Act of 1934 required listed companies to issue periodic financial statements, making accounting and auditing work the firm's raison d'être for the next forty years. During PW's early decades, the firm provided a wide array of services, just as it does today. In this respect, PW is returning to an emphasis on the consulting work that was at the core of its practice a century ago.

Fourth, the business environment for accountants is continually evolving, so that aspects of practice in the 1990s strikingly resemble those of a century ago. Now, as then, it is a volatile, highly competitive world, with much of the work risky and episodic. In 1890, the agency competed against other British accountants, and American accountants as well, to provide a little-known service. Similarly, in the 1990s, the firm must contend not only with the other firms in the Big Six, but also with information technology companies, large management consulting firms, and financial institutions to provide innovative products in new markets. By contrast, the interlude of 1934 to the 1970s saw a more ordered, less threatening practice environment that allowed many firms, and particularly PW, to grow powerful and influential.

The fifth theme identifies the public face of the firm's leadership. In a profession not generally known for its visibility, PW's leaders have consistently shown a high profile, and the firm's role as a leader in new approaches to accounting research and practice has greatly enhanced its prestige. From the first decades of the twentieth century to the present, the firm has attracted and developed individuals capable of assuming public roles, either as leaders of the profession, as public servants, or as spokespeople for the critical issues of their time.

A final theme is the firm's worldwide approach to its business. Although the U.S. firm grew to be the largest of the PW partnerships, it has always respected its relationships to the other PW firms around the world. Like the DeMond book, which ends the U.S. firm's first fifty years with the establishment of the Price Waterhouse & Co. (International Firm), this history closes with the American partnership's recognition that, more than ever, its interest lies with the worldwide PW organization and in a global strategy.

The structure of this book reflects the nature of the commission to the authors to present a narrative history of a single firm over a one-hundred-year period. This form has its clear virtues, including the opportunity to tell the full story of a significant institution and unlimited access to documents and records generally inaccessible to serious historians. The form also has its limitations, among them the obligation to be comprehensive, which limits the possibilities of exploring themes that might interest academic or other specialist readers. For example, this is not a history of practice, primarily, or of the ideas and techniques of the accounting profession. Rather, technical accounting matters are discussed to illustrate their impacts on PW's growth and on its policies. Similarly, the book does not make detailed comparisons between PW and its competitors. We did not have access to the inner workings of other large firms; as a result, our ability to collect data and draw conclusions on market share, client base, and strategy has been limited by the information available in the public record. A final constraint has been PW's obligation of confidentiality regarding specific client matters.

III

This book consists of eight chapters. The first two describe the partnership's origins in the United States as a one-person agency of the British firm, its subsequent establishment, and its eventual success in its own right. The next three recount the story of the firm's accession, after the securities legislation of the early 1930s, to the pinnacle of the profession and its dominance in a regulated environment through the 1960s. The final three chapters cover the period of global competition and disequilibrium from the early 1970s to 1990.

Although one theme of this history is the decentralized nature of the firm and the autonomy of its partners, we have chosen to organize the book in a "dynastic" manner. This reflects our view that there was a difference between the way the firm's policy and public role were established and the way individual partners and specific practice offices conducted their business. Incoming senior partners often fashioned policies and directions different from those of their predecessors, and partners often recall the various periods by the particular leaders, many of whom left their distinctive stamp on an era. Over time, however, a PW senior partner's highly personalized pattern of direction gradually gave way, as the changing service requirements of clients, the perfecting of automated information technologies, and the growing internationalization of business compelled the firm to experiment with more formalized and hierarchical organizational structures to ensure effective planning and control.

We also sought to place the firm's development within a larger context. PW's history is inextricably linked to that of a significant body of its clients—American big business in general—and to the environments in which they have operated. The unfolding dynamic of American business history over the last century provides a solid context for understanding today's challenges.

Chapter 1 establishes the origins of the British firm and the first ten years of its American agency. It describes the emergence of the accounting profession in Britain during the unfolding of the Industrial Revolution, as well as the birth of the British firm of PW in 1865. As British capitalists began to invest heavily in the United States in the 1870s and 1880s, they increasingly engaged their accounting firms to make periodic visits there. In 1890, PW established an American agency to handle these investigations. During its first decade, the two PW agents, Lewis Jones and William Caesar, struggled to establish their business on a secure basis. Chapter 1 closes with the death of Jones and the early retirement of Caesar, but with the establishment of a separate American partnership, whose practice was already the largest of its kind in the United States.

Chapter 2 relates the important role played by Arthur Lowes Dickinson from 1901 to 1911. Although an Englishman, Dickinson quickly grasped the importance of playing by American rules, even to the extent of relying on public advertising, much to the consternation of the British partners. During this period, the U.S. firm began to develop its extraordinary range of clients, encompassing the J.P. Morgan interests such as U.S. Steel, the large trusts, and significant government agencies. Until his retirement in 1911, Dickinson sought to secure an ever-greater measure of independence from London. George O. May succeeded Dickinson. As an administrator, he followed the directions set by his predecessor by opening new offices, hiring more local accountants, Americanizing practices and methods, and overseeing the rise of what is now called consulting work. Chapter 2 closes with the growing contemporary sense of PW as a native American accounting firm.

With Chapter 3 we begin our study of the second phase of PW's history. May's successor, William Campbell, led the firm through the

Crash of 1929 and the onset of the Great Depression until his untimely death in 1934. Of all the developments of this tumultuous period, the securities laws of the early 1930s played the most critical role in PW's destiny, for they initiated four decades of regulated equilibrium in the profession and pushed the audit to the center of the firm's practice. During this period, May's work as chairman of the firm and as a leading spokesman for the profession enabled PW to achieve and consolidate its pre-eminent reputation. John Scobie's subsequent senior partnership was almost immediately engulfed by the Securities and Exchange Commission's (SEC) investigation into the McKesson & Robbins matter in 1939—the first important case under the agency's authority. The affair also had an important effect on internal work patterns, for as a result, PW (and the profession as a whole) changed the way it staffed and managed audits and considerably reduced the nonprofessional temporary staff who had performed much of its work in the past. The peculiar circumstances of World War II made the few remaining, and aging, partners ever more independent and led to the hiring of college-educated women as auditors. Scobie's efforts to manage the crises of this period may have contributed to the decline in his health; he died in office in 1944.

Chapter 4, which covers the terms of senior partners Percival Brundage and John Inglis, depicts a golden age. Brundage and Inglis shared similar outlooks and goals, a convergence that made for fifteen years of stable leadership. Both also held important public and professional posts. Brundage served as president of the American Institute of Accountants and, after retirement, as President Dwight Eisenhower's budget director. Inglis contributed to the American Institute of Accountants in a number of distinguished capacities and became president of the National Association of Accountants. His noted insistence on a personal touch with partners and staff underscored their importance in a decentralized, democratic organization. The changing business environment and flow of capital to postwar Europe in this period led PW to establish the International Firm, and opportunities within the profession at home spurred it to a series of mergers with other, smaller firms. The chapter examines the growth and change in the firm's practice, particularly the creation of a small "systems" department to meet client needs for assistance with electronic data processing. The profession's relationship to the law can be clearly seen in the context of the tax practice, where important new legislation in the postwar period brought both increased demands for accounting expertise and sharp conflict with the bar.

Chapter 5 covers the 1960s and the senior partnership of Herman Bevis against a backdrop of the United States as the world's richest and most powerful nation. Price Waterhouse participated fully in the prosperity of this decade, although by its end, signs indicated that the professional environment had grown less tranquil. Corporate trends of growth, merger, and foreign expansion, the burgeoning computer industry, and competition from other large accounting firms figured prominently in the PW business environment. In meeting these challenges, the firm's SEC and international departments were enlarged, and its Tax Department expanded to handle the steady flow of congressional and Internal Revenue Service (IRS) enactments, while the new Management Advisory Services (MAS) Department struggled to secure sufficient computer staff to meet its assignments. On balance, PW competed reactively, pursuing the same course that had ensured its past success.

Within the profession, Bevis took a central, highly visible role in the debate over accounting principles, but he could not prevent either the lack of agreement that followed this debate or the demise of the Accounting Principles Board, the profession's standard-setting body. More positively, his decision to litigate for practice rights in Florida opened the way for all large firms to practice nationally, underscoring both the importance of the legal environment to the profession and PW's traditional leadership role. Within the firm, Bevis's management philosophy, particularly his emphasis on planned growth, led to much discussion about PW's unique nature, and his efforts to strengthen the partnership and develop its infrastructure left a strong mark on the era.

Chapter 6 sounds a different note as it opens the discussion of the third phase of PW's history. The 1970s were marked by contraction, disorientation, and intensified public scrutiny. The bear stock market of the late 1960s and early 1970s heightened criticism of the profession and led to an activist SEC, a full-scale congressional investigation, and the real threat of new government regulation. In addition, the legal environment, which in the past had been a source of opportunity for accountants, became a significant obstacle, as a wave of litigation concerning the financial statements of troubled companies swept the large firms. Within the profession, competition escalated, and reproposals were occasionally required by clients of long standing. Under the hand of John Biegler, PW met these challenges head on, and through his forceful representation, re-emphasized its claim to leadership of the Big Eight. Within the partnership, Biegler made important democratic reforms and established a distinct, centralized, practice-support National Office. Amid the tumultuous changes in the business and professional environment, PW initiated a federal government consulting practice and a public relations function and introduced a new emphasis on marketing and industry specialization.

Chapter 7 covers the decade of the 1980s and the administration of Joseph Connor. Globalization of the economy, the spread of information technology, and the restructuring of American industry emerged as the most significant forces driving the business environment of the 1980s. To address these forces, PW acted aggressively to develop and sustain a firmwide strategy for the future, emphasizing specialization. As in the 1950s, the firm contemplated mergers as a competitive strategy, although its plan to unite with Deloitte, Haskins & Sells did not succeed. Following the flow of capital, PW made an important commitment to strengthening its international practice. The ever-growing complexity of tax work, and more important, the rise of consulting services driven by the information technology needs of clients, assumed a more central place in the firm's plans for its future. In his efforts to provide more value-added services from the audit base, for example, Connor, like many PW leaders before him, emerged as a significant public figure.

Chapter 8 briefly reports on key events and themes in the period since 1988, when Shaun O'Malley became senior partner, and identifies aspects of PW's plans for the future. The Appendix provides a list of partners.

As the decade of the 1990s proceeds, American business is girding itself for the intensified competitive challenge to come. Part of that process is a frank appraisal of historical strengths and weaknesses, such as is contained in this history. It is our hope that out of such an inquiry will spring an understanding and an ability to grasp future opportunities. Like the oft-mentioned concept of the PW partner, nothing about PW's current position has developed in historical isolation. Present partners and staff will perhaps find a context for and an understanding of the firm's inherited strengths and its challenges for the future. Similarly, retired partners and former staff who find the firm's present organization or direction not readily understandable may learn that in fact there is a logic to the changes and a relationship to the firm's earlier days. Finally, the general public will learn how PW's rise to prominence fits into the larger trends of American business and economic history.

PART I

ESTABLISHMENT AND AMERICANIZATION

CHAPTER 1

British Parentage, 1850–1901

Following the American Civil War, the United States quickly emerged as a rapidly growing industrial power. Throughout the 1870s, and especially the 1880s, British capitalists invested heavily in the robust American economy. To oversee their financial interests, British investors increasingly engaged their accounting firms to make periodic visits to the United States.

It was in this buoyant economic context that the British accounting firm of Price, Waterhouse & Co. (PW) decided to open an American agency. Although at first the transatlantic outpost was closely monitored from London, distance and the impact of American conditions on the practice immediately exerted powerful influences on the new agency. During the tumultuous 1890s, the greater part of the office's British client base offered only nonrenewable work, but the wave of mergers in the United States allowed the agency to develop a new practice and, in so doing, to forge an enduring relationship with American big business. Fairly early on, the British firm recognized its United States agency as a distinct operation. The early history of PW in America is primarily the story of the changes in the relationship between the British parent and the American offspring.

DEVELOPMENT OF THE ACCOUNTING PROFESSION

Although accounting practice dates from antiquity, the formation of an accounting profession was closely tied to the rise of a modern industrial society in Britain during the late eighteenth century. The need for accounting services emerged slowly, but by the early decades of the nineteenth century a flurry of textbooks and handbooks on accounting had appeared, reflecting the impact of the Industrial Revolution. Several larger English cities also began to note a few "accomptants" among the listings of their inhabitants.

Accountancy was still an indeterminate calling in Britain as late as the 1830s. Men then engaged in accounting not only made simple accounts, but also found it financially necessary to act as auctioneers, appraisers, agents, and debt collectors. Those who called themselves accountants were held in no special esteem and possessed no monopoly in their services. Each of their skills provided occasional employment to many men engaged in other businesses. A method of distinguishing accountants had to come from an external source.

Perhaps more than any other profession in Britain, accounting was shaped by legislation. Throughout the nineteenth century, acts of Parliament came to describe more precisely the work and responsibility of accountants in the fields of bankruptcy, auctions, and making accounts, the tasks that provided a major focus for British accountants throughout most of the century. At the same time, legislation also changed and regulated the organization and conduct of business and in so doing helped to create the need for corporate accounting. Although industrialization was well under way by the mid-nineteenth century, legal restraints inhibited the size of enterprises and retarded their growth. The passage by Parliament of several "Companies Acts" released entrepreneurial energies by encouraging the creation of corporations with limited liability, which provided a new sphere of activity for accountants. While permitting many private companies to become publicly subscribed, the Companies Acts insisted on the creation of financial safeguards for a widening group of stockholders and the public at large. As a consequence, financial investigations and accounting and auditing for corporations, stockholders, and investors became increasingly more important areas of practice for leading British accountants after the mid-1860s.

Securing legal recognition of a sphere of professional activity for accountants was a slow, evolving process. The Bankruptcy Act of 1831 empowered the appointment of "Official Assignees," and for the first time accountants were specifically mentioned as qualified to hold such positions, although the work could also be taken on by "merchants and brokers." For the most part, however, accountants were mentioned in legislation only by inference and not by name. In the 1842 Act for the Relief of Insolvent Debtors, for instance, a party whose debts were less than £300 could present to the bankruptcy court a petition with a "full and true schedule" of debts. If the bankrupt could afford it, his listing of debts might be made out by an accountant.[1]

Other legislation in the 1840s more precisely defined accounting work and the role of accountants. The Act for the Registration, Incorporation and Regulation of Joint Stock Companies, passed in 1844, required joint-stock companies to file a list of company directors and an annual balance sheet with the Registrar of Companies. Outside auditors, working with an inside auditor appointed by the board of directors, were required to make a "fare and full" statement of the company's financial condition, reflecting the free access to the books that was accorded to them while compiling their report on the balance sheet. The 1844 Joint Stock Banking Act required that shareholders of joint-stock banks be provided with both an annual balance sheet and an accounting of profit and loss. In addition, shareholders were empowered to elect auditors, and the joint-stock banks were required to issue monthly statements of assets and liabilities.[2]

Other important developments affecting accountants soon followed. The 1845 Companies Clauses Consolidation Act went one important step beyond the Registration Act by granting company auditors the right, at the company's expense, to appoint accountants (or others they deemed proper) to assist them. In 1848, the Winding-Up Act effectively required a public accountant to serve as the official manager in liquidations. Within a relatively short time, therefore, a more well-defined occupation was available for accountants. No longer, in addition to preparing accounts, were they forced to seek employment as appraisers, auctioneers, agents, and debt collectors, all endeavors that many others could perform. There was now a growing sphere of activity in which their competence as auditors was both recognized and, in many cases, required.[3]

This change was reflected in the increasing number of individuals who called themselves accountants. In London, for example, the number of accountants listed in city directories between 1799 and 1860 increased from eleven to over three hundred, with most of that change occurring after 1840. The growth and permanency of the profession were evident in the opening of leading accounting practices in London. By the late 1840s, the antecedents of several modern firms—Deloitte, Touche, PW, and Ernst & Young, for instance—had been established. The first professional organizations soon followed. Accounting societies were formed by royal charter in Edinburgh and Glasgow in 1854 and 1855, respectively. In 1870, the Institute of Accountants was established in London, followed two years later by a rival organization, the Society of Accountants in England. By 1873, there was a professional accounting society in Manchester and, by 1877, one in Sheffield. In 1880, the Institute of Chartered Accountants of England and Wales was established.[4]

Other legal changes expanded the scope of the new accounting profession. Limiting the liability of stockholders had been prohibited by British law following the passage of the Bubble Act of 1720, legislation enacted at the zenith of an unparalleled speculative frenzy. As a result, most businesses in the eighteenth and early nineteenth centuries in Britain had been by legal, if not economic necessity, family-managed concerns or close partnerships that functioned without large sums of capital raised through stock subscriptions and without the services of accountants.[5]

The only exceptions under this restrictive legislation were canal and railroad projects, which both required vast sums of money that could be realized only through public subscription of stock. Such ventures sought special exemptions through private bills in Parliament. The record of their financial management, however, was often scandalous. Reflecting a concern for the stockholders of these enterprises, the Board of Trade gave notice in 1844 that before private bills for railway construction could be introduced in Parliament, full information, including "the estimate of cost of construction, of traffic and of working expenses," must be prepared, presumably with the help of accountants.[6]

By the mid-nineteenth century, it had become increasingly clear that if the British economy were to expand, other forms of commercial enterprise, particularly industrial concerns, needed access to wider sources of finance in order to extend their operations. With the passage of the Companies Acts of 1856 and 1862, Parliament sought to permit any business organization to raise capital by selling public shares and to protect the venture through limited liability. It also sought to safeguard investors by insisting that such businesses submit to extensive financial scrutiny. The 1862 Companies Act, for instance, contained provisions covering proper maintenance of accounts, balancing of books, and preparation and audit of balance sheets. The law made no mention of auditors, or of the qualifications of those taking on these financial responsibilities, but it became customary for professional accountants to do this work.[7]

The Companies Acts provided a new and growing market for accounting services. In the twenty years that followed the passage of the 1862 Act, some 18,000 companies were incorporated and registered, and by the turn of the century, an average of 8,000 companies were registered annually as corporations. The lifting of restraints on incorporation led not only to an increased need for auditing services, but also to a growth of insolvency work for accountants, particularly in times of economic downturn. In the two decades that followed the 1862 legislation, an estimated one-quarter to one-third of all businesses formed under its provisions failed. Nevertheless, by the 1880s, there was a general shift in fee income for major accounting firms from insolvency to audit work.[8]

In the years that followed the 1862 Act, limited liability and strict financial standards were applied to other forms of business organization in Britain, such as banks, building societies, and industrial and provident societies. The Companies Act of 1900 made an external audit compulsory for any company registered under the law, and the 1907 Companies Act authorized public access to corporate balance sheets.[9]

PW IN BRITAIN

PW was formally established in 1865, although the firm's history antedated its founding.[10] Samuel Lowell Price, the first senior partner, was born in 1821, the younger son of a Bristol salt-glaze stone potter. He began work for Bradley, Barnard & Co., a firm of Bristol accountants, auctioneers, and agents for bankruptcies. By 1848, that partnership had dissolved, and Price briefly entered into another partnership with William Edwards in London. Although Price and Edwards remained lifelong friends, their professional association lasted only a year. Notice of its termination was given in the *London Gazette* on December 24, 1849, a date since regarded as the beginning of what would later become the firm of PW.[11]

For the next decade and a half, Price apparently continued as a sole practitioner, until he decided to form a partnership in 1865 with a friend, William Hopkins Holyland. Holyland, who was born in 1807, had served as principal clerk in the accounting firm of Coleman, Turquand, Youngs & Company, where he had developed considerable expertise in liquidations and bankruptcies. Apparently both Price and Holyland, or at least the latter, felt that they needed a younger man in the new partnership. Holyland suggested Edwin Waterhouse, whom he had known when the two men both worked at Coleman, Turquand, Youngs & Company. Born in 1841 in Liverpool, Waterhouse was the son of a Quaker merchant family and was brought up in a "somewhat austere atmosphere."[12] Before embarking on a career in accounting, he had graduated from University College, London.

Although Waterhouse had left Coleman, Turquand, Youngs & Company in 1864 to practice on his own, Holyland saw him frequently in Leeds while on business, visits that gave him the opportunity to inquire into Waterhouse's interest in joining the new firm. Waterhouse recorded Holyland's proposal in his diary, noting its attraction. "I have been doing very well for myself during the last few months," he observed, "but the offer seemed to open out chances of quickly attaining a wider experience, whilst ensuring a more steady practice and affording me the advantages of assistance should I need it." After consultation with his father and business friends, he agreed to join Price and Holyland, and the partnership was made final on May 1, 1865.[13] By arrangement, Waterhouse and Holyland each received a 25 percent share in the firm and Price a 50 percent share. In addition, Waterhouse made cash payments of £1,000 to Price and £250 to Holyland. The partners established their offices at 44 Gresham Street in London, where the firm remained until 1899. It was known as Price, Holyland & Waterhouse until 1874, a few years after Holyland's retirement, and was thereafter renamed Price, Waterhouse & Co.[14]

Despite his junior status at the time of the partnership's founding, Waterhouse, more than his seniors, was responsible for building the practice into one of the most respected in England. Before Holyland's retirement in 1871, the partners had forged a strong traditional accounting practice in liquidations, bankruptcies, and arbitrations. In the newer fields of auditing and investigations, developed after the passage of the Companies Acts of 1856 and 1862, Waterhouse became a pre-eminent figure who played a leading role in the evolving accounting profession.

The firm's reputation was closely tied to the professional accomplishments of its partners. Waterhouse's important achievements began when he accepted the prestigious position of accountant and auditor for the London & North Western Railway. In this capacity he introduced significant improvements in operating statistics, which aided company personnel in making performance assessments and decisions involving resource allocations. More important, Waterhouse fought, and won against heavy odds, the battle to maintain separate capital from revenue expenditures, a distinction that reduced managerial discretion in reporting level of profits, which had sometimes been inflated to maintain shareholder confidence and the price of stock.

Waterhouse became widely known for his expertise in railroad work. In 1867, he was asked to investigate the accounts of a mismanaged railroad. This experience led to his playing a role the following year in formulating new legislation on railroad finance regulations. During the 1870s, Waterhouse was appointed auditor for several major joint-stock banks, including the London & Westminster Bank. In that capacity he served jointly with William Turquand, to whom he once had been apprenticed.

Price had been deeply involved with the Institute of Accountants in the 1870s until it and other small accounting societies were absorbed into the Institute of Chartered Accountants in England and Wales in 1880. Waterhouse emulated his partner's service to the profession by becoming a founding member of the new Institute. He was active in the Institute for the next thirty-five years, serving first in Price's seat on its council from 1887 until 1915 and as president from 1892 to 1894.

Throughout his later life Waterhouse applied his professional skills to public affairs. In 1887, for instance, he served, along with Frederick Whinney, as an adviser to the British government on an accounting reorganization of government departments. He later represented the Institute of Chartered Accountants on a government committee formed to investigate and develop legislation for joint-stock companies, an effort that led to the Companies Act of 1900. When an amendment to the law was being considered in 1906, his appointment to the formulating committee was endorsed by the *Accountant* magazine, which observed that "no one will be disposed to find fault with the selection of Mr Edwin Waterhouse, whose experience in company matters is unique."[15]

For its first twenty years, PW had only a handful of partners and grew modestly. Revenues from professional work between 1866 and 1887 increased from a little over £9,000 to about £15,000 per year. Between 1887 and 1890 there was a sharp rise, from £14,886 to £34,059, much of this increase attributable to American work. By 1900, revenues had increased to £47,842, again largely as a result of opportunities in America.[16]

The principal cause of this unexpected growth clashed squarely with one of Waterhouse's most cherished tenets, his belief that the partnership should not expand physically outside London. Waterhouse had misgivings about use of the firm's name on work that was beyond the control of the London office, and he always favored sending assistants to the provinces rather than opening new offices, in order to ensure uniform standards of practice and ethics. Opening an office in the United States would provide the exception, as well as an exceptional opportunity, but within Britain Waterhouse's policy remained intact for more than a decade. The first PW office outside London—in Liverpool—was not opened until 1904.[17]

BRITISH INVESTMENT IN THE UNITED STATES

The PW decision to establish an American office would not have taken place had it not been for the increase of British capital investment in the United States. British investment in its former colonies had a long and deep history, stretching back to the first settlements in the seventeenth century. However, aside from relatively small industrial ventures and the activities of British land companies, the first major spurts of investment occurred in the 1830s and early 1840s, when state governments sought funds for internal improvements, most notably for canals and railroads. Investment activity picked up again in the late 1840s until 1857, with increasing attention paid to railroads.[18]

The prodigious growth of British capital exports to the United States after the Civil War was the result of attractive American opportunities and also, more important, of the growth of an investment surplus in Britain.[19] The English middle class began to bring more capital into the market by mid-century, thus initiating an era of expansion that lasted until the beginning of World War I.[20] Much of this increased capital went to the United States. The level of all foreign investment in the United States, which had been about $380 million in 1853, grew to approximately $1.5 billion by 1869. (As a point of comparison, it was not until the 1880s that Congress authorized a peacetime budget in excess of $1 million.)[21]

Throughout the final decades of the nineteenth century, railroad securities attracted many British investors, as they had before the Civil War, with the peak of interest in railroads occurring in the 1890s and 1900s. Overseas investors were also interested in a wide range of other opportunities, many of which involved the exploitation of natural resources. Foreign-owned enterprises included dealings in land, mortgages, cattle, and oil, as well as with banking and insurance companies and various mining operations.[22] Large-scale industry, protected by limited liability, also attracted investors.

Meanwhile, in Britain, flotations and consolidations of British breweries—Guinness and Ind Coope in 1886, and, later, Watney with Combe & Reids—produced companies whose profitability increased significantly as a result of economies of scale in distribution.[23] British promoters sought out comparable opportunities in the United States. In 1889 alone, more than one hundred existing American breweries were consolidated into twenty-three British-owned breweries and liquor companies, involving $75 million in capital.[24] These and other flotations in the United States, which often mirrored changing patterns in British industry, came to occupy PW's early practice in America.

Although British investment in the United States was continuous, it was also variable, fluctuating in response to economic circumstances in both countries. The flow of British capital surged after the Panic of 1873 and crested in 1890, when Baring Brothers, which had been heavily involved in American investment for years, collapsed. British capital exports declined precipitously thereafter, worsening during the Panic of 1893, until about 1897, when they again turned upward, reaching a peak about ten years later.[25] This volatile change of fortunes had a dramatic impact on PW's American agency.

The growth of British capital exports also led to an increase in the number and kinds of financial intermediaries in the London money market specializing in foreign securities. Though the larger houses such as Rothschild, Baring, and Hambro were well placed to handle the loans for foreign governments and corporations, the aggregate monetary value and the market share of issues they undertook eroded after 1870. In their place came a wide range of issuing houses such as special-purpose syndicates, small companies with stock exchange connections, and joint-stock banks.

American company flotations at this time were largely handled by individuals or "ephemeral promoting groups" and, to a much lesser extent, by trust and financial companies. Larger financial houses were involved only rarely.[26] Since there was no permanent intermediate agency to evaluate new ventures, the issuing houses came to rely on accountants to make a report of earnings on the company in question. The accountant's report became an indispensable element of the prospectus issued by a promoter with his offer to the public.

Central to many American promotional activities in the closing decades of the nineteenth century, and particularly to those in which PW took part, was Henry Osborne O'Hagan, a London company promoter who founded the City of London Contract Corporation in 1882. O'Hagan had gained enough experience in his teenage years with a London promotional firm to set up his own independent company in the 1870s to specialize in the promotion of street car companies, coal mines, and breweries. A decade later, under the aegis of his City of London Contract Corporation, he expanded his interests to include numerous American companies at a time when the British investment market was buoyant.[27]

To help prospect for, negotiate, and settle several dozen American investment opportunities, O'Hagan relied on William D. Guthrie, a New York lawyer in the firm of Seward, Da Costa & Guthrie. (The successor firm, Cravath, Swaine & Moore, has served as outside counsel to PW's U.S. firm since 1890.)[28] Having decided that "the days of any dealings with English breweries appeared to be numbered," O'Hagan turned to the United States for comparable opportunities for his British clientele. His first American brewery flotation, completed in 1889, involved the amalgamation of three Rochester, New York, breweries into the Bartholomay Brewing Co. of America. In preparation for the merger, O'Hagan asked PW in London to make audits of the companies' accounts. George Sneath, who became partner in 1885, and Joseph Gurney Fowler, who became partner in 1887, were sent over, along with some of the London staff. The work was the first of a number of brewery mergers that PW investigated for O'Hagan, providing a critical volume of work for the firm in the United States between 1889 and 1891. Other work undertaken for O'Hagan in the following years involved meat-packing companies and various industrial concerns, as well as stockyard operations.[29]

The trip to the upstate New York breweries was not the first visit of PW partners to the United States on investigation work. These had begun as early as 1873. Subsequent firm visits, particularly by Sneath and Fowler, gradually increased in regularity.[30] Despite his strong disinclination to create branch offices, Waterhouse acknowledged by 1887 that "the business was growing and an American connection was springing up which made it necessary for us to send Mr Sneath, or a principal clerk, frequently across the Atlantic."[31] Repeated trips by partners and staff over the following three years, as well as the surge in investigation work in the United States, underscored the desirability of permanent American representation for PW.

THE AMERICAN AGENCY

PW was not alone in its decision to establish an office in the United States. A number of other British accountants followed British investment to the United States, particularly in the late 1880s, to undertake company investigations. As one English accountant observed:

> Toward the end of the year 1888 and the beginning of 1889, accountants in practice here experienced a feeling of much curiosity and surprise to find suddenly amongst them a number of English and Scottish engaged in special and important accounting work for a number of industrial undertakings in this country. . . . These operations were confined in the first place almost exclusively to American breweries, which in those days were undoubtedly large profit-making undertakings.[32]

The result of PW's efforts to secure investigation work for American brewery consolidations during the frenzied years between 1888 and 1890, including primarily O'Hagan's flotations and some others as well, were impressive. Among the eighteen brewing holding companies (consisting of more than seventy operating units) registered on the London Stock Exchange during that period, almost half were serviced by PW. With the prospect of other flotations in the months and years ahead, this concentration of work seemed reason enough for the partners to establish an American agency.[33]

To open the New York office, the firm selected Lewis Davies Jones, who had served on the London staff since early 1877 and who had been sent to the United States on several occasions. By an agreement drafted by New York lawyer William Guthrie and signed by Waterhouse, Sneath, Fowler, and Jones on September 11, 1890, Jones became the American agent for PW and manager of the "Agency or branch . . . established or about to be established in New York or elsewhere in America," effective on the first day of that month.[34] (At the time Chicago was also being considered as the location for the agency's office, as it was geographically closer to the flotation work that was being undertaken.)[35]

Despite increased business in the United States, PW approached the prospect of a permanent American office with caution and conservatism. The agreement with Jones allowed him to remain manager and agent until June 1894, unless the firm decided to terminate the relationship earlier with a three-month notice. The London office would supply him with working funds and a staff, and Jones was instructed to "undertake all work entrusted to him by the Firm in connection therewith, whether in North, Central or South America." Prospective work for the agency was classified as either "A business" or "B business." The former included "financial investigations" arranged by the London office or by any member of the firm in the United States, and "any other investigations or examinations made by the Agency" in which the firm name would be used in a prospectus or statement offering shares or securities. B business included audits for public or private companies, or of firms or individuals in the United States, or any other business not included in that outlined for A business.[36]

Jones, however, lacked the authority to handle American business on his own. He was instructed not to sign the firm name to reports or certificates "unless first specially authorized by the Firm in each case." This authorization could be given only by a visiting partner, such as Fowler, or by the London office after draft reports, with working papers, had been sent for examination and final approval. Jones was not allowed to take on work in his own name without prior consultation, and all fees from such activities went to the agency. Financial records had to be kept and copies of these sent to London periodically. It was agreed that Jones would receive a minimum salary, or 20 percent of the agency's profits, based on all of the income received from B business and on the value of time and expenses rendered by the agency on A business. Jones was credited with the gross receipts for his time and expenses, but partners who came to the United States in connection with either A business or B business were entitled to charge their time and expenses to the American accounts. In addition, the agency was charged interest on working funds.[37]

The American agency established its office at 45 Broadway in New York, and work was under way in the fall of 1890.[38] Its first bill, a

$3,000 fee written out in Jones's hand on September 25, covered an examination of the New York Belting and Packing Co. A month later, the office made an examination of accounts for the International Okonite Co. The agency also took part in two capitalizations that year, one of $25 million for O'Hagan's Chicago Junction Railway & Union Stock Yards Company, and the other of $3 million for the New York Belting and Packing Co. For the most part, however, brewery clients provided constant and steady work during the first year of operation.[39]

Jones was forced to contend with all the problems of a startup business. Important concerns involving personnel, costs, logistics, and management were made more difficult by his constant travel to supervise work. The London office sent over a steady stream of temporary staff to help with investigations and examinations. But ordinary living expenses, which Jones gauged to be twice as high in New York as in London, and travel costs for these men were not charged to clients, but to the agency, making its overall operation much less profitable. Jones appealed to London, asking if he could employ local staff, but the firm refused. The London partners insisted on using their own personnel, because they feared clients might raise objections if their accounts were examined by Americans.[40]

Jones's constant travel and attention to distant clients greatly concerned the London office. The pressing needs to manage the agency office and to respond to business opportunities were substantially alleviated in 1891, when the partners decided to send the agency William James Caesar, "an excellent man & capable of taking up all sorts of work."[41]

Caesar had already acquired considerable and varied experience in the United States. He had started out on his own in Edinburgh, and had worked as an auditor in London and Paris before being engaged to do investigation work involving American companies. He had formed, for some speculators, a British Florida land company and had served as its secretary. In this capacity, he had been sent to Florida with broad powers to reorganize the local management. This opportunity had also allowed him the occasion to engage in "other business for different parties," including a variety of bankers, lawyers, and speculators. On a later trip to Florida, he had been called on to make an investigation for a proposed railroad. Caesar believed that he had "more practical experience and knowledge of Americans and American business" than other British accountants with American connections because he had dealt with the details and features of many "different classes of business."[42]

Although both men were chartered accountants, Jones, an affable Welshman, and Caesar, a stern Scot, were a pair of contrasts. Reared in Lancashire, in the English Midlands, Jones was the more gregarious of the two and seemed to be genuinely appreciated by his clients. He took part in many professional associations and was considered a pioneer in American accounting circles, helping to form the Illinois Association of Public Accountants and becoming its first president in 1897. Caesar, the son of a Presbyterian minister, was born outside Edinburgh. Unlike Jones, he was a lifelong bachelor and remained aloof from most professional activities.[43] Resourceful, self-assured, and filled with "natural reserve," Caesar often expressed "his views with a note of finality" in discussions with clients. His letters to London indicated a tenacious, single-minded, and opinionated personality, often bordering on the dogmatic.[44]

Jones's initial efforts in America, in the ten months before Caesar's arrival, were impressive. Relying on himself and a few temporary accountants sent from London, the agency contributed approximately $18,000 to the firm, some 10 percent of its entire gross revenues.[45] This success continued at about the same level for the 1891–1892 fiscal year, prior to the opening of the Chicago office by Caesar.[46]

Jones and Caesar soon began to focus on developing indigenous American work.[47] They were quick to recognize that the different economic environment in the United States required more direct marketing to find clients than traditionally used by accounting firms in Britain. The agents broached to the London office their idea of expanding business through circulars describing their services. They proposed to send these not just to "friends and clients," but also to the "leading Legal Financial and Commercial houses" that were unaware of their existence or "the nature of our business." Prominent American banks advertised, they noted, adding that "generally quite a different view is taken of professional advertising or circularizing [here] to that held in England." The London office, however, frowned on such an undertaking and admonished the agency to "wait patiently and trust in getting known by degrees for doing good work and for not charging exorbitantly." "London rules" were to be followed even though PW was not so "well known in New York or Chicago as we are here in London."[48]

Given their initial success, this restriction was tolerable to Jones and Caesar until a series of events, long in the making, began to affect them at the end of 1893. The most important cause for concern was a decline in demand for investigations for British flotations of American companies. Ironically, Jones had arrived just as the investment frenzy of the previous decade, the very reason for the agency's initial success, was about to peak. A British financial crisis in 1890 caused investigation requests to decline by 1892. British investment interest in America did not revive again until about 1897 and then led to only a handful of new investigations.[49]

Although investigative work for flotations declined precipitously, the London office was able to provide other clients for the fledgling agency. Assignments consisted primarily of annual audits for floated companies, audits of American branches or subsidiaries of British companies, and special examinations of American railroads for British or European securities holders. These London introductions included only six clients in 1890, but increased to sixteen the following year, and to twenty-six by 1892. In subsequent years the number rose slightly, leveling out at about thirty clients per year, with the high point coming in 1899 with thirty-four clients. The work of London origin included services to breweries (both recurring and nonrecurring) and stockyards, as well as to packing, mortgage, insurance, railroad and car equipment, steel, publishing, and mining companies. The agency also provided help to an assortment of miscellaneous enterprises, ranging from brick and watch companies to companies in the chemical and food industries.[50]

Although London introductions managed to support the American agency, little American work was generated. None, apparently, was recorded in 1890; in 1891, the agency received $6,450 in fees from nine clients. In 1892, such fees declined to $4,700 from six clients for nonrecurring work. Conditions worsened in 1893, the year of the American financial panic and the country's worst depression to that date. Only four clients, requesting nonrecurring work, yielded a bare $2,600 in fees. A year later, only two American clients appeared, with one paying a fee of $200 and the other an unknown, though probably small, amount.[51]

By August 1893, the impact of these disappointments began to set in. Reflecting on the year's activities, Jones reported that "there have been practically no new investigations of any moment," nor would any likely take place until 1896, when the "vexed silver question is settled." Another result of the depression was the repurchase of foreign-owned businesses by Americans, who saw little need for retaining auditors, especially foreign auditors.[52]

Harder times also encouraged clients to seek lower auditing fees and to trim or eliminate the financial services that they required. The agents revived their earlier interest in promoting the agency through circulars in the face of competition for clients from cheaper and less skilled American accountants. These problems, together with the lack of American business, were augmented by difficulties that Caesar was experiencing with a Chicago lawyer who had referred substantial business to the agency. Misunderstandings abounded on both sides, exacerbated by Caesar's blunt personality and by differences in perceptions about auditing and accounting. To calm the waters, the agents decided, with the London office's approval, to move Jones to Chicago and Caesar to New York.[53]

Once these transfers were made in late 1893, Jones and Caesar began seriously to reconsider the nature of the agency and its future prospects. Recognizing that its life extended, unless renewed, only until the following June, they considered how they might revive its sagging fortunes. All sorts of issues emerged or reemerged in letters sent to London in early 1894, reflecting the frustrations of both men. On a personal level, they believed that they were undercompensated and overworked: minimum salaries and expenses that could not be charged to clients left their pockets empty and morale low. They needed to secure new business to alleviate these problems.[54]

Caesar, by this time the spokesman for their joint interests, boiled the issues down to a few salient points. Above all, he argued, they were too dependent on British business and yet unable to compete effectively for "purely American" work. The fees that the agency was compelled to charge for services, inflated by higher direct costs for London accountants, travel and living expenses, were the principal problem. Outside the few American companies that raised capital in London, there was little understanding of accounting in the United States and hence little domestic business. Jones and Caesar wanted to deal bare-knuckled with American competition in the promising but largely untapped indigenous market, but they believed that it was impossible "to make much progress in the way of securing new business during the remainder of the present agreement—at least under present arrangements."[55]

Caesar's proposal, in a letter sent in early 1894 to the London office and signed also by Jones, was simple and bold. The pair wanted the PW agency terminated, allowing them to set up their own business to compete openly for American clients on their own terms. They still wished to continue servicing firm clients in America under the existing arrangements. Although they would not sign PW's name on such work, they would "in all cases, where signing for you [was necessary, agree] to sign our own names and append thereto 'Agents for P.W. & Co.'" Caesar made other suggestions, including servicing the clients of other British accounting firms under the auspices of their own name and developing the interest of American companies in audits of their European subsidiaries. Principally, they asked PW to close the American agency but to retain them to carry out PW business in the United States.[56]

Caesar sent a second letter to London almost immediately, asking the firm to recommend him for a position as manager with the London Guarantee & Accident Co., if the earlier proposal was not acceptable. He followed up this correspondence with a personal visit to London, hoping to negotiate some settlement with the firm, since the agency was "not on a paying basis."[57] In the interim, the agency's life was extended for several months. The final decision was made in August.

"It is our intention," a letter from PW to the agents announced, to terminate "the Agreement in three calendar months from this date and to close our Agencies both in New York and Chicago on the 11th November next."[58]

JONES, CAESAR & CO.

After the official announcement of the agency's closing, plans to part company were conducted amicably. As a gesture of goodwill or a recognition that the London office would be unable to set up another American agency, PW generously gave their former agents "the option of taking up as much of the American business as [they] can obtain." The firm also offered advice, and was optimistic that Jones and Caesar would succeed, provided they remained together and consolidated their practice in either New York or Chicago.[59]

During the summer and early autumn of 1894, economic conditions in the United States began to change. In late September 1894, Caesar wrote to the London office asking if the closing of the agency could be postponed until June 30, 1895, the end of the fiscal year. He explained that completing agency business would occupy all of their energies until November, leaving no time for the final closing, for setting up arrangements to continue PW agency business, or for meeting with prospective clients. A flurry of interest had just begun for work by their own, new firm. They had been approached by a watch manufacturing company and had also been told that they would be asked "in a few months to examine the Accounts of a new Brewery 'Combine.'" There was also a "strong feeling," probably encouraged by Victor Morawetz of Guthrie's law firm, that "the coming winter will produce a new departure in the way of a demand for independent audits of all Railway Accounts." Caesar's intelligence reports, in fact, barely scratched the surface of what would shortly become an overabundance of work.[60]

In the meantime, Waterhouse and his partners reconsidered their position on the American agency, and on the acquisition of new clients in the American business environment, a subject that had been a frequent source of differences between the firm and its agents. No doubt encouraged by finding Jones and Caesar "fully occupied with work," the partners wrote to Caesar in October that they were willing to come to a new understanding, noting that:

> If we understood aright, your view was that if you were free to undertake work in your own name and on your own account, that work, together with the agency work for us, would produce to your-

selves a better income than we could afford to give under the present circumstances.[61]

PW agreed to continue the American agency under this arrangement. The partners stipulated only that "Jones, Caesar & Co." add to their office doors "Agents for Price, Waterhouse and Co. London," and that for PW work they would not sign "our name except under special authority." New agency terms were discussed, and PW suggested that it might assist the fledgling American accounting firm with startup capital expenses. The partners offered to take up any European work, under similar terms, that Jones and Caesar might develop.[62]

The decision to make this new arrangement had important and far-reaching consequences. Jones and Caesar were at last able to conduct their own business in the manner they saw fit. By agreeing to allow them to continue PW work in the United States, the British firm recognized that its share in such work, as profits during the next five years would show, would be minimal. However, the new arrangement kept the hope alive of future expansion by PW in the United States. Above all, the arrangement signaled the abandonment of a unitary system of organization, with London in complete control, and an implicit acknowledgment that accounting, in a worldwide context, was necessarily a decentralized operation.

The PW offer took Jones and Caesar "so Completely by surprise" that they were initially "at a loss what to do in the matter." After negotiating some points in the proposal, the new relationship, to remain in force for three years, was established on January 1, 1895. Agency fees of London origin had precipitously declined, contributing only a little over $550 in profit at the end of 1894, but they rebounded during the next six months. By the end of the fiscal year, fees approached those of the agency's first year in business, approximately $20,000. Agency fees continued at about the same pace during 1895–1896. They increased thereafter, reaching approximately $31,000 the next year and $45,000 during 1897–1898. Although Jones and Caesar took out a larger proportion than they had under the previous arrangement, the London office's profits soon justified the firm's decision to continue its American connection.[63]

The changing fortunes of both the PW American agency, and especially of Jones and Caesar, reflected the revival of the economy, coupled with a growing appreciation among American businesses of "the value of independent audits."[64] Although momentarily retarding the development of the accounting profession, the depression of the early 1890s ultimately led to the creation of many new opportunities for accountants. Many of the large American railroads that had gone bankrupt, for example, required investigations and audits for reorganization. In 1895, during their first year in business, Jones, Caesar & Co. took up thirteen matters on their own and serviced six others for PW. The next year was much the same, with twelve firm clients, and eight matters for the London office.

In 1897, the firm began a series of large-scale investigations and audits that signaled the beginnings of the merger movement in large American businesses—a phenomenon that lasted into the early years of the next century and in which Jones, Caesar & Co. played a significant role. During the 1890s, a new market for securities for industrial corporations had gained widespread acceptance among investors. The brisk market for these industrial stocks, listed on the New York Stock Exchange and traded all over the country, made it easier for businessmen to create large consolidations and combinations within industries. As a result, a great explosion of mergers took place. As one historian of the period has observed, "nothing like it was seen before or since in the history of the nation's economy." By 1901, many of the country's most influential corporations had been created.[65]

PW's American agents benefited greatly from these developments, forging an enduring connection with big business. "The firm was entrusted with by far a larger share of this work than that of any other," concluded George O. May, who arrived in the United States to begin work for PW.[66] One important connection was with the iron and steel industry. In 1897, Jones, Caesar & Co. started auditing some twenty-five to thirty companies that were later merged into the American Steel & Wire Co. Instructions for the work came from J.P. Morgan, and fees collected were in excess of total billing for any of their first five or six years in America.[67] Two years later, another examination of the same companies was made, as well as one of a large group of companies that were consolidated into the National Tube Co. Other merger work came from a wide diversity of businesses. In 1899, engagements were undertaken for nine or ten street railway companies and two railway construction companies in St. Louis, six milk companies in Chicago, nineteen railway supply companies, and six companies that were later merged into Allis-Chalmers Co.[68] The sheer volume of work required the skills of more British accountants, and the London office sent over May, Edward Stanley, George R. Webster, Henry W. Wilmot, and others who provided critical continuity for PW in subsequent decades.[69]

Besides consolidations, Jones, Caesar & Co. also secured work directly or indirectly from current or former clients. Earlier brewery investigations were followed by audits for many private breweries through 1898. Brewery connections in St. Louis led to enough other engagements in that community for the U.S. firm to consider opening an office there.[70] The decision was postponed until 1901, after Caesar's retirement. Referral business occurred elsewhere. The firm began annual examinations of the Omaha Stockyards and related enterprises in 1896, expanding on their earlier work done for the Chicago Stockyards. Conducting an audit for the Norfolk & Western Railroad in 1895, "a class of work which seems . . . more desirable than any other," led to audits or special examinations for almost a dozen other lines in the five years that followed.[71]

The revival led the London office to suggest a new arrangement in the fall of 1897. Its proposal was as bold as that made in late 1894. It envisioned the establishment of "a *separate* American [PW] Firm," in which both Jones and Caesar would be partners. Although Caesar believed that, "from a purely business point of view," such a firm would not attract any more clients than "under an agency arrangement," he was also of the opinion that "the establishment of an International House would prove a great success."[72] Again, and perhaps more clearly now, the London partners proposed, this time with no prompting from Jones and Caesar, a more decentralized structure in which to carry on its international business.

This proposal met with an enthusiastic response from Jones and Caesar.[73] Difficulties soon arose, however, including a new American law prohibiting foreign contract labor, which effectively prevented PW from sending its contract accountants to the United States. Caesar also came to believe that the current financial arrangement was unsatisfactory and that, even if it were possible to bring over more British accountants, they were too expensive to make PW business profitable. In addition, Caesar's reports of anti-British sentiment in the United States and of increased competition in the accounting field, combined with the new legal restraints, seemed to preclude an alternative course of action for the time being. Although some of these issues were relevant, it may have seemed to Waterhouse, Sneath, and Fowler that Caesar was trying to protract discussions.[74]

In the end, calmer sentiments prevailed, and the relationship struck in 1895 continued throughout 1898. Discussions for a new arrangement resumed in the fall of that year.[75] Responding to a new proposal, Jones and Caesar argued that the different names of both firms should continue, being "advantageous to you and practically a necessity for us." Caesar went on to note that they felt that PW would "always be looked upon in this country as a London firm and that no amount of legal technicalities will remove this impression and its consequences." Nevertheless, they were "willing to Combine and divide the profits of both businesses on the basis arranged with Mr. Fowler." The London partners agreed to Caesar's points, seeing the continued existence of two firms "as being as satisfactory a means as seems available in dealing with any local prejudices that may exist or that may hereafter arise." Still, they cautioned that this was in no way to imply or "result in, a less measure of influence by ourselves over the manner in which the entire business is conducted in America."[76]

Having reached a level of general approval, Jones went to London in December 1898 to conclude matters. On his return home, he stopped in New York, where he and Caesar examined and approved the draft memorandum of agreement and began planning financial reporting information, letterheads, and other details for the new partnership.[77] However, by the time Jones reached Chicago, he was very ill. Despite his sickness and his preoccupation with new work, Jones returned the signed articles of partnership to London. Shortly thereafter he became bedridden and died a few days later, on February 2, 1899, apparently of diabetic complications, at the age of forty.[78]

In the aftermath of Jones's death, Caesar placed his assistants in new positions, putting Charles J. Marr in charge of the Chicago office and May in New York. A.H. Pogson was assigned to handle all western work outside of Chicago. With these working arrangements in place, Caesar took "charge of all business now on hand or that is likely to arise in the immediate future." Over the next several months he was constantly on the road, handling most matters on his own. Although the state of the partnership agreement had become unsettled with Jones's death, it was a question that Caesar felt could be postponed. "My impression is that the main thing to do now," Caesar wrote to London, "is to overtake the business on hand and after the busy season is over to correspond in regard to future arrangements."[79]

Still, some issues could not wait for long. Caesar was willing to discard the recently concluded partnership agreement and ready to reconsider the whole matter. He was also confident in the abilities of the three managers, who might be "more useful as partners than almost anyone who could be sent over" and who, having recently been promoted to wider responsibilities, were "more than satisfied" with their appointments. Making any change in this arrangement in the near future, Caesar thought, would be a mistake.[80]

The London office, however, was insistent that Caesar should bring in another partner, possibly even more than one. "Our experience here would never for one moment allow us to consider it possible for one accountant by himself to carry on any considerable business & the circumstances of America render it far more difficult there." Since Caesar believed that his current managers were too inexperienced for partnership, he acceded to this concern by suggesting that they send a specially suited candidate on a trial basis. Then, abruptly, Caesar nominated Henry W. Wilmot, employed with the firm since 1894, for an American partnership. The two had met while Wilmot was assigned to the United States on wire company audit work the previous year. In July 1899, after preliminary details of the partnership had been sorted out, Wilmot joined Caesar in New York for further discussions.[81]

As in the past, Caesar waged a long battle with the London office over provisions in a proposed new partnership agreement. Many of the issues were familiar, but in one aspect they took on a new dimension. Caesar was very aware that the U.S. firm had grown spectacularly during the previous two years. Now, without his former colleague, he pressed for an even larger financial arrangement than that provided under the agreement arranged by Jones.[82] An outline completed in May was followed by drafts in September and October and by the final document on December 22, 1899.[83] In addition to the delays caused by his incessant and voluminous demands, Caesar had also needed some time to work out a partnership relationship with Wilmot. Despite the London office's urging to give the matter of choosing a partner sufficient time, Caesar apparently saw no reason to look beyond Wilmot, and he worked out an arrangement with him during July and August.[84]

In its broad outline, the partnership agreement followed the larger vision contemplated in 1897. A U.S. PW firm was created, consisting of the four London partners and Caesar, who had the right to introduce Wilmot (to whom he was to sell part of his interest) and others into the partnership, with the consent of the London partners. The new firm would conduct business under either the name Price, Waterhouse & Co. or Jones, Caesar & Co. Resident American partners had the right to sign the PW name on certificates and other documents. In addition, the agreement allowed a substantial payment for goodwill when Caesar either died or retired. This benefited him, or his heirs, with a sum equal to half the entire net profits of the American business during the two years prior to either event, or for the entire net profits of the first year under the agreement, should he die or retire earlier. The agreement was made retroactive to July 1, 1898.[85]

The reorganization occurred amid continuing good fortune. The 1899–1900 fiscal year was probably the busiest and certainly the most profitable on record. Fees generated by Jones, Caesar & Co. reached $75,000, and those originating from PW rose to $58,000.[86] Although future prospects seemed promising and expansive, Caesar, amid his heavy work load, informed London in June 1900 of his intention to retire within a year.[87] Confirming this decision several months later, he encouraged the London partners to look for his successor in the American offices.[88]

The news of Caesar's plan to retire aroused consternation over provisions made in the agreement.[89] His payment would require a substantial sum and, coming so soon after Jones's death, it might put the U.S. firm in a precarious situation. Spirited correspondence, firm revenue figures, and eventually a visit by Caesar to PW's new London quarters at Frederick's Place, Old Jewry, after his retirement were necessary to resolve the financial arrangements.[90] London had little reason for concern, however, about Caesar's successor. By late October, Arthur Lowes Dickinson had arrived in New York to get "a footing" among Caesar's wide and intimate "connections" in New York's legal, banking, and investment communities. A transition was in place well before Caesar, at the age of forty-one, left to retire in France.[91]

A NEW CENTURY

In the last years of Caesar's connection with PW, he prided himself on the pioneering accomplishments that he and Jones had made in the United States. In the fall of 1898, months before Jones's death but after their change of business fortunes, Caesar called their practice "the largest office in the country." Two years later, he viewed "the business being now permanently established at the head of the profession in the country."[92] Despite his characteristically bold and brash tones, Caesar's familiarity with American business life allowed him to gauge correctly the importance of such solid accomplishments.

On the other hand, rapid growth had left numerous serious shortcomings unaddressed. There were significant organizational concerns, especially those related to the development of a professional work force. Jones, Caesar & Co. had employed dozens of men over the decade, but few stayed, probably because of poor pay and lack of opportunity. The founding generation was slow to divest its authority, and the drive for profits was seen as more important than better compensation for the accountants. Turnover in the last few years of the decade well illustrated the problem. Among the eighteen staff accountants employed in December 1897, only seven remained when Caesar departed in June 1901. Throughout that period, the firm had hired thirty-seven men, but only seventeen of them remained on the staff, and their service length was, on the average, less than one year.[93] Turnover represented an even more acute concern when applied to skilled and experienced young managers like May, Marr, and Webster, who would be needed to provide organizational stability in the years ahead. Repetition of events like the Wilmot selection or Caesar's abrupt departure had to be avoided if the firm was to provide stability and a future for such men.

The sources of firm income posed still other problems. Despite the meteoric rise in revenues during the closing years of the decade, those gains came disproportionately from merger work, which was a highly lucrative but risky and nonsustaining basis for firm income. In the 1897–1898 fiscal year, for instance, more than 55 percent of fees came from wire company work.[94] Although such assignments helped propel the firm financially, greater attention was needed to find consistent, reliable, and recurring clients. With public, and especially business, banking, and underwriting opinion coming to recognize the importance of accounting work, the U.S. firm was in a good position to develop a more stable business. Dickinson had just such thoughts in mind when he wrote his early observations of America: a "great deal yet remains to be done," he noted, "before the business can in any way be compared with yours in England."[95]

CHAPTER 2

The Americanization of the Practice, 1901–1926

During the years 1901 to 1926, the small, two-office Price, Waterhouse & Co. American outpost grew into a self-sustaining, highly regarded, and distinctively American enterprise. Two senior partners, Arthur Lowes Dickinson and George Oliver May, led PW's American practice through this formative period, and each left his own imprint on the new partnership. Many enduring characteristics of PW's culture emerged during this time, including the individual authority of partners so central to the firm's governance, the selectivity of the partnership, and the leading role of PW senior partners in professional and public affairs.

Dickinson was responsible for the Americanization strategy. During his eleven-year tenure, he established the U.S. firm as a viable entity in a tumultuous and uncertain environment, often by adopting practices wholly at odds with British accounting firms' traditions. Under his guidance, PW opened new offices elsewhere in the United States as well as in Mexico and Canada, to enable the firm to respond more effectively to local business opportunities and client needs. Dickinson sought out, hired, and promoted American accountants. He also persuaded the London office to take an increasingly smaller share of the U.S. firm's profits. Finally, he responded to the need to promote the firm's name and to stimulate demand for accountants' services, imperatives in the United States that were barely countenanced in Britain, where PW and the profession were far more established. The U.S. firm moved into new areas such as systems work and took on innovative engagements. These included the creation of the first major consolidated financial statement, the policy of submitting quarterly financial data to stockholders, surveys of accounting and auditing systems of large government organizations, and recommendations for financial accounting for whole industries. Such activities drew public attention, often for the first time, to the work of accountants. When Dickinson stepped down, he was replaced by May, who served as senior partner for fifteen years and whose influence endured even longer. When May assumed leadership, PW's security was assured, and its name had become widely synonymous with excellence. He was left free to emphasize a more exclusive approach to new business and to new partners and to safeguard the firm's distinctive professional reputation. To accomplish this, he drew on his own strong ties to the London office and its emphasis on quality and tradition. His unparalleled expertise in accounting and tax matters allowed May to play a leading role as spokesman and theorist for the accounting profession as a whole.

THE DICKINSON DECADE

At first glance, Arthur Lowes Dickinson seemed an improbable choice to head PW's practice in the United States, and even less likely to serve as the agent of change that transformed it into a distinctly American entity. A graduate of an English public school, Dickinson completed his formal education in 1882 at Cambridge University, where he took a first in mathematics. He taught briefly in a school near Edinburgh before embarking on a traveling tutorship to Algiers. His decision to marry a short while later hastened his choice of a permanent occupation, and in 1883, Dickinson became apprenticed to an accounting firm for three years.

In an age when there was little formal accounting education, with few books on the subject, and when the monotonous nature of the work generally dispirited those who had attended university, Dickinson swiftly achieved distinction. He was exempt from the Institute of Chartered Accountants' preliminary examination because of his university degree, but he took the second or intermediate examination eighteen months into his apprenticeship. The examinations covered many aspects of professional work, ranging from bookkeeping and accounts to principles of the law of arbitrations and awards. When the results were announced, Dickinson had placed first. A year later, in December 1886, he took the Institute's final examination, which covered the same subjects but was designed "to exclude those individuals who did not possess intellectual or personal qualifications considered requisite for practice." Dickinson again did well, this time tying for first place with another candidate. He was admitted into the Institute of Chartered Accountants of England and Wales in 1893.

Dickinson then joined Lovelock and Whiffin, a small London firm, as a junior partner. During his years there, he traveled to the United States for a London company, the Riverside Trust Co., Ltd., which operated a 3,500-acre land development project in southern California engaged primarily in the production of citrus fruit. This investment venture had first attracted Wilson Crewdson, one of Dickinson's Cambridge University friends, and shortly thereafter, Crewdson's uncles, Edwin and Theodore Waterhouse. The company was organized in 1889 with Edwin Waterhouse as its chairman, and with Crewdson and Dickinson serving on its board. The Riverside enterprise required periodic audit visits, which Dickinson made during the 1890s. His experience with, and increasing knowledge about, American business, coupled with his frequent reports to Waterhouse on Riverside matters, led to PW's offer that he serve as the U.S. firm's senior resident partner when Caesar decided to resign. Dickinson arrived in New York in April 1901, three months before Caesar's retirement.[1] Although Caesar remained with the firm as a consultant until the fall, Dickinson acted quickly and decisively once he took the reins.

Shortly after his arrival, Dickinson had assessed the American business environment and judged it to be dramatically different, and much less predictable, than that in Britain. American business was in the midst of a massive corporate merger movement at the time, and important opportunities had arisen from the investigations required in preparation for the mergers.[2] This work, however, proved unreliable, and the firm's economic fortunes fluctuated widely during Dickinson's first few years. At first, assignments of prodigious and unprecedented size came in, but business opportunities declined thereafter, at least for a brief time. Dickinson was forced to take urgent measures such as opening new offices (sometimes without waiting for the London office's approval), developing an American staff, experimenting with marketing and promotional activities, and providing new services. The downturn lasted only a few years before the firm was engaged in large-scale, although very different, projects for industry and government. In short, the American business was much more opportunistic, and required a readiness to take chances. Dickinson, to his credit, was willing to do so.

Getting Grounded

By the end of April 1901, less than two weeks after his arrival, Dickinson had decided that the firm would remain in New York, "which must always be the most important office," but that Wilmot should be posted to Chicago to develop the practice there and to train assistants "who may, as junior partners, gradually take charge of the Western business." To create depth in the organization, he proposed to make George O. May and Charles J. Marr junior partners. May initially served in the New York office. Marr, who had been with the Chicago office since 1895, was Jamaican-born but had spent his entire professional life in the United States, starting as an accountant for the Chicago, Milwaukee & St. Paul Railroad. He had rapidly become known for his attention to detail and for the long, exhausting hours he devoted to client matters. Both May and Marr became partners on January 1, 1902.[3]

Dickinson had quickly grasped one of the realities of American business life, the fact that many prospective clients were concerned only with fee considerations. In these circumstances, the only way to compete successfully was by creating branch offices "within a night's journey either of New York or Chicago" where clients were located. By keeping a manager and small staff at these offices, "we should be able to carry out local work without any travelling or hotel expenses and at the same time the staff at these offices would be equally available with that at our head offices for work at distant points."[4]

Dickinson's first step toward geographical expansion was to open the St. Louis office in November 1901. At that time, St. Louis was booming. It was the fourth most populous American city, fourth in the gross value of manufactured products, and fifth in the amount of capital invested in manufacturing. In addition, all eyes were trained on St. Louis as it prepared for a World's Fair in 1903 to celebrate the centennial of the Louisiana Purchase.

Opening a St. Louis office had been considered at least as early as 1899, but it had been delayed because Caesar was unwilling to take a risk of loss against future profit. Once Caesar decided to resign, he saw even less reason to commit resources to a course that might affect his final financial settlement with the London partners. Dickinson, on the other hand, was under no such constraint, and he saw not only an opportunity, but an urgent business necessity. Although he had wanted to consult with London before taking action, it was clear that unless an office were created quickly, many clients would be attracted to another newly formed local audit company.

The St. Louis office was founded under the more familiar name of Jones, Caesar & Co. and was successful from the start. Client engagements covered a wide variety of services, ranging from the firm's first bank examination to an investigation for sixteen Midwest candy companies that were being consolidated. Within a matter of months, manager Edward Stanley reported that "the firm is now very strong in St.

Louis, stronger than any other accounting concern."[5] By 1904, its activities in the St. Louis area had attracted such wide attention that a local newspaper wrote: "first-class public accountancy has had only about three years' existence in St. Louis. Jones, Caesar & Co. were the first to introduce it. They came here with the prestige of known Eastern connections." The firm had also been at least partially responsible for a new understanding of what accounting could do. "The old idea of accountancy," the newspaper noted, "was a man who investigated books when fraud was suspected. Its uses have become much more varied and include periodical audits, investigation of accounts on behalf of intending purchasers and the institution of new methods of accounting."[6]

Dickinson also was learning to appreciate the unpredictability and uncertainties of the American business environment. Good work for a client did not necessarily lead to a permanent relationship. As he explained to the London partners, work in America was more "speculative" than he had realized.

> By this I mean that annual audits which in England are always the backbone of a business are comparatively few in number and the largest of them being dependent on the caprice of a few individuals cannot be considered as certain in their recurrence as they are with you.

Having just lost the American Steel & Wire audits, and with bleak expectations of continued work from National Tube Co., he suggested that "the prospects of our getting any annual auditing work from the [newly created parent] U.S. Steel Company are for a similar reason somewhat remote."[7]

To combat this situation, Dickinson felt that the firm must advertise its name in circulars to prospective clients or by announcements of office openings and personnel changes in newspapers. The issue, which clearly distinguished American professional etiquette from conventional British practice, had long disturbed the London partners' sense of propriety. Dickinson, nevertheless, sent out 36,000 announcements of his joining the U.S. firm to "the leading bankers, lawyers, and merchants in the principal towns to which our business extends." The notice was sent to the "leading financial papers" as well.

To soothe London's fears, he reminded the partners there again how different conditions were in America.

> We cannot afford to sit down and wait for business to come to us as you can in England; our competitors are all much in evidence and consequently better known than we are . . . even assuming that we

> have a better reputation and do better work . . . does not go far with people like the majority of the Commercial classes here . . . who have very little knowledge of the subject and do not know good work from bad.[8]

The British connection, however, was not without value. In February 1902, stockholders of U.S. Steel unexpectedly selected PW rather than Jones, Caesar & Co. as the company's auditors. Choosing the British firm name was somewhat surprising, as the appointment came less than a year after the corporation's formation from an amalgamation of various steel producers, several of which had been clients of the Jones, Caesar & Co. firm since the late 1890s.[9]

The consolidation that gave rise to U.S. Steel was the largest of the mergers that took place between 1895 and 1905 and produced the first billion-dollar corporation. It controlled three-quarters of the steel business in the nation and easily overshadowed all of its competitors. The U.S. Steel engagement instantly gave PW priceless recognition and secured its relationship with the banking firm of J.P. Morgan, arguably the most powerful factor in the American economy at the beginning of the twentieth century.[10]

PW's audit had to be pathbreaking, given the company's unprecedented size, and in order to give proper accounting expression to the company's technical and managerial innovations.[11] Dickinson's work for U.S. Steel was innovative in precisely this way and was the first effort in what would become a PW tradition of developing measurement conventions to facilitate American technological and managerial development. Because of the complex relationships between U.S. Steel and its many subsidiaries, Dickinson believed that stockholders could be informed adequately of the corporation's relative financial condition only through a consolidation of accounts. The U.S. Steel comptroller later noted that Dickinson's "sound and experienced judgment were of great value and benefit to us." He taught us, the comptroller recalled,

> many fundamental principles which should properly be observed in the presentation of the affairs of a corporation through its accounts and likewise in the composition of accounts. We were profited materially from his counsel and advice.[12]

U.S. Steel's 1902 consolidated statement rapidly became a landmark in accounting history.[13] *Scientific American* wrote that it was "the most complete and circumstantial report ever issued by any great American corporation," noting that the company's total assets of over $1.5 billion dwarfed the $50 million appropriated by Congress for the Spanish-American War several years earlier. James T. Anyon, a British-trained accountant who practiced for Barrow, Wade, Guthrie & Co. in the United States, regarded the report as "an event that perhaps contributed more to creating a realization on the part of the business world here as to what accounting and auditing really meant than any other occurrence at that time." Dickinson gave lectures on the theory and practice of consolidated statement preparation in 1904 and 1905 and wrote articles about some aspects of his experience that appeared in the British journal, *Accountant*, as well as in the fledgling American *Journal of Accountancy*.[14]

Although PW had made consolidated accounts for other clients during the 1890s, this practice gained wide acceptability after the U.S. Steel engagement. It also hastened Dickinson's decision to open an office in Pittsburgh, which, like his move into St. Louis, was done without the London partners' prior approval. The opening of a new office again raised the question of advertising. Wilmot believed that St. Louis manager Edward Stanley would "not have done so well [there] except for his little burst of advertising. Everyone in St. Louis knows us." He reminded London that "America is not England, and it is no use thinking it is. We have just to think about ourselves the same as every other accountant." Dickinson concurred, noting that "there is no use pretending that our name is as well known outside of New York as those of either Haskins and Sells or the New York Audit Company." He suggested that all that was necessary in the way of advertising was to place the firm's business card in the newspapers for a short period. "I am satisfied that once our name is sufficiently well known we can, by keeping up the quality of our work, secure all we want without further advertising." Although London apparently frowned on the general practice of promotion, it saw "no objection to circular [announcing] new office." Interestingly, Deloitte, Dever, Griffiths & Co., another British firm with offices in the United States, objected to notices in a St. Louis newspaper that announced the selection of May and Marr as partners. Deloitte's interpreted the notices as advertising in contravention of the principles of the British Institute of Chartered Accountants.[15]

By the fall of 1902, the firm was prospering. Despite the loss of a number of clients since Dickinson's arrival, particularly among the railroads, the firm acquired an increasing volume of work from elsewhere following the U.S. Steel audit. In October 1902, Dickinson decided to take much larger accommodations in New York. The number of New York office employees had grown from fifteen in 1901 to seventy-three in 1903, when the office moved from 54 Wall Street to 54 William Street. The Chicago office was growing as well. Work there began in 1902 in connection with the "Big Four" meatpackers, which were then considering a merger. J.P. Morgan also asked the Chicago office that year to examine the accounts of five farm machinery entities that were later merged into the International Harvester Co.[16]

But success spawned personnel problems, many of which, again, clearly separated the American from the British practice. During 1902, the number of clients quadrupled, and the size of the staff more than tripled from 44 to 166, forcing Dickinson to seek out accountants everywhere, including a return to his predecessor's practice of procuring them from Britain, which he did not want to do. Dickinson preferred to promote those who had served the U.S. firm well during the late 1890s rather than to create friction by introducing new British accountants for partnership. In 1907, he flatly informed the London partners that "we do not think it good policy or fair to our own men to bring in outsiders to fill the good positions which come up from time to time." Although foreign-born accountants dominated the firm for several decades, the lower staff ranks were increasingly filled by Americans. Dickinson advocated that partners become naturalized Americans, a course he himself took in 1906.[17]

Gradually, as a result of new financial incentives, increased contact among partners, managers, and younger accountants, and more opportunities in new branch offices, Dickinson developed an experienced, stable body of accountants. He proposed to the London office that assistants be placed on a compensation scheme that combined a guaranteed salary and a percentage of the firm's profit. "In England this might not be necessary," he conceded, "as it is much easier to retain men in your service there than it is here, where the number of really good men are limited and there are numerous opportunities always open for them to better their position." Dickinson also noted that "by collecting around us men who have grown up with the business, and are themselves interested in the results, we have a body from whom we can select future partners."[18] He focused on finding experienced people "who could be trusted to take up matters at a distance & complete all the detail work without any supervision." For in contrast, "a raw Englishman coming out here, however good an accountant, has a good deal to learn before he can be left entirely to himself." Dickinson registered a strong preference for self-starting Americans who could see tangible evidence of a promotion policy.[19]

Dickinson regularly reminded the London partners how difficult it was to get good, experienced accountants and noted that such men commanded higher salaries in the United States than in Britain. Moreover, as business picked up, it became increasingly necessary to reward talented staff with a stake in the business. He consistently believed that this stake should not come wholly from the American partners, who were taking on increasingly larger workloads that did not yield a commensurate return on their share of the business, but from the "sleeping partners," as he termed them, on the other side of the Atlantic.[20] His argument became a constant refrain, and one that he gradually won. His protégés became staff accountants, managers, and partners and continued to serve the firm for three and a half decades after Dickinson's departure in 1911.

Increased client demands underscored the need to create a stable professional organization that could withstand the death, resignation, or retirement of its senior management. An initial step in that direction was the organization of annual meetings of partners and managers to discuss common problems. At the first meeting, in June 1903, Dickinson revealed a bonus scheme, payable to employees below partnership rank who had worked for PW a minimum of one year. The fund was to equal 7.5 percent of the firm's profit, with a guaranteed profit base of at least $50,000. He was convinced that the scheme would benefit "the business in every way by the increased zeal, industry and keenness of all our staff" at a time when it was increasingly difficult to attract and keep good people.[21]

Much of PW's growth in staff and clients had been the result of investigative and audit work for large mergers. The firm's fortunes from merger work expanded spectacularly in 1902 and 1903, when profits soared to $184,500, a threefold increase over the previous year.[22] Securing new work when these projects ended was difficult, however, underscoring once again the differences between the American and the British practice. In America, increased promotional effort was required at greater geographical distances and under more intense competitive pressures; it was "missionary work [that] does not result in immediate profits." In addition, the cost of doing business was much greater in the United States than in Britain. In 1904, the U.S. firm's profits tumbled to about 40 percent of the previous year's high. This decline had a serious impact on the senior partners of the firm, who had no guaranteed salary and who had based their investment in the practice on an expected annual profit of twice the 1904 figure.[23]

Dickinson later recalled the difficulties of these times. The two years after the merger movement collapsed, he noted, were "for us years of much hard work, continuous strain and poor results financially. We had," he added,

> practically to reconstruct our business and adopt methods of promotion most distasteful to me, but entirely necessary if we were to maintain our position; and we had to do a large amount of work at comparatively small fees, with salaries rising all the time.[24]

Rebound

In 1904, PW began to pursue a number of promotional activities and to develop new services in order to regain lost ground. The firm entered into the relatively new field of municipal accounting, where it quickly achieved distinction. Overhaul of city accounting and bookkeeping methods and systems was a prime objective of the National Municipal League, a Progressive Era city improvement organization. The league developed a model municipal program in 1899, and its Committee on Uniform Accounting Methods (1900–1905) was composed of some of the country's leading municipal accounting academics and practitioners. The committee's work in creating uniform accounting methods, municipal budgeting, and accounting systems was one of the most important and permanent reforms of the era.[25]

PW's first municipal work was an engagement in late 1903 for the city of Minneapolis to "overhaul its entire accounting and bookkeeping system and establish its finances on up-to-date and sound business methods." The result was praised in the *Commercial and Financial Chronicle* as "certain to attract a great deal of attention and . . . most assuredly worthy of careful examination and study." The system of accounting, the publication also noted, was "the work of a firm of public accountants of international standing and reputation." The efforts of the partner-in-charge of the work, Henry Wilmot, were so noteworthy because he placed the city on a revenue and expense basis. The city now operated under a balance sheet, and the accounting system put every fund in view; income from city services was classified as "operating profit." The *Chronicle* viewed the Minneapolis system as a model for other cities and a "perfect system of accounting" for public finances. "In time," it noted, "we may be sure the public will insist upon having the profitableness or unprofitableness of government work in the mercantile field clearly and fully revealed." A year later Wilmot wrote up his experience for the *Journal of Accountancy*.[26]

Despite such success, the firm was in serious competition with other accounting firms for this business. Edward Stanley, who now managed the Pittsburgh office, noted that "Haskins & Sells have at present a monopoly of state and municipal work and they are prepared to fight by any means whatever, any attempt at competition." Stanley echoed a concern increasingly felt that "in this country the only effective work seems to be done by lobbying and working before the real work comes into play." He was convinced, with respect to municipal work,

> that our stickling at professional etiquette, as we by English tradition have come to understand it, is doing us an infinity of harm, is impeding our progress and is making us something of a joke, and a sort of an easy mark for our competitors.[27]

Obtaining new work increasingly relied on fee considerations, broad experience in municipal work, and marketing efforts such as endorsement letters from satisfied clients and pamphlets describing the Minneapolis experience.

Under Dickinson's direction, the firm sought to increase its name recognition through the new "Information or Intelligence" and "Promotional" efforts initiated at the 1905 partners' and managers' meeting. By far the most aggressive activities were those undertaken by an accountant acting as a fact-gathering consultant for the firm. He traveled to several locations, including upstate New York and Philadelphia, where he met with leading citizens, chambers of commerce, and individual businessmen. His detailed and systematic reports indicate that he spent time introducing PW to prospects and sought to arrange for future visits.[28] A more traditional approach to marketing was handled by the Promotion Department. It placed articles in professional publications and newspapers, arranged for papers to be read at congresses of different professions and trades, and encouraged the firm's attendance and discussion at these meetings. The 1909 partners' and managers' meeting decided to discontinue the firm's practice of inserting its business card in trade newspapers, however, "except such as is indispensable, as for instance public directories and other books of reference, and that in these cases no display insertions of any kind should be authorized."[29]

The firm also sought to create goodwill by taking an active role in developing an accounting profession. Dickinson assumed a leadership position in the Illinois Association of Accountants, an organization of British accountants and their American counterparts.[30] An opposing faction of American practitioners was led by Charles W. Haskins of Haskins & Sells and based in the New York Society of Certified Public Accountants. Attempts to end the rivalry led in 1902 to the founding of the Federation of Societies of Public Accountants in the United States. Despite this effort, the two groups continued to disagree, and the New York Society voted to withdraw. Faced once again with the prospect of a divided profession, the federation sponsored the first International Congress of Accountants in St. Louis in 1904. Dickinson served as the federation's president that year, and the congress proved to be an important organizing vehicle for the profession on a national basis. In 1905, when the federation merged with, and took the name of, the American Association of Public Accountants (AAPA), Dickinson continued to serve on committees.[31] PW's professional activities not only provided an important boost at a crucial and formative time, but also enhanced the firm's position among its peers and with businessmen.

Despite the disappointing experiences of 1904, PW was able to continue its expansion and opened an office in San Francisco, a move urged by the London partners for several years. Although the firm had some long-standing brewery work there and had provided services for other clients on the West Coast, Dickinson decided the least expensive course of expansion was to acquire the San Francisco accounting practice of Frank G. Phillipps. This move would ensure sufficient work for the office during its early years and thus avoid the necessity of a costly promotional effort to secure additional clients for an entirely new office.[32]

No sooner had many of its promotional activities been undertaken than PW was again faced with a rush of work. In the summer of 1905, the firm was asked to participate in a financial investigation of the Equitable Life Assurance Society of the United States in the wake of a New York state legislative probe into the insurance industry. The investigation centered on the financial practices, the relationship with security syndicates, and the handling of loan arrangements within the state insurance industry. Equitable's chairman asked PW and Haskins & Sells to investigate the company's financial condition from the time he took office in June 1905. The joint investigation covered a wide-ranging array of activities, including expenses, real estate investments, record-keeping improvements, and Equitable's relations with other financial institutions. A system was created to account for the amount of premiums collected and of insurance in force. So significant was PW's role in systems development that PW manager William E. Seatree was offered the Equitable comptrollership, which he declined. The Equitable investigation became so extensive that PW had to seek short-term financing to meet cash flow problems. Although it created temporary stress on financial resources, this engagement helped the firm rebound and then exceed past performance.[33]

Although Dickinson's subsequent efforts to secure legislation to compel insurance companies to make annual financial filings and to undergo annual examinations by independent auditors were unsuccessful, these investigations led to the revival and expansion of business for the firm. In 1921, George O. May would recall their propitious effect:

> The disclosures of what had been going on in the insurance companies led to doubts as to the status of other companies which were not

> supposed to be as highly respectable as insurance companies had been considered; people were naturally suspicious and audits became much more general.[34]

A similar joint effort with Haskins & Sells was launched at the request of the chairman of the New York Life Insurance Company at about the same time.[35]

Other significant work followed. As part of the efforts of Congress to reorganize the U.S. Post Office in 1907, the Joint Congressional Postal Committee asked Deloitte, Plender, Griffiths & Co. and Jones, Caesar, Dickinson, Wilmot & Co. to investigate methods of accounting and expenditure and to recommend improvements. Dickinson himself supervised the Post Office investigation. Later that year, the two firms submitted a 300-page joint report in which they analyzed existing conditions, compared them with those of private enterprises, and made recommendations on improving the Post Office's systems, accounting methods, and the work of its divisions. Some of the more important recommendations involved the use of labor-saving devices and machines as well as a cost-accounting system in order to track the cost of various postal services.[36]

The volume of the firm's systems work increasingly distinguished the American practice from that of its British counterpart. Systems development, which involved both consulting and the installation of accounting systems, as at Equitable Life and the U.S. Post Office, became a popular activity during the early decades of the twentieth century as a result of a greater interest in accounting and a growing appeal for efficiency in business. Spokesmen for efficiency ranged from Frederick W. Taylor and his study on "scientific management" to Arch W. Shaw, editor of such prominent periodicals as *System: The Magazine of Business* and later *Factory*, which focused on developing and promoting principles and techniques for better business management. It is impossible to assess accurately the volume of fee-based income derived by the U.S. firm for systems work, but it was clearly extensive at this time, with clients ranging from government agencies to large retail stores. Certainly it was of a greater order of importance than any comparable work done in Britain; for example, another large contemporary English firm recorded that "special work" in Britain, which probably included more than the installation of accounting systems, never exceeded more than 5.6 percent of their fee income.[37]

American technological development also provided new and different specialties for PW accountants. Most striking in this early period was the firm's role in the new motion picture industry. In the first two decades of the century, PW examined the accounts of eight motion picture companies, as well as those of film producers, theaters, and trade organizations. From these experiences the firm was able to devise accounting systems and to establish accounting procedures for the industry. In 1916, PW published manager Frank W. Thornton's *Memorandum on Moving Picture Accounts*, the first accounting treatise on the industry.[38]

Although the firm's rising workload was gratifying, Dickinson informed the London partners of the need for an entirely new partnership relationship. He felt that the current form had proved inadequate to cope with the increased demands of the business. Not only were there long hours of work for all, but there was increased competition from rival firms for personnel. He himself showed signs of wear:

> I sometimes doubt whether I can keep it up for another 5 years, and if any really good offer were made now in some other line I should feel very much disposed to ask you to release me altogether and accept it.

Dickinson was concerned about losing his staff. There were two men he wanted to promote to partnership and others that he wished to make managers, but not at the expense of his own shares in the business. Dickinson finally cajoled the London partners into selling some of their shares to incoming U.S. firm partners on the grounds that they had received, and would continue to reap,

> a handsome return on the amount of your investment quite apart from the prestige which your London business gets from the growth of the American business and the profits which you make on work which the American business is able to send you.[39]

PW had become the best-known and most prestigious accounting establishment in America, Dickinson wrote to London. It had reached "the head of the profession, not so much in size (although it is so in this respect too) as in quality." In addition, the work of the partners and staff was increasing its "value all the time and spreading it over the country here, where it is safe to say it is now as well known as in England." The firm's reputation was primarily attributable to "our hard work and energy." It was unfair, he insisted, to pay London an ever-increasing sum as the business grew, in exchange for the PW name "which you and your predecessors made in England, and which we by our exertions have added to enormously here." At the same time, Wilmot also wrote to remind the London partners that this question was no different from that raised by Caesar:

> Now it is raised by Mr. Dickinson and myself. After us it will be the same question with Mr. May and Mr. Seatree, and even if you were

> to send some new Partner from London to take our places, I can sincerely assure you from my deepest conviction that in three or four years the same question would be raised over again.[40]

Plainly, according to Wilmot, the U.S. firm was no longer a "mere child dependent on London. It has a personality of its own, and it is we who have created this personality and, given the proper recognition, we know we can continue to build it up."[41]

Dickinson's persistent objections to London's share in the U.S. firm as a sleeping partner, an arrangement that affected the financial fortunes of the American partners and their ability to admit new partners, were ultimately met by concessions. With the induction of Seatree and George R. Webster into the partnership, a compromise was reached whereby the London partners began to decrease their share in the business. Whereas in 1901 the London office held a one-third interest in the firm, by the time Dickinson retired in 1911 the London share had declined to one-eighth, primarily as a result of the increase in the number of American partners. By 1919, the firm had grown to fifteen partners, further diluting London's role to a 7.5 percent interest.[42] (The British firm's financial interest in the U.S. firm ended in the early 1930s, after the passage of American securities laws.)

Hitting Stride

Once revenues and business opportunities were restored, PW experienced another burst of expansion. In 1907, after consulting with his partners, Dickinson invited Philadelphia accountant Joseph E. Sterrett to merge his firm with PW and become the first American-born partner. Sterrett, who had joined the office of pioneer Philadelphia accountant John W. Francis in 1891, had practiced under his own name following his partner's death. With Sterrett's acceptance, the firm acquired a Philadelphia office and staff as well.

Sterrett brought great luster to the firm, and throughout his career he served in numerous important professional capacities. He was chairman of the first International Congress of Accountants in St. Louis in 1904, a founder and later president of the Pennsylvania Institute of Certified Public Accountants from 1904 to 1906, and president of the American Association of Public Accountants in 1909. He took an active role in discussions that led to the merging of the latter organization with the American Institute of Accountants (AIA) in 1916.

In speeches and published articles, Sterrett was a leader in efforts to upgrade the profession through education. In 1902, he was instrumental in establishing an evening school in Philadelphia with courses in accounting and finance designed to help prepare students for the Certified Public Accountant (CPA) examination. This school later merged with the Wharton School of Commerce. He also played a prominent role, along with Dickinson, in establishing the *Journal of Accountancy* as the leading source of technical guidance to accountants. In an article on "The Education and Training of a Certified Public Accountant," which appeared in the inaugural issue of the journal in 1904, Sterrett encouraged readers to see an accountant's work as more than "sublimated bookkeeping." It was, he wrote, "preeminently the profession of business advice." In a later article on professional ethics, he opened a pioneering discussion on accountants' duties to clients, to the general public, and to their peers. Sterrett also was co-author of the first book-length treatment of the role, functions, and organization of the trust company, an institution that had become a prominent factor in the financial world. *The Modern Trust Company* went through several reprintings and editions.[43]

The firm also established three additional offices at this time. For several years PW had been interested in establishing a presence in the Pacific Northwest, and a decision was made in the fall of 1906 to open an office in Seattle in January 1907. A year later the firm expanded into Montreal, Canada. "We are afraid," wrote Dickinson to London, "that if we delay the opening of a Canadian Branch for a few years it might then be found that we had missed an opportunity." Similar reasons were expressed in 1909 when a Boston office was set up. "We have many good friends in Boston," Dickinson noted, "but it seems to be quite impossible to get work from them unless we are on the spot."[44]

Distance and increased specialization of services led PW to develop ways of exploring and reporting on developments of general concern to the entire firm. With the support and involvement of partners and managers, Dickinson developed more uniform office procedures and better communication among offices. The New York office increasingly served as the coordinator of information and communications, and it became a source of limited guidance on issues such as quality control.[45]

At the 1909 partners' and managers' meeting, committees were created to deal with cash audits and defalcations; banking, finance, and insurance; costs; industrial companies; railroads and public service corporations; statistics; general audit programs; and steel companies. Committee reports were to be submitted at the subsequent annual meeting, and information was also to be presented to the newly established Statistical Department, which functioned as a kind of research and information center. Following the 1909 meeting, it was decided that all offices would have a "partner-in-charge" to avoid

> the waste of partners' time and also the inconsistency of policy which results from similar matters being taken up with different partners and often with several partners where one could act equally satisfactorily and dispose of the matter.[46]

Throughout the Dickinson period, and prior to it, firm accountants often faced difficult conditions, pressures, and frustrations in conducting their work, which frequently involved dreary and extended periods of travel. As early as 1891, Jones's inability to be in both New York and Chicago simultaneously cost him an important but impatient prospective client, although he philosophized that "I don't think that the fact of [my] being too busy at that time to undertake a matter at an hour's notice will in any way prejudice the chances of our being employed by them at some future date."[47] A few years later, Caesar found himself at railroad stations in Salt Lake City and St. Louis, waiting "day and night" for the next trains out to his destinations. Such inconveniences seemed to be the lot of accountants. Dickinson, too, discovered that traveling to the West Coast, with many stops along the way to visit clients and offices, was a time-consuming but necessary activity that took him away from New York for periods of four to six weeks and prevented him from addressing New York matters properly until his return. Other firm members faced even greater problems. Partner Frank Belser, for example, was required to travel to Mexico on business for an American oil company on trains that were frequently robbed by bandits.[48]

Getting to an engagement's location was sometimes only the first obstacle. In 1907, for example, Belser was assigned to install an accounting system for a mining company in Kennett, California. "Kennett was a typical mining town built on one street along the railroad tracks," he recalled later. "There was a general store, some saloons, and a 'hotel' in the center of town, and the inevitable red light district trailing off on the outskirts." Since Belser was accustomed to travel frequently on assignments, he had brought his wife with him, only to discover that finding a place in Kennett for them to stay "presented quite a problem." He recalled that

> the hotel could hardly be termed luxurious. The partitions between rooms were built of rough lumber with gaps between the boards over half an inch wide. Evidently privacy was not one of the main considerations of the builders. As to its cleanliness, the less said the better.[49]

There were also occasionally natural disasters to cope with, such as the 1906 San Francisco earthquake. Frank G. Phillipps, the local San Francisco office manager, was able to commandeer a boat in Sausalito several days after the quake but found, on his arrival in San Francisco, that the city was under martial law and that the Mills Building, where the firm had offices, was closed for safety reasons. A short while later the Mills Building was engulfed in flames, and all records, working papers, and clients' reports were ruined. Phillipps assured New York that the staff was safe, although the office and business district of the city had been completely destroyed. PW, like many other businesses, relocated across the bay in Oakland. For several weeks Phillipps relied on the telegraph and the mail to obtain enough working capital, typewriters, paper, and other office supplies to resume operations.[50]

The firm's professional staff grew sixfold between 1901 and 1911, from 24 to 145 individuals, while the number of offices increased more than fivefold, from two to eleven. PW accountants enjoyed their infrequent opportunities to socialize. In 1907, Dickinson instituted annual dinners in New York, and in 1909, they were expanded to include not only partners and managers, but also past and present members of the New York, Philadelphia, Boston, and Montreal office staffs. These dinners became a strong tradition for three decades, until the firm became too large to maintain them.[51] Individual offices socialized as well. For instance, the Pittsburgh office held a dinner party for partner Alexander B. Brodie in 1911 shortly before his departure to the Montreal office. The "jollification" provided an opportunity for more than a dozen accountants to present speeches that not only gave insight into their lives, but also revealed their sense of humor. The speech titles included "Farming in Missouri to Auditing in Pittsburgh—How I Achieved It"; "On the Impossibilities of Playing a Championship Game of Golf with the Necessity of Earning a Livelihood as a Handicap"; "Working Late as an Aid to Physical Culture"; and "Rich Politicians I Have Known, or Why Should an Irishman Remain in Public Accounting?"[52]

In St. Louis, an annual "frolic" dinner was held for the professional staff. Originally established as a conclusion to the annual office training program, these dinners soon became black tie affairs, and in later years included after-dinner plays, prepared months in advance. "In these skits," a St. Louis partner recalled,

> everyone from the partners to the office boy got razzed, which had a wholesome effect on everyone, and on more than one occasion the skits presented furnished a liberal education to the partners on what was going on in the office.

One of the more unusual plays involved an incident where a teetotaling firm manager had been asked by a client to deliver two bottles of liquor to another firm member. Since Prohibition was then in effect, he promptly destroyed them instead. The incident was memorialized in a courtroom skit in which the offending manager was "sentenced to ten years hard labor with the firm." The St. Louis office also sponsored both a golf tournament for employees and two softball teams, one called "The Assets" and the other "The Liabilities."[53]

FROM DICKINSON TO MAY

In June 1910, Dickinson announced his retirement as senior partner, effective at the end of June 1911, a decision made largely for family and health reasons. He had discussed his plans a year earlier with both Wilmot and May, the likely candidates to replace him. According to the partnership agreement, the London office had the final determination in such situations; in time, a London partner arrived to survey the partners' opinions. But before any further action could be taken, Wilmot took himself out of the running by deciding to retire at the same time as Dickinson. In retirement, he left the accounting profession and entered business, soon becoming a successful New York sugar importer.[54] With Wilmot's withdrawal, George O. May became Dickinson's virtually certain successor. Earlier friction, apparently caused by a concern that May would want to increase his number of shares after becoming senior partner, was removed when he informed the partnership that he would not pursue that course.

May's early years as senior partner closely followed the direction laid out by Dickinson. He doubled the number of offices around the country and continued to hire American accountants. The Americanization of accounting practice and methods also continued into the 1920s. As early as 1904, Dickinson had observed that Americans demanded more of their accountants than did clients based in other countries:

> The majority of the people here require something more than the bare statement of facts, and cannot understand why, if an accountant has formed in his own mind an opinion about certain matters, he cannot give them the benefit of this opinion.[55]

Dickinson was convinced that the "same rigid rule" that confined English accountants' "reports and certificates strictly to matters of ascertained facts" could never prevail in the United States because of the "utterly different conditions existing, particularly in the minds of ones [*sic*] clients and the public generally." May agreed with these sentiments. He pointed out that for the U.S. firm, the balance sheet audit comprised the "great bulk of the firm's work," whereas this was "quite unknown" in Britain, where there were few very large companies with an elaborate internal organization.[56]

When Dickinson left, the firm's future seemed reasonably assured. One result of the great merger movement was that, by 1910, America's economic structure had been reconfigured, and large companies, many of which eventually became PW clients, dominated the scene. These industrial giants included petroleum companies such as Standard Oil and Texaco; rubber producers such as U.S. Rubber and Goodyear; metals firms including U.S. Steel, Bethlehem Steel, American Smelting and Refining, Jones & Laughlin Steel, Anaconda Copper, Phelps-Dodge, International Nickel, and National Lead; the electrical manufacturers General Electric and Westinghouse; food processors such as American Sugar, Nabisco, United Fruit, Swift and Company, and Armour; and many others including American Tobacco, Du Pont, Pittsburgh Plate Glass, American Can, Allis Chalmers, International Harvester, Singer, and Eastman Kodak.[57] Their sheer size required a large, national accounting firm like PW, with the necessary personnel and the resources to conduct their audits. The promise of the U.S. Steel audit had borne fruit; PW was well positioned to serve the largest and most prestigious clients in American industry.

As the pressures of Americanization steadily increased, it seems ironic that the U.S. firm name gradually receded into insignificance, while that of PW became the accepted standard. At the turn of the century, Jones, Caesar & Co. was the better known, and, as a result, both firm names were used after Caesar's departure in 1901, depending on the client relationship. Foreign clients with American interests often preferred PW, whereas many American clients favored Jones, Caesar & Co.

Gradually, however, the Jones, Caesar & Co. firm name began to fade in importance. The first important development in this direction was the choice by U.S. Steel of PW as its auditors, not Jones, Caesar & Co. This choice also marked a change by J.P. Morgan, who had used the services of Jones, Caesar & Co. while he was consolidating the various small companies into what would later emerge as U.S. Steel. Apparently Morgan wished to connect U.S. Steel with a firm whose name was also well known in Britain, as a sizable portion of the underwriting subscription for the merger came from Europe.

Many engagements, especially those conducted for government agencies, continued to insist on the services of Jones, Caesar & Co. Gradually, however, this name was altered to reflect the change in partners. In 1904, Jones, Caesar & Co. became Jones, Caesar, Dickinson, Wilmot & Co. When Sterrett joined the firm in 1907 it became known as Dickinson, Wilmot & Sterrett, although "formerly Jones, Caesar & Co." also appeared on the letterhead. With Dickinson's departure, the Jones, Caesar

& Co. name was dropped for all intents and purposes, although two separate firms remained in the 1911 Partnership Agreement. Under the Partnership Agreement of 1920, all reference to Jones, Caesar & Co. and its successor firms vanished, as the firm became simply PW.[58]

This decision reflected the growing perception that PW was a native accounting firm. Two stories related by Sir Nicholas Waterhouse, son of Edwin Waterhouse and a partner in the London firm, suggest that the transition occurred shortly before World War I. Waterhouse recalled that in 1907 the U.S. Navy approached PW, following the completion of its work for the U.S. Post Office, to ask the firm to undertake a large-scale investigation of the Navy. However, the U.S. Senate disapproved of using a "foreign" organization, and the proposal languished. A few years later, Waterhouse recalled, on a return voyage to England, another London partner was engaged in conversation by an American businessman. On learning that the latter was a London partner of PW, "the Yankee exclaimed in surprise, 'Sakes alive, you're not telling me those guys have a house in *Europe* too!'" The firm even then had an American nickname. The same man was in "a spot of trouble" with New York bankers concerning an overdraft, and the bankers had threatened to "'let loose those waterbugs on him' to make an investigation" if he did not provide more security.[59]

Building on Strength

In 1911, May succeeded Dickinson as senior partner, a position he would retain until 1926, although he subsequently returned to the senior partnership in 1934. May was modest about his accomplishments:

> Caesar created for accounting, as represented by the firm, a high standing in the financial world[,] Dickinson set the firm on a sound footing and built up a real staff[, and] I, with no interest in administration, built successfully on the foundation he had created.[60]

In fact, May contributed to the firm in other, equally important ways. Up to that time, no other individual at the firm had developed such a degree of technical skill; not only did May become a specialist in financial accounting as an outgrowth of his auditing experience with large publicly owned corporations, he also became one of the most important authorities in the tax field.[61] Moreover, this expertise was not buried away within the firm, for May continued PW's tradition of public and professional service as a spokesman for accounting thought.

May did not originally intend a career in accountancy. He was born in England at Teignmouth, Devon, in 1875, attended a local English public school on scholarship, and planned to attend Cambridge University. However, his cousin, a provincial solicitor, persuaded May to abandon his university plans for the "rising profession" of accountancy. He entered the office of an Exeter accountant in 1891 and embarked on five years of training as an "articled pupil," for which his father paid the sum of £100.[62]

The Exeter firm offered few practical experiences for May except in the bankruptcy field, so when he began to study for his first Institute examination "almost all . . . subjects . . . had to be learned through coaching." His results were so successful that he continued his preparation for the final examination with coaching classes in London. There he freely entered into classroom discussions and debates, impressing his coaches and fellow students alike. In the end, May took first place in his final examination, correctly answering a tricky question involving an obscure aspect of English bankruptcy law. One of his coaches encouraged him to pursue law, but May decided to find employment in a larger London accounting firm in order to gain two or three years of experience.[63]

Despite his lack of experience in the audit and investigation fields, May was immediately hired by PW. He later learned that Edwin Waterhouse "liked to bring into the office men who had taken good positions in the examinations, and to place heavy responsibilities on them to see how they stood up under pressure." May entered the London firm's offices in February 1897, several weeks after being admitted as an associate of the Institute on completion of his articles.

His career in London, however, proved to be short-lived. In the summer of 1897 London received a request from Jones, Caesar & Co. for help with their mounting consolidation work. May decided to go to the United States as an "experiment," one that would provide him with valuable experience for two or three years before he returned to practice in England.

May quickly took on important responsibilities for Jones, Caesar & Co. and became a favorite of American clients. Within a few years, George Eastman offered to make him treasurer of Eastman Kodak at an initial salary of $7,500, some five times higher than his salary at PW. May, however, decided "to stick to the career that I had planned for myself." With the installation of Dickinson as senior partner in 1901, and with assurances of May's promotion within the U.S. firm, any wavering doubts about where he would make his career vanished. Early in 1902, he returned from England with an English bride, as a partner in the U.S. firm.[64]

As part of Dickinson's efforts to expand geographically, he transferred May to St. Louis in 1902. Dickinson felt that May needed to gain maturity: "May is a very clever fellow & we all like him personally," he wrote to London, "but he has too high an opinion of himself at present & is very young." Dickinson believed that the midwestern assignment might be useful for May's career development.

> His weak point is not I think ability to organize, but a disinclination to sit down & do it if Some one else will do it for him. . . . Unless he is put in a position where he has got to do it, or fail in getting through his work, he will not do justice to himself or develop into a thoroughly capable man.[65]

Whereas Dickinson saw the move as an essential career step, May, on the other hand, regarded it as an "exile," because the move came "at the height of the consolidation movement, during which I would have been much more valuable in New York as junior partner to Dickinson."[66]

Nevertheless, during his midwestern sojourn May began to develop the skills in writing and the interest in professional activities that would become central to his later career. He helped to organize the first International Congress of Accountants, which met in St. Louis in 1904. Two years later, as he was about to return to New York, he published, in the *Journal of Accountancy*, the first of more than 150 professional articles. His second article, a response to a noted accountant, appeared in 1906 and established May as a practitioner who was willing to defend his opinions.[67]

Despite May's disclaimer that his early years as senior partner were "comparatively uneventful," the firm grew enormously during this time. Many new branches were opened, doubling the total of existing PW offices, including a Los Angeles office in September 1911, the first office of any national accounting firm in that city. In 1914, PW opened an office in Milwaukee, followed a year later with one in Detroit that, like San Francisco, was established through the acquisition of a local partnership. In 1919, PW acquired more office space in New York and in 1921 moved into larger quarters at 56 Pine Street. Firm revenues also rose prodigiously. In 1910, the year before May assumed leadership, profit amounted to $235,000, an average of $33,571 per partner. This had increased to $1,278,000 ($79,875 per partner) by 1926, when May relinquished his executive duties.[68]

PW was also expanding abroad. In the original 1890 agreement with Jones, the London firm had allowed the American agency to undertake all work in North, Central, or South America. This stipulation remained intact until 1913, when the London firm opened an office in Buenos Aires, and later other offices throughout South America. By 1912, two more offices were established in Canada, at Winnipeg and Vancouver, by the U.S. firm. Two years later, in 1914, a separate Canadian firm was formed, although until 1924 Canadian matters were still discussed at the U.S. firm partners' meetings, and Canadian-based partners remained as partners in the U.S. firm. By the beginning of World War I, what had been broadly called the "American" firm had become (except for Mexico, Venezuela, and the Caribbean region, which remained within its sphere of operation) more accurately known as a "United States" firm.[69]

May sought to consolidate Dickinson's gains by expanding the partnership and creating incentives for the rest of the professional staff.[70] In 1914, he announced the selection of seven new partners, thus doubling the size of the partnership. These promotions recognized those men who had helped to build the firm's reputation during the Dickinson era. May also sought to improve the prospects and to increase the interest of junior staff.[71] He arranged, with the assistance of Dickinson, who was now a partner in the London firm, for "an interchange of a certain number of the more promising juniors" to expose them to broader experiences. This exchange program between the two firms provided an invaluable cultural and professional experience for its participants.[72]

May also agreed with Dickinson that PW's high standards provided ideal training for accountants and an influential educational experience, regardless of whether these individuals rose to partners, entered business, or established their own firms. "I rather welcome the idea of a constantly growing number of graduates from the office bringing the same traditions and ideals into business life and into the smaller practices in the country," he wrote. PW was "a training ground for men who may be able to do better on their own account than they can with us."[73]

May was distressed that many accounting treatments in the United States were defined not only by practitioners but often by clients as well. Only the most established firms such as PW could remain invulnerable to client pressure. One of May's first American assignments had been an audit of the Louisville & Nashville Railroad. The work, ordered by August Belmont & Co., resulted in a qualified certificate, which, although it did not please the client, did not lessen Belmont's regard for PW.[74] Later, May, working with Caesar, had examined the accounts of the Northern Pacific Railroad. Although the assignment came from J.P. Morgan & Co., both Jones and Caesar resisted this influential client's insistence that they change their method of accounting for certain items.[75] These formative experiences did much to mold the young May's attitudes, which became, by virtue of his later influence, a central part of the firm's culture.

May found it critically important to maintain the firm's reputation, and he cautioned his partners from lending "our name to any enterprise or to say more in a certificate than we feel entirely warranted," either to keep a client or to obtain a new one. May felt free to turn away business in order to maintain quality standards, noting that "we have now reached the point where it is far more important to improve the character of the business than merely to increase its volume."[76] May's position became PW dogma and was endorsed by the partners at their 1922 meeting: "The policy of the firm is not to increase its business unless such increases in business can be undertaken on the high standard that has already been set for our work."[77] Partners noted that "there is often a danger that branch managers in their effort to build up the gross business of a young office will accept instructions on undesirable business and thereby injure the good name of the firm as a whole."[78]

For Nicholas Waterhouse, May's greatest accomplishment was his ability "to carry on and instill in the minds of the younger generation in America the traditions of the old Firm and all that it stood for." For May, the outstanding reputation of the British firm was an essential part of that tradition. He instilled these values in American accountants through public service and by speaking on public and professional issues. At Dickinson's request, he gave his first series of lectures on this subject in 1908, at the newly established Harvard Graduate School of Business Administration. He also regularly, and effectively, testified as an expert witness. His viewpoint in a 1912 case involving the imprudent disposition of stock shares by an executor, for example, became a classic statement on the valuation of goodwill.[79]

In 1916, the American Institute of Accountants was created as part of a reorganization of the older AAPA. Not a federation of societies, the AIA concentrated power in the hands of a central executive committee dominated by large national firms. May's career as an accounting spokesman took on added significance that year, when he was appointed by the new AIA to serve on a committee organized to create a standardized form and method for the preparation of balance sheet audits to be used by businesses to borrow money from banks. The committee and Federal Trade Commission (FTC) officials decided that the best way to provide this information was to prepare a statement that could be published in pamphlet form. After the committee unsuccessfully attempted to draft the pamphlet, May turned over a report written by PW's John Scobie several years earlier for internal firm purposes. The committee members "were favorably impressed" and agreed on the text. This document was transmitted to the Federal Reserve Board for publication in the April 1917 issue of its *Bulletin*, reprinted in 1918 in pamphlet form, and then revised in 1929. Not only was this report the first step in what would ultimately lead to the development of formalized auditing standards in the late 1940s, but it was also the only attempt to set down a compendium of accounting principles, aside from articles in the *Journal of Accountancy* and special bulletins published by the AIA, until the 1930s.[80]

America's entry into World War I brought further opportunities for public service. May, Sterrett, and Seatree, the firm's three senior partners, went to Washington to serve in government positions, where knowledge of accounting was critically needed to manage war-related activities. Seatree became a member of the War Industries Board and was later an adviser on taxation. After spending time on war-related activities in France, he became a partner in PW's new Continental (European) firm. Sterrett served as a member of several tax advisory bodies created by Congress and the Treasury Department that sought to formulate tax regulations for the administration of the 1917 excess profits tax law. He was also a member of two tax appeals boards.[81]

For May, in particular, the Washington experience "opened up a new era" in his life. He was asked to become part of the War Loan staff in the Treasury Department, where he monitored the loans to, and expenditures of, foreign governments. Before long, May and a small group of other volunteers were also engaged in consulting for the Treasury. He developed extensive congressional, executive, and political connections and was exposed to many "new fields of related activities which after 1926 [would absorb] the time [he] had previously devoted to [firm] administration."[82]

Although May's full-time duties in Washington allowed him only weekends in New York to carry on his responsibilities as senior partner, PW continued to flourish in his absence. The firm took on more tax work as a result of the excess profits tax. This part of the firm's practice had begun with the enactment of the corporation tax law of 1909 and had increased in 1913 with the passage of the individual income tax amendment. Although the general significance of the early tax work was quite limited, the very "modesty of its beginnings" provided the key to the accounting profession's early involvement. At the time, income taxes were closely tied to general accounting principles, techniques, and concepts, and all professional practice was done with the Treasury Department's sanction. Lawyers showed no interest in income tax work, which they referred to accountants. Each successive increase in tax rates or change in tax law reinforced the importance of accountants to the business community, and the practice steadily grew.[83] Additional prewar measures affecting corporate taxation created a "sudden and widespread necessity for professional [accounting] assistance." World

War I regulations accelerated this trend, as accountants were required to bring their large corporate clients into conformity with excess profits tax and depreciation laws.[84]

PW's tax "business expanded with great rapidity" during the war. As partner Frank Belser noted, "There seemed to be unlimited need for accountants in war industries and on tax matters which now for the first time assumed importance." Novel tax questions and new rulings and decisions kept accountants "very fully occupied," and this pressure only gradually declined in the years following the war. Belser experienced firsthand that "the meaning and application of the new laws presented no end of difficulties, particularly in cases of subsidiary companies and on questions arising under invested capital."[85]

On his return to the firm full time at the end of the war, May assumed the general supervision of tax work. Its novelty challenged his intellect, and he became involved in many difficult cases. By 1917, he had already entered into public discourse over methodological difficulties he found in the excess profits tax law. Taxation became a second area of expertise in which May would serve as spokesman for the firm and the profession in the years to come.

The demands of the war and its aftermath seriously burdened the firm's resources and imposed an undue strain on the partners and managers. By 1921, May noted that the firm had grown "thirty or forty times as great as it was when I joined it [as partner] twenty-one years ago."[86] In 1925, PW decided to refrain from any new growth and directed its efforts to consolidating its position, replacing war and tax work with that of a more permanent character, thus "increasing the margin of security and comfort in the conduct of its business."[87] The partners decided to adhere to a conservative, nonexpansionary policy: only work of the highest quality would be provided, and the firm would grow only through advancement from within. "It is the practice of the firm, which is very seldom broken, to fill higher positions by promotion." Every partner, except Sterrett, had first served as a staff member of PW.

In 1923, when two partners withdrew from the firm to become partners in the newly independent Canadian firm and two others retired, a group of senior partners reviewed the names of possible candidates to fill the four vacancies. They considered "the idea of admitting at least one partner on the basis of exceptional promise rather than seniority," but this suggestion was rejected by the partners as "unfair." After 1914 and until 1923, for instance, only five additional partners were admitted. Three had been associated since the earliest years of the century, with one becoming a partner after working seventeen years for the firm, another after eighteen.[88] Only four men were made partner during the remainder of the decade, and the total number of partners increased only by three between 1923 to 1929.[89]

Reluctance to name new partners was based on May's belief that the partnership should remain small. In a small partnership, with a highly decentralized organization, individual partners were the key to success. In distant locations, they were virtually autonomous and served as the firm's ambassadors to clients. To clients and the general public alike, each partner operated as an independent spokesman for PW. With firm revenues rising rapidly, May's formula for success—retention of a small partnership (though increasing the number of support staff), a reluctance to grow as fast as the market would bear, a rising reputation, and a determination to take on the most profitable clients—provided the firm with a powerful strategy. As attractive and effective as this policy was, however, the small size of the partnership had disadvantages. As May noted, the prospect of opening new offices was often rejected "because we could not spare the men to take charge of them and still have sufficient first-class men to take care of the work attached to the offices already established."

Operational issues continued to grow more important as PW expanded in the early 1920s. Partners often discussed the growing concern for "securing uniformity in office practice and seeing that the firm's rules were being followed and its standards adequately maintained." One of the retired partners undertook "reviews of reports in different offices (such as he had made in the past with valuable results) and any other kindred matters which might arise." In 1925, the firm published its *Manual for Use of Office Managers*, a guide especially prepared for those offices where a manager, rather than a partner, was in charge. Concern about "the dearth of good juniors" and a need for "more systematic training" led to the operation of an "accounting school" in the New York office for several years.[90]

The partners also considered office practices concerning understandings with clients. Meetings and memoranda were devoted to discussions about the clear and unambiguous scope of work as reflected in the instructions, wording, and substance of client reports, policy on balance sheet audits, and systems of internal checks. These measures were necessary, in part, because of difficulties that had arisen with clients. Belser recalled that a number of clients were "arbitrary and dictatorial" and that jobs often "ended in a bitter wrangle over adjustments. A favorite device of the client," he noted,

> was to tell his bankers what the profits showed on his own closing figures, and it is easy to see what a hurdle that presented when we

> afterward insisted on changes. And always we were faced with the suggestion, express or implied, that if we did not wish to pass the accounts as they stood there were plenty of auditors who would. And as a matter of fact that was the bitter truth.

Belser also recorded that in his experience, the firm had "lost many pieces of work for large clients and potentially large clients over this question of adjustments or qualifications in the certificate." Despite such losses, Belser was "whole-heartedly supported" by the office partner-in-charge in every instance.[91]

Such confrontations in the early 1920s reflected not only the growing use of audited statements by businesses, but also, and more important, their increasing misuse and an accompanying widespread public cynicism over the credibility of the public accountant's claim to professional status. The seeming inability of the profession to standardize financial accounting encouraged businesses to shop and bargain for their audited statements. Furthermore, "innovative modes of financing and organizing business" in the Roaring Twenties "had created a host of accounting problems whose solutions had been left to the discretion of practitioners and their clients." This had given rise, in the public's mind, to a strong "perception of the inadequacy of corporate financial reporting." This issue came to dominate May's thoughts and actions in the years immediately following his decision to relinquish his executive duties as senior partner.[92]

A New Senior Partner

May had often asked his fellow senior partners, Webster, Seatree, and Sterrett, who all had equal interests in the partnership, what they would do if he resigned or became incapacitated. "Each suggested that one of the other two were to succeed me if that event should happen in the near future," May noted. In the mid-1920s, however, Sterrett began to encourage May's tentative desire to leave his post, suggesting that it would allow "an opportunity for a younger man to assume broader responsibilities" while permitting May to take on activities in the public sphere that he had long desired. Sterrett ruled out both himself and Robert O. Berger, then the only other senior partner. He noted that Berger had long been preoccupied with client work and showed no ambition to manage the firm.

Sterrett had someone else in mind, proposing William B. Campbell, "an exceptional man." This younger partner, he noted, "has not only ability of an outstanding order, but also a personality that has endeared him to all his associates. He commands the respect of the staff and he enjoys the confidence of the clients." In Campbell, Sterrett saw an opportunity both to provide "added recognition and responsibility" to younger partners and to retain the traditions and values important to their seniors. He felt that operational issues and exploration of "the broader questions of policy ought to be initiated by the younger men and worked out in consultation with the older group." Sterrett's plan also envisioned that May and the other senior partners would then be able to involve themselves "in consulting work and to some extent in advising clients along lines which at times may somewhat depart from ordinary accounting practice."[93]

By encouraging May to change the course of his career, Sterrett was also pointing out the path that he himself had taken after 1917. Besides his years of service on tax advisory bodies and tax appeals boards during the war, Sterrett's postwar activities had brought him, and PW, national and international recognition. He was a member of the Reparations Commission in Paris. After Congress passed the Revenue Act of 1921, he returned to Washington to serve on the Tax Simplification Board. In 1924, he went to Berlin for three years as the American member of the transfer committee, established under the Dawes Plan, that supervised German reparation payments to creditor nations. In the years that followed, Sterrett took on other international responsibilities. In 1928, he completed an investigation, with Joseph S. Davis, a professor at Stanford University, of Mexico's financial condition. Mexico had defaulted on its bonds and other obligations, and a group of bankers, headed by J.P. Morgan & Co., were attempting to negotiate some arrangement with the government for payments of principal and interest. The Sterrett and Davis study provided the basis for these negotiations. In 1929, Sterrett made a report on the financial and accounting organization and methods of the German state railways. The following year, he acted as their financial adviser. For his services throughout the world, Sterrett received numerous awards, as well as recognition for PW.[94]

May took Sterrett's advice. In November 1926, he advised the partners that he would step down from day-to-day administrative duties to devote "more time to economic studies and to the broader problems of financial and business affairs." The partners recommended that Campbell become "senior executive partner." While Campbell assumed executive duties and chaired semiannual partners' meetings, May continued to hold as many shares as any partner, though he did reduce the number to a level equal to Campbell's increased proportion. He also still attended partners' meetings and other firm affairs and provided valuable insights and contributions.

By the end of May's tenure, PW had become a truly American firm. A selective partnership, with its guarantee of a distinctively high level of client service, had been created. The firm had begun to exhibit some of its other distinguishing characteristics as well, including the public role played by its leaders and its international approach. As Campbell took the helm, he could hardly have anticipated the enormous changes that would face the country and the profession during the coming decades.

PART II

Regulated Equilibrium

CHAPTER 3

Coming of Age, 1926–1946

By the late 1920s, Price, Waterhouse & Co. was no longer an agency of a British firm, but a distinctively American firm in its own right. Many enduring elements of its culture—its decentralized structure, geographically dispersed offices, and autonomous partners—were in place. The firm's elite status was also solidly established. In 1932, *Fortune* praised PW as "easily the world's foremost accounting firm in size, in reputation, in number of clients."[1] Indeed, its client list was the envy of rivals: among the 700 corporations whose securities were then listed on the New York Stock Exchange (NYSE), PW represented 146 of them—more than twice the number of its nearest competitor. William B. Campbell, who succeeded George O. May in 1926, was determined to carry on in these highly successful directions.

The 1930s were landmark years for the accounting profession. The Great Depression rocked the industry's client base, while the U.S. government's response to the crisis included regulatory statutes and the creation of administrative agencies such as the Securities and Exchange Commission (SEC). The enactment of federal securities laws permitted an oligopoly to form in the accounting profession. The new laws redefined the role of accountants, guaranteed them clients, and elevated the audit over all other accounting services. The new SEC encouraged the profession's efforts to promote uniformity of practice in areas formerly characterized by complete lack of standardization. Growth statistics attested to this remarkable coming of age: between 1930 and 1970, the accounting profession grew by 271 percent, compared with 73 percent for the medical profession and 71 percent for the legal profession.[2]

During this period, PW seemed destined to establish a pre-eminent position in the field. May emerged as a prominent economist, an expert on tax matters, a prolific author, and an influential spokesman who testified before numerous government agencies and investigative bodies on the leading questions of the day. He contributed broadly to the development of the profession by seeking wide acceptance for fuller disclosure in corporate financial statements, for annual audits by independent accounting firms, and for the formulation of accounting principles. His great prestige, along with the firm's clients and pre-eminent reputation, made PW unique. According to *Fortune*, the firm seemed "as unapproachable as royalty, entrenched in tradition and pride as well as professional ethics."[3] Within the firm, senior partners, including Campbell, May, John C. Scobie, and others, helped the partnership to develop stronger organizational standards, greater continuity of leadership, and a more clearly defined system of governance.

Even the firm's difficult experience arising out of the McKesson & Robbins engagement had a larger positive impact. The SEC's inquiry called into question the auditing standards and procedures that all firms employed in conducting their engagements and ultimately resulted in major changes in practice. By encouraging a wider scope of inquiry beyond merely auditing company assets, the McKesson & Robbins affair pointed the way to new services by, and new roles for, accountants. The events of the 1930s transformed the profession; by the early 1940s, audit work had become a fully accepted and regulated part of American business life.

THE AUDIT PRACTICE IN THE 1920s

In 1926, William B. Campbell succeeded to the firm's leadership on May's retirement as senior partner. Like his predecessors, Campbell had been born in Great Britain. Although he became a member of the English Institute in 1905, he emigrated to Canada a year later and then moved on to Buffalo, New York, where he worked for several small firms. In 1911, he applied to PW's New York office and was immediately assigned to the Chicago office. He remained there until 1915, when the firm acquired a Detroit practice and placed Campbell in charge. He was admitted as a partner within two years, when that office grew to rival others in size. During World War I, Campbell was attached to the Treasury Department. In the 1920s, he also held several important positions within the American Institute of Accountants, most notably chairman of its Special Committee on Cooperation with Bankers.[4] When he became senior executive partner of PW, Campbell carried on the Dickinson tradition of geographical expansion, opening offices in Buffalo and Atlanta. Much of his attention was devoted to the firm's increasingly complex administrative issues and to the implementation of firm policy, often in cooperation with selected New York office partners.[5] Campbell was frequently assisted by executive assistant Frank W. Thornton, who compiled numerous studies of the firm's administration and finances.

Minutes of partners' meetings of the late 1920s record discussions about the firm's competitive position, including probes into the quality of its client base and into ways to improve client relations. The question of whether or not to specialize was often raised. In 1927, Campbell led a discussion of whether the "class" of the firm's activities should be reconsidered. Some partners asserted that PW "was the only firm that is really ethical at the expense of earnings," whereas other firms went "after the business and were not too full of scruples about how they got it." Partners also expressed concern over the lack of personal contact with clients. One emphasized the need to keep clients advised of the progress of work and the accumulation of fees. Others raised the possibility of training staff for specialized branches of accounting such as banking, investment banking, and brokerage, moving picture, municipal, and public utility work in order to obtain greater market share.[6]

In the 1920s, PW's audit work schedule, like that of other firms, was highly seasonal. The bulk of its practice consisted of audits of year-end balance sheets. As a result, work "was very slack during the summer and exceedingly arduous during the busy season." One partner recalled that "from November to April the office was open every night until eleven, and we had arrangements with the night watchmen to run the elevators." The firm had to hire dozens of additional staff during these months, and typically 80 percent of these would leave by May of the following year.

While some of the temporary staff were college graduates with careers to pursue, many returned year after year from colorful "offseason" jobs that included cutting diamonds, clerking at racetracks, and counseling at summer camps. The competence of the temporary staff varied widely; one retired partner recalled a totally incompetent auditor who was, however, a skillful plumber. While working at PW, temporary staff, both college graduates and plumbers, seldom knew whether their status would become permanent. All reported for work and waited for assignments in the "available" room, where they gossiped, pitched pennies, or played cards. Being too "available," however, might result in unemployment:

> If the phone rang and you picked it up, the senior personnel man, whose name was Williams, would say "Who is this?" and you would say, "This is Smith," and he would say "Come on in Smith," and fifteen minutes later you would be out the door. That's how . . . [PW] selected who was going to be fired. So you got yourself friends around the staff and got yourself buried doing something so you would not go to the available room.[7]

All temporary staff performed the same boring tasks. One partner called it "donkey work," as it involved reconciling bank accounts, matching checks against the manual check register, stuffing envelopes so customers could confirm their accounts receivable, and reviewing endless pages of detailed inventories.

> You literally copied hundreds of documents rather than any photocopying process [as you would today]. . . . We made red and blue checkmarks, very pretty papers. Over time, January, February and March, you couldn't see straight.[8]

The few available adding machines were manually operated. Hard and long hours also resulted in costly mistakes, as when a whole evening's effort was accidentally discarded because of exhaustion.

Another annoying "waste of time" grew out of PW's long-standing requirement that all work be done in ink. Not only did this make for tedious recopying when errors were made, but it also encouraged too much attention to details that had little relation to good auditing: "Old-timers, particularly ones that weren't good accountants—that were just first-class bookkeepers—prided themselves on how neat their working papers were instead of what was in them."[9] Despite all of these drawbacks, few employees complained. College-educated juniors knew that this kind of work was required training for an accountancy career. As the Great Depression struck, many felt fortunate to have jobs at all.[10]

THE DEPRESSION YEARS

The stock market crash of October 1929 has come to symbolize the start of a decade of depression that demoralized the nation and devastated the business community. At its low point, the gross national product of the United States dropped 30 percent, wholesale prices fell 32 percent, roughly 9,000 banks failed, and national unemployment reached 25 percent.

The initial impact on PW was less severe than on many other businesses of the time. Between 1926 and 1930, firm profits climbed from $1,278,000 (or an average of $79,875 per partner) to $2,131,800 ($118,433 per partner), accelerating at a pace two-and-a-half times greater than the pre–1926 rate.

The firm fared much worse during the rest of the decade, however, although by contemporary standards PW partners continued to live well. By 1932, a decline in demand for special work and requests for reductions of past fees and current audits caused profits to fall to $1,210,900 ($67,272 per partner) and a year later to $1,031,700 ($57,317 per partner), which was less than half the level of 1930. Five years later, the firm rebounded, with profits reaching $1,820,200 ($75,842 per partner), though these declined somewhat by 1939 to $1,499,190 ($57,662 per partner).[11]

Varied demands for services and regional economic problems also had their effect; although business increased in the East, it declined in PW's western and midwestern offices, except Chicago. Decisions to open new offices were rescinded, and a few branches were closed. The three-year-old Atlanta office shut down in 1931, apparently a casualty of timing. "The establishment of a new office is a long and arduous task," one partner noted.

> There is so little one can ethically do to attract business and new clients come with painful slowness. Therefore there is a long period of losses year after year, and as many of our partners were definitely allergic to red ink, it was not many years before it was decided we were ahead of the times in Atlanta.[12]

The Great Depression experience served to reinforce PW's conservative approach toward growth. It also reinforced its tradition of loyalty to managers with long years of experience and its unwillingness to admit new partners until absolutely necessary. Any thoughts of expanding the partnership came to a halt in 1929, when the matter was referred to a committee of the New York partners. No new partners were added during the year, and during the following year, the firm promoted only two men—seasoned veterans, each of whom had served more than two decades with the firm.

PW depended more and more on its experienced professional staff. The number of permanent professionals grew from 401 to 472 between 1923 and 1932, when it was reduced because of economic conditions. The proportion of seniors in this group rose from 29 to 43 percent of the total, whereas that of the less experienced first and second assistants declined. These figures, exaggerated by the effect of the Great Depression, also illustrate the increasing lack of advancement to partnership ranks.[13]

The Accounting Profession Comes of Age

Although Campbell became senior partner in 1926, May remained as chairman of the firm. Over the next decade and a half, he played an important role in debates over changes in auditing and accounting procedure and acted as a spokesman for the profession in response to public criticism.

During the 1920s, the accounting profession had come under attack, as educators and commercial bankers criticized accounting practices and the "certification" of corporate financial statements. The tradition of nondisclosure and the nonstandard accounting practices that prevailed throughout the securities industry came under particular fire. Some companies did not issue any reports or information. The multiplicity of possible accounting treatments worsened the situation, making it impossible for accountants to come to agreement on generally accepted standards. Although the rules of the stock exchanges required that listing companies submit a substantial amount of information, enforcement was uneven. As a result, large accounting firms were unable to standardize accounting practices for their clients. Although it is not clear how useful this type of financial data would have been to the small investor of the late 1920s and 1930s, the absence of such information increasingly undermined the credibility of the securities industry.[14]

The issue of lack of disclosure was highlighted in a growing debate over physical inspection of inventories, a factor that would figure prominently in the McKesson & Robbins affair in the late 1930s. Critics challenged the treatment of inventories under the 1917 *Federal Reserve Bulletin*, "Uniform Accounts," which had been based on a PW internal document. The *Bulletin* had gained influence and strong acceptance throughout the 1920s, and with the publication of its third edition in 1929 became known as the "accountants' bible." Although it helped to promote uniformity of the audit process, its critics argued that it granted "an extraordinary amount of discretion to the auditor in the selection and extent of tests," and that it did not require personal observation of inventories, especially in large companies, where it would have been "arduous and perhaps impracticable." Likewise, the *Bulletin* held that confirmation of accounts and notes receivable was optional, dependent on the time available and the client's consent.[15] Backed by this authoritative source, business managements could refuse to allow accountants to make discretionary tests or inventory inspections on the grounds that they were merely incidental or too costly. In addition, the 1917 *Bulletin*'s heavy emphasis on balance-sheet data, a concern of lending banks, also resulted in a virtual exclusion of earnings reports, which would have been useful to investors.

To counter critics in the contemporary banking community, Campbell joined May in public discussion. He defended the prevailing practice on the grounds that there was a scarcity of accountants, and that even if physical inspection came "within the scope of an accountant's duties, they could not find the necessary staffs" to undertake it. Taking inventory required "the services of a very large number of people for a few hours or days once in six months or once a year," making it impossible for an accountant to take the inventories of any substantial number of clients. Furthermore, Campbell added, it would be impossible "for the accountant to carry on his staff men having sufficient technical knowledge of materials and products," ranging from jewelry to chemical company inventories.[16]

In several important articles that appeared in the *Atlantic Monthly* in 1926, Harvard University economist William Z. Ripley took the profession to task. He charged that insufficient information was provided to stockholders concerning the companies in which they had invested. Ripley especially criticized the work of accountants, which represented an important nexus of communication between management and the shareholder. He noted that the demands of aggressive companies that accountants add ambiguous qualifications to their certificates diminished both the profession's stature and the general public's ability to follow and interpret business practice. Ripley called for active intervention by the federal government to compel uniform and timely reporting by all public companies.[17]

Ripley's first article, "From Main Street to Wall Street," which targeted the accounting practices of a number of current and former PW clients, provoked a reply from May. May questioned the practices that Ripley had given as illustrations, but agreed that stockholders should receive adequate information about the companies in which they had invested. Above all, May noted that every balance sheet and income account was, in large measure, a matter of estimate and opinion. He warned his readers

> that if those on the inside in a corporation desire to profit at the expense of those on the outside, it is often as easy for them to achieve their purpose by issuing statements which are adequate and correct according to every accepted canon as in any other way. No amount of regulation will make a dishonestly managed company a satisfactory investment.[18]

Despite his skirmish with Ripley, May quickly became a strong supporter of more complete disclosure in financial statements. In a speech at the AIA annual meeting in September 1926, he asked the organization to consider working with others to determine "what are the proper responsibilities of auditors and what can be done to hold them to such responsibilities and to put them in a position to assume all the responsibilities which they ought to assume."[19]

May became involved in developing a strategy to address concerns about financial reporting and about the implications of the increased ownership of securities by the general public. In the late 1920s, a number of private interest groups, including the stock exchanges, the investment bankers' association, and the accounting profession, began working for greater disclosure. May joined with other leaders in business, government, and education interested in sponsoring research aimed at identifying solutions to the problems involved in greater disclosure, and he also served as chairman of a special committee at Columbia University's Council for Research in the Social Sciences. This work drew May into closer contact with Ripley, who was grant administrator for the project, and introduced him to its researchers, Adolf A. Berle, professor at Columbia University Law School, and Harvard graduate economics student Gardiner C. Means. Although many involved in the project initially supported a more active role for the government in regulating financial markets, their viewpoint gradually shifted, under May's influence, toward a solution devised by the profession and private institutions.[20]

May sought to implement the ideas that he developed as chair of this committee by working under the AIA's auspices to persuade the New York Stock Exchange to require full disclosure in the financial statements of its listed companies. In early 1927, he met with the new executive assistant of the exchange's Committee on the Stock List, J.M.B. Hoxsey, who had been appointed to his post in 1926 to review financial reporting by listed companies. The New York Stock Exchange ultimately declined the AIA's initiative, but it retained PW, with May in charge of the engagement, as consulting accountants on accounting questions that arose relative to the listing of securities.[21]

During the 1920s, May recalled, "the public appetite for securities grew insatiable and undiscriminating."[22] Whereas in 1899, half a million people owned stocks, by 1930, this figure had grown to ten million.[23] With the precipitous decline in the value of securities after the stock market crash in October 1929, public complaints against accountants over their widely differing approaches of reporting corporate financial information reached a new level. A wave of litigation began, and many leading firms became embroiled in stockholder suits. Under the glare of public scrutiny, the New York Stock Exchange agreed to reforms, and in 1930 May was finally able to assist the AIA in establishing a

Special Committee on Cooperation with the New York Stock Exchange.[24]

Within two years, a number of important events occurred that prepared the way for radical changes in the securities industry. In 1932, the Kreuger & Toll scandal broke and helped to fan the flames of public discontent. Kreuger & Toll, Inc., whose stocks were the most widely held securities in the United States and in the world, was an international match monopoly run by Ivar Kreuger, known as the "Match King." Hailed as "the greatest financial genius in the world," Kreuger was an icon of the Roaring Twenties, an adviser of kings and presidents and a lender to foreign governments.[25]

The Great Depression unraveled this empire, revealing that Kreuger & Toll was nothing more than a gigantic pyramid scheme. Kreuger committed suicide in March 1932. Within a month of his death, PW, which had been hired to conduct a thorough international investigation, issued the first of fifty-seven reports revealing the true state of affairs. Kreuger had owned, operated, or had an interest in more than four hundred companies; investigating this tangled and fraudulent empire was a massive undertaking that took five years.[26] Throughout the process, PW performed with characteristic reserve. May told a *Fortune* reporter who was then writing a story about Kreuger & Toll that the firm "should much prefer to see no reference to PW & Co. except anonymously as the international accounting firm which was called in by the Swedish Government."[27]

The inquiry revealed that nearly a quarter of a billion dollars in assets reported by Kreuger never existed. Through misstated balance sheets and income statements, Kreuger defrauded hundreds of thousands of individual investors, many university endowment funds, and hundreds of banks. Innocent investors lost hundreds of millions of dollars. Since the frauds occurred in Sweden, no American accountants could have had access to the records, and they were not held responsible. Serious doubts had been raised, however, about the effect of financial reporting and independent audits in general. Within two months of Kreuger's death, Congress began to consider legislation to stop future frauds of this kind.[28]

The second key event of 1932 was publication of Berle and Means's landmark study, *The Modern Corporation and Private Property*, based on their Columbia research. Although their book is best known for its analysis of wealth distribution in the United States in the 1920s and of the implications of the growing separation of ownership and control in the modern corporation, Berle and Means also stressed the need for more objective financial information to ensure the equitable and efficient functioning of financial markets. In their book they argued that the groups primarily responsible for adequate financial disclosure were investment bankers, corporate directors, and managers. To make certain that these sectors operated in the public interest, the researchers called for increased regulatory powers of organizations like the New York Stock Exchange. Reflecting May's influence as chair of the Columbia University committee, Berle and Means also specifically cited the necessity of requiring large public companies to file audited financial statements and of mandating some accounting principles to prevent the flagrant abuses that had plagued reporting. The authors identified public accountants as key agents in ensuring the efficient functioning of these regulatory mechanisms.[29]

Alliance with the SEC

With the Great Depression looming in the background, the election of President Franklin D. Roosevelt in 1932 made the enactment of federal securities laws inevitable. Among the legislative proposals passed in the first "Hundred Days" of the new administration was the Securities Act of 1933, which regulated the issuance of new securities and provided for "full and fair disclosure" in registration statements for large, interstate flotations of securities. This law was designed to strengthen the financial system and to assure probity by defining stricter responsibilities for the various professional groups on which it depended. Many of Berle and Means's proposals became public policy; the new law required, for example, that detailed financial information be provided by companies in their registration statements, which had to be audited by an independent public accountant.[30]

The Securities Act of 1933 also imposed more responsibility on accountants for negligently failing to discover "untrue statements or omissions of material facts." Under the standards that previously existed at common law, a purchaser of stock had the burden of proving the negligence of an accountant in a court of law. The new act changed this standard; now the purchaser did not have to prove the accountant's negligence, but only that he or she had suffered a loss as a result of the purchase, and that the financial statements on which the accountant had reported were misstated. The accountant bore the burden of proving either that the purchaser's loss resulted from reliance on information other than that contained in the registration statement, or that the accountant was not negligent.[31]

The Securities Act of 1934, also known as the Securities Exchange Act, followed the next year. This statute, whose broad objective was to mandate continuous financial disclosure for all public companies, required periodic financial reports, similar to those specified by the earlier law, by companies whose securities had been previously issued to the public.[32]

The 1934 Act also created the Securities and Exchange Commission and gave it complete authority to determine the accounting practices used by corporations in their financial reports. Accountants were initially alarmed by the SEC's wide authority. At PW, for example, partners worried about the direction that government intervention would take and the degree to which efforts to regulate financial markets would affect their professional autonomy. They expressed deep concern about the prospect that compulsory audits imposed by government might eliminate the public accountant's function. This had already happened in the railroad, banking, and insurance industries, as well as in some state and local governments that had created their own audit bureaus. But the many accountants who at first bitterly protested the liability provisions contained in the new laws soon recognized that the statutes provided enormous overall gains for them. The new responsibilities of accountants concerning disclosure, for example, gave those who needed it the leverage to challenge unscrupulous clients.[33]

In 1935, the SEC hired its first chief accountant who, by virtue of his position, became the most important individual regulator of accounting practice in the United States. The chief accountant's mandate was to lead the profession in a drive toward more vigorous audits, to impose more serious sanctions to deter violators of accounting principles, and to promote uniform accounting statements.

The most pressing question before the SEC was one of implementation: how to make the marketing and trading of securities safe and legitimate for the American public. The new commission decided to pursue this goal by working pragmatically through existing structures rather than by overseeing an army of its own auditor-regulators deployed throughout America's large companies or by attempting to force results with direct government action. PW played an important role in establishing basic reporting packages and formats to be used by the SEC, and the firm provided a model for the SEC's cooperative work with the accounting profession in the areas of standard-setting and financial reporting. Volunteer accountants and the professional societies helped devise the SEC's filing forms. The SEC relied on previous work done by the profession and the stock exchanges to formulate six fundamental rules or principles of accounting (which later became known as "generally accepted accounting principles"), to promulgate guidelines on financial statements for listed companies, and to set forth a foundation for the standard form of an auditor's report. These standards appeared in a 1934 AIA booklet entitled *Audits of Corporate Accounts*, and the principles, commonly referred to as GAAP, immediately came into common usage. Although May, who helped devise GAAP, hoped that all listed companies would be required to assert publicly which principles they used, this requirement was not imposed until the early 1970s.[34]

Despite these promising developments, accounting practices continued to be quite diverse. In 1937, the SEC's chief accountant began to issue Accounting Series Releases (ASRs) to inform the profession about acceptable methods and procedures. In the following year, the SEC issued ASR No. 4, stating, in effect, that it would expect accounting practices used in reports filed by corporations to have "substantial authoritative support." The profession realized that unless it acted to provide the SEC with such support, the implementation of GAAP would become the responsibility of a federal regulatory agency.[35]

This threat had a salutary effect on the accounting profession. In 1937, the American Institute of Accountants, which represented large national accounting firms, agreed to merge with its rival, the American Society of Certified Public Accountants, which had split off in 1922 and which represented many smaller local practitioners. This merger enhanced the AIA's efforts to assert its professionwide authority through the promulgation of professional standards, as well as its leverage in dealing with political leaders. The unified AIA could also work to limit any further efforts by regulators to encroach on its autonomy.[36]

Committees were quickly established to formulate standards for financial accounting and auditing. In 1938, the AIA created a twenty-one–member Committee on Accounting Procedure (CAP), which had the authority to issue pronouncements called Accounting Research Bulletins (ARBs). May played an instrumental role as vicechair of the CAP until 1941 and, from 1939 to 1947, as head of the AIA Committee on Terminology, which developed several reports that were later issued as ARBs.[37]

Following the profession's successful efforts to retain its self-regulatory powers, leading accountants continued to develop accounting principles and broader objectives. Acknowledging the overlap of interests, the SEC supported the guidance given by the CAP's bulletins and did not attempt to set professional standards itself.[38] The SEC worked instead through regular meetings with AIA committees and through confidential meetings with corporate executives of companies whose accounting practices it had questioned, and by promulgating standards in ASRs and in speeches and writings of the chief accountant and the agency's commissioners.[39]

By 1940, a united and vigorous accounting profession with a wide degree of self-regulation had emerged, and the concept of the "independent" outside auditor had come of age. The securities laws of 1933 and

1934 had placed the accounting profession at the center of American business life, and accountants who served large corporations became integral to the efficient functioning of financial markets. These laws also guaranteed a stable market for the audit. By the mid-1930s, more than 90 percent of the companies listed on the New York Stock Exchange were audited. Its high proportion of NYSE–listed clients (which were already required by the exchange to be audited by independent public accountants) meant that PW had less need than other accounting firms for legislation that ensured a steady client base. Nevertheless, the firm benefited from the securities laws, and its continuing prosperity seemed assured at the end of the 1930s.[40]

In addition to his work in the regulatory developments of the 1930s, May also contributed knowledge and insight concerning a number of other important public issues throughout this period. For example, he testified before the Senate Finance Committee in 1936 on a proposed Treasury Department tax bill, quietly but relentlessly attacking it as ill-considered and unnecessary. Embarrassed Treasury aides seated near the press tables admitted to reporters that the criticism was telling because May was "one of the highest authorities on the subjects of finance and taxation." His statements caught the attention of headline writers who reported "Tax Bill Unsound and Not Needed, Expert Testifies," and, more succinctly, "May over [Secretary of the Treasury Henry] Morgenthau."[41]

In the years following his retirement from PW in 1940, and from the CAP in 1941, May remained a perceptive commentator on accounting principles and practices. In retirement, until his death in 1961 at age 86, he wrote more than a hundred professional articles and continued to speak on accounting issues before government bodies and professional audiences and in academic forums. Although he was perhaps best known for his work in formulating GAAP, May's most enduring legacy to the profession was considered by many to be his insistence that an accountant use personal judgment, rather than simply apply rigid and unvarying rules.

> Accounting conventions must take cognizance of the social and economic concepts of the time and place. Conventions which are acceptable in a pioneer, free-enterprise economy may not be equally appropriate in a more mature, free-enterprise economy, and may lose their validity in a controlled economy.[42]

May was sometimes referred to as G.O.M., or "the Grand Old Man"; his life and practice spanned a whirlwind of change in the profession.

LEADERSHIP IN TRANSITION

Although Campbell had been named senior partner in 1926, by the early 1930s his health had irreversibly declined. In looking for a successor, PW partners were aware that a leadership vacuum loomed as the older generation resigned, retired, or died. Many partners had spent their early careers under Dickinson, and few had advanced to partnership without long years of service as managers. Many were nearing the age of 60 at the same time. To redress this problem, five new partners were admitted in 1933, and another five were selected a year later. These actions proved inadequate, however. Several PW partners, including May, were forced to manage the firm while younger successors were groomed.[43]

The veteran partners were not mere caretakers, however, and they made significant changes in PW's governance. To help May deal with the operational issues that Campbell had handled, one senior partner from the St. Louis office and one from Los Angeles were transferred to New York. In July 1934, a month after Campbell's death, May established an ad hoc Executive Committee. Such a committee had been provided for in the 1920 Partnership Agreement, but apparently never had been convened. Until this leadership crisis, it had not been needed, since the size of the partnership had always averaged fewer than two dozen members, and most of the important business had been handled in semiannual partners' meetings.[44] May sought advice from leading partners in staffing the Executive Committee and then appointed four members, including the two senior partners who had recently been transferred from St. Louis and Los Angeles. May served as chairman. In 1936, at his suggestion, the committee was expanded to include four additional members, including two younger men, who the older partners hoped could eventually take over the firm's leadership.

Confusing the issue of leadership throughout this period was the term "senior partner," which had never been adequately defined and which was often used indiscriminately to refer to any older and experienced partner. Although Campbell had acted as a chief executive officer for the firm and was called the senior executive partner, May had apparently retained the title of senior partner and, in 1936, a "Silver Jubilee Party" commemorated his quarter-century of service in that capacity. By the 1940s, after May's retirement and following the permanent establishment of the Executive Committee, the term "senior partner" came to be associated with the chairman of that committee.

Although May resumed his role as chairman at partners' meetings in 1934 and presided over the Executive Committee's deliberations, he was, according to many, "virtually retired." The management of the firm devolved on John C. Scobie, with such help as the other members of the Executive Committee could provide. Over the next several years, the older members of the Executive Committee gradually departed through retirement and resignation. One of the two promising young partners who had been elevated to the committee resigned. Management was left in the hands of Scobie, only three years junior to May, and Percival (Percy) F. Brundage, seventeen years younger than May.[45]

The Executive Committee tried to open up the partnership by developing a retirement policy linked to a retirement income program. Although retirement at age 60 was an unwritten precept at PW, few partners could afford to leave. With the formal adoption of a plan devised by the Executive Committee and accepted by partners in their 1937 spring meeting, the near-uniformity in the age of partners, perceived as constituting a definite weakness in the firm's organization, at last began to break. Under the arrangement, retired partners could continue to serve the firm as consultants, and younger men were admitted to the partnership on a more regular basis. Over the next ten years, twenty-eight new partners were admitted, while ten retired. This was a significant change for a firm that had admitted only forty-two partners during its first forty-seven years.[46]

The McKesson & Robbins Matter

During this period of leadership transition, PW was sorely tested by a notorious and embarrassing case. The firm had been involved in some litigation during the 1930s, but most cases were relatively minor affairs, involving losses suffered from defalcations. Since the firm had advised clients of the limitations of its work, little came of these suits. As a protection, however, partners regularly discussed the scope and wording of certificates, resolved to talk more directly to clients about the issue of defalcation, and worked to provide an adequate record of the firm's position on these matters in its files. Since dissemination of information was crucial in light of the charged, litigious atmosphere at that time, it was decided that the New York partners should systematically send out information of interest regarding legal cases to the other partners.[47]

None of these efforts prepared PW for its role in the McKesson & Robbins scandal, an event that had an immediate impact as well as deep lasting repercussions. It was the first instance in which auditing practices were subject to significant public comment, criticism, and judgment. Ultimately, the SEC's investigation forced a long-overdue appraisal and, later, a reorientation of audit priorities throughout the profession.[48]

The facts surrounding PW's audit of McKesson & Robbins were highly unusual. The original McKesson company had been founded in

New York City in 1833 as a manufacturer of drugs and liquor. It remained in family hands until the mid-1920s, when changes in the industries it served required the company to build its own national distribution system. Unwilling to make this investment, family members sold out in 1926 to F. Donald Coster for $1 million. At that time, no one in the company knew that "Coster" was, in fact, one of many aliases for Philip Musica. Under different identities, Musica had entered into questionable business activities that led, eventually, to convictions for bribery and grand larceny. In the early 1920s, for instance, he had purchased a pharmaceutical manufacturing company to provide a legitimate facade for a bootlegging operation.[49]

Under Musica's aggressive leadership, McKesson grew to become a complex $82 million corporation. In addition to a crude drug manufacturing division, the company also controlled, after the repeal of Prohibition, the country's largest wholesale distributor of wines and liquors, a distillery, a liquor importation business, and a wholesale distribution business, or "jobbing" of drugs, including those of other manufacturers. The wholesale business, which developed through the acquisition and consolidation of forty-nine of the country's largest drug-jobbing houses, grew to be ten times bigger than that of any other drug wholesaler in the United States.

Musica's relationship with PW began in 1923, when, after acquiring a small New York pharmaceutical company named Girard & Co., he hired PW to conduct its annual audit. Throughout the next fifteen years, neither Girard's directors and lending banks nor PW were aware of Musica's previous crimes or ongoing fraudulent activities. As *Fortune* later noted,

> Girard & Co. was undoubtedly a sort of laboratory in which Musica perfected the technique of his later, larger frauds. He was experimenting with the limitations of accountancy and directorships, and the experiment was a great success.[50]

Musica consolidated McKesson with Girard and he moved all the machinery and stock of the newly named "McKesson & Robbins of Connecticut" to Bridgeport, Connecticut. He rapidly expanded, weathered the initial years of the Great Depression, and gained tighter control over the company's operations. Only in 1937, when the board of directors voted to cut the level of inventories in the company's divisions, which had risen in value over one year to $10 million, did Musica's embezzlement begin to emerge. When the corporate treasurer questioned Musica about the company's foreign crude drug manufacturing operation, he learned that, although its profits were the highest of all the

McKesson & Robbins divisions, they were always reinvested into new supplies and failed to produce cash for the operation.[51]

When the treasurer found that further questions yielded only elusive replies from Musica, he began an investigation that eventually uncovered an elaborate fraud. Musica responded, inexplicably, by placing McKesson & Robbins under receivership in Connecticut. Several of the company's directors reacted swiftly and successfully reorganized the company under New York law. McKesson & Robbins securities were suspended from trading. A quick investigation by the SEC revealed Musica's shady background and led to his arrest. He committed suicide in December 1938, after having defrauded the company of about $2.9 million. After his death, newspapers dug into his past, uncovered the breadth of his corruption, and discovered that he had been blackmailed by individuals familiar with his earlier activities.[52] For the next several years, McKesson & Robbins was run by a receiver appointed by the court.

A subsequent investigation revealed that the company's foreign crude drug business was largely fictitious. The scheme had employed a complex setup of false suppliers and buyers who carried on their business with McKesson & Robbins from back offices in Canada, where the nonexistent inventories were supposedly held. At the time, physical inspection of inventories was not regarded as part of an accountant's responsibility, and PW auditors were not inclined to undertake the task at McKesson & Robbins partly because several of Musica's brothers, each using a different assumed name, readily supplied the firm with the information it had needed to conduct its audits. "Robert Dietrich," the youngest Musica brother, prepared false inventory sheets for the auditors and produced count sheets when these were requested by PW. "Dietrich" also forged credit reports on the dummy companies, and created elaborate sets of documents that deceived both PW and the McKesson & Robbins directors. Musica had not interfered with other company operations, including the wholesale domestic drug division that accounted for most of the company's profit at the time.

To grasp the difficulties PW faced in this case, it is important to understand how an audit was conducted in the 1920s and 1930s. At that time, an auditor examining a company's books was interested primarily in figures and documents. To verify cash assets, the auditor wrote to the bank to see how much cash the company had and reconciled that figure with deposit records and canceled checks. For accounts receivable, the auditor took a sampling and checked the documents on each sample group as evidence that bona fide sales had been made. Although confirmation of accounts receivable and the observation of inventory were all recognized procedures of the period, their use in practice was not mandated. The lack of any body of professional standards at this time meant that the application of these procedures depended on the judgment of the practitioner in a particular circumstance. As a result, auditors often did not get independent confirmation of receivables from customers. With regard to inventories, auditors often determined how goods on hand were counted and valued, but they did not personally count them.[53]

In January 1939, the SEC began several months of public hearings on the McKesson & Robbins matter. Witnesses testified that PW had adhered to generally accepted auditing procedures as prescribed by the AIA, such as those found in the 1917 *Federal Reserve Bulletin*, "Uniform Accounts." PW auditors had matched customer credits with entries in cash receipts books and had compared crude drug sales with inventory records and copies of customer and shipping invoices. However, as witnesses explained, many of the documents on which PW had relied were forged, so even though the auditors had conformed to prevailing auditing standards, they did not uncover frauds involving managerial collusion. Requests by PW to perform further testing might have produced only more forged documents, witnesses asserted, similar to the signed inventory sheets and written confirmations by the company's Canadian "suppliers" that had then been checked against purchase orders. It was also noted that McKesson & Robbins had formally certified the condition and quantity of inventories on its balance sheet.[54]

In its 1940 report on McKesson & Robbins, the SEC had some harsh words for PW. It questioned existing auditing standards that could fail to detect $19 million in fictitious receivables and inventory. "The time has long passed," the SEC noted, "if it ever existed, when the basis of an audit was restricted to the material appearing in the books and records."[55] The SEC called for a "material advance" and a tightening of auditing procedures, so that facts disclosed on paper were verified through physical inspection or independent confirmation. In addition to calling for confirmation of receivables and physical inspections of inventory, the SEC report also sought better reviews of systems of internal checks and controls, greater auditor responsibility to stockholders and management in the audit process, and clearer representations on the scope of work in certificates. The SEC noted with approval the work of the new AIA special committee on audit procedure and its report, *Extension of Auditing Procedure*, which emphasized more thorough audit testing of receivables and inventory.[56]

PW defended itself in a short written response to the SEC's report, maintaining that the scope and procedure of its examinations substantially conformed to professional standards at the time of its engagement and describing the newer standards "developed largely as a result of this particular fraud as clearly inapplicable to this case." The firm's position was later affirmed by an AIA Committee on Professional Ethics in 1941, which, though concluding that a more careful investigation by "resourceful auditors" should have revealed the gross inflation in the accounts, acknowledged that cases involving the same degree of managerial manipulation were "so rare that there is no economic justification for the amount of auditing work which would be required to increase materially the protection against it."[57]

May was particularly embittered over the McKesson & Robbins affair. During the height of the SEC hearings, he noted that it was "almost impossible for anyone, now, to distinguish between foresight and hindsight." He thought that the enlarged base of accounts receivable and inventories should have been recognized by the group of bankers, which included an ex-director of the company, who were hired in 1933 by Musica to study McKesson & Robbins's financial soundness. These bankers, who turned against Musica once they began digging into the records, "had full investigating powers and spent months on the Company's affairs." According to May, although they were "anxious to get rid of Musica and raised questions on many points with us, they raised no question in regard to these inventories and accounts receivable or the crude drug division generally." For May, the key to McKesson & Robbins was its singularity: "the fact that a group of criminal brothers succeeded in establishing themselves in controlling key positions in a large company." As late as 1955, he still believed that the SEC had drawn the wrong conclusions from the matter by introducing procedures that greatly increased the cost of audited financial statements yet would still be ineffective in McKesson-like cases of forgery.[58]

The SEC, on the other hand, maintained that its suggested reforms were effective. In its final McKesson & Robbins report in 1941, the SEC declined to recommend that the government begin defining and issuing detailed regulations governing audit procedures. Instead, it praised the profession for adopting new procedures and expressed its belief that new audit standards would be developed and adapted as conditions required.[59]

The SEC's 1944 *Annual Report* continued in this vein, noting with approval that the securities laws had caused fundamental changes in accountants' responsibilities, requiring significant alteration in the profession's approach to accounting problems. The SEC found that accountants were making important progress by freeing themselves from the "stigma of managerial influence in their selection or approval of accounting principles," by developing a "philosophy of accounting" to establish a rationale for principles, and by accepting the need for full disclosure in financial statements. The SEC also approved of the growth of an authoritative body of literature regarding accounting principles.[60]

The McKesson & Robbins matter served to force a final break with an older British tradition, common throughout the American accounting profession, of "auditing the assets" instead of "auditing the business." With auditing standards changed to require inspection of inventories and confirmation of receivables as part of a general expansion of audit responsibility, the tendency of audits to become, at their worst, little more than superficial credit investigations was reversed.[61]

The McKesson & Robbins matter also raised an important issue of auditor independence. Although it was standard practice at the time, PW had been engaged by McKesson's president and controller and not by the company's board of directors, leaving the firm open to criticism that it was engaged by the same management group whose assertions, in the form of financial statements, it was to certify through an audit. Based on the findings in this case, the SEC would later recommend that boards of directors, in their capacity as primary fiduciary agents to shareholders, take responsibility for engaging independent public accountants.[62]

The McKesson & Robbins case, in fact, changed the nature of an auditor's work. The new normal starting point for an audit was a review of a company's internal controls, and the results of that review largely determined the extent of subsequent testing required. For example, where sampling indicated that a reliable internal control system existed, the detailed verification procedures so characteristic of earlier audit staff work could be nearly eliminated. At the same time, McKesson & Robbins broadened the scope and content of accountants' inquiries, and the auditor's concept of internal control expanded to include the totality of a company and its operations, and even questions of managerial policy.[63] In choosing to evaluate internal control beyond its direct effects on the accounting system, auditors positioned themselves to diagnose and suggest solutions for a client's operating problems. Both the modern audit and the origins of today's management consulting services provided by accountants emerged as post–McKesson & Robbins developments.[64]

NEW DIRECTIONS AND WARTIME DEVELOPMENTS

In May 1939, a month after the conclusion of the SEC's McKesson & Robbins proceedings, PW created a formal Executive Committee. Unlike its predecessor, which was called into being in response to an emergency, the new body permanently assumed the general supervision of the partnership's affairs, recommended policy changes in partners' meetings, and had the authority to borrow money and execute deeds. In the new Partnership Agreement completed several months later and embodying these developments, the U.S. firm, on the advice of counsel and because of the SEC's proxy rules, severed its profit-sharing arrangement with the British firm.[65]

The partners selected John C. Scobie to serve as chairman of the new Executive Committee and as senior partner. Scobie was born in Edinburgh, Scotland, where he received a university education and served his accounting apprenticeship. In 1903, he wrote to the London firm to apply for a position on the American staff, noting that "I am desirous of going out to the States in order to better my position—as business is very dull here." That same year he joined the U.S. firm in New York, where he spent nearly all of his career except for a three-year sojourn as manager of the Pittsburgh office beginning in 1911. He was admitted to the partnership in 1914.[66]

Scobie's immediate objectives as head of PW were to work out a settlement with the McKesson & Robbins trustee, to visit important clients to discuss the case, and to implement some important internal reforms. Throughout the whole ordeal, the partners saw Scobie as "a tower of strength to us all during these difficult times. He never for a moment conceded that any fault attached to us and fought valiantly for his viewpoint."[67] As a sign of good faith, Scobie offered the McKesson & Robbins trustee a sum equivalent to the engagement fees over the previous six years; the money was accepted. Scobie spent a great deal of time traveling and meeting with clients, discussing the events and circumstances surrounding the McKesson & Robbins matter, and assuring them of the firm's integrity and reputation. As a result, their concerns gradually diminished. While PW did lose a few clients, they were those, as one partner later recalled, who were "merely seeking an excuse to get rid of us anyway." One was National Dairy Co., whose CEO had viewed PW as "a thorn in the side" for years. Outside the New York office, the McKesson & Robbins case "caused barely a ripple," and it is doubtful that it caused the firm any considerable losses in the other offices.[68]

Scobie's travels were also intended to reassure partners and especially the firm's staff. A Los Angeles staff member who later became partner-in-charge of that office recalled a visit from Scobie at this time. The senior partner discussed the McKesson & Robbins affair frankly and openly and encouraged the young accountant to remain with the firm. Most young staffers apparently had no reservations about PW as a result of the McKesson & Robbins case and did not sense a change in client relations after it; the experience apparently had little impact on revenues in the early 1940s.[69] It did, however, prompt a number of internal changes. Scobie established a committee to study client annual reports "with a view to making these documents more useful to an ever-widening body of interested parties." He also sought to develop more uniformity of practice, though he, like May, recognized that "wide divergences in business enterprises necessitated the arrangement of financial data in a form which, to the partner in charge of the engagement, seemed most logical and informative." Scobie worked to make adjustments in PW's techniques of evaluating clients' systems of internal control, and he enlisted the help of partners to investigate and recommend changes. Working papers were made clearer and more comprehensive. Some of these efforts were of such general interest that they were presented at professional meetings or published in accounting journals.[70]

In May 1939, Scobie recommended expanding the partnership in order to guard against personnel shortages. Eight senior managers in charge of important client work were admitted as partners during the next year and a half. He also suggested that certain senior managers be promoted to the new position of "principal," giving them full responsibility for the assignments they supervised and allowing them to sign the firm name on correspondence and accounts. Creating this new group was an acknowledgment of the small partnership's inability to deal effectively with the details of client work. Many partners felt that what had occurred on the watch of Geoffrey Rowbotham, the partner-in-charge of McKesson & Robbins, might easily have happened to them. Rowbotham had given

> the job about the same degree of attention as the partners generally did. Large pieces of work were in direct charge of trusted senior managers, since the partners could not pretend to go deeply into the details that were supposed to be dealt with by the men directly on the work.[71]

The introduction of principals was intended to remedy this apparent lack of supervision.

Staff members were also given better training. In 1941, PW instituted scheduled staff conferences, in which one or two dozen employees were trained under the direction of a junior manager. These courses relied on a wealth of practice material written by partners and staff over three decades, the most important sources being Arthur Dickinson's *Accounting Practice and Procedures*, Robert Berger's *Organizational Ethics and Teamwork*, Ward Reynolds and Frank Thornton's *Duties of the Junior Accountant*, and Thornton's *Duties of the Senior Accountant* and *Financial Examinations*.[72]

Finally, the McKesson & Robbins matter prompted efforts to end PW's use of "temporary" employees and to move toward year-round auditing work. In fiscal year 1938, for example, the number of staff had oscillated from a low of 940 individuals in the summer to a high of 1,666 in January, and levels remained high until the spring. Previous attempts to secure work in the summer, or other kinds of interim work, had made practically no progress.[73] Yet even as PW sought to make changes in all of these important areas, the firm was temporarily deflected from its efforts by the personnel challenges of World War II.

INTERLUDE: PW DURING THE WAR

Unlike the pivotal events of the 1930s, the securities acts and the McKesson & Robbins crisis, World War II did not have a lasting, structural effect on PW or on the profession. The changes it brought to PW were chiefly a result of the loss of personnel and the flood of new and different business. Many partners, managers, and other staff members entered military service or left for government jobs, in which they made notable wartime contributions, particularly in accounting areas. Heavy demands were placed on those who remained, and innovative solutions were devised to handle the work.

To the usual, recurring client needs was added a significant amount of new business, particularly consultations on war contracts and other war-related services. Many of these engagements, often involving "cost-plus" contracts, emergency plant facilities, systems work, and tax measures that collected up to 80 percent of client income, were additionally complicated because few rules had been established to govern them.

Increasingly complex wartime Treasury and Internal Revenue Service (IRS) regulations resulted in an ever more specialized tax practice that diverged widely from general accounting principles. Military requirements spurred constant modifications to the 1939 Internal Revenue Code, both to achieve social and economic objectives and to raise money.

In addition, mechanized clerical routines, auditing tests, and internal control procedures developed after McKesson & Robbins were widely introduced in defense-related systems, spurred by the war's tight deadlines. Joseph Pelej, who later became the first PW systems partner, recalled

> the tremendous demands made on industry in converting to war production, expanding, and meeting incredible schedules. . . . We were plunged, together with all management throughout the big industries, into problems of administration, production and control that had never been faced before on such a scale.[74]

At the war's onset, PW still relied on seasonal workers, but as the conflict gathered in intensity, even the supply of "temporary men" dried up. The Detroit office, for example, grew so desperate that it hired a 76-year-old man for audit work.[75]

Faced with the most serious personnel crisis in its history, PW initiated an innovative program to recruit college-educated women as auditors. In the spring of 1943, the partner-in-charge of the Chicago office hired a Northwestern University professor as a recruiter. Of the sixty-five women recommended to this professor by deans of midwestern colleges, twenty-one were accepted into an eleven-week, all-expenses-paid training course in accounting and auditing at Northwestern. A year later, the professor arranged second, larger training courses at Northwestern and at Connecticut College for Women. A majority of these women recruits worked on the staffs of the New York and Chicago offices, with about twenty-five women assigned to each. In addition, many other, smaller offices also recruited college-trained women, who composed 30 to 40 percent of PW's accounting staff during the war.[76]

Available data on the number of women in the accounting profession in general during this period are contradictory. A 1943 survey taken by the War Manpower Commission stated that a total of 821 women were employed in public accounting at that time. Although this was an increase from 480 in 1941, the survey noted that women comprised only 9 percent of total professional accounting staffs in 1943. Another study found 18,265 women holding positions as accountants and auditors in 1940, with their numbers rising to 55,660 by 1950, perhaps by including accountants, auditors, and bookkeepers, rather than only women engaged in public accounting.[77]

Servicemen returning to PW in 1946 brought an end to the firm's experience with significant numbers of women auditors for several decades. The professor who had recruited the women asked the firm to keep them on in the postwar period, reminding PW that trainees had been assured that "at the end of their neophyte period of one year they would be in competition with other men and women on the staff and have the same opportunities for a successful career with the firm."[78] PW had encouraged college women to major in accounting, and he warned the firm against discriminating against women by failing to employ those whose records were outstanding "in the same way we expect to take topnotch men graduating in the field." Nevertheless, only a "few women still remained in responsible positions on the staff" at PW five years after war's end.[79]

In July 1944, Scobie died after a long illness. Although senior partner for only five years, he had achieved much through his tireless efforts, serving as spokesman during the McKesson & Robbins controversy and guiding PW through a series of permanent internal reforms. He also met the accounting demands of the war in a creative and innovative fashion. His decisive actions left PW stronger than he had found it, and better able to meet the challenges of the postwar world.

The 1930s and early 1940s were pivotal for the accounting profession and for PW. While the events of the first thirty-five years of the firm's history influenced its establishment and Americanization, those that followed after 1929 created an entirely new era. The stock market crash threw the business world into an economic convulsion of unprecedented magnitude and, for the next decade, PW and the profession were at the forefront of dramatic institutional changes.

With the enactment of the landmark securities legislation of the 1930s, annual audits of public companies became mandatory, and the role of accountants in the business world was institutionalized. The threat behind the legislation also forced a divided and fragmented group of practitioners to unify themselves into a stronger profession. The new laws helped to create a number of widely recognized audit and accounting procedures, which were, in effect, a first step toward a body of professional knowledge. The movement toward professionalism was further underscored by the aftermath of the McKesson & Robbins affair. As accountants began increasingly to audit business procedures, a broader scope of inquiry and new service opportunities arose. In addition, the legislation brought accountants from large firms into an important alliance with their regulators at the new Securities and Exchange Commission. The economies of scale involved in audit work for large public companies allowed the sizable firms to consolidate their grasp on this lucrative and dependable new work. All of these changes led to the formation of a monolithic industry structure that endured for the next fifty years.

PW underwent important internal changes as well. It began this period as a simple partnership dominated by one man, George O. May. Having endured a leadership crisis following the premature death of May's successor, William Campbell, and a personnel crisis caused by World War II, the firm introduced changes in management and staff development to guard against future discontinuities. PW ended this period as a professional organization that was better able to meet and resolve problems arising out of leadership transitions, the size of the partnership, and the morale of younger partners and staff. With these changes effected, and against the backdrop of accountancy's new and important role in American business life, PW strengthened its position as the profession's pre-eminent firm.

CHAPTER 4

A Golden Age, 1946–1961

As World War II came to an end, Americans braced themselves for economic downturn and a return to depression conditions. Instead, by 1959, the United States had become the "affluent society," and the accounting profession participated fully in American economic prosperity. The seeds of the field's many postwar opportunities had been planted during the war, when accountants grew accustomed to working directly with management, advising on internal systems, tax matters, and corporate policy. In addition, as electronic data processes originally developed for the military were adapted for office use, accountants assisted in the widespread mechanization of clerical tasks and accounting information. The profession's close relationship with regulatory authorities ensured growth parallel to that of government, and its longtime leadership in the income tax area enabled accountancy to maintain this practice even under challenge by the bar.

Price Waterhouse reaped the benefits of this prosperous era, and its leaders played important roles. George O. May continued to influence the development of accounting thought and practice and senior partners Percy Brundage and John Inglis both served in highly visible public and professional capacities. The similar perspectives of Brundage and Inglis made for almost two decades of continuity in outlook and direction. Their notable achievement was to establish the foundation for a truly national partnership. Brundage initiated the transition of PW away from a highly decentralized collection of local practices into a firm possessing the rudiments of an integrated, nationwide organization. He broadened its perspective, transforming a self-sufficient, "closed shop sort of fraternity" into an enterprise characterized by greater interdependence and reliance among partners. His attention to client needs also led to the forging of new links abroad in an ambitious new organization, the International Firm.[1]

Inglis, Brundage's successor, a man of extraordinary personal warmth, carried on in these directions. Inglis's strong interest in staff and partners made an enduring impression, and his efforts to run PW as a team facilitated a functional specialization. This approach served the firm well as its practice became increasingly complex. Although the audit constituted the core practice, promising opportunities arose in the areas of management consulting and tax work. During this time, too, the concept of the PW partner achieved greater definition and assumed a more central role in the firm's culture than ever before. Overall, this was a golden age of confidence, prosperity, and unquestioned professional leadership.

THE POSTWAR BOOM

The years following World War II marked the rise and widespread public acceptance of the mixed economy. During the war, problems such as rationing and the allocation of scarce resources required business and government leaders to work closely together. These cooperative efforts were extremely successful: war materials were produced, prices and wages kept in control, and essential civilian needs met. By the time the conflict ended, many business leaders had grown accustomed to working with government. At the same time, government management of the economy acquired a new legitimacy.[2]

Legislation and government spending largely determined the direction of the postwar economy. Passage of the landmark Employment Act of 1946, which committed the federal government to the philosophy of maintaining "maximum employment, production, and purchasing power," was spurred by Congress's concern about a return to the mass unemployment of the Great Depression. Government spending was increasingly used to modulate the business cycle, to promote general prosperity, and to foster entire new industries. By the 1950s and the advent of the Cold War, a permanent new sector of the economy had been established; the steady growth of peacetime defense spending amounted to 10 percent of the gross national product in this period. National security also provided the rationale for enormous federal expenditures in highways and the space program. General research and development, greatly stimulated during the war, was sustained by substantial postwar federal investment channeled through educational institutions. Government spending promoted growth in new geographical

areas, new industries, and new economic segments, particularly those based on data processing, aircraft instruments, chemicals, rubber, and plastic products. At the same time, the finance and service sectors also expanded. What began as intervention to promote stability evolved by the mid-1950s into widespread participation in the economy, with the government acting as a "guarantor of growth." By 1960, it had assumed an apparently permanent role in overall economic management through intervention and support of private enterprise, increased regulation, laws aimed at reducing unemployment, and funding for the goods and services of private enterprise.[3]

The mixed economy cushioned the nation against a major depression and served as the backdrop for a period of prosperity. Each time a recession occurred in the early postwar years, as it did in 1949, 1954, and 1958, the federal government intervened with a combination of accelerated highway construction, increased unemployment benefits, and liberalized housing credit. Recessions and a slow national growth rate notwithstanding, the postwar period saw a doubling in personal income that, combined with a shorter work week, produced a higher standard of living. The affluent society was born amid this unprecedented surge of real wealth.[4]

As might be expected, these years proved bountiful to the accounting profession. Technological, managerial, and accounting innovations developed during the war promised a new, expanded role for accountants. Wartime experiences with computers provided a foundation for exciting postwar applications, and on their return to civilian life, businessmen brought a new respect for sophisticated internal controls and statistical analysis. Postwar accountants were expected to assist in the mechanization of accounting and clerical procedures and to transform accounting and reporting systems into more useful management tools. Similarly, public accounting firms were expected to be conversant with these innovations and to adapt their methods to the new electronic processes.[5]

Other important trends created pressing needs for quick, reliable information. Professional management of publicly owned corporations, larger business units, substantial investments in plant and equipment, increasing labor and material costs, higher tax rates, and greater competition gave new impetus to cost-effective measures such as "quality control" and "operations research." The latter, which looked to the tools and methods of other disciplines including accounting, mathematics, engineering science, and physics, allowed management to determine the basic relationships that underlay decisions within an enterprise as well as across an industry.[6]

Business machines and innovative management practices helped create a new business environment. Decision making could be facilitated by faster data processing and advanced mathematical techniques. In

addition, automation could handle masses of clerical work at high speeds, eliminating the need for extra personnel and providing a powerful computational tool for reports, schedules, and forecasts.

Advances in automation came at a propitious time, when business was struggling with an explosion of office personnel and paperwork. The number of clerical workers in 1950 was equivalent to two-thirds of the factory labor force. While the number of factory workers had increased 53 percent since 1920, the clerical work force had increased by almost 150 percent and was continuing to rise. By 1954, one-tenth of the nation worked at "recording, transferring, summarizing, and analyzing information," although the volume of paperwork was growing much faster than either the economy or office workers' efficiency. In desperation, industry looked to automated business machines to assist in cutting costs and holding down the size of the clerical staff. It was not disappointed. A boom began in new typewriters, dictating devices, check signers, and automatic desk calculators. The first advanced, large-scale, general-purpose computer was delivered to the Bureau of the Census in 1951. As these "giant electronic brains," as they were called at the time, began to make their appearance in the mid- to late 1950s, some business leaders saw a "second industrial revolution" on the horizon.[7]

Auditing and accounting were deeply affected by changes wrought during the war. The value of continuous information on production and distribution carried over into peacetime; clients wanted to access accounting information throughout the year. Accounting work slowly ceased to focus on the balance sheet and began to extend beyond a frenzied few months. Some companies changed their fiscal calendar to a more natural business year, and others began to take their inventories several months prior to the traditional date of December 31. The McKesson & Robbins experience, too, had profoundly affected auditing procedures. Accountants realized that they needed to perform more detailed reviews of inventories and accounts receivable throughout the year. Clearly, "the bell was tolling for the ink-stained, green-eyeshade type of accountant."[8]

These changes reflected a wider transformation in the postwar accounting profession. As a whole, it was larger, better trained, and more articulate about its role in business and world affairs. The number of CPAs had doubled from 1941 to 1951, increasing by 5,000 annually as a result of service opportunities generated by government-related activities, expansion of America's industrial plant, increases in tax work, and the complexities of wage and price controls. Not only were more accountants practicing, but they were better educated and more mobile. Entry-level staff in major accounting firms during the postwar period

were increasingly drawn from colleges and universities; a bachelor's degree became virtually mandatory.[9]

The profession reveled in its growth at the half-century mark but approached its responsibilities seriously. AIA president Edward Wilcox saw the profession as playing an important institutional role in maintaining the "great temple" of a democratic society:

> We can contribute to it through services to business management that aid production, through financial statements increasingly useful to society as a whole, through services which will bring labor controversies a step nearer to sound and fair settlements, through public services in the fields of taxation and governmental accounting, and through zealous guardianship of that conscience of a free economy which is our especial trust.[10]

Since "the greatest causes of war are economic injustice, economic slavery, and economic distrust [which] feed on obscurity and distrust in financial representations, [and] perish in the light of honest publicity," Wilcox noted, accountants could ensure peace and prosperity by maintaining a vigilant stance against these elements.[11]

Others saw accountants, as a result of their training and independence, as uniquely capable of reconciling conflicting interests within a democratic society. Accountants provided help in resolving disputes arising between labor and capital, the government and taxpayers, or producer and consumer because of their ability to "develop and report the financial facts in the most useful manner so that a common starting point for discussion is possible."[12] Accountants could promote "the confidence necessary for the smooth running of our business economy" and provide "a means for the transmission and understanding of information about large corporations to the numerous individuals that own them."[13] Many accountants would have agreed with May's observation that "accountancy had developed from a service department of business to a social force."[14]

Brundage: Strengthening the Foundation

Percival F. Brundage led the firm through the end of World War II and into the postwar period. Under his tutelage PW took a number of important steps toward establishing itself as a national accounting firm through changes in recruiting and personnel development, by strengthening its committee structure, and by creating the International Firm and the Systems Department.

People who worked with and under Brundage differed in their recollections about his management style: some remembered an aloof, autocratic, and even Olympian style patterned on May, whereas others recalled a more informal, even casual, manner. Consensus existed, however, concerning Brundage's method of making decisions: partners recalled him as "impetuous" and "bursting with ideas," rather than deliberative. All agreed that he personified PW's tradition of public and professional service. In 1948, Brundage became the first PW senior partner to serve as president of the AIA. Later, President Dwight Eisenhower appointed him assistant director of the budget from 1954 to 1956, and director until 1958.[15]

Brundage ascended to the top of his profession in a straightforward manner. After graduation from Harvard Business School in 1914, he worked at a New York public accounting firm, where he earned $5 a week. Two years later, he joined PW's New York office, but he left after one year to become civilian head of the New York Depot Quartermaster's Office, assisting with military purchasing for World War I. After the Armistice, he returned to the New York office, where he remained until 1924, when he was transferred to Boston. Six years later he became the firm's fourteenth partner and Boston's partner-in-charge. In 1936, May selected Brundage for membership on the Executive Committee, and thereafter the Executive Committee named him secretary of the partnership. In that capacity, he maintained the firm's confidential administrative and financial records. In 1943, senior partner John Scobie appointed Brundage senior executive partner. Upon Scobie's death a year later, the Executive Committee elected Brundage as its chairman.[16]

Brundage's first task as senior partner had been to get through the war. He then faced the postwar environmental changes that, spurred by the McKesson & Robbins affair, forced a transformation in the firm's thinking about the audit and accounting processes as well as in its approaches to training and to developing future audit partners. Rather than pursue the more traditional task of uncovering fraud by company employees, the firm deliberately refocused its postwar mission on rendering opinions on sets of financial statements. To create a year-round professional staff and to ensure the quality of new staff throughout the entire firm, Brundage began by centralizing PW's personnel function in the New York office in 1946 and by naming a national recruitment director.[17]

Hiring imperatives challenged local practice office autonomy and also underscored the growing recognition of the importance of partner selection, training, and development. In 1946, Brundage presided over a group of loosely connected practices sharing the PW name rather than over a unified firm. This situation was a natural outcome of the firm's pattern of growth, which World War II had exacerbated by thinning the partnership ranks and allowing the remaining, seasoned, and aging partners to become ever more autonomous. Local partners-in-charge believed themselves answerable to no one outside their "fiefdoms" and felt that their offices' rewards stood or fell on their own economic successes. Moreover, "each office had a jealous protection of its own sovereignty," and local partners attempted to shield their clients from other PW contact. Part of each fiefdom's sense of autonomy and self-sufficiency was its authority to hire its own staff, although this meant that sometimes the best candidates were not selected. Not all offices were equally able to develop young juniors into seniors, or later, into managers and partners.

To meet its recruitment needs, the firm considered the possibility of gaining approval as a training institution under the G.I. Bill. It found, however, that the trials of bureaucratic oversight outweighed the $60–$90 per month the government would provide for each veteran. Instead, the national recruitment director coordinated individual efforts at recruitment by alumni at several universities such as Bowdoin, Dartmouth, and Stanford.[18]

Active recruiting also reflected the firm's greater heterogeneity. Its early years had been dominated by English and Scottish accountants, and as PW grew, it continued to attract recruits of similar northern European backgrounds, particularly to the New York office. But by the 1940s, more prospective recruits were applying for jobs in finance on Wall Street than in accountancy with large firms. Reflecting this change in demographics, PW admitted its first Jewish partner in 1937, and its first Catholic partner in 1941.[19]

Once staff members were recruited, they needed to be trained. After the war, Brundage and the Executive Committee instituted a number of internal changes, including the firm's first major effort in staff training in 1948. A junior staff member who was asked to help develop teaching materials was astonished by how little of the administration of the practice was documented; he found that staff training materials had traditionally been composed of fictitious company documents provided by a commercial publisher. Utilizing twenty pounds of general ledger documents and other materials drawn from a real company whose identity was concealed, he then developed a substantial case, "Pick Typewriter Company." The first run of copies for distribution to the training classes weighed "a little short of five tons and the New York City fire marshall gave the head of the PW Multilith Room . . . 72 hours to get it off the 6th floor!"[20]

The Pick Typewriter course ran for four weeks and was initially given in New York, Chicago, and Houston. Lasting a week longer than similar courses given by other firms, Pick Typewriter was seen as an aid to recruitment. By the mid-1950s, having been rendered anachronistic both by its terrific bulk and by the advance of punched cards, Pick Typewriter was superseded by the shorter and simplified "Best Chair Company" case.[21]

Although staff training had become sufficiently important by 1950 for the firm to appoint a group of managers to prepare course material, the firm always viewed engagement demands as having absolute priority, and these managers could be, and were, sent off at any time to an audit. Until 1953, when one manager was permanently assigned to the area, "staff training was more or less administered as a 'voluntary' special effort—off the cuff."[22]

Between 1946 and 1952, Brundage coordinated the Executive Committee's effort to centralize more PW operations. The new position of controller was created to assist the financial partner in centralizing the firm's accounts. In 1951, the Executive Committee asked a retired manager to examine inconsistencies in office accounting firmwide and to recommend improvements in the reporting of information. Two years later, after affirming the need for harmonizing the partnership's fiscal operations, he developed an accounting manual for use by all PW offices, another sign of the inroads being made into practice office autonomy.[23]

Brundage also oversaw the expansion and strengthening of PW's committee structure. Prior to his term, the firm had only three standing committees of partners: the Executive Committee, and the contract and the salary committees, which together made annual reviews of employee compensation and performance. However, the partnership's steady growth meant that new problems and issues needed attention. In 1946, the Executive Committee created eight new committees, four covering the practice areas of audit, tax, and systems, and four others handling administrative matters. The systems committee and tax committee considered the problems and policies of those specialized departments; the auditing committee and the technical (later accounting) committee did the same for the audit staff. The growing administrative details of the partnership were handled by the reports, defalcations, expense allowance, and staff committees. Individual offices, particularly the larger ones, also had committees, composed of managers or partners, or a combination of the two. For example, the New York office had a committee composed of five managers, who reviewed the performance of each audit staff member in order to recommend promotion or salary increases for the coming year.[24]

Throughout the postwar years, the Executive Committee tinkered with its nominating process, although changes reflected what was still only an illusion of democracy within the partnership. Prior to the war, new members could be added to the Executive Committee only by the senior partner; postwar leaders worked to create a mechanism for orderly succession. A nominating committee was first appointed in 1947 to consider candidates and, in 1948, the partners resolved on a procedure that allowed the Executive Committee to propose names to a nominating committee, giving partners the opportunity to make their own additions or deletions before voting on the slate of candidates. The nominating committee was required to consider all suggestions made by partners, including members of the incumbent Executive Committee.[25]

As the partnership expanded and business opportunities flourished over the next decade, the partners grew more comfortable about speaking their minds regarding firm affairs. In 1958, the Executive Committee moved to assert greater control over the nominating process by resolving to dispense with the nominating committee altogether and to fill vacancies directly. In a memorandum to the partnership, John Inglis explained that with the partnership at eighty members, "it is practically impossible for many of the partners to be well acquainted with their other partners and more particularly with their qualifications for the Executive Committee."[26] Moreover, under the existing system, when the Executive Committee made its nominations for the nominating committee, the nominees assumed, perhaps erroneously, that they were excluded from consideration for service on the Executive Committee. In addition, since the Executive Committee nominated candidates for admission to partnership, it also presumably would have the expertise to fill its own vacancies. The partners rejected the Executive Committee's proposal to dispense with the nominating committee, however, on the grounds that it "smacked of self-perpetuation." They chose instead to keep the existing method, but to require that nominating committee elections take place as soon as possible after vacancies to the Executive Committee became known, rather than on the first day of the annual partnership meeting.[27]

Amid these democratic stirrings, other traditions endured. The New York office continued to play the lead role in the firm, for although all partners and offices were theoretically equal, New York was still *primus inter pares*. Certainly it had an overwhelming lead in terms of chargeable hours, logging six times more than Chicago, its nearest competitor. New York also boasted specialists, such as Paul Grady in accounting and Leslie Mills in tax, who "had the broader experience and knew the answers to tough questions." Promising managers were often required to spend time there, in order to avail themselves of the superior experience New York offered and to be tested and reviewed by the firm's leaders.[28]

Tension existed between New York and the other major offices, manifesting itself in various ways. In 1944, to protect other offices from New York's dominance, any one office was prohibited from gaining a majority on the Executive Committee. New York partners were perceived to be less understanding of the competitive pressures felt elsewhere. Even established partners from other offices were wary of the personalities and politics in New York, and a subtle discrimination was thought to exist against inviting non–New York partners to take leadership positions within the firm. In 1969, John Biegler became the first senior partner who had not spent a considerable portion, or all, of his previous career in the New York office.[29]

Another lingering tradition was the formal interpersonal style and hierarchical working environment derived from PW's English and Scottish heritage. Some partners still addressed peers and staff by last names, and high decorum marked the firm's meetings.[30] For many years, the partners had held semiannual meetings in May and October in the boardroom of the New York office at 56 Pine Street. Business aspects of the practice formed the agenda for the spring meeting, whereas in the fall partners focused on "professional requirements in preparation for the year-end audit examinations." Meetings were stiff, very cut-and-dried, all-day affairs allowing little discussion and dominated by the senior partner. When George O. May led the partnership, he alone sat at the head table, permitting only five-minute inspections of the accounts. Similarly, in John Scobie's time, he, or someone at his request, made the only nominations for committee positions. These nominations were always adopted.[31]

PW's formality was also reflected in its dress code. The accountant soberly clad in dark hat and overcoat depicted on the cover of the firm's recruiting brochure exemplified the conservative stereotype of the 1950s. At times, this conservatism had humorous consequences. Staff hired in this era recalled, with some exaggeration, that a hat was a sine qua non.

> We were introduced to a manager who then attended to hiring. . . . After four or five minutes he said he'd give us a job. . . . His parting comment was—he never asked us . . . whether we owned a pencil or pen—he did ask us if we owned hats. None of us owned hats. He said, "Well, have a hat when you show up for work."[32]

However, what may have been de rigueur in New York was inappropriate elsewhere. The cover of the recruiting brochure caused great consternation in San Francisco, as "nobody out here" wears "overcoats in the first place, and they sure [don't] wear hats!"[33]

Against a generally austere background, Brundage began to add a note of equality and informality. In 1944, he moved the spring partners' meeting to the Seaview Country Club on the New Jersey shore. Business meetings took place in the morning and the afternoons were devoted to golf. Young partners received greater personal exposure to Brundage and other senior partners at these meetings than they did on the job; social and business conversation flowed more freely. In 1946, Brundage initiated a dinner dance after the fall meeting in New York City, including wives in a PW function for the first time in many years. These meetings strengthened personal bonds across the country.[34]

Managers' meetings were also held out of the office, at the Westchester Country Club in New York. Audit managers attended on a rotating basis, every third year, and tax managers attended the year they became managers. In addition to being social affairs, these meetings provided opportunities for young managers to display their talents. Brundage's innovations took hold: social events became a traditional part of partners' meetings, serving an important function as the increasing number of partners meant less internal cohesion.[35]

The pace of the partnership's growth quickened throughout the postwar period. Although only one or two partners had been admitted annually throughout the 1930s and 1940s (and in some years, none at all), this trend was reversed by the 1950s. Four new partners were admitted in 1951, nine in 1952, six more in each of the next two years, and nine in 1959. By then, the firm was already well on its way to a dramatic doubling: from 53 partners in 1954 when Inglis became senior partner to 101 when he retired in 1961.[36]

The International Firm

The American partnership's origins as the agency of a British accounting firm gave PW a strong international perspective. Prior to the 1930s, however, the connection between the associated firms around the world that shared the PW name was solely through informal, personal ties. Relationships developed out of shared professional backgrounds, cooperation on an international case like the Kreuger & Toll fraud, or participation in an exchange program. In 1932, partners drawn from each of the associated firms had formed an International Committee, with May acting as chair. The committee's powers were only advisory, and its charter was limited to working toward uniform practice standards and policies among associated firms. The outbreak of World War II prevented any further collaboration; as the war progressed, meetings were suspended, and even communication by mail became difficult.[37]

When the war ended, the American partnership faced an unprecedented volume of overseas work for its clients. Brundage urged the British firm's leaders to help develop a plan for an international organization, and representatives of all the firms met at frequent intervals to discuss this matter during 1945 and 1946. In July 1946, they established what was then known as "Price Waterhouse & Co. (International Firm)." Eight partners—two each from the United States and Britain and one from each of the associated firms in Canada, continental Europe, South America, and Australia/New Zealand—composed the new entity. Its annual meetings were held alternately in New York and London, underscoring the American partnership's prominence within the worldwide organization. The International Firm's existence allowed the American partnership to accept foreign assignments for other American accounting firms that lacked international ties. In 1950, for example, the International Firm agreed informally that its associated firms would do work for Coopers & Lybrand in some foreign countries.

During the late 1950s, the International Firm entered into "correspondent" relationships with other, smaller firms that were formerly PW agents in countries such as India, Japan, the Philippines, and Hong Kong. By 1959, the American partnership could proudly state that it was "part of what is today probably the largest professional organization in the world, having offices in 134 locations in 43 countries, and correspondents in 8 countries."[38] Exhibit 4.1 shows the extent of the international network in the PW International Firm organization chart of 1958.

Notwithstanding its far-flung structure, the International Firm was still more of a theory than an actual working entity. It did not take a direct role in the affairs of its associates, which remained completely autonomous, and it did not have any financial control over the individual partnerships. Rather, its efforts centered on encouraging uniform standards in all those using the PW name, strengthening personal links, and promoting cross-training by transferring staff members between countries. The International Firm's most visible manifestation in the postwar years was the exchange program that had been reinstituted in the late 1940s between British and United States staff and their families.[39]

Expansion of Services

Another important opportunity for PW was the explosion in systems work that occurred after World War II. Across the country, clients began to ask for help with office and tabulating equipment and in evaluating their accounting controls. The partner-in-charge of the Chicago office had developed systems work there and was a strong advocate of establishing it firmwide. In 1946, PW created a Systems Department, its first management consulting function. The new department was run by Joseph Pelej, an Austrian who had emigrated to the United States after World War I. Pelej had learned about the accounting profession while

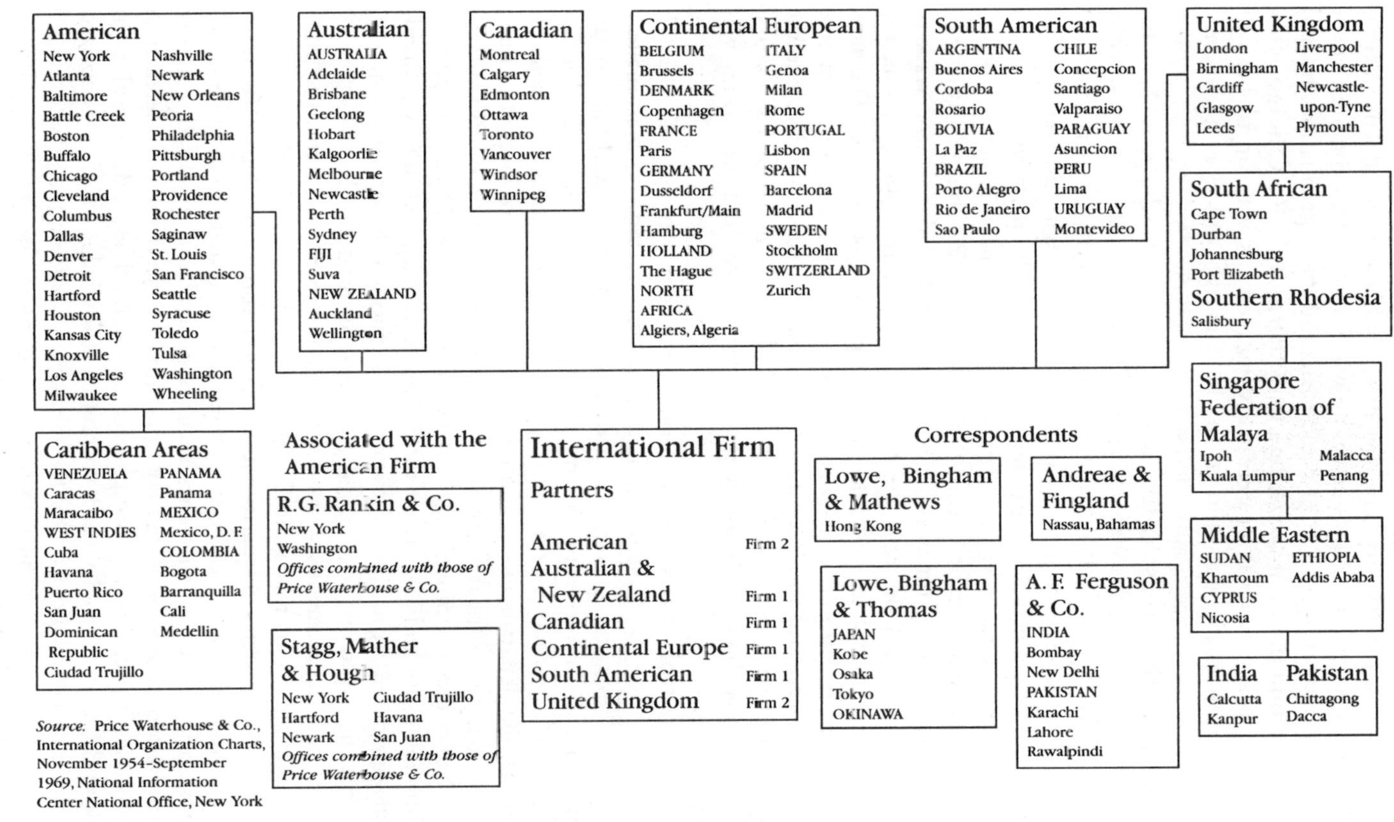

Source. Price Waterhouse & Co., International Organization Charts, November 1954–September 1969, National Information Center National Office, New York

EXHIBIT 4.1 Price Waterhouse (International Firm) Territorial Organization, January 1958

working as a factory stock boy, and he took a correspondence course to earn his certificate. At the time, he was impressed by the high salary of $100 per week some CPAs could earn, and upon graduation, he quit his job to find the right accounting firm. Hired by PW's Chicago office as a temporary man, Pelej eventually worked his way up to become audit manager. He was known in the Chicago office as a dynamic salesman with a special aptitude for systems work.[40]

Some of the firm's leaders were supportive of the new Systems Department, but others were skeptical of its ability to become profitable. One pioneer later recalled, "there was some merit in each position," noting that the new function had been introduced with little fanfare, no statement of expectations, and no incentive for the partners to support it. Some consultants within the firm were initially reluctant to ally themselves with the new entity. Although the Pittsburgh office had done systems work for years, for example, it did not, at first, want to be identified with the new department. To ensure against failure, the Executive Committee instituted two important safeguards. The new group was monitored in its first year by a systems committee of five audit partners, and the Executive Committee agreed to underwrite the Systems Department's losses up to $25,000 for the first two years. Reservations about profitability proved unfounded, and the money was never required.[41]

Pelej's notable charisma served him and the department well. In 1947, one year after the Systems Department was started, he was made a partner. Three years later, the growing needs of clients required the Executive Committee to expand the department's operations, and it appointed the first systems staff, a young manager to assist Pelej. Although the department's headquarters and library were located in New York, regional offices were soon established in Chicago, Pittsburgh, and San Francisco. Since early systems work was considered "90 percent common sense and 10 percent technical," it was carried out by individuals borrowed from the audit staff and supervised by an audit partner. The name "systems" was initially quite appropriate: at least 75 percent of the new department's work dealt with accounting systems, recorded either manually or mechanically.[42]

But the Systems Department was soon forced to depart from its exclusive reliance on audit personnel. Even tabulating machines, the most complex office machines then in general use, required a highly trained consultant, because they "operated by electrical and mechanical principles which [were] complicated in themselves, but [were] even more difficult to understand without a knowledge of the specialized technical terms developed by the tabulating machine manufacturers."[43] By the early 1950s, the department had hired its first non–CPA, a "mechanization" specialist, and later it hired an industrial engineer. With this staff, it could provide services in office layout, materials handling, warehousing, and the physical aspects of inventory and production control. As the industrial engineer began working with cost accountants, projects that developed labor standards, piecework rates, and work measurement followed. Thereafter, the Systems Department hired an operations research specialist, who provided expertise in inventory control, scheduling, break-even analysis, and in other special situations where mathematics could be applied.[44]

The Systems Department grew rapidly, developing and training staff in the analysis of organizational structures and in methods of general and mechanical bookkeeping, cost accounting, financial and statistical control, budgeting, and reports. It also created and circulated questionnaires or checklists on accounts payable and purchases. Client employees were accustomed to visits from their audit firm, and they often felt more comfortable using PW's systems personnel for special work rather than a management consulting firm. Eventually, the department added marketing experts and executive recruiters. By 1953, it had grown so large and had so much potential new work that the firm admitted two more systems partners.[45]

To reflect the continual broadening of its expertise, the Systems Department was renamed the Management Advisory Services (MAS) Department in 1954. By then, seventy-four full-time specialists were engaged in MAS work throughout the firm, half of them in New York. The practice fell into fifteen general categories, ranging from revision and design of general accounting systems to assistance with plant and office layout.[46]

Although PW's initial policy toward MAS had been "to limit its practice to those fields in which the work can be supervised adequately" and approved by an audit partner in the firm, the growing complexity of the MAS Department's work made this policy impractical.[47] By the mid-1950s, a team of operations research experts had been developed in response to increased client demand. These experts applied mathematical techniques in a number of areas, including the determination of the number, location, and control of warehouses; the rationalization of railroad maintenance and equipment; and the maximization of profits by scheduling intake and output of petroleum products. In addition, six systems specialists maintained close contact with developments both in the United States and abroad. In a typical systems project, the MAS Department assisted the National Bank of Detroit in determining whether electronic devices could be adapted to the bank's paper-handling problems.[48]

Not surprisingly, given the highly technical and scientific nature of its work, finding personnel to handle new engagements and to replace those who resigned was a serious problem for MAS. High turnover was fairly routine, partly because most of the staff was located in New York, and travel schedules were often demanding.[49]

MAS personnel themselves had a great deal of ambivalence about the practice. Many felt that its growth was inhibited by concerns about the department's possible impact on the firm's relationships with audit clients. MAS engagements tended to involve change and controversy, and some audit partners considered them "no-win" propositions: "you do a good job and you lose a good man [to the client]; you do a poor job and you lose a good client." Disagreement between an audit client and MAS staff, even when the MAS position was correct, sometimes led an audit partner to withdraw personal and professional support from the MAS Department. Inglis admonished the department at the 1957 annual meeting to "lean over backward" to ensure that its work did not disturb an audit partner's relationship with his clients.[50]

As a result of the wariness of the British firm and local professional rules, distribution of the first MAS brochure was limited to an in-house audience. A later effort to test the waters for a larger circulation was roundly criticized by other PW senior partners, leading Inglis to cancel it.[51] The Executive Committee asked Pelej for assurance that any MAS work done in nonaccounting areas would be performed by fully qualified MAS senior partners. The department itself took a go-slow approach despite its strong desire to grow. It criticized Arthur Andersen's aggressive use of "a colored film and other 'props'" and unanimously agreed to refrain from such "sales tactics" and to confine its efforts to "conservative and ethical promotion methods." The firm's cautious approach toward MAS reflected the realities of the postwar profession and its own view that work that deviated from traditional accounting and auditing might well be appropriate, but only after careful deliberation and study.[52]

Inglis: Personalizing the Partnership

The mid-1950s saw an orderly transition of leadership at PW. In 1953, when Brundage reached the firm's automatic retirement age of 60, the partners asked him to remain for another two years. He agreed, but in order for him to devote his energies to general policy and professional affairs, the Executive Committee elected John B. Inglis as executive partner with responsibility for general operation of the firm. In 1954, the Executive Committee elected Inglis as its chairman and the firm's senior partner.

"Jack" Inglis quickly distinguished himself within PW. Born in New Zealand, he began working in the New York office in 1924, originally planning to stay in the United States for only two years in order to learn new accounting techniques.[53]

He acquitted himself so well in the firm that he stayed on and made his career in the New York office.[54] He was admitted to the partnership in 1939 and four years later was appointed to the Executive Committee. As a young partner, Inglis so excelled at handling personnel matters that Scobie entrusted him with "extremely delicate missions." He was responsible for introducing benefits, such as the first life insurance program for partners and staff, and he was chosen in 1946 as one of the American partnership's two representatives to the International Firm. Inglis also served in distinguished capacities outside PW. The AIA was renamed the American Institute of Certified Public Accountants or AICPA, in 1957, and Inglis was the organization's treasurer from 1956 to 1958.[55] He also represented the firm on the AICPA's Committee on Accounting Procedure from 1958 to 1961 and was president of the National Association of Accountants in 1958–1959.

As a young partner, Inglis made a name for himself, both inside and outside the firm, in the controversial area of accounting for depreciation. U.S. Steel, his client at the time, was struggling with serious postwar inflation, and in its 1947 annual report, the company reported its implementation of a version of replacement cost depreciation. Although Inglis found this method acceptable, he was outnumbered by May, Brundage, Paul Grady, and several other influential partners who were "ardent advocates" of historical cost depreciation. As a result, PW issued a qualified opinion. The following year, after extensive meetings between Inglis and various committees of U.S. Steel personnel, a new, trailblazing policy for depreciation was worked out and a mutually acceptable certificate issued.[56]

Inglis, who modeled himself on an older generation of senior partners, could often intimidate the younger staff and be dogmatic and authoritarian with contemporaries. The name tag he donned at managers' meetings reinforced this image: "Name: J.B. Inglis. Nickname: Mr. Inglis." Yet many realized that this crusty exterior was mostly a bluff. As one partner recalled, "he was very warm-hearted. He had a cold gimlet eye, but a heart like a marshmallow." Indeed, Inglis's overwhelming talent, and the foundation for his management style, was his rare and unforgettable personal warmth. He made it known that he was always available to all partners or staff. As a matter of policy, he visited all the major offices once a year, and the smaller ones biennially, although this meant that he traveled at least 50 percent of the time.[57]

> I wanted to see how the partners worked in their offices and observe their relations with their staff. Also I wanted to know if they had any

> special problems with their clients. I wanted to get to know the managers because many of them would be future partners.[58]

Inglis's management style suited the dynamics of a swiftly growing partnership. His youthful experiences as a foreigner in the United States and as an "unknown junior" within PW had made him more sensitive. "I felt at the time and many years thereafter, that the then partners showed little interest in the welfare of the individual members of the staff," he recalled in his autobiography, *My Life and Times*. "I resolved then as a young man that if I ever became a partner, I would interest myself in their welfare and progress." As senior partner, he recognized that the firm was growing rapidly, and in fact the partnership more than doubled between the time he became senior partner and the time he retired. Despite this growth, Inglis tried to manage the firm with the camaraderie and closeness of earlier days. He believed so strongly in the importance of personal contact that he knew not only all partner names, but often those of family members as well, and he had more than a passing familiarity with the names and backgrounds of New York office staff.[59]

Inglis's hands-on approach extended to client relations. He was unwilling to give up his audit clients, because he thought they were "essential to give me some first hand feeling of what was going on in the field and in the practice." Not until his last year as senior partner did criticism by other members of the Executive Committee, and ultimately, a vote by the partnership, force him to give up the five extremely significant accounts—Corning Glass Works, National Cash Register, U.S. Steel, West Virginia Pulp & Paper, and Babcock & Wilcox—that he still retained.[60]

Inglis "devoted a considerable amount of personal attention" to bolstering the firm's personnel and recruitment functions. As a result of a series of events, including a business downturn, the Korean conflict, PW's desire to retain its small partnership, and the more aggressive recruiting by some of the other large firms in the late 1940s and early 1950s, PW's recruitment figures had flattened until 1954, when the Executive Committee made a number of important changes and raised starting salaries. Acknowledging the importance of coordinating these efforts broadly, the firm reappointed a national recruitment director and created the new positions of national personnel director, who was responsible for contacting graduating college seniors, and staff training director, who visited the firm's offices around the country. Both new positions reported directly to the Staff and Executive committees. Also in 1954, PW created and published its first recruitment brochure, *Career Opportunities in Public Accounting*.[61]

These changes reassured many partners that the firm was taking a more effective, rational, and competitive approach to recruiting at a time when there was a larger personnel shortage in the profession as a whole. Many accounting firms were having immense difficulty finding qualified staff. They suffered from an inability to offer salaries and benefits competitive with industry and from their reputation for excessive overtime and travel. In response, the AIA appointed a committee to conduct a recruitment campaign and to develop a motion picture for high school and college students.

PW was wrestling with turnover, as well. The partner-in-charge of staff reported in 1957 that each year the firm retained less than half of the professional staff hired five years previously. Personnel and recruitment problems affected not only the staffing on engagements, but also overall profitability. Although PW raised its billing rates and posted the highest number of chargeable hours in its history in 1954 and again in 1958, profits were less in these years than before because of substantial increases in salaries and expenses.[62]

Inglis also sought to delegate many leadership responsibilities. May, Campbell, and Scobie had dominated the partnership and had made all key technical and operational decisions themselves. Brundage had overseen a loosening of this policy and the designation of new committees, but the committees could only make recommendations and were unable to make decisions on problems requiring immediate attention. PW's growing size and organizational complexity made Inglis "determined to operate the firm on a team basis." He initiated a policy of "designating certain areas of the firm's practice to specially designated partners," and he created functional specialties in technical accounting, SEC filings, taxation, and international matters. Inglis became involved only when policy decisions arose or if a problem needed resolution by the senior partner.[63] By so doing, Inglis continued and expanded the movement started by Brundage of delegating decision making within the firm's leadership.

Tax Accounting: Opportunities and Conflicts

Increased government regulation of the economy broadened and deepened the profession's tax specialty, providing another example of the changing nature of accountants' services. Tax accounting, spurred by new legislation, enjoyed sustained growth unrelated to war-related opportunities emerging from the excess profits tax and wage and price controls. However, as the tax practice expanded in scope, it increasingly met resistance from lawyers who also provided tax services, making for sharp disputes over the acceptable boundaries between the two professions. Because accountants were well established in the field, lawyers eventually found it impossible to remove them or to restrict their influence.[64]

In the postwar era, one tax accountant observed,

> our basic federal taxing statutes are complex and difficult to understand, due primarily to the fact that there is such a wide divergence between the statutory and economic concepts of income. . . . The problem is further complicated by the fact that our present tax code is not the result of a carefully thought out plan of taxation designed to produce a comparatively simple but efficient law. It is the result of piling amendment after amendment on top of the original law until now the structure is so top heavy, unwieldy and unnecessarily complicated that the mere mechanics of preparing and filing a return is a terrific burden on business.[65]

This complexity "made the services of the CPA indispensable," and "sophisticated investors as well as general business managers soon discovered that it was unwise to engage in even routine transactions without first consulting their tax advisors."[66] As a result of the confusion, tax work mushroomed: AIA office practice statistics compiled in the 1950s indicate that of all work, tax planning and advising was growing the most rapidly.[67]

As postwar tax work became more lucrative, lawyers sought to bar accountants from the field. The legal profession had lodged complaints regarding income tax practice against accountants in 1935. Efforts at reconciliation had achieved little result. "Realizing that this situation was not in the public interest," the American Bar Association (ABA) and the AIA created the National Conference of Lawyers and Certified Public Accountants in 1944. Comprising five members from each organization and jointly headed by AIA president Percy Brundage and ABA president John D. Randall, its purpose was to seek agreement on certain cooperative principles.[68]

Although the conference initially made considerable progress, its operations were suspended with the 1946 filing of the *Bercu* case by the New York County Lawyers' Association. Three years later, New York's highest court found that accountant Bernard Bercu was illegally practicing law when he engaged in research and prepared a memorandum advising a client (for whom he rendered no other services as an accountant) on the advisability of a federal income tax deduction. *Bercu* left accountants not only extremely disappointed, but also deeply suspicious that lawyers were using their monopoly over the legal system to eliminate the 40-year-old right of accountants to do tax work. While acknowledging that they were not entitled to give advice on matters of general law, accountants had "generally assumed that questions such as the deductibility of proposed expenditures for tax purposes were matters of tax accounting, on which certified public accountants were fully qualified to advise."[69] Although the *Bercu* decision was limited to New York and made no mention of the long-held right of accountants to a Treasury practice, the accounting profession was dismayed at the forces marshaled against it. It noted that the New York County lawyers who brought *Bercu* were assisted by three other influential groups: the Bar Association of the City of New York, the New York State Bar Association, and the American Bar Association. Accountants found the exclusionary rationale that lawyers were supporting absurd and unrealistic. They noted that the Treasury's own staff was composed of accountants, not lawyers, and they pointed to the significant roles played by George O. May of PW and Robert Montgomery of Lybrand, Ross Brothers, & Montgomery in the early development of the income tax law. Nevertheless, the legal profession seemed bent on hostility. Even the name of the ABA body designated to carry on discussions with accountants, the Committee on the Unauthorized Practice of Law, was a "subtle source of friction."[70]

Relations between the two groups grew worse before they improved. After deteriorating into what contemporaries described as an "unseemly quarrel," the National Conference of Lawyers and Certified Public Accountants ceased to meet. Ill will was deepened by two proposed congressional bills filed with the ABA's support, one limiting the ability of accountants to practice before federal agencies by requiring special proof of qualification, and the other seeking to deprive accountants of the right to practice before the Tax Court. Finally, in 1951, the AIA and the ABA resumed efforts at reconciliation by adopting a Statement of Principles, recognizing that lawyers and CPAs were both professionals whose services were necessarily sought by business and acknowledging the interrelatedness of their work, particularly in the area of income taxation. The two groups also conceded their mutual right to prepare and render advice on federal income tax returns and to practice before the Treasury.[71]

These attempts at cooperation were dealt a severe blow by yet another court decision adverse to accountants. The 1954 *Agran* case in California, unlike *Bercu*, dealt directly with the Treasury practice issue by holding that certification to practice before the Treasury did not permit the accountant to perform services that would constitute the practice of law, even if the accountant represented clients only before the IRS. This decision, later affirmed by the intermediate appellate court, was based on an "unprecedented interpretation" of Treasury Circular 230, construed to permit local courts to limit the scope of practice before the Treasury to the extent it might constitute the "practice of law" under state law.[72]

Agran shocked accountants. Although like *Bercu*, *Agran* was only a state court case, they found its implications ominous and feared that other jurisdictions would invoke it as precedent. Should enough states do this, accountants could lose their substantial tax practice, and almost half of the 65,000 practitioners enrolled with the Treasury Department were CPAs. In the face of *Agran*'s backing by the California Bar Association and the growing evidence of the hostility of local bar groups, "Many CPAs felt they were the object of an organized campaign to push them out of a major part of their tax practice so that lawyers could take over."[73] Accountants grew militant and made plain their intent to appeal *Agran* to the U.S. Supreme Court if necessary and to support legislation in Congress seeking clarification of their right to practice.[74]

With the ill will generated by *Agran* at the top of the agenda, the presidents of the ABA and the AIA met to see if differences could be resolved. Although special committees were appointed to look into the matter, the parties deadlocked over differing interpretations of Treasury Circular 230. In 1956, the Secretary of the Treasury issued a long-awaited clarification, affirming the right of accountants to a Treasury practice and indicating that "there presently appears no reason why the present scope and type of practice should not continue as it has in the past." He admonished the two groups to "accept their responsibilities of determining when the assistance of a member of the other profession is required."[75] Following this Treasury statement, mediators carved out some neutral ground in 1957. Both sides agreed not to engage in further court contests and to refer disputes instead to a special committee composed of representatives from both professions. A 1959 AICPA and ABA Joint Statement acknowledged that it was often in the public interest that the services of both professions be utilized and described a dispute resolution procedure.[76]

In 1963, accountants were greatly relieved by a U.S. Supreme Court decision superseding state court cases on this issue. *Sperry* v. *Florida* held that an accountant who was enrolled to practice before the U.S. Patent Office could carry on his practice in Florida. Even though Sperry was not a lawyer and his activities constituted the practice of law, the Supreme Court ruled under the pre-emption doctrine that Florida had no right to prevent him from doing what the Patent Office had authorized him to do. By freeing accountants to practice before federal agencies without fear of state intervention, *Sperry* underscored the critical importance of law to the accounting profession's fortunes.[77]

Although neither the Treasury nor the accounting and legal professions ever explicitly defined their respective responsibilities—an impossible task by the late 1950s, in any case—an accommodation was reached. No discussion concerning the dispute appears in the professional literature of the next decade, when the debate shifted from the fundamental right of accountants to practice in the tax area to narrower questions concerning the tax accountant's role as adviser or advocate, and the propriety of dual practice as both a lawyer and an accountant.[78]

Within PW, the tax practice, whose historical origins were found in wartime expertise in excess profits tax work, had long suffered from an image problem. "Getting transferred to the Tax Department was the kiss of death," one partner recalled. However, although the audit function remained the firm's raison d'être, major changes in federal tax laws in the 1950s lent the tax practice tremendous legitimacy, as well as a long, accelerated growth.[79]

The tax area developed real momentum and a larger client base as a result of the comprehensive revision of the Internal Revenue Code in 1954. The new law not only codified the previous fifteen years of case law, but also effected a

> complete overhaul of the basic tax law structure involving major changes in basic philosophy as to procedure, taxation of various types of income, tax accounting principles, and the tax approach to various entities (partnerships, fiduciaries, etc.) and to corporate organizations, re-organizations, liquidations and separations.[80]

The 1954 Internal Revenue Code completely dominated tax practice into the next decade and required a tremendous assimilative effort. The new laws required experts, not just auditors with an interest in taxation, and the code's high concentration of accounting content catapulted accountants into a central, interpretative role. Its favorable depreciation and LIFO (determining inventory by a last-in, first-out method) provisions also gave it a pro-business orientation. Analysis of these provisions and their implications for companies became very important. The PW Tax Department maximized its opportunities by printing informational brochures and making speeches and presentations; over 3,000 copies of memoranda analyzing specific parts of the new code were produced and sent to interested clients. As the code's provisions became more familiar, the PW Tax Department moved into planning and shelter work. Positive client response led the firm to pay more attention to the tax practice and to assist offices where there were no tax partners.[81]

In 1951, the Tax Department was led by Leslie Mills, a reserved Scotsman with an intellectual approach to tax work. He was already a partner in another accounting firm and had achieved an outstanding reputation when he joined the New York office in 1950. Mills was well connected with the Internal Revenue Service and the Treasury, and he was hired to specialize in tax work and problems connected with government contracts. Brundage and Inglis recruited Mills expecting that he would bring a new point of view. Although the partners had "contentious debates" concerning his outsider status, Mills became a partner in 1951; he was given responsibility for coordinating tax work among all the offices, as well as for laying the groundwork for tax managers and departments in all major offices.[82]

In the mid-1950s, the practice's growing complexity led the Executive Committee to appoint a manager for the tax research area. An early project was to develop a formal reference file. At the time, tax reference material consisted of little more than internal questions and memoranda addressed to the New York office regarding unusual problems and copies of important correspondence. The tax research area organized this information by condensing the important points into relevant data files, which were then organized under section headings derived from the Internal Revenue Code. The new reference system drew on the department's knowledge, insight, and experience and became a centralized repository readily available to the offices. Tax research's second major project involved the creation of a tax "subject" file, which recorded the firm's current tax work. This file was organized conceptually and was not "sanitized" as was the reference file, but simply contained the raw work product. A milestone was reached in 1956 when Mills was appointed chairman of the Tax Department and the firm admitted three tax partners in one year, nearly doubling the number devoted to the practice.[83]

Auditing and Accounting: Strengthening the Partnership

The center of the PW postwar practice, nevertheless, was its auditing and accounting work. The firm made a number of important changes to strengthen audit skills and to improve techniques, as well as to provide reference and research support. These developments marked a significant milestone in the partnership's history, as it moved toward greater interdependence.

Other than George O. May, the partner who best exemplified the firm's pre-eminence in this area was Paul Grady, chairman or partner-in-charge of "technical accounting." Grady had been a partner at the Andersen firm for ten years and was considered by many to be the heir apparent to Arthur Andersen himself. However, as a PW colleague recalled, Andersen "cut Grady off at the knees when he got close to the throne," and Grady went to work for the Department of the Navy.[84] In 1943, Scobie and the Executive Committee brought Grady into PW, and he became a partner one year later. Grady was a figure of great professional stature. From 1944 to 1948, he chaired the AIA's Committee on Accounting Procedure which, under his leadership, produced *Tentative Statement of Auditing Standards: Their Generally Accepted Significance and Scope*, the first authoritative statement of generally accepted auditing standards. From 1957 to 1958, Grady served on a special committee appointed to develop a blueprint for the newly created Accounting Principles Board (APB) and its research division. After Grady's retirement from PW in 1960, he acted for a year as the AICPA's director of accounting research. During this year, he wrote his landmark study, *Inventory of Generally Accepted Accounting Principles for Business Enterprises.*[85]

Although Grady's outstanding qualifications made him a potential PW senior partner, internal opposition apparently blocked his election to the Executive Committee because he had not come up through the firm's ranks. Disappointment on this score did not prevent Grady from making many outstanding contributions to the firm. His expertise in accounting for utilities emphasized the value of specialization. His training had given him a keener marketing sense than many PW utilities partners, and, as a result, he was a significant business developer. He regularly expressed opinions at partners' meetings, mentored young accountants, and was remembered with great warmth by many who became future firm leaders.[86]

Grady's greatest strength, perhaps, was that he was a consummate professional accountant. As chairman of the firm's technical accounting committee, Grady knew the answers to tough questions, and he used both his high ideals and his technical skill to stiffen the backs of partners whose clients were pressing to achieve certain results. His "Outline for Staff Training" was one of three standard references given to all new professional personnel. Grady oversaw preparation, in 1955, of an extensive amount of desk-reference material relating to financial statements and short- and long-form reports. These materials were distributed to all partners, managers, and seniors in 1956. May respected Grady's expertise and welcomed his assistance in preparing *Memoirs and Accounting Thought of George O. May* for publication.[87]

By the late 1950s, the firm's accounting and auditing research needs had grown too extensive, even for someone of Grady's technical virtuosity. Partners and staff in different offices, often faced with similar accounting problems, lacked an organized method of sharing information and expertise. They also had difficulty keeping abreast of the CAP's new releases. These factors, combined with the firm's long-range interest in developing a broader, national approach aimed at reducing unwarranted differences in accepted accounting practices, led Inglis and the Executive Committee to create an Accounting Research Department in 1957.

The new department grew quickly, as did the range of its work. Carl Tietjen, who had worked with Grady and who was known as an excellent technical resource, was named director and given the assistance of one part-time manager. The Accounting Research Department's mission was to provide "thorough and objective study of many important new accounting problems with which PW and the profession are confronted" to ensure that the firm retained its "leadership in accounting thought in the U.S." To accomplish this agenda, the department's work was divided into two areas: "practical" research on specific accounting matters for partners and staff, and "basic" or theoretical research on new ideas or approaches, which was considered the primary objective.[88] PW expanded the department's activities in its second year by making it responsible for "communications." This task was defined as maintaining the firm's reference, subject, and industry files, as well as serving as a clearinghouse for technical speeches and articles. As part of this mandate, the department updated the one-volume reference file originally created during Grady's tenure. The new "Auditing and Accounting Service" emerged as "the basic reference material used by a partner and staff on the job" and eventually grew to fifteen or twenty looseleaf volumes, updated each year. The Accounting Research Department grew sixfold within a decade, with staff employed full time on research problems. Young managers who did a two-year tour of duty with the department were considered to have "prospects." It clearly filled a need, for within two years, 170 important problems in 39 different subject areas had been referred to it by partners and staff.[89]

The postwar Accounting Research Department and the Tax Department's research function were important steps in the direction of a more centralized firm and a more interdependent partnership. Their existence symbolized the requirements posed by an increasingly complex and specialized profession, one in which no one person could claim to have all accounting knowledge. The era of a rugged individualist like partner Charles Carruthers—who could take the witness stand in 1925 and state, "I do as I please in my own office"—had passed. Yet even as the research departments provided partners with access to critical technical information, data, and assistance, they simultaneously preserved individual partner autonomy. Because partners could be confident in achieving a more consistent approach firmwide, they could still display a Carruthers-like assurance to the outside world.[90]

Sharing information was becoming more important for another reason as well. The problem of accountant liability had arisen once again. PW's indemnity insurance had increased dramatically in the early 1950s after bankers brought suit against another national accounting firm and received a $1.4 million settlement. By 1955, the American partnership was warning its international associates that "recent cases against accountants in the United States made it imperative that the firm take every step to insure that procedures being followed are adequate." Spurred by the threat of litigation, PW worked throughout this period to improve the effectiveness of its audit procedures and to verify that the firm's high standards were being maintained. Groups of managers and partners from other offices were designated to review working papers in each office once every three years, and partners were also urged to reach an understanding with clients regarding the limitations on the scope of a regular examination.[91]

Another important element in PW's continuing effort to improve audit techniques and avoid litigation was the development of a sophisticated, mathematical approach to statistical sampling. Traditional sampling had been done by an accountant's "horse sense"—for example, by checking every tenth piece of data out of five hundred. The use of formal rules of statistical sampling was necessary to guarantee that the laws of probability would control the selection process. In 1955, the firm invited a statistics professor from New York's City College to assist it in reconsidering its sampling techniques. The professor met with partner Henry P. Hill and staff to form a committee noted for its "lengthy and productive debates." In 1958, they introduced new sampling techniques and required that the professional staff learn to apply them to audit tests. In encouraging scientific sampling, the committee sought to limit "traditional means" of auditing selection only to those "obviously preferable" instances. *Sampling in Auditing*, prepared by the committee as an in-house publication, became a highly successful book, selling more than 50,000 copies and generating significant royalties for the firm.[92]

A New Order of Competition

The perception of new opportunities in the postwar business environment led some large accounting firms to break with traditional practices and to embark on entirely new strategies for growth. As the market leader, PW saw little need to change, but some of its major rivals aggressively pursued a variety of marketing, service, and expansion strategies to gain new clients. Although more heated competition occurred later, the expansive postwar market allowed firms to develop their own niches or specialties without adversely affecting their peers.

Arthur Andersen and Peat, Marwick, Mitchell were two such examples: Andersen chose early to strengthen its consulting practice and specialize, whereas Peat, Marwick adopted a growth-by-merger plan. Both were notably successful.

Andersen's management laid the groundwork for growth in consulting services before the conclusion of World War II. Its wartime Administrative Services Division specialized in the mechanization of accounting and clerical work, including applications of punched cards to accounting and reporting systems. This division's leader revealed the depth of his commitment to new technology in his impressions of a computer prototype in the early 1940s: "It took no genius to see that we had before us a device that would outrun, outpower, and outmode every device that preceded it." He became a man "with a mission. It was to convince everyone I encountered . . . that this day I had seen a vision of what would soon become a revolutionary reality."[93]

Demand for computer applications increased in the postwar era. Andersen built from within the firm by developing a few highly qualified electronics experts who then trained new staff. At a remarkably early stage, Andersen began working with computers. Although the firm was warned by manufacturers against "wasting its time" in seeking broad applications of computers for business use, Andersen's perseverance in this area paid off. Out of its landmark 1952 General Electric UNIVAC work emerged the first major computer applications for the processing and recording of business transactions and "the beginning of a dramatic firmwide growth" in the consulting practice. By the early 1970s, Andersen's MAS department clearly emerged as the largest.[94]

The strategy of Peat, Marwick, Mitchell, by contrast, was simply sheer growth. It began with a size advantage: in 1947, its practice had partners spread throughout thirty-three offices in the United States. At the time, PW had twenty-one, Arthur Andersen, sixteen, and Touche Ross, ten. Although Peat, Marwick's size and organization were impressive, it had not yet distinguished itself in a profession where PW had the "dominant reputation" and Haskins & Sells, along with Lybrand, Ross Brothers & Montgomery, possessed the "strongest voices in the professional organizations."[95]

William Black, the senior partner at Peat, Marwick from 1947 to 1965, was the architect of the growth strategy. Rather than entice clients away from other firms, Black looked for new business in industries unaccustomed to traditional audits or in those requiring highly specialized work. He conceived a strategy of merging with smaller firms that possessed a particular expertise and whose clients were already being served by a competent and experienced local staff. Peat, Marwick's postwar merger program gave it an entree into new areas, including transportation, insurance, and the savings and loan industry. In addition, notable mergers such as that with the prestigious small accounting firm Barrow, Wade, & Guthrie in 1950 had a distinct psychological impact on the profession. They led many independent CPAs with smaller, specialized firms to seek to combine with Peat, Marwick to obtain access to energetic young assistants, a wider range of contacts, and superior resources. Black's strategy was successful: Peat, Marwick's domestic and international mergers totaled fifty-three during the 1950s, and by the mid-1960s, Peat, Marwick led the profession in volume of business.[96]

Arthur Andersen and Peat, Marwick adopted the most distinctive, and perhaps the most extreme, strategies of all the major accounting firms during this time. PW partners identified Andersen's assertiveness and the mergers of the 1950s as events that would initiate a major transformation of the profession. Within PW, the aggressive actions taken by others led to differences of opinion over the firm's future strategy. Younger partners and staff were increasingly troubled by what they saw as too conservative an approach to the changes in the profession and questioned whether PW was "getting its full share of new work." At the 1953 spring partners' meeting, one group, committed to attracting new clients, forced a decision to create a Business Research Committee (BRC). During its approximately ten-year life, the BRC pressed hard for implementation of several new directions for the firm, the most important of these being industry specialization. Although PW had a long tradition of developing generalists who were broad-based CPAs with a wide variety of experience, business people in the 1950s sought expertise tailored to their own industries. "Practice development," PW's genteel term for marketing, was the other significant item on the BRC agenda. Committee members traveled from office to office, educating partners and staff on sales and marketing techniques, compiling a firm-wide client list for the first time in six years, and distributing monthly schedules of new inquiries and new work to all offices. BRC questionnaires sought information on procedures followed by competitors in attracting new clients, business obtained during the past twelve months, and plans for improvement. Once a year, the committee issued a report at the partners' meeting containing the results of its activities, its observations on practice development by the offices, and its recommendations for obtaining new work. Partners and staff were urged to build their reputations through public speaking and writing professional articles, and the BRC asked the Executive Committee to establish a budget for this purpose.[97]

Given PW's dominant reputation and prestige, its leading partners saw no real need for a marketing strategy like that proposed by the BRC. Neither practice development nor industry specialization was endorsed by the Executive Committee, and the BRC could never fully implement its agenda. It had other proposals that were also ahead of their time. The BRC chairman repeatedly but unsuccessfully urged the Executive Committee to encourage all offices to expand their executive recruitment services. Requests that the Executive Committee hire a dynamic public relations organization to make a study of PW also received no action, partly because of the ambivalent attitude, not only of the firm itself but also of the accounting profession as a whole, toward public relations. In moving slowly on the BRC suggestions, the partners were following the traditionally conservative approach of PW toward attracting new business and the firm's philosophy of client relations, which was, in essence, to keep the biggest and best companies and give them good service.[98]

PW's attitude toward competition in the mid-1950s was well illustrated in the remarks made to the Executive Committee by the senior partner of the British firm. In recounting a conversation with the chairman of a large London company who was displeased with his current auditors and sought to change to PW, this British senior partner told the Executive Committee, "I talked him out of it. He had a fine firm, and 'you don't switch auditors. Forget it!'"[99]

The British firm reacted negatively when the American partnership was asked to participate in the newly televised Oscar awards ceremony. Notwithstanding the strength of the British viewpoint, the U.S. firm declined to withdraw, noting that if PW relinquished the engagement, another large American accounting firm would certainly seize the opportunity. The Executive Committee later noted that participation in the Oscar awards ceremonies undoubtedly helped to make PW's name and reputation for integrity well known outside the business and finance communities.[100]

On balance, however, the British firm's conservative perspective was deeply embedded in the U.S. firm's heritage and met with approval. During this period, PW played the game as respected professionals played it. May, for example, never actively sought new business; prospective clients approached the partnership in his era on the strength of the firm's reputation. This strategy still worked: of the 457 inquiries for new business in 1953, more than three-quarters came through the firm's reputation and its outside contacts and only one-quarter were the result of partner and staff business development.[101]

The firm's success led, not surprisingly, to a sense of complacency. Inglis had no reason for concern about the partnership's health and prospects when PW had clients like Standard Oil, Shell, Gulf, and U.S. Steel, the giants of American industry, and the firm led the profession in clients listed on the New York Stock Exchange and in the *Fortune*

500 list. Clients were very loyal, often entrusting their PW auditor with the highest responsibilities. Carnation, for example, a long-time client of the Los Angeles office, had worked out a contingency plan in the case of nuclear attack—a concern that gripped both the nation and the corporate community during the 1950s and 1960s. Should California become the target for such a bombing, making it impossible or impracticable for the board of directors of Carnation to function, the PW manager in either Phoenix or Tulsa, whoever had survived the blast, was designated to help manage the company in the interim.[102]

Moreover, the firm was simply not inclined to increase its size. Growth in numbers was not, and had never been, a primary aim of the firm, and as a matter of policy, partners had agreed to limit expansion until qualified personnel existed to supervise new offices. Although several other firms were growing larger, most older PW partners at this time were not worried about the implications. One partner later characterized this attitude as "We're doing all right; biggest ain't necessarily the best." Another recalled that nobody "looked to the right or to the left as far as competition was concerned. We said, 'We're not going to worry about them. Let them worry about us . . . we [are] Price Waterhouse.'"[103]

Nevertheless, many in the firm were disturbed by the changes in the profession, particularly by the increasing number of mergers. PW had not taken part in any mergers at all during the previous twenty-five years and officially deplored this trend. When the firm finally altered its policy, it did so only in a highly selective way, and merged with only ten firms between 1955 and 1967, compared to Peat, Marwick, which merged with fifty-three firms in the 1950s alone.

When PW decided on a merger, it did so in order to gain a special expertise or a practice area, not for the sake of growth alone. A merger might be sought to bring in blue-chip clients, or to provide entree into selected geographical areas—as long as it did not disrupt the firm's partnership philosophy. By the 1950s, approaches by smaller firms, especially those with clients of international or national importance, could not be ignored. One very successful union in 1963 involved Pogson, Peloubet & Co., whose senior partner, Maurice Peloubet, was a PW alumnus, and whose mining company clients (Anaconda, Phelps Dodge, Newmont, and others) were among the most prestigious mining companies listed on the New York Stock Exchange. Similarly, the single most significant merger in PW's history, with R.G. Rankin & Co. in 1955, brought in blue-chip clients, including IBM, Woolworth, Ingersoll-Rand, and Bristol-Myers, that wanted to work with a large firm once Russell Rankin retired. The 1956 merger with Osborn & Page of Tennessee was sought not only because of the company's outstanding reputation, but also because it was a convenient way to open an office in Tennessee.[104]

The firm's careful merger policy was based on its philosophy of "hire and grow." Partners believed that it was better to start with young staff and develop them in accordance with the firm's standards than to attempt to fit partners acquired through a merger into the PW mold. (As lateral hires, Paul Grady and Leslie Mills were rare exceptions to this rule.) Experience had shown that partners from other firms were integrated with difficulty. They often found it hard to adjust to the heavier responsibilities, greater number of clients, and increased independence expected of PW partners, and they were reluctant to yield clients they brought with them to the newly merged partnership.[105]

In addition to shifts in domestic practice, signs of change had begun to appear in the international arena in the mid-1950s as well, as other large accounting firms created their own international organizations. Intense competition for foreign work ensued when these firms opened an aggressive campaign of advising their clients regarding foreign developments. PW was forced to relinquish some international assignments that it had previously performed regularly, and it lost some of its foreign clients at this time to their regular U.S. auditors at Coopers & Lybrand, Arthur Young, and Arthur Andersen.[106]

An industry profile published in *Fortune* in 1960, the first in thirty years, also sent tremors throughout the firm. Acknowledging that PW was still considered the most prestigious firm, the profile nevertheless made much of Peat, Marwick's position as the largest in terms of partners and gross revenues. It pointed out that PW had the second smallest number of partners, and the fourth largest gross revenues, among the major firms. For some at PW, this news

> hit the firm like a thundercloud because it's one thing to say, "We don't worry about the competition," it's another thing for a publication like that to come out and say, "You're no longer number one, quantitatively speaking."[107]

Overall, however, PW's unquestioned professional leadership in this period and its superb client list insulated the firm from any real need to develop a competitive strategy and, in fact, encouraged an inward-directed focus that lasted through the 1960s. Since the postwar period was one of apparently boundless opportunity, PW's efforts, as an elite institution acting to maintain its elite status, were reasonable. The firm chose not to grow rapidly and to concentrate on maintaining its reputation. Although this decision caused the loss of some market share, the firm nonetheless expanded at a heady clip and maintained profitability.

Under these circumstances, tampering even slightly with PW's successful formula or risking any shadow on its pre-eminent reputation did not seem appropriate. Instead, the firm explored those options most promising, and least threatening, to what it did best.

Unlike a more centralized entity, PW's leaders deferred to the concept of an independent partnership and, as a result, could be responsive and closely attuned only to evident needs. Even senior partners could do no more than the rest of a conservative Executive Committee and partnership permitted. And the partners overwhelmingly valued qualities that appeared incompatible with rapid growth, including the warmth of a smaller partnership and the maintenance of the highest standards. Although in hindsight it appears that PW's culture and history constrained it from responding to some of the challenges and opportunities posed by the postwar business environment, it would be decades before some of the effects on PW's competitive position were felt.

CHAPTER 5

THE CHALLENGE OF GROWTH, 1961–1969

The 1960s were a prosperous time. Price Waterhouse entered the decade with optimism and confidence, feelings encouraged by its leading partners and reinforced by America's political and economic dominance. Herman Bevis, another in a long line of senior partners committed to highly visible roles in professional affairs, led the firm from 1961 to 1969. During these years, the strong American economy encouraged the partnership's domestic expansion, and worldwide accounting services flourished in response to opportunities abroad. Electronic applications began to proliferate and expand the range of services that accountants could offer, and a blizzard of revenue enactments stimulated the expansion of the tax practice. It was a decade of great promise, the culmination of the postwar period's steady growth, and an apparent affirmation of the superiority of the American way of life.

Yet there were many disquieting signs for the accounting profession amid this prosperity. By the end of the decade, an overheated stock market and runaway inflation gave rise to a disturbing sense of unease. In addition, computer consulting demanded an unprecedented degree of technical sophistication. Three changes in the practice environment were also very important. First, a wave of mergers and acquisitions eroded once rock-solid client bases. Second, competition among firms for clients as well as for new staff grew markedly more aggressive. Finally, the debate over accounting principles ended in a failure to reach agreement that spelled the demise of the profession's standard-setting mechanism and foretold the end of the monolithic structure of large-firm practice that had been established by the securities legislation of the

1930s. Indeed, the issues raised in this debate link together many of the themes of this book, including PW's relationship to its clients, its leadership role in the profession, and the place of the profession in the larger society. By 1969, the future seemed distinctly less certain than it had at the outset of the decade.

For PW, the 1960s marked a watershed. As the manifold changes outside the firm gave rise to calls from within to expand, the partnership made a deliberate decision not to grow for growth's sake but to focus on providing service of the highest quality.

Hewing to the steady course charted by early leaders like George O. May, PW steered clear of many of the excesses of the period. It assumed that its time-tested strategy would withstand most changes in the business environment. In this assumption, the firm was soon to be challenged; even as PW participated fully in the growth and prosperity of the 1960s and enjoyed the benefits of its place at the head of the profession, so too did it make an important choice about growth. The effects of its decision were still felt in the late 1980s.

THE "GO-GO" YEARS

President John Kennedy took office in 1960 promising growth. Although the tax cut he sought was not implemented until 1964, in the early days of Lyndon Johnson's administration, the tax reduction policy had the desired stimulative effect, accelerating growth without serious inflation. "Growth became almost a slogan for U.S. industry, manufacturing and financial, in that period," recalled Herman Bevis. "Everybody was for growth, not necessarily paying attention to why, or what the consequence might be." Although a flood of "unseasoned" equity offerings climaxed and crashed in a stock market break in May 1962, the industrial stock market averages surged back by 1965, breaking records each successive year until the end of the decade.[1]

American companies, meanwhile, pursued headlong expansion abroad; the rapid growth of multinationals was a distinctive phenomenon of the decade. American overseas investment had been accelerating since the end of World War II, when the government sought to promote private investment in friendly countries in the belief that free enterprise, economic growth, and industrialization would provide the foundation for a democratic world. The unique opportunity to expand overseas encouraged a substantial number of companies to take advantage of the access to raw materials, cheap labor, and low-cost plants that they found abroad, and by the late 1960s, most large American corporations had at least part of their operations abroad. During this period, two hundred American multinationals, growing at twice the rate of domestic corporations, accounted for more than half of the direct investment made by American companies abroad and generated $180 billion a year, 15 percent of the gross production of the noncommunist world outside the United States.[2]

The conglomerate was another corporate phenomenon of the era. Throughout most of the 1960s, stable economic conditions led many firms to expand operations and to diversify outside of their own industries. Abandoning the older belief that corporate activities should be technologically or market-related, some managers assumed "they could efficiently supervise almost any sort of business that promised to turn a profit."[3]

These conglomerations of various unrelated businesses were sanctioned by new tax laws that rewarded prosperous companies for merging with unprofitable ones in other industries and encouraged by antitrust laws that forbade mergers in the same line of business. Perhaps the most important factor behind this new type of merger was an unshaken belief in prosperity. The stock market boomed as many new business ventures brought their securities into the market, synergistically fueling and feeding what would become a conglomerate craze. Twice as many mergers occurred in 1968 as in any previous year, with inflated stock prices allowing for false profits and encouraging other ingenious merger and acquisition deals.[4]

THE COMPUTER COMES OF AGE

The dizzying pace of change in the 1960s was accelerated by the widespread introduction of computers into the business world. Electronic data processing (EDP) became a revolutionary force. Throughout the decade, business people debated the role of computers, but by 1969, it was clear that large firms that lacked internal computer capacity and computer consulting expertise would be left behind. Computers enhanced the operation of a multidivisional, decentralized corporation by allowing it to monitor operations on a much larger scale. Well over 50 percent of the top five hundred industrial companies had extensive EDP operations by 1964, 65 percent having been installed within the previous five years.[5]

Computers posed a dilemma for accountants, presenting both a profound threat and a dynamic opportunity. On the one hand, the speed and accuracy with which they verified transactions and their enhanced ability to control corporate operations and information were obvious. A tabulation and verification job that had required 3,125 hours, or approximately seventy-eight weeks, to complete manually could be done in a little over two hours on a computer. Assisted by computers and EDP, auditors could become an "intelligence unit" that provided increased quantitative counsel to managers planning the long-term profitability of their enterprises. Computers allowed auditors more latitude and sophistication. Not only could auditors assess internal control systems, but they could focus on management structure, efficient use of personnel, and evaluation of EDP departments as well.[6]

Some accountants, however, saw only a threat. Computers could eliminate their traditional function and demote them to an advisory role. Accountants who had formerly played an integral part in a company's internal information system might have to relinquish their supremacy to the statisticians, technicians, and other specialists who now seemed essential to the financial information system's overall functioning. To maintain their unique and favored role, accountants needed to develop a general understanding of the statistical operations offered by computer software and at least a general familiarity with the working of computers.[7]

Whether EDP was viewed as a threat or a promise, it was clear that it had the potential to change significantly the audit environment. By the late 1960s, auditors had two options when a client used a computerized system of internal control: either auditing "around the computer" by tracing a number of representative transactions that previously had been processed by the client, or auditing "through the computer" by using the computerized system itself to generate data. Auditing was rarely done through the computer at this time because it required knowledge of computer operations and the creation of an accounting computer software program to run in the client's data base. Nonetheless, it was seen as the way of the future: cheaper, more efficient, and more accurate.[8]

The number of management advisory services involving computer expertise that were provided by accounting firms mushroomed in the 1960s as the impact of computer systems on accounting and records systems increased. Favorable economic conditions, complex government programs, and the increased ability of audit partners to identify opportunities for MAS work all contributed to the enlargement of the scope of MAS services during this time. By the early 1960s, all major accounting firms had MAS departments, with most containing more than two hundred consultants and staff. Sanguine MAS partners predicted that "the future of management consulting belongs to the accounting firms because of our continuing, close, confidential relationship with our clients."[9]

By the end of the 1960s, computers were providing the foundation for the growth of big-firm MAS practice and were having an important effect on the audit and accounting sphere as well. The rapid rate of change in EDP technology and the difficulty in securing knowledgeable personnel ensured that only those firms with a strong will to succeed in this area would in fact do so.

HERMAN BEVIS AND ADMINISTRATIVE REFORM

Herman Bevis, who became senior partner in 1961, fit the mold of his predecessors. Marked for success early in his career with the firm, he brought to the position a sober dignity that comported well with PW's reputation for probity and integrity. Not only did he assume a number of important professional leadership positions, but his internal efforts on a multitude of fronts to improve the firm's administrative processes and information flow also formed an enduring contribution to its management. Through his skillful leadership, Bevis helped to shape PW's autonomous offices into a more cohesive whole.

Bevis entered his profession at a difficult time. Raised in Alabama, he graduated with Harvard Business School's 1932 depression class. In those dark days, the only prospective employers interested in more than one graduate from the business school were "Gulf Oil Corporation for service station attendants and Daltum Hosiery for door-to-door salesmen."[10] Bevis wanted a position at PW, but he took a job at a southern utilities company until an opening appeared in the New York office a year later.[11]

Known as a serious student of accounting, Bevis spent his entire career in the New York office. In 1946, he was admitted to the partnership. He distinguished himself by consulting as a financial adviser to the Air Force, in conjunction with Touche, Niven, Bailey & Smart. In addition, he also served the AICPA in numerous distinguished capacities; he was chairman of its committee on national defense in 1957 and a member (1956–1961) and chairman (1959–1961) of its special long-range objectives committee on the future of the profession. He also served on the AICPA executive committee. In a unique, early example of industry specialization, Bevis pioneered PW's successful statistical survey of law firms. In 1958, he was elected to PW's Executive Committee, where he soon was viewed as Inglis's heir apparent. Three years later, he was elected committee chairman and the firm's senior partner.[12]

Almost immediately, Bevis made a number of important administrative changes. He issued the firm's first set of written policies, delegated the operational details of leadership to a managing partner, and sought to make partners more accountable for hours and billing. Because of their great respect for Bevis, partners were willing to accept his management innovations, even when they were burdensome. They gave their full support to Bevis's championing of flexibility over specific rules, although they found this a drain on the firm's resources.[13]

Bevis sought to strengthen the traditionally decentralized partnership by publishing firmwide policies. When he had joined PW in 1933, its thirty partners knew each other well. Families were friendly, and the concept of a larger "PW family" was an important part of the firm's culture. Policies were informal, building on these personal relationships. By 1960, when Bevis was elected senior partner, the firm's family had grown to more than one hundred partners, and the personal bonds that had knit the group together were dissolving. Word-of-mouth policies had become inadequate and even harmful, as contradictory practices were followed in different offices. The traditional decentralization of each office, with each partner-in-charge a virtual ruler of his own fiefdom, exacerbated the problem.[14]

In 1961, Bevis circulated to each partner the firm's first written expression of policy, known as Policies and Administrative References (PAR). PAR was the result of Bevis's two-year study of the minutes of all Executive Committee and partners' meetings and of special reports. PAR covered all aspects of the firm—partnership, contract and staff, and operations—with each section containing a summary of present policies supported by excerpts of minutes from committee and partners' meetings. To understand the circumstances that had led to policy development during previous decades, a partner could turn to the office copy of PAR Background, which listed the history of each policy over time. PAR Background brought the policy alive, allowing partners to research, for example, the firm's rule on partnership retirement at age 60 or to find information on the scope and power of the Executive Committee. By creating and distributing an objective guide for the firm's decision making, Bevis sought to strengthen PW by checking the discretionary power of any single office or partner-in-charge, and by providing a new foundation for policy decisions.[15]

Other important changes grew out of the twin currents of delegation and centralization that Bevis initiated. Discussing PW's future at a week-long retreat in 1962, the Executive Committee decided to create a new position to handle internal operations, leaving Bevis free to deal with external relationships, professional problems, and firm policy. Bevis chose O. Kenneth Pryor, partner-in-charge of the San Francisco office

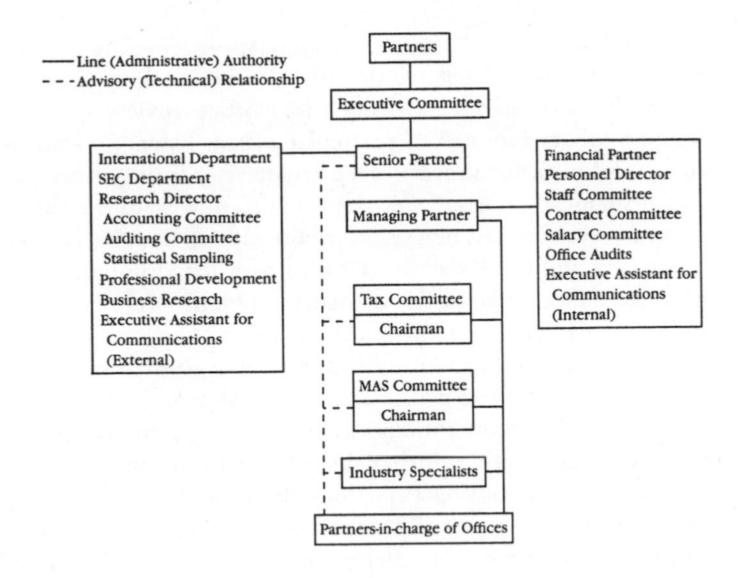

Source: Price Waterhouse, Executive Committee Minutes, Office of the Firm Secretary, National Office, New York (March 14–16, 1962), 1 and Appendices.

EXHIBIT 5.1 Organization Chart, March 1962

since 1945 and member of the Executive Committee since 1957, as the firm's first managing partner.[16] The firm issued its first organization chart at this time, which is shown in Exhibit 5.1.

The managing partner was responsible for administrative functions and supervised the firm's finance and personnel areas. In order to keep close rein on internal functions and to determine the extent of problems in the firm's financial organization, the managing partner often sent letters to partners indicating that accounts receivable were overdue, that billings were too slow, or that staff cuts were needed. Policy questions or client problems went to Bevis.[17]

Creating the position of managing partner continued a process that Bevis had begun when he transferred all of his own clients to other partners. In doing so, he deliberately departed from the model created by Inglis who, while serving as senior partner, continued as principal audit partner for major clients and also ran the New York office (with another partner, Chester DeMond). Freedom from both client concerns and operational details gave Bevis more time to deal with external professional problems and firm policy.[18]

Bevis also revised PW's reporting structure. Although Inglis had visited as many partners as possible, personal contact became increasingly difficult for Bevis as the partnership approached two hundred members. Over time, he delegated the job of visiting offices to members of the Executive Committee. During these office reviews, Executive Committee members assigned to particular offices listened to problems and gave advice on office morale, client matters, administration, competition, and financial affairs. Later they reported back to the full committee. This process created newer, more formal reporting relationships between partners and the Executive Committee, for although in theory all partners had a direct line to Bevis, many problems were handled first by the designated Executive Committee member.[19]

These delegations of responsibilities did not give Bevis complete freedom to devote himself to professional leadership and policy making. The growing complexity of running a large firm and the controversies surrounding standard-setting during the 1960s forced him to relinquish his position on the Accounting Principles Board in 1966.[20]

In 1962, PW moved its headquarters and the New York office for the first time in forty years. The change from 56 Pine Street, described by one partner as "a horrible old building, inefficient, costly to operate, un-airconditioned," to 60 Broad Street around the corner symbolized the new leadership style.[21] In the new building, a distinctive carpeted and paneled suite of offices housed Bevis, Pryor, Weston Rankin, the chief financial partner, Paul E. Nye, the partner-in-charge of staff, William T. Hazelton, the partner-in-charge of the New York office, and Alden C. Smith, the head of the International Department. This small but highly visible area physically drew the different departments together and symbolized the true beginning of the firm's National Office.[22]

Another small but important manifestation of the National Office was the Communications Department, which was set up in 1961. Its principal activity was to edit and publish a "family of periodicals" to meet the information needs of a "variety of audiences." *PW Review*, first published in 1955, was directed to staff as well as clients. It reflected the firm's major activities and served as a forum for professional articles. *PW Staff News*, first distributed in 1961, informed staff members, particularly those below manager level, whereas the *Executive Letter* transmitted information specifically relevant to partners and managers.[23]

In 1967, two years before the end of his term, and in recognition of the rapidly growing complexity of firm leadership, Bevis made a final organizational change, naming John Biegler to the new position of deputy senior partner. The managing partner retained authority over all firmwide administration, as well as responsibility for the Financial and Personnel departments and for the staff and contract committees, while Biegler supervised all substantive and technical matters arising out of the practice offices. He was also responsible for staff functions like the

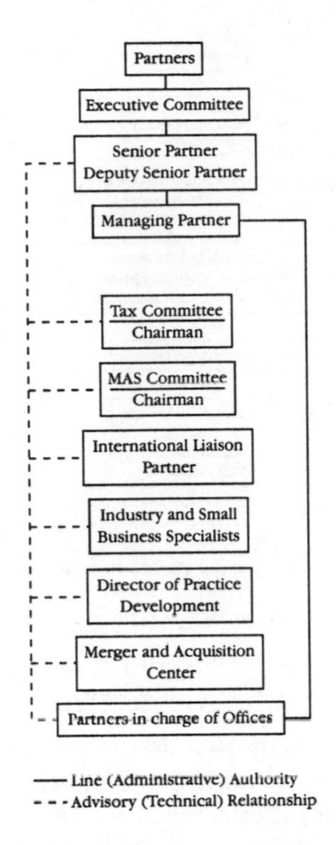

Source: Price Waterhouse, "Policy and Administrative References, Background Material" (PAR Background), 1961–1978, 075.12, Office of the Firm Secretary, National Office, New York.

EXHIBIT 5.2 Organization Chart, December 1967

Research and SEC departments, and the accounting and auditing committees. Only the most senior individual in each practice area reported to Bevis.[24] These 1967 reporting relationships are shown in Exhibits 5.2 and 5.3.

Bevis was interested in measuring PW's profitability and productivity and focused on operational details in order to make the firm more accountable. As the partnership expanded and personal contact and observation grew more difficult, he increasingly relied on statistical data and formal reporting requirements to obtain information. PW had never before systematically collected and processed operating or statistical data from each of the offices, but EDP now provided the opportunity to do so.[25]

PW's lack of systematic financial accountability within the firm was rooted in practice patterns dating back to the 1940s and 1950s, when

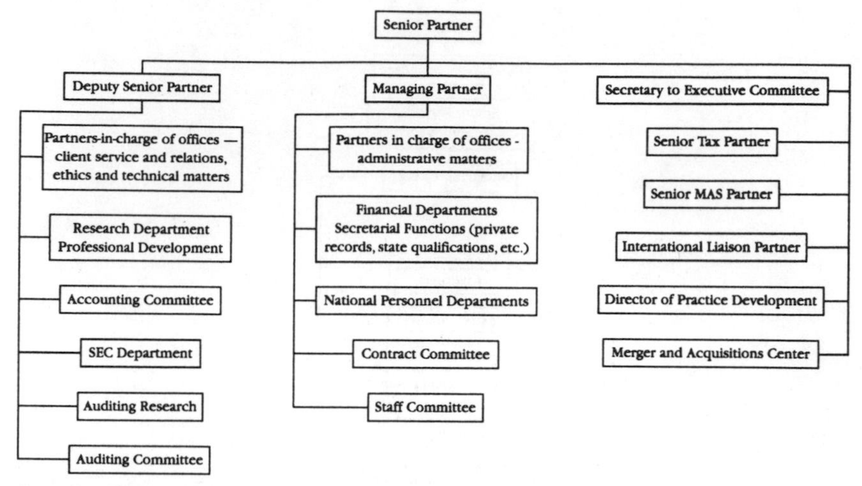

Source: Price Waterhouse, PAR Background, 075.13, Office of the Firm Secretary, National Office, New York.

EXHIBIT 5.3 Organization Chart, 1967

audits were structured with up to a dozen juniors working in a client's offices and supervised by a full-time, on-site senior. A manager had ultimate responsibility for the effectiveness and completeness of the audit and for review of the working papers, and clients rarely saw a partner, since managers were responsible for supervising the fieldwork. There were fixed and identical rates for each class of staff and for partners. The firm did not dun clients for overdue bills in the belief that clients knew the quality and value of the work they had received and would pay without argument or undue delay. In any event, no one, even strong-willed leaders like Inglis, enjoyed exchanges over fees.[26]

This system had been sufficient in the past, but new business imperatives required changes in how audits were conducted, how partners spent their time, and how these events were reported internally.[27] Bevis sought to change the firm's traditional working patterns, and he became known as a "demon" for getting partners to pay more attention to their clients and to charge more of their time on client work. He developed a standard worksheet, which included information on the number of chargeable hours compared with time spent on professional activities. Each partner received a listing, in declining order, of all partners' chargeable hours—no names attached—with a red arrow next to his own. Pryor sent letters to all offices listing the total chargeable hours that partners had billed in the previous year, and if performance was below par, he would often note, "it stinks!" Offices began to submit goals and budget projections to the financial partner, who then discussed them with the Executive Committee.

By the end of Bevis's term, the MAS Department was involved in improving the firm's financial planning and reporting system. Internal bookkeeping schedules were completed by each office, providing a solid basis for firmwide statistics. An office income statement was devised that included revenues, expenses broken down by salary and occupancy cost, the office's realization or underrealization percentage, and its contribution to firm profit. After this information was processed, the New York office distributed it throughout the firm, for some of the partners "loved to get data and sometimes they'd get more data than they knew what to do with." For many years thereafter, "every partner was getting the results of every office."[28]

Over the course of his senior partnership, Bevis bridged two very different worlds. His austere mien and magisterial manner epitomized the reputation of PW for integrity and quality. He saw his role as conservator of the firm's great traditions and articulator of accounting standards. Bevis assumed control of the firm, however, in a decade when larger environmental issues required a new definition of leadership. As the firm's fortunes and place within the profession appeared to be as solid as ever, it is not surprising that Bevis's initial efforts were directed primarily at solving management problems. The firm was certainly better managed and administered as a result of his reforms, and for the first time the firm had a centralized direction and control. But this inner-directed focus may have diverted some attention from competitive issues facing the partnership in the 1960s. As the decade wore on, reports from the field and the relentless pace of change made the implications of such an institutional stance ever more problematic.[29]

STAFFING THE TAX DEPARTMENT

PW's tax practice grew enormously during the 1960s. Innovative training, as well as efforts to allow partners greater independence, were used to try to fill the personnel gap resulting from the pressures spawned by growth.

Increases in tax work were the result of new legislation—proof, if such were needed, of the importance of laws to the accounting profession. A trend toward more numerous, complex, and specific tax laws, which had begun with excess profits tax legislation at the time of the

Korean War and the 1954 Internal Revenue Code, continued into the 1960s, creating a very favorable business environment for tax accountants. Tax work brought the profession its largest public audience in the 1960s and became the second most remunerative part of the CPA practice; a 1963 study showed that 25 percent of the typical CPA's gross income was based on tax services.[30]

Congress's unparalleled activity during the early 1960s created many opportunities. The Revenue Act of 1962 had a major effect on taxpayers with international operations, and until the Treasury and the IRS issued their own bulletins, the burden of interpreting the act's provisions for clients fell on accounting firms' tax departments. Even more critical was the Revenue Act of 1964, described by a congressional spokesman as "the most important single domestic economic measure of the last fifteen years." The act's revisions in the determination of taxable income made "radical changes in a host of tax provisions affecting business and individual taxpayers alike," and tax planning responsibility for business clients mushroomed. The PW Tax Department closed out the decade extraordinarily busy, as "feverish activity concerning tax reform" took place in Treasury and congressional circles.[31]

The Tax Department suffered from a severe lack of personnel throughout the 1960s. It had always obtained its staff from the audit practice, and a history of friendly competition had grown up between the two areas for the "best" people. But pressing client demands and a shortage of experienced staff forced the Tax Department to take increasingly inexperienced recruits. The director of technical tax services, at this time partner Albert Cohen, became alarmed at the experience shortage at the various promotion levels, and he responded by introducing several new tax education programs in 1966. Cohen and a team of partners developed an intensive, two-week, full-time course for new audit transfers called "T3" or "technical tax training," and a week-long program for more experienced, nonmanagerial staff called "Select." Each year more courses were added, until twenty-five were available to new personnel below the managerial level. When Cohen and his team were satisfied with the content and usefulness of the first two levels, they focused their attention on the existing three-day managers' meetings. By 1968, they had introduced a demanding technical education program at managerial level as well.[32]

The sophistication of the Tax Department's educational program put it at the forefront of the firm. The push for continuing education reflected sensitivity to a central PW tenet: the pride and independence of a small partnership. Cohen did not try to impose his programs on the partnership, but sought to make useful education available and thereby to increase the ability of every member of PW to serve clients.[33]

MAS MAKES ITS WAY

PW's MAS Department spent the 1960s establishing itself as a consulting practice and a viable part of the firm. Its task was made more difficult by rapidly changing EDP technology, which formed a large part of its work, and the need for trained, non–CPA technical staff. In addition, the tension that existed between the audit and consulting practices forced the latter to adhere to a more circumscribed focus. Overall, however, the firm was content with the progress of its consulting practice.

One thorny issue created by the department's growth was the large number of MAS staff with primarily nonaccounting skills. In the 1950s, it employed a few punch-card specialists, to whom there were no serious objections. The MAS Department's needs were clear, and it assured the firm that these specialists would be supervised by CPAs. This compromise was shattered "by the arrival of the computer, its complex technology, and the concomitant expansion of services outside the accounting function."[34] As a result, in the 1960s, "MAS went from being a department made up almost 100% of CPAs to one in which non–CPAs constituted about two thirds of the staff."[35] This situation raised important questions of authority and responsibility.[36] Computer-literate personnel for the department could be garnered or developed from three sources: by retraining punch-card specialists already on staff, by hiring individuals working for computer companies, or by training transfers from the audit staff. It was difficult for PW to attract and especially to retain computer experts, since a non–CPA could not become a partner. PW did not award partner equivalent status for non–CPA MAS consultants until the 1960s, when it created the new category of "MAS principal" to recognize those who were fully qualified to be admitted as partners except for their lack of a CPA certificate. MAS principals were treated internally like partners in most respects, though they did not have the right to vote on partnership matters.[37]

As computers became smaller, more efficient and reliable, less expensive, and more closely intertwined with telecommunications and other programming systems, their use spread. As a consequence, PW's MAS Department grew and dispersed geographically, developing a regional organization. It also sought staff talented in a number of areas beyond systems and accounting, including manufacturing, marketing, purchasing, and personnel. MAS consultants with manufacturing skills, for example, assisted in inventory problems, and operations research experts were valued for their mathematical and statistical abilities.[38]

As accounting systems became more integrally related to computer systems, and as computer software grew more sophisticated, a gap developed between an auditor's knowledge base and that of a specialized

MAS consultant. Auditors sought the MAS Department's help, but in these early days, a consultant's lack of audit expertise and ignorance of fraud control issues often made the effort unproductive. A program was developed by PW auditors and the MAS Department to help auditors to audit through the computer, showing how electronic records could be counted and audited, accounts receivable totaled, and items selected that failed to meet certain criteria. The firm used this program for several years and made it available to a number of clients' internal audit departments.[39]

During the 1960s, the MAS Department serviced large numbers of government clients, did important work for the firm itself, and expanded the PW executive recruitment function. Although government work at first was largely confined to the state level, it widened rapidly to include federal and local entities. Government work, however, was generally fraught with difficulty and hard to make profitable. It was a very competitive area, and proposals often had to be made without adequate knowledge of existing conditions, personnel, or the level of cooperation.

The MAS Department worked for the firm itself during its slack periods on tasks such as office layout, filing systems, and records retention. In addition, it assisted Bevis in his efforts to gain control of PW's internal record-keeping and profitability. In 1966, the Executive Committee transferred the executive recruitment function, formerly part of the Personnel Department, to the MAS Department. Closer identification of this service with the MAS Department was thought to be a more effective means of filling client openings for controllers and chief financial officers, because these needs were related to the identification and solution of larger organization and compensation problems. The transfer was extremely successful; by 1969, the work had "increased dramatically."[40]

Large, unusual, and interesting MAS engagements proliferated during the 1960s. The department reviewed the ten years of EDP development for American Mutual Liability Insurance, for example, and studied EDP worldwide for International Nickel. As the decade continued, the scope of work widened. The department developed and implemented major innovations in customer claims, credit, and collections for Consolidated Edison, assisted in redesigning a subscription fulfillment system for Curtis Publishing, and developed a mathematical model to plan mining operations for Minera Frisco.[41]

One of the best examples of the MAS Department's specialization and profitability was the litigation support practice that began in the 1960s in the Los Angeles office. PW's auditors had always been active in litigation support work, which often centered on the calculation of damages. The catalyst for the new practice was an article in a legal journal describing an executive compensation study that PW partner Francis C. Dykeman had prepared for trial. His careful approach and his detailed analysis of the propriety of business decisions, based on Dykeman's expertise as both a lawyer and a CPA, helped to win the case, no small accomplishment since the claim for compensation had been rejected by four previous judges as excessive. Over time, the MAS Department sought to widen the focus of litigation work to encompass antitrust, divorce, breach of contract, Internal Revenue Service actions, and mergers. It developed an interdisciplinary staff, that included mathematicians, computer experts, industrial engineers, and psychologists. This work also brought the firm special assignments from nonaudit clients such as General Motors and Coca-Cola.[42] By 1973, PW had been involved in more than a hundred litigation support engagements concerned with expert witness testimony.[43]

In June 1966, the MAS Department gathered in Boston to celebrate its twentieth anniversary. Chargeable hours had increased twelvefold since its founding in 1946, and the staff numbered 250, having grown 50 percent within the previous two years. The department noted that the

> formula for this success is simple to state and hard to emulate—a million business ideas a minute, a willingness to think and talk aggressively with clients, a lively interest in and contribution to the engagements themselves and a (reluctant) willingness to accept the emotional and technical ups and downs of a typical engagement as normal.[44]

The Philadelphia office was singled out as a particularly bright star, with business rising "from a trickle to a torrent" in just two years.[45]

The MAS Department's overall scope of services slowly expanded in the 1960s in line with Bevis's policy, which was generally viewed within the department as concerned and constraining, but fair. Early computer assignments concentrated on answering two fundamental questions for clients: Should they get a computer and, if so, what kind? Once these decisions had been made, with relatively few exceptions the MAS Department did not advise clients during the implementation or post-installation and evaluation stages of computer use as did some of its competitors. It was not permitted until 1969 to develop and sell EDP software packages designed by PW, and even then permission was given "tentatively and subject to modification," despite the Executive Committee's acknowledgment that "sale or lease of these packages was already widespread and [the] future potential was great."[46] PW's software packages were tailored to a variety of uses and many, like the general ledger package, were developed exclusively for sale to clients. The department had also created software for its own work in areas such as bank information systems, executive salary evaluations, and records management.[47]

The consulting practice had unique burdens. Computer capability was still a major challenge, and questions and differences regarding responsibility for consulting engagements remained unresolved. In the end, PW's MAS Department concluded the decade as a solid contributor to the firm.

AUDITING AND ACCOUNTING

Unlike tax and MAS, PW's audit and accounting services had never been gathered under the umbrella of one department or managed by one particular partner. Instead, different individuals headed up various committees, departments, and support services and reported to the Executive Committee in a decentralized system. This organization reflected PW's view of itself as an audit firm that also happened to have two other distinct, and smaller, specialties. Despite the growth pressures of the 1960s on the audit and accounting side, the firm took a deliberate approach there as well, building on basic structures, creating new support areas, and rechanneling resources where needed.[48]

The chief accounting support area, known as the Research Department, expanded to meet new needs. Its noteworthy projects of the early 1960s included a collaboration with the firm's auditing committee, which had been created in the 1950s by the Executive Committee. They produced a report entitled "The Objectives of Audit," with a companion piece on implementation. In 1961, the Research Department prepared a "Guide to Practical Business Approach Auditing," recommending changes to the firm's existing audit methods. Among its suggestions were that

> the three major ingredients of modern audit, knowledge of the business, knowledge of controls, and audit tests, [be] woven together in such a way that all *must* be covered in order to complete an examination [and] the auditing approach [be organized] by basic functions (marketing, production, etc.) instead of by the traditional method of captions (cash, accounts receivable, etc.). This should make it easier for assistants to view the company as a set of books and records.[49]

The partners welcomed the Guide, believing that its suggestions, which promised "a major change from the firm's present methods," would be an addition to its prestige; "If PW can lead the way, it will not only enhance the firm's reputation, but continue PW's leadership within the profession."[50] By 1964, each member of the firm's auditing committee had applied the Guide to one or more engagements on a trial basis.

During the mid- to late 1960s, the Research Department substantially increased its emphasis on long-range research by assigning one partner, five managers, and one senior to handle this work. The focus of the department's responsibilities shifted almost entirely to accounting matters, and a typical project included research related to AICPA revisions of its Accounting Research Bulletins.[51]

The auditing committee was responsible for introducing reforms and regulating procedures in the firm's audit approach. It worked throughout the 1960s to improve audit techniques and to assist in the professional staff's adaptation to computers. Between 1959 and 1962, it issued the firm's first ten checklists "designed to guide the less-experienced assistants and to prod the experienced staff to bring to bear their knowledge of the business."[52] In 1961, it "endeavored to anticipate problems in areas of accounting and reporting" and noted that work on the "'incentive' depreciation proposals of the Kennedy administration" and "problems involved in changing the form of the firm's opinions" were among those that required its attention.[53] Beginning in 1963, the committee worked to devise material that would "assist managers to meet their responsibilities efficiently," and it recommended that the firm's existing "audit checklists" be completely revised.[54]

Because PW's philosophy required that audit checklists be used only as guides for preparation of tailor-made audit programs for each client, the committee created a set of basic and general checklists useful as guidance for both large and small examinations. In addition to the checklists themselves, the committee generated a companion text, which included explanations and instructions on how to develop and carry out audits under various circumstances. This text codified all existing checklists as well as standard references such as Paul Grady's "Outline for Staff Training." Work continued on the checklists throughout the decade, and after some delays because of lack of personnel, the new system was field-tested in the fall of 1968.[55]

In 1967, the first full-time audit research partner, Wyman Patten, was assigned to the area, initially to respond to problems and questions raised by partners and staff involving auditing standards and procedures as well as audit-related litigation matters. The committee was renamed, and the new "audit research" committee's responsibilities embraced the continuing development of computer-based technology, participation in AICPA audit research, expansion of the firm's quality control system, and development of audit reference support.[56]

In 1969, for example, the new Audit Research Department introduced its "Audit Guide Series," developed by John Farrell, a young partner.

The series, which represented nearly two years of work, emphasized a more business-oriented audit approach. It covered more than ten separate areas, including, for example, the preliminary audit survey, sales and receivables, and auditing in an EDP environment, and discussed "many of the factors previously considered on an intuitive basis," including formal recognition of environmental factors and construction of audit programs responsive to differences among individual companies. The material became a desk reference, rather than an on-the-job checklist, since it was broad in theory and useful in the initial design of audit programs and checklists for new clients.[57]

By the late 1960s, computer technology spurred the Audit Research Department to further innovations. In cooperation with the Research Department, it developed computer audit training material. In addition, responding to a 1968 challenge from Haskins & Sells's newly developed software, the Audit Research and the MAS Departments devised a generalized audit program on computer tape, a departure from the tradition of programs designed specifically for each individual engagement. The tape program utilized an audit language that allowed CPAs to write out audit steps that could then be executed through a computer. It was "completely and successfully tested against a client's live data file" a year later.[58]

Audit Research also developed guidance and safeguards to help stem the rising tide of litigation against accounting firms. For example, the committee considered a policy for outlining the limits to the scope of an examination in the usual representation letter obtained from clients. Yet, though some other large accounting firms were outlining certain limits to the scope of their examination of accounts, PW retained its policy that engagement partners were to be specifically responsible to "see that a proper understanding exists," based on a thorough discussion with clients and documentation. As lawsuits against accountants continued to plague the profession, the committee recommended new procedures for screening potential clients and joined in developing, with the AICPA, model representation letters for the profession as a whole.[59]

In 1967, another support function, staff training, was renamed "Professional Development" and given its first big push in twenty years. Within a short time, Professional Development's budget was doubled, and by 1969, a partner was assigned to this area.[60]

One of the most dynamic sides of PW's auditing and accounting practice in the 1960s was its international work. The needs of the firm's worldwide clientele for new services, and the increasing interest of American business people in the "potentialities of foreign operations" led PW to create an International Department and an International Tax Department in the late 1950s. In 1962, the two departments moved to adjacent offices on the same floor at 60 Broad Street, "so clients doing business abroad will have the services of both departments easily available in conferences. It is expected that the two departments will work together even more closely."[61] The International Tax Department, which operated under the direct supervision of Leslie Mills, senior tax partner at this time, rendered services to clients and to other offices concerning the more sophisticated areas of the tax practice involving foreign operations. The International Department, a subsection of the firm's audit practice, served as a liaison between PW foreign offices and their clients' headquarters in the United States when these enterprises were not clients of the U.S. firm. In the mid-1960s, PW offices abroad carried out work for more than two hundred American companies that were not clients of the U.S. firm. With offices in many foreign countries, some of these nonclient companies preferred to send instructions to the U.S. firm and to depend on the International Department to disseminate the instructions to the various PW offices abroad. The International Department also served to settle disputes in handling audits between international offices.[62]

Among the successful and widely known ventures produced by these two departments were the *Information Guides* and the *Guides to Doing Business Abroad*. When the federal tax laws changed in 1958 to require that citizens working abroad file income tax returns, the partner-in-charge of the Venezuela office approached the New York tax partners to request a guide clarifying this change for his expatriate community. The Tax Department's initial booklet, published as *Guide to 1958 Income Taxes for U.S. Citizens Abroad*, was widely circulated and, by 1962, had developed into a series of information guides on doing business abroad covering twenty-eight countries. Another booklet, the *Information Guide to Foreign Exchange*, covered forty-one countries. In addition to being very useful within the firm and for existing clients, these guides helped attract inquiries for work overseas.[63]

The purpose of technical support and of auditing and accounting committee work was, above all, to assist partners with clients. For PW in particular, this assistance often concerned issues arising out of audits of large multinational corporations, as the firm had consistently had the lion's share of major international clients. PW had always been the unquestioned leader in petroleum industry clients as auditor of more large oil companies than any other accounting firm. Its expertise led to a special engagement by the U.S. government in the early 1950s to assist in evaluating the qualifications of small oil companies that were participating in the oil discoveries in the Middle East.[64]

Numbered among PW's clients, in order of assets in the 1960s, were Standard Oil of New Jersey (SONJ), Gulf Oil Corporation, Standard Oil of California, Standard Oil of Indiana, Shell Oil, Tidewater Oil, Richfield Oil, and Superior Oil.[65] The firm's long history of work for

SONJ shows the vast scope and myriad administrative details involved in a large multinational audit.[66] The relationship with SONJ began in 1932, when PW was hired as a consultant to develop a comprehensive manual to ensure comparability in the financial statements of all SONJ subsidiaries. In 1934, PW was appointed SONJ auditor and carried out SONJ's first consolidated audit pursuant to the new Securities Exchange Act. At the time, some thirty PW offices took part.[67] Three decades later, in 1965, the SONJ work had grown enormously; the New York engagement partner oversaw the work of some seven hundred staff members in seventy-three offices worldwide. Having ultimate responsibility for work done throughout the globe, this partner was required to visit all the company's principal offices, as well as PW practice offices, to ensure that examinations were conducted effectively and that all necessary information was provided.[68] The New York office handled all project administration, coordinating instructions to all other firm offices and resolving unusual accounting problems. It developed an administrative manual just for this engagement, as well as an extensive memorandum of general instructions and audit guidelines to inform other firm offices of the scope of the examination. New York was also responsible for ensuring that the company's own audit and accounting manuals were accurate and up to date.[69]

During the 1965 engagement, PW issued or reviewed an immense number of reports involved in some way with either SONJ's consolidation or its financial management. In all, the firm played an important role in some 560 reports to the public and to management regarding the company's 1964 financial information, including review, by the New York engagement partner-in-charge, of 184 memoranda on examinations, 139 statutory accounts and annual reports to shareholders, and 100 reports rendered by internal auditors to local management. Throughout the year, SONJ controllers discussed major procedural changes affecting the accounts with PW, as well as the proper treatment of major transactions.[70]

A specialized area of the audit and accounting practice was its SEC work. Originally created in 1952 to ensure a coordinated approach with the SEC, the SEC Department had

> routinely participated in prefiling conferences with the SEC staff, conducted prefiling reviews of draft material to be included in registration and proxy statements, attended due diligence meetings, and participated in a number of other activities relating to SEC filings with clients, underwriters, and attorneys.[71]

Throughout the 1960s, the SEC Department faced unprecedented challenges brought on by the bullish stock market. When filings for public securities by Far Eastern companies began in 1961, it played an important and innovative role in assisting Japanese companies to obtain capital from American financial markets. The firm had a large number of Japanese clients that sought assistance, including Sony, Mitsubishi, Toshiba, and Nippon Electric. To ensure that these foreign companies would be permitted to sell their securities in the United States, the SEC Department and other partners and staff traveled to Japan, where they introduced consolidation accounting and developed all the necessary formats. In addition, they worked with Japanese accountants to bring their financial statements into compliance with SEC requirements. This was arduous, round-the-clock work that involved many first-time consolidated audits of Japanese enterprises, and it was often done under extreme time pressure, with the added burden of a language barrier.[72]

The complexity of developing the five-year financial presentations that the SEC required of these companies, usually with a hundred or more subsidiary and associated companies, was daunting. In the early 1960s, the Japanese accounting profession was in its infancy. Audit standards and practices were sketchy. Japanese accountants prepared financial statements under statutory rules that largely mirrored income tax–based accounting and lacked group or consolidation features. Indeed, consolidated financial statement practices and presentation were neither followed nor generally known.

The SEC required that the financial statements in these filings be prepared and audited in accordance with American accounting principles. The differences between U.S. and Japanese accounting were substantial; the Japanese "free share" distributions, for example, the absence of deferred tax accounting, and the lack of consolidation methodology, among other variances from American practice, all contributed to the need for a unique, tailored approach in the SEC filings. PW, in effect, set the financial reporting standards for these early filings and for a time enjoyed a monopoly of the large Japanese public offerings in the United States.

This special work contributed substantially to the reputation and the growth of the newly established PW office in Tokyo, which had resulted from the acquisition of the Lowe, Bingham & Thomas correspondent practice there in 1962. This combination of practices, with its experienced Japanese accountants and Americans on temporary assignment in Japan, contributed significantly to accounting and auditing educational efforts for the staff and for other professionals, as well as for client and nonclient company personnel. It was not uncommon, recalled a partner who participated, for a team composed of an American and a Japanese PW manager to teach courses in consolidated accounting, after hours, to client officers and employees. "After hours" often meant from 8 to 11 P.M., after the client and PW personnel had already worked a 12-

hour day in the seven-day work weeks customary in these initial offerings. PW's initial offering work and its educational leadership in this area provided the most important spurs to the eventual widespread adoption of consolidation accounting in Japan.

Back in the United States, the SEC Department responded to requests for consultation and information by issuing new support material for partners and staff. In 1964, it updated and distributed its "Reference Service," first issued in 1957, which contained selected SEC rules, regulations, and forms, and which was described as an "authoritative reference work based on the cumulative knowledge and experience of the SEC Department in the New York office." This work contained the most comprehensive guidance then available in the profession on theory and standards for presentation of pro forma financial statements used widely in merger and refinancing prospectuses.[73]

The market continued to spiral upward. From 1950 to 1965, the number of shares of stock listed on the New York Stock Exchange increased 502 percent, and the market value of all corporate stock rose sixfold. The 59 percent increase in public registrations in 1968 over 1967, the biggest percentage gain since 1933, was exceeded by a 67 percent increase in 1969. Although the record-breaking securities market of the 1960s ensured higher firm revenues, PW observed these developments with caution and, in the end, with no small measure of prophecy; "Capital markets are erratic and unstable in 1966, yet never before had securities been sold publicly in such volume and seldom before had conditions been so unattractive."[74] The upsurge in defense spending to finance the Vietnam War had thrown off the balance achieved by the 1964 tax cut. When no additional revenues were raised to offset the additional expenditures, the economy overheated and an inflationary spiral began. Economists urged raising taxes, but Congress delayed until 1969, when it approved a 10 percent increase. By then a downturn had already begun, and escalating inflation overtook the economy. These events put an end to the merger craze, for they "provided a test of the conglomerator's management abilities and most failed."[75]

THE DEBATE OVER GROWTH

The inevitable result of the external pressures on the profession in the 1960s was a shifting in relative size standing among the large accounting firms in the United States. During PW's first fifty years, the firm had no real competitors. Arthur Andersen emerged in the 1960s, however, as the most dynamic, aggressive, and fastest growing of the Big Eight. (The Big Eight were Peat, Marwick, Mitchell, Price Waterhouse, Arthur Andersen, Coopers & Lybrand, Haskins & Sells, Touche Ross, Arthur Young, and Ernst & Whinney.) Although a significant portion of PW partners were troubled by this change, the firm's deliberate strategy, given its pre-eminent status, was to make few institutional changes.

By the mid-1960s, PW recognized that Andersen was by far the strongest competitor in all respects. In 1965, partner John Biegler reviewed an Andersen publication listing their partners, offices, and revenue numbers to discover what factors accounted for their growth rate since World War II. Comparing the Andersen and PW data for the same twenty-year period, Biegler concluded that "they were walking all over us in terms of growth."[76]

In 1968, PW distributed an in-house study listing the auditor changes made over the previous seven years by 869 significant American industrial and merchandising companies. Its conclusion must have been disquieting:

> While PW maintained a significant lead among the companies studied and in fact increased its percentage of the total, Arthur Andersen's growth performance has been quite spectacular. In a declining field, it was the only firm to increase the absolute number of clients. Of 69 companies identified as having changed accounting firms directly, (other than through merger, etc.) 17, or nearly 25 percent selected Arthur Andersen. (About 19 percent selected Peat and 16 percent PW.) During that same period, that firm lost only 3 clients via that route. Of the 30 clients gained by Arthur Andersen, 22 were lost by other "Big Eight" firms; this again exceeded the performance of the other firms.[77]

Andersen's success stirred pride as well as concern inside the firm, for Arthur Andersen had started out in PW's Chicago office. He was aggressive even then, and when he left PW to become controller of the Joseph Schlitz brewery in Milwaukee, he was able to negotiate a handsome bonus of $100. When he began his own firm in 1913, Andersen concentrated on developing a specialty in utilities accounting.[78]

During the post–World War II years, the Andersen firm had expanded dramatically, competing with PW to hire the best college graduates and often offering slightly higher salaries or an earlier, faster road to partnership as part of an intentional program to invest partnership profits in new personnel. As one PW partner recalled, when he later asked prospective recruits,

"Why did you go to Arthur Andersen?"

"Well," they'd say, "they offered more money. I couldn't tell the difference between you two. You both talk great. . . . You both have good practices, both well known."[79]

In the business arena, Andersen was aggressive as well. Although PW respected Andersen's technical expertise, its method of seeking client opportunities was quite different from Andersen's. One often-told story recounts an exchange between Andersen's senior partner Leonard Spacek and PW's Jack Inglis:

Inglis: "Leonard, I didn't much like your visiting U.S. Steel."
Spacek: "Jack, I'll visit anywhere I'm asked to visit."
Inglis: "Yes, but do you have to send eight partners?"[80]

By the 1960s, Andersen's success had convinced a number of PW partners that relying on prestige was no longer enough. To attract new recruits and new clients, more had to be made of the firm's blue-chip reputation and client base. Some partners thought it more important to preserve PW's traditions and culture than to compete for clients and personnel. Although Bevis warned against "complacency, sleepiness, and self-satisfaction," he also stressed that accountancy was "a profession, not a competitive industry." He publicly disapproved of the "aggressiveness on the part of some firms to bring themselves and their services to the attention of the business public."[81]

Bevis represented an older view that, at its extreme, disdained marketing and held that the firm's professional stature was based on its reputation, which was best promoted through "articles and speeches and good service" as well as "word of mouth" from existing clients and bankers. He quoted with approval May's statement that PW's best references were from those clients that had fired the firm in anger. Although he realized that PW would lose the client, he backed the partners and staff who refused to accept Newmont Mining's financial statements because, in PW's view, they did not fairly present its financial position and operating results. PW's examination of Newmont's accounts revealed a significant disparity between Newmont's reported income and the amount that should have been reported had a subsidiary been consolidated with Newmont. PW recommended that Newmont report its pro rata share of the subsidiary's loss in its financial statements, rather than report as income the dividends it received from the subsidiary for the year. Newmont's CEO refused and fired PW as the company's auditor. Arthur Andersen was hired and supported the CEO's position.[82]

The emphasis on maintaining quality was deeply ingrained, even though it posed an occasional threat to the firm's client base. PW still lived by the credo: "We're doing all right, and these other firms, they've got a right to live, we're not going to steal their clients." In keeping with this philosophy, typical practice development speeches sought to determine how new clients could be attracted while PW stayed within the bounds of professional ethics.[83] To be sure, the general prosperity of the 1960s blunted the incentive of most firms to compete against each other. The market for accounting services was continually expanding and being redefined, providing room for many different firms pursuing different strategies. PW, in particular, had historically ignored the competition, although its rejection of growth for growth's sake was a viewpoint shared by some other firms.

As PW surveyed the competition, its partners focused less on the techniques that other firms were using to grow in size, client base, and revenues and more on the public debate over accounting principles in which PW and Andersen became engaged. This focus, important as it was to the evolution of accounting principles, occupied much of Bevis's time during a critical period when PW might have been developing ways to counter growth initiatives of the competition.[84]

One stimulus of competitive initiatives, however, was the feverish corporate merger and acquisition activity of this period. In the mid-1960s, PW audited 108 of the *Fortune* 500 companies, 71 percent more than the number audited by any other firm. PW also audited 216 of the New York Stock Exchange's listed companies, again considerably more than any other firm. However, as a result of this impressive client base of large companies, whenever a sizable merger occurred, PW was likely to be involved at least 25 percent of the time, often on the wrong side.

> The PW stable of clients were the cream of the crop—New York Stock Exchange companies. They were basically very conservative companies, and they didn't for the most part engage in mergers and acquisitions. So we watched . . . a number of our clients being swallowed up by others, rather than our clients swallowing up others.[85]

By 1967, the pace of mergers had accelerated so rapidly, and so many PW clients were involved as either buyers or sellers, that the firm created a mergers and acquisition center in the New York office. The partner-in-charge provided technical assistance in accounting and tax problems arising out of merger negotiations and analyzed the firm's experience in gaining and losing clients as a result of acquisitions. In 1968 alone, twenty-six of America's *Fortune* 500 companies disappeared. Older, established PW clients in the steel industry like Jones & Laughlin, Youngstown, and Wheeling; motion picture studios like RKO, Warner Brothers, and Paramount; and meat-packing companies like Armour, Wilson, and Morrell were acquired by newer companies that had other auditors.[86]

PW saw only a limited role for marketing its services. Bevis centralized the firm's marketing function in the New York office when he named a full-time director of practice development in 1961. As late as 1968, the Executive Committee decided against preparation of a series of booklets describing PW's specialized services. The firm created a high-quality descriptive brochure and prepared an organization chart so personnel could connect names and titles with functional responsibilities. PW rejected recommendations for a merger with a management consulting company and for a pilot industry specialization operation for one industry as too risky or too expensive.[87]

Although the leadership exercised restraint in its approach toward marketing, certain offices did not. Philadelphia's practice development, under the leadership of John B. O'Hara, was considered by some as "probably the most vibrant in the firm." Philadelphia had already gained some momentum in the 1950s when Du Pont, in an unprecedented move, became a regular client. Du Pont's customary practice in the early decades of the century had been to follow a policy of rotating among national firms annually and, thereafter, at intervals from two to nine years. By coincidence, PW had rotated off when the McKesson & Robbins scandal broke, creating the misperception that Du Pont had fired PW because of the McKesson matter. When PW once again had the opportunity to serve as auditors, Paul Grady became deeply involved in the engagement, and the Philadelphia office "put a lot of power on that job, into trying to keep Du Pont happy." The increased scale and complexity of Du Pont's worldwide operations, the fact that very few auditing firms could handle such work, and the tremendous effort made by PW and Grady's "ministrations" convinced Du Pont to end its rotation policy and to remain permanently with PW.[88]

As Philadelphia's partner-in-charge, O'Hara instituted various techniques to attract and keep clients. He circulated business clippings from seven local papers, highlighting changes in management and ownership or other news that might provide opportunities for PW. Articles were consolidated into a central library file, where they served as valuable background information once a job prospect materialized. When Philadelphia proposed on Narco Scientific,

> we had a tremendous amount of information on this company. They called at 11:00 in the morning and wanted to see us at 3:00, which they did. At the end of the meeting in the afternoon, they said, "You know

much more about our company than Lybrand does, and they're our auditors." We got the job.[89]

Another example of O'Hara's philosophy in action was his successful pursuit of Curtis Publishing. In the early 1960s, Curtis sought new auditors from among the major accounting firms. According to an account written by Curtis's chief executive, O'Hara made

> a detailed examination of Curtis financial statements and found that Curtis was not handling "deferred subscription income" in the same accounting method as *Time*, *McCall's*, and other publishing companies used. . . . After O'Hara discovered this Curtis omission and prepared himself well, he made a presentation at our request. Superior in person and presentation, he got the assignment and performed magnificently for Curtis. O'Hara engineered a multimillion dollar tax refund, changed our methods and procedures, and was able to report several months later that Curtis financial controls were equivalent to those in the top third of PW's clients.[90]

By the mid-1970s, O'Hara's successful methods were widely adopted by other PW offices.

Although PW partners were cautious about adopting new business development strategies, they took a clear leadership role in defending national practice rights for all big firms. For six years, the partnership engaged in a court battle against the Florida state board of accountancy. A number of southern and western states, including Florida, Louisiana, Kentucky, and Arizona, had sought restrictions on practice by out-of-state auditors like PW. In Florida, for example, PW work for its out-of-state clients engaged in interstate commerce could be done only under the authority of temporary certificates. Although these certificates had been routinely issued by the board for many years, PW's work had grown so much by 1962 that permanent offices and personnel were located in Miami and Tampa. When the board notified the firm that it would deny any further temporary certificates as long as PW maintained full-time staff in Florida, the firm filed suit. The Florida courts upheld the ruling, but PW continued to appeal until the U.S. Supreme Court ultimately ruled that the firm's appeal failed to present a substantial federal question. During its battle, PW found strong support in a *Wall Street Journal* editorial:

> It's hard to see how [this regulation] benefits anyone except the Florida accountants, who are protected from high-powered competition. . . . Floridians should question why their legislators have twisted a public law to serve purely private purposes.[91]

Not until 1969, when Walt Disney Productions threatened to withdraw projected plans for its Disney World complex in Florida because PW could not perform its audit work, did the Florida legislature pass a bill permitting national firms to practice there.[92]

PW deliberately took up the gauntlet in Florida as the profession's most prestigious firm. By challenging local interests, despite the expense and duration of the litigation, and by bringing to bear the prestige and resources of its clients, which were major companies seeking an integrated audit by a large firm, PW opened the way for national practice rights.[93]

Planned Growth

Pressure from competitors and the prosperous atmosphere of the 1960s encouraged calls for change from within PW. Discussion crystallized into what became perhaps the most controversial issue of the Bevis era, the debate over planned growth. In the end, the firm made a deliberate choice not to expand the partnership beyond the perceptible demands of the 1960s and to stay relatively small and concentrate on quality instead. Some direct results of this decision, such as partner shortages and the inability to develop particular specialties, manifested themselves within the next decade.

Becoming a PW partner in the late 1950s and 1960s was not easy. Partners were admitted at an older age in PW than in other firms in order to ensure greater maturity and breadth of knowledge. They could not take charge of an office unless they were largely self-sufficient. The firm prided itself on its rigorous and selective twelve-to-fifteen–year partnership track and on the experience that partners brought to the job. A firm member had to spend six to eight years as junior, first assistant, and then senior assistant before even reaching the rank of manager, and five to seven years as manager before becoming partner. As one partner put it: "It was a pretty tight shop in those days." Membership was for life in this exclusive club, for only a rare serious offense or a drinking problem would prompt separation.[94]

The business climate of the 1960s, however, began to make vastly increased demands on partners. PW prided itself on its ability to accept an unexpected audit of a huge new client such as Allied Chemical, Westinghouse, or American Express, and such an assignment could result in unusual and heavy workloads. The buoyant economy that boosted firm profits did so by continually absorbing new staff. In addition, the national expansion of large corporate clients, and the migration of oil companies to the Southwest and to the Pacific Coast, required the firm to set up new offices and hire new personnel. The new offices also needed partners-in-charge, for experience had shown that, in many cases, partners, not managers, could best open up new geographical areas and attract new clients.[95]

PW's selective admissions policy caused it to have fewer partners than most other national firms, some of which had more than twice as many. Peat, Marwick, Mitchell, for example, had 340 partners in 1965, compared with approximately 150 at PW. But even as staff recruitment goals steadily scaled upward from five hundred in 1961 to nine hundred in 1969, the firm still faced a desperate shortage of partners. This hampered PW's ability to target new markets, to develop new services, or to focus on industry specialization. Partners were either stretched too thin keeping up with existing clients or not deployed in the right places. To resolve this issue, the Executive Committee voted unanimously in 1968 for planned growth coordinated on a firmwide basis.[96]

As part of this process, Bevis circulated a memorandum to the partners, describing his concerns and soliciting their views. Although he resisted growth for growth's sake, he believed that "not growing would be fatal to the long-run health of the firm." He was concerned to "dispel any misapprehension about the partners now on board getting rich out of that growth." As he noted,

> per partner incomes are not appreciably increased by additional volume of work. For each increment of chargeable hours, we must have that many more partners, managers and staff. Even our overhead increases [are] in large measure proportionate to volume. Therefore the fees from the work increment go pretty well to the additional personnel and facilities which service it; the other partners get no more. In fact, if the additional work does not meet our fee scale, the partners may get less because of it.[97]

Bevis attached detailed statistical studies to his memorandum illustrating the number of staff needed to produce a partner twelve years later, calculating how many chargeable hours of partner, manager, senior assistant, and staff hours were required for each assignment without sacrificing "good PW principles of careful auditing and good client attention." As he noted, "If *all* the partners *really* went all out to attract any and every new client, our chargeable hour growth rate over a period of years could be 15 percent per annum or more." With these calculations in hand, Bevis concluded that a reasonable projection of growth would be an increase of 7 percent per annum compounded. Considering the likely net increase of new partners and senior managers, he predicted that chargeable hours would likely outstrip resources, leaving the firm short of twenty-four to fifty-one partners by 1979, unless partners took on additional billable time to fill the gap.[98]

Bevis's projections appeared to be a reasonable compromise between extremes of higher and lower growth rates. He postulated conservative but modest expansion while acknowledging that the firm could increase even faster. In fact, he was relying on a specific model, derived from his work with law firms:

> Why not keep PW like a Sullivan & Cromwell in the legal profession: a relatively small, distinct, super-quality operation, dealing essentially in mega-clients, and preserving that by constantly improving our quality?[99]

Although he realized that change was taking place, Bevis adhered to his own more cautious instincts, noting later that he "wasn't for making any moves just to grow."[100]

For the critical mass of new, younger partners who had been named since 1960, however, Bevis's idea of restricted growth was insufficient. Ambitious, questioning, and dissatisfied with the status quo, many had tested themselves during World War II and believed in their ability to manage. There were many debates at the partners' meetings over whether the firm should retrench and seek to maintain quality or grow. A number of partners rejected Bevis's approach and chafed against restrictions set by PW's "reputation syndrome." At these meetings, partners questioned where their opportunities lay. If PW was going to add only a handful of partners every year, they argued, where would the firm be in twenty years?

Although willing to concede that growth did not necessarily increase the bottom line per partner, some partners argued for the synergies of growing, noting that "you keep the whole operation rolling, progressing, building, enthusiastic, with good morale and lots of key responsibilities taken care of."[101] Not surprisingly, 23 of the 116 respondents to Bevis's memorandum warned that "any plan which is expressed in terms of inhibiting the firm's growth would damage staff and partner morale, as suggesting reduced opportunities and incentives."[102]

Even as the partners disagreed, the debate had an inward-looking aspect: the need for growth was discussed in terms of the quality of client base, the firm's personnel shortage, and the preservation of local office autonomy. Only six respondents to the memorandum noted concern with keeping abreast of external competition, an argument that assumed center stage in the next decade.

The planned growth debate clearly displayed the partnership's divided attitude toward expansion as well as the strength of the firm's traditions. Planned growth fit PW's style, with its emphasis on quality clients, a small independent partnership, and a lack of concern about competition.

In fact, the partnership increased only to five hundred partners by the end of the 1970s, as Exhibit 5.4 shows. This figure was fairly close to the Bevis estimates.[103]

Partners also began to demand more policy information. As the annual partners' meetings became larger, their ability to communicate, give feedback, and accomplish substantive tasks decreased. Partner complaints on this score led the Executive Committee in 1962 to institute sectional meetings to provide interim reports on firm activities. Annual sectional meetings, composed of about twenty-five partners, were held over weekends at seven or eight locations around the country.

Some partners also sought, for the first time in PW's history, to penetrate the secrecy surrounding the distribution of shares:

> the only information we got was how many shares the partners were admitted with. We had no concept of what everybody had altogether. We younger guys said, "To hell with that, whose firm is this?" For a long time [we felt] it was the Executive Committee's firm and we worked for them.[104]

Although the firm charted a cautious course on growth, the partners decided to open the partnership in an important way. In 1969, in acknowledgment of the significant number of highly capable younger staff, the shortage of partners, and the perception that PW's traditional apprenticeship period was too lengthy, the partners decided to eliminate the requirement that only individuals over the age of thirty-four could join the partnership. Coming at the end of Bevis's tenure, and at the conclusion of the debate over planned growth, this vote was a bow to the inevitable. PW changed its tenure rules to allow for "a professional organization decreasing in maturity" just as a demographic bulge on an unprecedented scale loomed on the horizon.[105]

The Executive Committee also changed at this time. Under Inglis, it had been heavily involved in day-to-day operations, but PW's increasing size and growing specialization necessarily meant that the group spent less time executing the firm's activities and more time developing policy. Long before its name was changed to the Policy Committee in 1971, the Executive Committee had ceased to run the firm and instead concerned itself with "how the firm ought to be run." In 1964, after considerable debate, the partners voted to increase the maximum number of Executive Committee members to eight and to allow members a five-year term. All except the senior partner were eligible for re-election when their terms expired.[106]

The decision on planned growth set PW's course for the future. The choice not to rely on sheer size, but to hitch its star to the firm's tradition

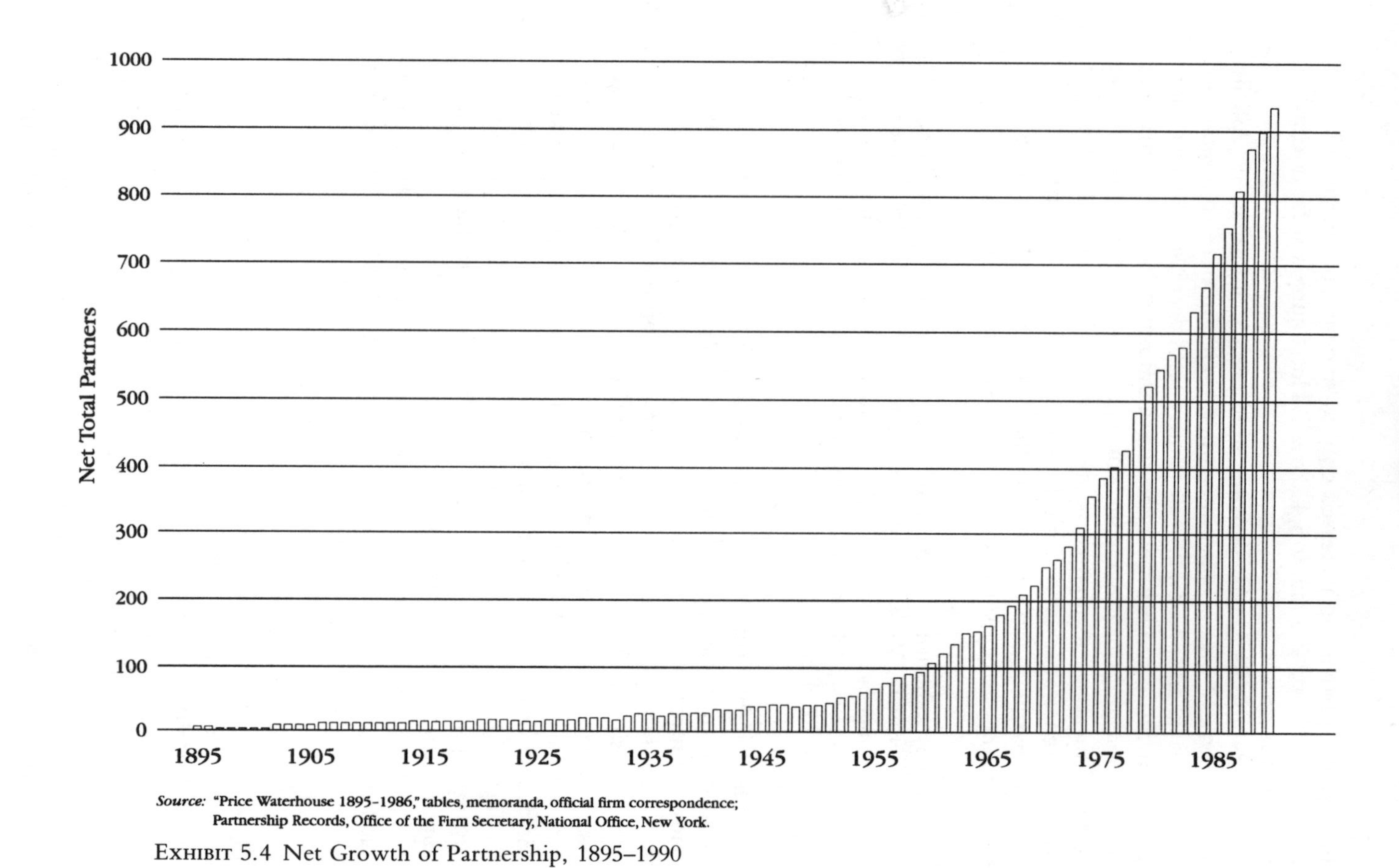

Source: "Price Waterhouse 1895–1986," tables, memoranda, official firm correspondence; Partnership Records, Office of the Firm Secretary, National Office, New York.

EXHIBIT 5.4 Net Growth of Partnership, 1895–1990

of quality proved more transitory than predicted at the time. PW kept its blue-chip reputation, but it was not able to ignore indefinitely the larger economic and political trends shaping the profession in the 1970s.

THE DEMISE OF THE APB

The 1960s saw the rise and fall of the Accounting Principles Board. One portent of its demise was the debate between Herman Bevis of PW and Leonard Spacek of Arthur Andersen over accounting principles. As he did in the planned growth discussions within PW, Bevis took the more conservative, although generally accepted, position. The very fact that Spacek could challenge Bevis and PW directly, however, was a sign of how much the profession had changed, for if the controversy had arisen during May's term, it would have been briefer and not so confrontational. That Bevis and Spacek debated so vigorously also underscores the deep divisions that had arisen in the profession as a whole; twenty-five years earlier, May could accurately represent the views of all accountants in his discussions with the stock exchanges. Ultimately, the same forces that made the two senior partners of two leading accounting firms unable to agree on accounting principles also paralyzed the profession's standard-setting body. The Spacek-Bevis debate represented an initial breakdown in consensus that characterized the entire profession by the end of the decade. These divisions endured, and standard-setting was eventually shifted to a more public forum, the Financial Accounting Standards Board (FASB), in the 1970s.

The APB was not the first standard-setting body for the accounting profession. The securities legislation of 1933 and 1934 and the fear of further government involvement in the profession had led the American Institute of Accountants to take an important leadership role in setting accounting principles. In 1938, an AIA Committee on Accounting Procedure, headed by George O. May, was enlarged and formalized. Charged a year later with the authority to issue pronouncements in accounting, the CAP issued more than forty Accounting Research Bulletins setting forth its understanding of generally accepted accounting principles on a variety of problems during the next two decades. Some dealt with the particular problems raised by World War II such as the excess profits tax, while others concerned more basic issues such as inventory pricing and the calculation of earnings per share. The authority of the ARBs rested not in any professional sanction, but on their logic and their general acceptability. In 1949, the SEC's chief accountant recommended that the CAP work toward a comprehensive statement of principles, but efforts that year, and those later in 1953, were abandoned as impractical.[107]

Criticism of the CAP and its method of determining accounting principles began to be heard in the 1950s. In 1957, Arthur Andersen's senior partner, Leonard Spacek, had launched his career as the profession's gadfly when he gave a public address for which he was accused of "impugning the integrity" of the CAP and another AICPA committee. In response to what was perceived as the "serious embarrassment" of Spacek's charge, the AICPA's president appointed a committee to investigate the allegations. Although the committee ultimately determined that the claims were unfounded, Spacek was on his way to becoming the profession's most visible and well-known critic.[108]

The AICPA president sought to calm the controversy by recommending that the Institute establish a formal research organization to "conduct continuous re-examination of accounting principles" and to "develop authoritative principles." He also suggested that accounting principles would gain greater legitimacy if they were seen as arising from "pure" research, and that decisions flowing from the research program should be binding on AICPA members.[109]

In the fall of 1959, the CAP was disbanded and the new APB came into being. Charged with "narrowing the areas of difference and inconsistency in practice," and supported by a greatly expanded research program to assist it in taking the lead on unsettled and controversial issues, the board was composed of thirteen practicing accountants (among them the senior partners of each of the Big Eight firms), three accounting professors, three industry representatives, one government official, and the AICPA research director.[110]

As APB members, Spacek and Bevis quickly entered into a serious and public debate over accounting principles. Continuing into the mid-1960s, the two senior partners staked out their opposing positions, reflecting a tradition in which big-firm partners, most notably George O. May, had regularly engaged in "reasoned advocacy on standard-setting and accounting principles." These arguments, usually aired in professional journals and treatises, were considered significant at a time when very few accounting principles were detailed or definitive. For a principle to be widely accepted, proof was required in the form of "substantial authoritative support" in speeches, articles, and books, as well as evidence of widespread use. Spacek and Bevis were the last two senior accountants to debate accounting principles in order to create a body of advocacy literature that could influence accepted practice. Serving on the APB through the early 1960s, they both outlined accounting principles compatible with their views. Spacek demanded greater uniformity, whereas Bevis stood for the application of considered judgment to particular situations. These positions reflected their own experiences and the traditions of their two firms.[111]

Within the profession, Spacek was well known for his iconoclasm and combativeness. "Uniformity" was his watchword, derived from Arthur Andersen's utilities practice. Spacek demanded that accounting principles be uniformly applied so that financial statements would be comparable within particular industries, and he decried the profession's wide latitude of choice in selecting alternatives. He produced examples showing that for the same transaction, accountants could choose from a number of acceptable alternative principles, producing widely different results. Spacek found it absurd that his firm could

> certify the statements of three major oil companies—Texaco, Superior, and Skelly—as being in accord with generally accepted accounting principles when each accounts for drilling costs in a different manner, and each method can make millions of dollars difference in net income reported for shareholders.[112]

With such a system, Spacek claimed, direct comparability of companies' financial statements was difficult for members of the public, as was an appraisal of a particular enterprise over several years. He proposed the creation of an accounting court equivalent to the U.S. Supreme Court, a suggestion dismissed by critics as a self-serving way to have himself appointed as chief justice. Overall, Spacek's activities, though generating a good deal of publicity, put Arthur Andersen "in a position where it was heartily disliked by other national firms." Since absolute, uniform rules were considered not only impracticable but dangerous by many within the profession, Spacek pitched his argument to those outside it who were unaware of the kinds of choices that accountants made. His remarks made an impression on this audience.[113]

Bevis's opposition to uniformity grew out of his own interpretation of the profession's expanding role in the 1960s and his personal experience at PW, where partner autonomy and judgment were deeply valued. Bevis was influenced by May's conviction that "the world of business" was "subject to a constant and sometimes violent change and full of uncertainties," and therefore "the work of accountants cannot rise higher in the scale of certainty than the events they reflect."[114] In the words of another partner, "PW senior partners believed that the accountant served his function best if he were free to apply good judgment to the accounting treatment in the financial or operating circumstances of the particular company."[115] In challenging Spacek, Bevis was articulating central PW tenets adjusted to the demands of the 1960s.[116]

In a series of articles, a book on corporate financial reporting, and two "white papers," Bevis articulated the basis for his position. He began by carefully defining accounting in broad, conceptual terms as "the measurement and communication of financial and other economic data." Accounting's end product was "not merely to provide a financial statement, but to assist in formulating judgments and making decisions." Since accountants dealt not with absolute, universal truths, but with data based on human actions, he believed that "data must always be measured and communicated in accordance with a set of man-made standards."[117]

Bevis went on to argue that because significant differences among businesses "had pronounced effects upon accounting standards which may be appropriate for them," more than one way was needed to treat any given set of data. The potential number of users of accounting data was vast, precluding the possibility that they would all have the same desire for uniformity. A reliance on judgment grew out of answers to the broad questions of which standards, for which issuers, and for which users. Bevis related his approach to the fundamental strength of the American economic system, where, he felt, "Diversity was more characteristic than uniformity in any beyond the broadest areas while the free enterprise system continues."[118]

Bevis sought to preserve a high degree of management judgment while still insisting on full disclosure. Truth and accuracy were guaranteed, in his opinion, by the "long-standing decentralization of responsibility to corporate managers and directors for full and fair financial accounting and reporting." Just as America's free-market system needed no centralized coordination, Bevis argued, the financial reporting system must rely on a persuasive "consensus as to the preferred accounting or reporting treatment in a given situation." For the consensus to be equitable and legitimate, he added, "the principle of full and fair disclosure must remain the keystone of successful corporation-stockholder and corporation-society relations."[119]

As befitted the man considered to have the most prestigious place in the profession, Bevis's viewpoint found substantial contemporary support. Yet whether his position ultimately prevailed is far from clear. During the 1970s, a trend developed toward regulation and narrow procedural standards expressed in greater detail. With many people demanding more of accounting, specifically that it create an accounting world without significant options, Bevis's position came to be seen as supporting the status quo. An effort to serve the public interest by demanding a high degree of disclosure while also championing individual judgment in framing accounting methods began to seem paradoxical. Within ten years, when public and stockholder protection became a primary political and regulatory goal, preserving the accounting profession's power to choose between alternative methods appeared excessively favorable to company management.[120]

Yet Spacek could not claim victory, either. Over time, it became apparent that the imposition of strong accounting uniformity in certain regulated industries did not result in better information or protection. Rather, the principle of uniformity worked best when similar events were reported similarly and different events were reported differently. Although the APB's successor, the FASB, put greater emphasis on rule-making, accounting practices did not become as uniform or as comparable as Spacek's vision might have implied. Moreover, critics maintained that the FASB's "cookbook" approach, instead of promoting particular criteria, encroached on professional judgment and that its standard-setting process was too bureaucratic.[121]

The brisk public debate over uniformity was one manifestation of the APB's deeper structural problems, and foreshadowed its declining ability to establish generally accepted accounting principles. The division between Bevis and Spacek symbolized the dilemma inherent in standard-setting for a group of increasingly diverse and independent-minded professionals. Soon after the APB's founding, it abandoned its original philosophy that "through reasoned discussion of the conceptual underpinnings of accounting, the superiority of particular accounting principles and practices would be demonstrated." Those members supporting "applied" practical study, rather than the "pure" research originally envisioned by AICPA president Alvin Jennings, took control. This development proved to be the rock on which the APB foundered, for once it conceded that accounting principles were to be defined in terms of existing practice, the need to gain consensus among the Big Eight firms was crucial. On most issues, this proved to be impossible. As one PW partner noted, although generally accepted accounting principles were not written down in one place, everyone at PW "knew what they were." He added that "the guy from Arthur Young did too, but his list was not the same as my list." As a result, when representatives of the various firms "got on the APB they fought like tigers."[122]

Not surprisingly, the APB found itself embroiled in controversy over its first substantive decision. A provision of the 1962 federal tax bill allowed a business to subtract from its federal taxes as much as 7 percent of the cost of equipment purchased in a year. Known as the "investment tax credit," the measure was a tax incentive designed to stimulate capital investment. Forced by the bill's passage to act quickly, the APB could not gain consensus on which of the two options, deferral or flow-through, should be used to handle the new tax credit. The APB in its Opinion No. 2 opted for deferral and recommended that the "investment credit should be reflected in net income over the productive life of the acquired property and not in the year in which it is placed into service." Over industry's objections, the APB rejected the flow-through option, which would have increased reported net income by the amount of the tax savings, chiefly in the year the tax credit was claimed.

In the end, only a bare two-thirds majority in the APB approved the deferral option, with the Big Eight firms split evenly. Supported by the APB chairman, Bevis led the Big Eight dissenters, three of whom indicated that the overwhelming majority of their clients used the flow-through method. Spacek led the majority and accused his opponents of working to foster "misleading financial statements." As it turned out, the APB's decision incurred the wrath of both business people and Washington policy makers. After intense lobbying, reflecting a great diversity of opinion, the SEC intervened and issued its own Accounting Series Release permitting both methods. This seriously undermined the APB's authority to set accounting principles. In addition, the SEC warned the profession that unless greater uniformity were established in corporate reporting, it would begin setting standards itself. Thereafter, the APB followed the SEC's lead, and in its Opinion No. 4 in late 1964, both options for handling the tax credit were treated as generally acceptable.[123]

The investment credit controversy was the first in a series of issues that illustrated the APB's lack of authority. The APB had never been given enforcement power, and a serious question existed as to whether its pronouncements were authoritative. Any belief that the APB could set standards after the investment credit debacle was further undermined by the AICPA. A 1964 AICPA council proposal providing that APB opinions be the only generally accepted accounting principles was voted down by those who "viewed enforceability as an additional step toward the elimination of professional judgment in the financial reporting process." To reach a consensus, the AICPA council compromised, conceding that, although opinions of the APB were considered "generally acceptable accounting principles" with "substantial authoritative support," other principles that differed from APB opinions could also have substantial authoritative support. The council then voted a requirement that auditors disclose material departures from APB recommendations in their financial statements or their reports.[124]

In the second half of the decade, the APB continued its struggle to set accounting standards, often in the glare of publicity. Another controversy arose in 1967, this time over an exposure draft published by the APB on deferred taxation. PW surprised many in the profession when it issued its first "white paper" directly contrary to an APB draft. The white paper contained a study of how a hundred PW clients accounted for their income taxes from 1954 to 1965 and showed that, as a practical matter, companies rarely repaid tax savings because their physical plant kept expanding. As a consequence, reported earnings were reduced unnecessarily by reserves for added tax liabilities that never materialized. Once again, the APB seemed to stumble. Its Opinion No. 11 on deferred taxation was published despite Treasury opposition and in the face of the SEC's express lack of support.[125]

Investment tax credit controversy continued. After Congress abolished the tax credit in 1967, and in anticipation of its restoration in the Revenue Act of 1971, the APB convinced the SEC to support its position on the deferral method for the investment tax credit. However, when the APB issued its exposure draft proposing this method, so many companies lobbied Congress that the Revenue Act was amended to allow for both methods.[126]

The continuing inability to articulate broadly supported accounting principles led to a growing sense of crisis and disorientation within the APB. It was criticized for failing to maintain adequate communication with business leaders, to give sufficient consideration to operating problems involved in applying accounting principles to diverse business situations, and to integrate long-term research into the development of accounting principles. Also faulted were its inadequate pronouncements, its ever-expanding disclosure and reporting requirements, its unwieldy size, its requirement for a two-thirds vote to carry a decision, and the lack of outside participation in its decision making.[127]

The APB was a victim of the times, particularly of changing perceptions of conflicts of interest. Since

> a large majority were practicing public accountants, they were ultimately deemed to be in a position that was untenable because on one hand they spent four days a week or three weeks a month . . . dealing with their clients, and the other part of their time they were expected to go out and set rules that precluded their clients from doing things their clients wanted to do.[128]

Members were criticized as "shills for their clients," yet as one former APB member recalled in his frustration, "There was no point pointing out: 'How do you do that when the two clients disagree? or How can I possibly shill for both of them?'"[129]

A final illustration of the dilemmas facing the APB was the controversy generated by the "pooling of interest" method of accounting for business combinations. Pooling required companies to carry forward assets at the premerger amounts shown on the two corporations' books, as if the two had been one; thus the level of earnings was calculated as if it were one company. The purchase method, by contrast, required restating the assets acquired and gave rise to higher depreciation in the future, with lower earnings. Pooling helped to encourage the conglomerate craze of the late 1960s, because business combinations could be effected while earnings levels consistent with the past were maintained. Conglomerates could preserve assets by offering stock, not cash; they could carry forward the historical cost basis of the assets of both companies, thus avoiding the higher depreciation of assets and amortization of goodwill that would have had to be fair-valued under the alternative purchase method.

Favorable stock market conditions also accelerated the use of pooling and its abuses. Some conglomerates posted significantly higher earnings, sold stock, and bought other companies in a deliberate pyramid scheme. The practice could conceal operating losses. The profession was not sufficiently united to forestall the abuse, and marginal and questionable applications of the pooling concept proliferated.

Beginning in 1968, pressure from both industry and government to restrict pooling became especially intense and unrelenting, and the APB began to consider a tentative proposal to abolish it. But the APB became paralyzed by competing viewpoints and was unable to agree on content and language for the opinion. PW, for one, had always been a strong proponent of the concept of pooling in appropriate circumstances, and its representative on the APB consistently advocated that position and strongly opposed any abolition of pooling as not in the best interests of business and other interested groups. Finally, amid "much dissent and criticism," the APB split the issues into two opinions with majority support (Opinion No. 16 on business combinations and Opinion No. 17 on intangible assets) in November 1970, long after the conglomerate merger movement ended. The financial press blamed the accounting profession for the lack of consensus within its standard-setting body. Intense pressure was brought to bear on the APB, giving rise to a final call for reform and its eventual dissolution in June 1973.[130]

Just as the two positions espoused by Spacek and Bevis could not be reconciled, so the failure of the APB represented the inability of the profession to reach consensus any longer. The APB's demise was another example of the end of the monolithic industry structure established by the securities laws of the 1930s and underscored a fundamental break with the past.

By the end of the 1960s, intimations of a new era at PW were appearing. Although the decade's dramatic growth and expansion were certainly positive, a number of factors in the 1960s combined to make the world seem less secure. Record numbers of mergers and acquisitions, a high-flying stock market, rapid advances in computer technology, aggressive competition within the profession, and failed standard-setting together with the accelerating pace of change set the stage for what would become a new environment by the early 1970s.

The PW partnership was not impervious to these changes and recognized the need to respond. To address them most effectively, it needed to loosen the strictures imposed by its distinguished past. Herman Bevis had led the firm and the profession in the best PW tradition. The times now required a different style and strategy. With the election of John Biegler as senior partner in 1969, "a generational change in management" occurred that would build on Bevis's managerial and organizational accomplishments and position PW for the future.[131]

PART III

Challenge and Redirection

CHAPTER 6

A Turbulent Era, 1969–1978

The 1970s brought a dramatic break with the previous thirty years. When the 1960s ended in market collapse, disillusioned investors clamored for explanations, and some sued the accountants who had audited the reports of newly bankrupt companies. Meanwhile, the financial press, reflecting a heightened public interest, reported critically on a profession that had rarely made news. Pressure on accountants intensified as a result of three successive congressional investigations and as the feeling grew that "accounting issues had become too important to be left to accountants alone." Even the Securities and Exchange Commission, with which the profession had peacefully coexisted for nearly forty years, took a more activist stance. With every aspect of the accounting profession under review, from its organizational structure to its independence and basic competence, contemporary observers believed that it had reached "the most critical stage in its history."[1]

Dramatic change also characterized senior partner John Biegler's era at Price Waterhouse. The security and pride of place that came with leading the profession's pre-eminent firm were challenged by the events of the decade. Most Big Eight firms struggled with mounting operating expenses, uneven MAS and tax revenues, fluctuating chargeable hours, slowly growing share values, intense competition, and a flood of costly lawsuits.

Unquestionably, this was a new age, and Biegler took actions that would have been unthinkable within PW a decade earlier. He instituted significant internal changes, including two structural reorganizations and major democratic reforms. He led the partnership to remarkable innovations, including publishing annual reports of the firm's financial data and hiring a rival to perform a peer review of professional practice procedures. In the end, PW, like the other large accounting firms, surmounted the difficulties of the 1970s; the story of the decade's events was one of challenge, crisis, and ultimate success in a new, less hospitable world.

JOHN BIEGLER AND DEMOCRATIC REFORM

PW's new senior partner came to the firm, he recalled, "by accident." On leaving military service in 1946, and armed with a BA in accounting from the University of Illinois, John Biegler sought work at the large Chicago accounting firms. He received responses from PW and Arthur Andersen. When he appeared as scheduled for his Arthur Andersen interview, however, a mix-up led the firm to say that it was not hiring at that time. Biegler "walked out and up the street to PW and told them, 'O.K., I'm your man.'" Although an apologetic Arthur Andersen representative called him back three days later to explain the error, Biegler stayed with PW.[2]

He quickly distinguished himself in the firm. In 1952, Biegler was selected to go to London for six months on the staff exchange program. He then returned to Chicago until he was sent to New York in 1955 to help start the SEC Department. In 1958, Biegler was admitted to the partnership, and because he had so ably assisted the partner-in-charge of SEC work and of the Royal Dutch Shell account, he assumed responsibility for both when that partner retired two years later. His reputation grew as he coordinated SEC matters involving clients all over the world. In 1965, he was elected to the Executive Committee, and two years later he became vice chairman and deputy senior partner responsible for client services and relations, ethics, and technical matters. In 1969, the Executive Committee elected him its chairman.

During his nine years as senior partner, Biegler upheld the long-standing PW tradition of serving the profession in several leadership positions. He was the profession's sole representative on the Wheat Committee, which was instituted in the early 1970s to consider the process by which accounting principles should be established. In 1977, he served as president of the board of trustees of the Financial Accounting Foundation, the body responsible for financing and overseeing the profession's new standard-setting body, the Financial Accounting Standards Board.[3]

As senior partner, Biegler's noteworthy contributions to the firm were the institution of democratic reforms that permitted all partners to participate in the selection of a new senior partner as well as of nominees to the Executive Committee and the establishment of a strong and effective national office organization. The structural foundation for Biegler's democratic reforms was an organizational study he made in 1967 while deputy senior partner that synthesized the views expressed in myriad comments, opinions, and recommendations solicited from partners.

Among the organizational issues that surfaced was the composition of the Executive Committee. Despite the firm's growing diversity and the strength of its nonaudit lines of business, only audit partners sat on the committee. Some partners had grown cynical about the "self-perpetuating" selection process; both the Executive Committee and the senior partner had the right to inform the nominating committee of their "best judgment as to nominees," and only these preselected names were tendered to the partners for a vote.

So many questions arose about the nominating committee's lack of independence that Biegler determined to create a more democratic, participatory process. In 1970, he ended the Executive Committee's practice of informing the nominating committee of its views on nominees, thus allowing all partners to participate in selecting a new, more representative Executive Committee. At the same time, he enlarged the Executive Committee to ten members, changed its name to the less autocratic-sounding "Policy Committee," and altered its duties as initial steps toward making the committee more analogous to a board of directors.[4]

Biegler's decision to open the nominating process was very popular, and the 1971 elections dramatically reflected the partnership's sense of its own diversity. The requirement that the nominating committee "represent a broad spectrum of partners" enabled two nonaudit partners, William Miller (tax) and Henry Gunders (Management Advisory Services), to be elected to the Policy Committee for the first time. The elections created a more balanced, representative body and highlighted the evolving demographics within PW. The seven members of previous Executive Committees had always been drawn from the largest offices: New York, Chicago, Detroit, Los Angeles, St. Louis, San Francisco, and Pittsburgh. By 1971, although some of these offices had grown significantly, their work had declined as a percentage of the firm's total business as clients moved out of these cities and into the southern and western United States. Chargeable hours during the 1973 fiscal year in the Houston office increased 21 percent over 1972, and work in the Dallas–Fort Worth, Jacksonville, Nashville, and Memphis offices was expanding rapidly. Although these offices did not comprise large numbers of partners and staff, their growth was an indication of the vitality of the smaller cities and geographical regions with which PW was now concerned.[5]

Biegler's reform of the Policy Committee selection process did not stop there. Previously, the chairman of the Executive Committee had always been chosen by his predecessor and this choice ratified by the committee. The chairman's name was then presented to the partnership for pro forma election as senior partner. Having been "designated" by Herman Bevis, Biegler felt he did not have as strong a mandate as he would have had if he had been elected democratically. In 1971, he proposed that the senior partner be eligible for two terms of up to five years each and that an independent nominating committee seek the views of all the partners on the choice for senior partner. Again, his inspiration was his faith in democratic processes; he noted that "if you get a true consensus of the partners on any issue, they will come up with the right answer." Under the new system, members of the nominating committee visited each partner individually, heard and weighed the comments, deliberated, and then presented a name to the entire partnership for election. The existing senior partner's role was strictly limited to informing the nominating committee if he had knowledge of a nominee's serious medical problems.[6]

Biegler's decision to limit the chairman's tenure to no more than two five-year terms was another change in this area. His reason was pragmatic: "I didn't think that anybody should be senior partner of the firm for more than ten years, on the grounds that if you can't get your program accomplished in ten years—forget it!"[7]

Biegler's final critical structural reform, also in 1971, was the creation of the National Office, a move that reflected his strong desire to centralize and coordinate the firm's administration. The National Office was intended to provide advice and technical services, to monitor performance, and to act as a communication center; its technical experts and staff were designated to support practice partners. Biegler felt that it was critically important to be able to "honestly tell a client that they are having the benefit of the firm's total experience—not just the guy who is handling that account."[8]

Until the National Office was created, partners acting in committees such as in the staff, contract and salary, or auditing and accounting committees handled all administrative matters. "We had all kinds of committees doing staff work," noted a partner who for six years chaired the contract committee, which was required to approve the annual compensation adjustments of managers, a group that had expanded to 701 individuals by 1969.

In 1971, Biegler created three national directors, Arthur B. Toan, William C. Miller, and Henry P. Hill, to provide staff and technical support for the respective practice areas of Management Advisory Services, Tax Services, and Accounting and Auditing Services (A&AS).[9] He also made a full-time national director of administration responsible for internal accounting, budgeting, and treasury functions. Kallman Nashner managed a staff of approximately 130 people, including a partner, 10 managers, 12 technically trained staff aides, and some 100 clerical, secretarial, and service assistants. Biegler rounded out the new administrative structure with several other appointments, including Albert H. Cohen as national director for professional development, with overall responsibility for professional development activities in Audit, Tax, and MAS, and Robert E. Field as national director for manpower and special services, responsible for supervising specialized activities such as mergers and acquisitions, government contracts, the International Department, and industry specialization. The firm's first general counsel, Eldon Olson, was hired from its long-time legal advisers, Cravath, Swaine & Moore, to be part of the new National Office structure. The 1971 National Office organizational structure is shown in Exhibit 6.1.

In 1972, the National Office moved into the Exxon Building at 1251 Avenue of the Americas, where several satellite administrative offices around New York City were incorporated into one facility. This physical relocation sent two strong symbolic messages to the partnership: first, that the National Office had nationwide responsibility, and second, that the New York practice office was now no different from others. Subtle but very important changes in psychology and vocabulary occurred as problems now were discussed with "National," rather than with "New York."[10]

Biegler appointed Thomas Ganner as vice chairman of the Policy Committee and as managing partner. Ganner had been partner-in-charge of the New York office and Biegler's closest rival for the senior partner position. Biegler considered him invaluable. "He had the right instincts and was an excellent judge of people so I could rely on his evaluations" of partners, Biegler noted.[11] Often Ganner served as Biegler's point man, dealing with troublesome situations and reporting back with recommendations.[12]

Biegler's democratic thrust and inclination toward greater dissemination of information led to a significant break with the firm's tradition of secrecy in the area of partnership compensation and retirement benefits. In a speech early in his term as senior partner, he provided statistics concerning the general pattern of shareholding throughout the firm. "You never saw so many pencils fly in your life," noted one partner.[13]

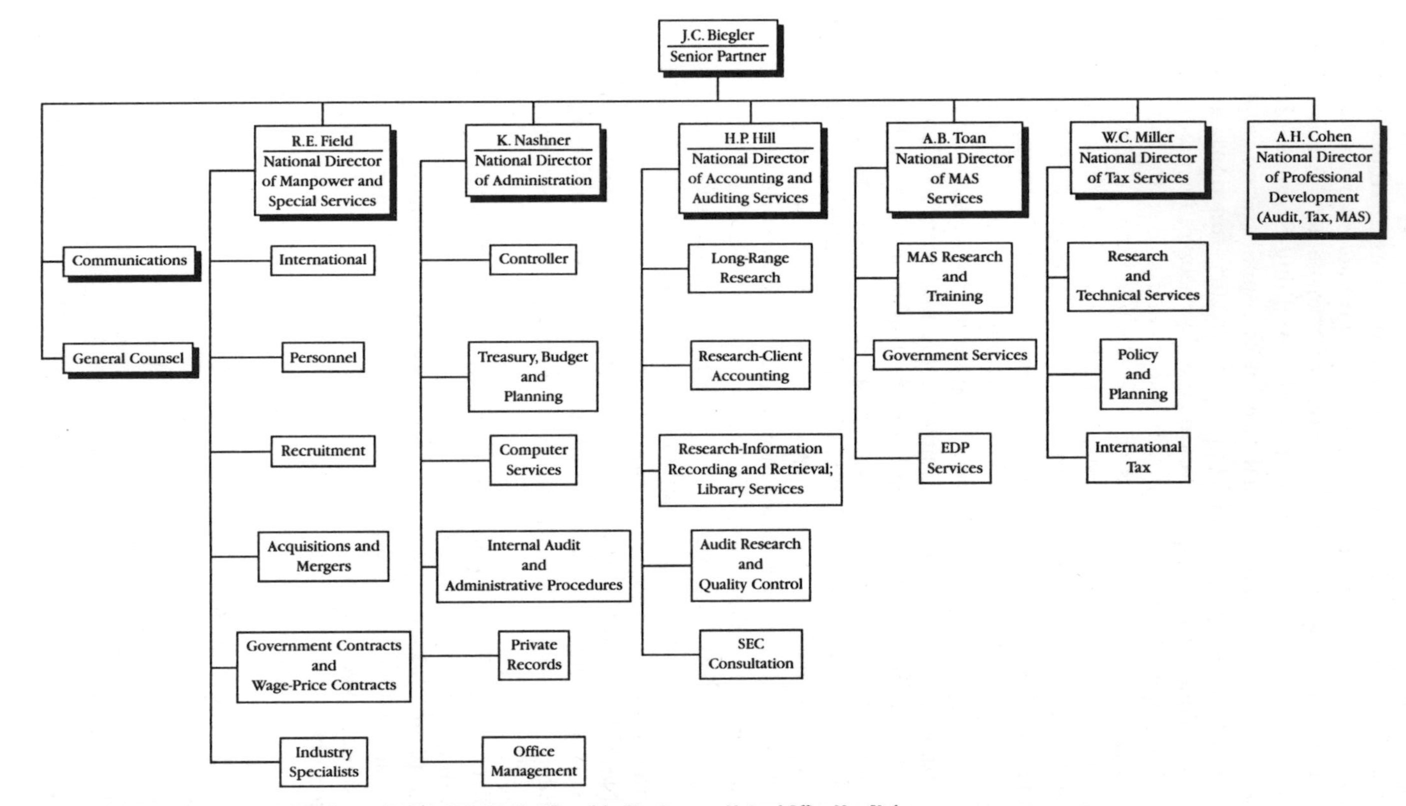

Source: Price Waterhouse & Co., "PAR Background," 1961–1978, 078.20, Office of the Firm Secretary, National Office, New York.

EXHIBIT 6.1 National Office Organization, 1971

Like his predecessor, Biegler came to power with a very specific set of reforms. During his first few years in office, the world outside the firm changed dramatically. Public dissatisfaction, economic instability, an explosion of litigation, and cutthroat competition eventually combined to consume Biegler's time, attention, and direction. By 1973, he felt that his "creative work was over," and he spent the rest of his term "just fighting crises as they came up."[14]

THE PROFESSION ON THE DEFENSIVE

The 1960s were a decade of social turmoil and unrest. The civil rights movement, opposition to the Vietnam War, and environmental activism were vehicles for the expression by many Americans of a general dissatisfaction with the status quo. In the accounting profession in particular, a major re-evaluation was prompted by company failures, new social attitudes, and, especially, a rising tide of litigation. When the long bull market came to an end in 1970, in the first sustained break in twenty-five years, some of the most spectacular losses occurred in those companies that had prospered in the 1960s: conglomerates, computer leasing companies, electronics companies, and franchisers.[15]

The sheer number and extent of losses on the stock market shook the investing public's confidence not only in business but also in accountants. It seemed to many that accounting rules had clearly failed to deal with earnings manipulations. Policy makers and angry investors sought to establish a connection between faulty financial reporting and business collapse, demanding to know "where was the independent auditor?" A disillusioned public greeted annual reports skeptically after a number of companies faltered despite reporting high earnings. Only "imaginative bookkeeping," it was said, allowed Penn Central to show a $4 million profit just before it went bankrupt. Terms like "accountability" and "full disclosure" began to appear more and more often in financial and accounting publications of the time, reflecting demands for socially responsible corporate and government conduct as well as for greater disclosure. Like many other American institutions during this period, the profession became politicized. Critics claimed that discretionary considerations often played a part in what the public believed to be "subjective" accounting techniques, and that public accountants were not "independent" as their title implied but were, in fact, inside players in the corporate, global business game. As in the 1930s, corporations and, by extension, their accountants, were being asked to adhere to higher standards.[16]

The stock market collapse was not the only problem in this period. The inflation that had begun in the late 1960s began to have serious adverse effects on the economy, and government efforts to curb it resulted in "stagflation," a combination of rising prices and increasing unemployment. De-escalating the Vietnam War and reducing government spending in nonmilitary areas put more people out of work. In 1971, President Richard Nixon initiated the first peacetime wage and price controls. However, the 1973 oil crisis and subsequent high energy costs derailed the government's efforts to get the economy back on track. By 1974, the nation was experiencing its worst inflation since 1947, and prices jumped 38.2 percent from 1971 to 1976. All of these problems, in combination with President Gerald Ford's decision to slow down the economy in 1974–1975, created the most serious recession in nearly forty years.[17]

Searching for causes of the slump, some critics blamed outdated inflation accounting methods for failing to portray the true state of business affairs. Accountants were encouraged to discontinue accounting conventions that valued business assets in terms of old dollars spent months or years before, which, some maintained, allowed companies to overstate profits and understate depreciation expenses. Implementing the untested "price-level" method, which restated old costs upward and brought profits, adjusted for inflation, tumbling downward, was highly controversial and not generally accepted. The profession's inability to agree on inflation accounting techniques prevented consensus on improved ways to report corporate profits. By 1978, the SEC's chairman, a strong price-level advocate, cautioned that "fully one third of the earnings that companies reported for 1978 were an illusion—gains generated by inflation and out of date accounting methods."[18]

The accounting profession, with urging from the SEC and financial analysts, subsequently developed a supplementary price-level reporting methodology. Millions of dollars were spent by the profession and reporting companies to develop, maintain, and publish these supplementary price-level data regularly. But after mandating this reporting requirement for a period of years, the FASB found that its continuing research disclosed serious questions concerning how widely and well the price-level data were being used in practice. No strong advocates emerged from the user groups and consequently the mandatory requirements were withdrawn.[19]

PW, as were the other Big Eight firms, was unprepared for the economic contraction. As Biegler recalled, "We had come into the 1970s with every expectation of doing well. We were in a growth mode." As a result, the downturn "hit us cold." As the economic crisis deepened, "all of the growth trends of the 1960s turned on a dime."[20] In the fiscal year 1970–1971, recruitment goals were halved, from 1,300 to 652 new hires. Before the firm could regain its equilibrium, it was devastated by the billing-rate freeze required by the federal government. Nor did

HE ECONOMIST. 74

n London, and The First National Bank, The Illinois Trust and Saving
ny in Chicago, will receive Subscriptions for the undermentioned Capital.
7th day of June, and Close on or before the 10th June, 1890.

cago Brewing & Malting

mpany, Ltd.

E CAPITAL - - £1,250,000

into 62,500 Eight per Cent. Cumulative Preference Shares of £10 each, £625,000; 62,500 Ordinary Shares of £10 ,000. In addition to the above Shares, there will be issued by the American Corporation 3,166,000 dols. (equivalent of ,000) of 6 per Cent. First Mortgage Bonds of 1,000 dols (equivalent of £205) each at par.

The Bonds will be payable £10 per Bond on application, £90 per Bond on allotment, and the balance of £105 per Bond two months after allotment, or the whole may be paid up on allotment. The Shares will be payable 10s per Share on application, £4 10s per Share on allotment, and the remainder in two instalments of £2 10s per Share at two and four months respectively, after allotment. Of the foregoing Bonds the American Vendors, their customers and friends, take 2,094,000 dols. (being the equivalent of £430,009), and of the Share Capital £275,650. The remainder of the Bonds and Shares are now offered for subscription.

TRUSTEES FOR BOND HOLDERS.

The Northern Trust Company of Chicago, Illinois, U.S.A.

DIRECTORS

WILLIAM JAMES FORD, Esq., Messrs Hoare and Co.'s Brewery, London (Director of Nalder and Collyer's Brewery Company, Limited).

EDWARD THOMAS HELME, Esq. (Director of Ind, Coope and Co., Limited).

SAMUEL LUCAS, Esq. (Director of Parker's Burslem Brewery Company, Limited).

(Directors of the Bartholomay Brewing Company (of Rochester), Limited).

WILLIAM M. WROUGHTON, Esq., Cannon Brewery, London.

WILLIAM HOARE, Esq., Messrs Hoare and Co.'s Brewery, London.

*RUSSELL H. MONRO, Esq., London.

* Will join the Board after Allotment.

DIRECTORS OF AMERICAN COMPANY.

WILLIAM C. SCEIPP, Esq., President, President of the C. Seipp Brewing Company and Director American Exchange National Bank.

THIES J. LEFENS, Esq., Vice-President, Treasurer of the C. Seipp Brewing Company and Director of the Traders Insurance Company.

JOHN A. ORB, Esq., Vice-President, and Treasurer of the West Side Brewery Company.

FRANCIS J. DEWES, Esq., President of the F. J. Dewes Brewery Company.

L. C. HUCK, Esq., Treasurer, President of the L. C. Huck Malting Company.

GEORGE BULLEN, Esq., President George Bullen and Company (Incorporated)

F. S. WINSTON, Esq., Director of the Michigan Central Railroad, and Chicago Breweries, Limited.

BANKERS.

Lloyd's Bank, Limited, 72 Lombard street, London, E.C.

First National Bank of Chicago.

Illinois Trust and Savings Bank, Chicago.

Merchants' Loan and Trust Company, Chicago.

BROKERS.

Messrs Panmure Gordon, Hill and Co., Hatton court, Threadneedle street, London, E.C.

Mr Charles Henrotin, President Chicago Stock Exchange, Chicago.

SOLICITORS.

Messrs Ashurst, Morris, Crisp, and Co., 6, Old Jewry, London, E.C.

Mr F. S. Winston, Adams' Express buildings, Chicago.

AUDITORS—Messrs Price, Waterhouse, and Co., 44 Gresham street, London, E.C.

SECRETARY (pro tem.)—Mr Frank Buchanan.

OFFICES.

London: Warnford court, E.C.

Chicago: Adams' Express building.

ABRIDGED PROSPECTUS.

This Company has been formed for the purpose of acquiring the Shares of an American Corporation which is to own five of the largest Breweries and Malt Houses situated in the City of Chicago, and carry on the businesses under one management.

Chicago is well known to be the most progressive of all American cities. A small Indian trading post in 1830, it reached a population of 300,000 in 1870, and over 500,000 in 1880. To-day Chicago is a city of 130 square miles, with a population estimated at over 1,100,000.

THE CONRAD SEIPP BREWERY.

This has always been the largest Brewery in Chicago. Established in the year 1854, its progress each year has been marked by a steady increase, the output of 1889 having reached the immense figure of over 230,000 barrels.

The Brewery is situated in the south division, which is the wealthiest portion of the city. It is on the shore of Lake Michigan, from which it draws its own supply of water independent of the city water works. Between the Brewery premises and the lake are the tracks of the Illinois Central and the Michigan Central Railroads, from which the Brewery has its own sidings, thus affording facilities for handling and transporting materials and beer with a minimum of expense and delay. At the present time this Brewery sells nearly [illegible] The

are located at Kensington, Illinois; South Chicago Illinois; Matteson, Illinois; Hammond, Indiana; Whiting, Indiana; and Kalamazoo, Michigan.

This Brewery sells Beer to 675 licensed houses, of which over [illegible]06 are in the City.

THE WEST SIDE BREWERY.

This Brewery is in the Western portion of the City, and occupies nearly a whole block on North Paulina, Augusta and Rumsey streets. It is a commanding structure of stone, brick, and iron, and was built in the year 1881, and is a fire-proof building.

The Brewery, having been recently built, contains every modern appliance for manufacturing Beer on the most scientific and economical principles. Although only organised in 1881, the excellence of the Beers has caused it to take a high position among the best of the Chicago Breweries, and it now occupies the sixth place in the sales of the city.

The plant is so constructed that the output can be doubled without any further outlay except a slight increase in the storage room. The sales at the present time amount to over 96,000 barrels per annum.

This Brewery has a prosperous branch at Springfield, Illinois, the capital of the State; and there are numerous freehold and leasehold saloons tied to the Brewery.

THE DEWES BREWERY.

This Brewery is situate on West Chicago and Hoyne Avenues in a section of the City of comparatively recent settlement, but which is growing very fast in all directions. No part of Chicago has felt the increase of trade and prosperity more than that in which this Brewery is now established.

This Brewery is celebrated for a special Beer called Munich Beer, which is sold at two dollars per barrel more than the usual price of Lager Beer, and which is not only sought after in the neighbourhood, but is attaining a large sale all over Chicago and the suburbs.

The Brewery is of modern construction, and the plant is conveniently arranged for continuing a progressive trade, the sales of each of the last three years having increased upwards of 23 per cent. on the year preceding. The sales at the present time amount to over 61,000 barrels.

There are a number of valuable leaseholds in addition to the freeholds.

THE HUCK MALT HOUSES.

The Malt Houses are on the corner of Canal and Eighteenth Streets, and are among the best Maltings of the United States. Amongst the customers are the principal Brewers of New York, Philadelphia, Boston, Washington, Cincinnati, St Louis, New Orleans, Chicago, and many others.

The Malt Houses have five railway tracks, aggregating over one mile of railroad on the premises, and connected with all the trunk lines of Chicago. The barley is brought by the Railways into the Elevators, and by steam power unloaded at rate of 4 000 bushels per hour.

New works have been erected for Saladin's Pneumatic Process, introduced for the first time into the United States by L. C. Huck in 1886, which enables malting to be carried on all the year round by cylinders working in water and keeping the temperature at 60 degs Fahrenheit; the moist and cool air is then forced into the Malt Houses, where there are constructed numerous compartments of 400 bushels capacity each, which malt 1,200 bushels per day, or equivalent to 360,000 bushels per annum on this system.

The annual sales for the last two years have been over 1,000,000 bushels, 200,000 of which have been sold in the City of Chicago itself. The property is of great value, and consists of nearly three acres of ground in a most improving part of the city.

THE BULLEN MALT HOUSES.

These Malt Houses and Elevators are situated only one block from the docks along the Chicago River, and within one mile of the business centre of the city.

The Malt Houses are of brick, with stone foundations six stories high, and, with the basement, making up seven fully-equipped malt floors. The Elevators are also of brick, and considerably higher than the Malt Houses, and the machinery comprises every necessary for first-class Malt Houses. The Malting capacity is upwards of 1,000,000 bushels per annum (equivalent to 125,000 quarters), and the storage capacity in the elevators is upwards of 650,000 bushels

The United States Internal Revenue Returns also show that the sales for the seven months from October 1, 1889 to April 30, 1890, were 201,455 barrels as against 175,402 barrels in the corresponding seven months of the previous year, showing an increase of about 15 per cent.

The output of the Huck and Bullen Malt Houses has exceeded 2,000,000 bushels per annum since 1886, when the improvements and additions were completed.

The books of the Breweries and Malt Houses have been examined by Messrs Price, Waterhouse, and Co., on behalf of the Company, whose certificate attached shows that the net profits of the five corporations for the last two years have been as follows:—

For the year 1887-8	£192,414
For the year 1888-9	205 066

Thus showing a steady increase in the profits.

Taking, however, the rate of profits at £198,740 per annum, the average of the last two years, the following results will be shown:—

To pay interest on £650,000 bonds at six per cent. will require	£39,000
To pay interest on £625,000 preference shares at eight per cent. will require	50,000
To pay dividend on £625,000 ordinary shares at fifteen per cent. will require	93,750
	£182,750

Leaving a surplus of £15,990 per annum for management, expenses and reserve; or taking the profits of the last year, a surplus of over £22,000 per annum.

The several properties have been surveyed and valued by Mr S. B. Chase, the public assessor, elected by the citizens of North Chicago. Mr Chase appraises the real estate and buildings, and fixed plant, with the several railroad facilities at the aggregate valuation for the five properties of £1,214,500.

The price to be paid by the Company for the shares of the new American Company, which requires the property purchased, is £1,900,000.

The following contracts have been entered into:—A Contract dated May 7th, 1890, between William C. Seipp, Emma A. Seipp, Thies J. Lefens, Marie Lefens, Hattie Baries, Emma Seipp, Clara Seipp, John A. Orb, Catherine Seipp, individually and as guardian of Elsa Seipp, Alma Seipp, and Conrad Seipp of the first part, and Henry M. Bigelow of the second part, and the Conrad Seipp Brewing Company and the West Side Brewing Company of the third part. A Contract dated April 24th, 1890, between Francis J. Dewes of the one part and Henry M. Bigelow of the other part. A contract, dated 24th April, 1890, between Louis C. Huck of the one part and Henry M. Bigelow of the other part. A Contract, dated 22nd April, 1890, between George Bullen, A. N. Young, and W. A. Montgomery of the one part, and Henry M. Bigelow of the other part. Four Contracts, dated 29th May, 1890, between Henry M. Bigelow, of the one part, and Russell Henry Monro of the other part, for the re-sale of the above properties, and a Contract, dated 3rd June, 1890, between the said Russell H. Monro of the one part and the Company of the other part, for the re-sale of the properties to the Company at a profit; and other arrangements have been entered into by the said Russell H. Munro with various persons with regard to the division of such profits and as to the payment of the aforesaid charges and expenses, and for guaranteeing the subscription of capital, which may constitute Contracts within the meaning of the 38th section of the Companies Act, 18 7; and there are also various Contracts connected with the Breweries as going concerns, which, from the nature of the business, it might be injudicious to publish. Applicants for Shares and Bonds will, therefore, be effected with notice of the existence of such arrangements and Contracts, and will be deemed to have waived the insertion of the dates and names of the parties thereto, and in order to prevent any questions, must accept the above statement as a sufficient compliance with the requirements of the said section or otherwise.

A Stock Exchange quotation will be applied for, both in London and Chicago.

Prospectuses and Forms of Application can be

By the late 1880s, the British firm of Price Waterhouse had audited so many accounts of American companies as part of investment schemes by British capitalists (such as the Chicago breweries described here) that it decided to open an American branch in 1890.

Samuel Lowell Price and Williams Hopkins Holyland welcomed Edwin Waterhouse into their partnership in 1865. Several years after Holyland's retirement in 1871, the partnership changed its name to Price, Waterhouse & Co.

An Agreement made the 11th day of September one thousand eight hundred and ninety, between Edwin Waterhouse, George Sneath and Joseph Gurney Fowler, carrying on business in partnership under the firm or style of Price, Waterhouse & Co. as Chartered Accountants, at 44 Gresham Street in the City of London (hereinafter called the Firm) of the one part, and Lewis Davies Jones, formerly of 44 Gresham Street in the City of London, of the other part. —

1. The said Lewis Davies Jones shall become and be from and after the first day of September, 1890, Agent for the Firm and Manager of the Agency or branch of their business established or about to be established in New York or elsewhere in America. —

PW's London partners name Lewis D. Jones as American agent of the firm on September 11, 1890.

Lewis D. Jones, Price Waterhouse's first agent in America.

Despite his efforts to bring the firm more in line with American practice, to the local accounting community PW partner Arthur Lowes Dickinson exemplified the proper British accountant. Here, he is humorously depicted with an American-born rival, Elijah Watt Sells. *Source:* Program of the 1906 Annual Meeting of the American Association of Public Accountants, Columbus, Ohio, AICPA Library, New York.

Partners and staff posing in Dickinson's office, New York, 1910. From left to right, (front row) G.R. Webster, H. Wilmot, A.L. Dickinson, G.O. May, C.S. Marr, W.E. Seatree, J.E. Sterrett; (second row) D. McClelland, J.H. Bowman, J.E. Masters, J.C. Scobie, J.R. Lynn, D.L. Grey, J. Medlock; (third row) C.A. Moore, unidentified staff members, R.O. Berger, W.E. Lovejoy, A.B. Brodie.

Young George O. May with British fiancée Edith Slocombe. They married in 1902, when he became a partner in the U.S. firm.

High-flying accountant William B. Campbell in the cockpit, circa 1918.

Humble beginnings: Price Waterhouse opened its office in Oruro, Bolivia, in 1921 with correspondents Faller & Co.

John C. Scobie steered Price Waterhouse successfully through the McKesson crisis of the late 1930s.

President Dwight Eisenhower welcomes PW's Percy Brundage as Director of the U.S. Bureau of the Budget in 1956 as Mrs. Brundage looks on.

New York office personnel of 1960 show off their midnight blue jackets with the PW symbol on the breast pocket.

Out with a blast: The partners applaud John Inglis on his retirement in 1961, surprising him with a firecracker.

The Price Waterhouse accountant depicted on the cover of a 1960s recruiting brochure epitomized the "establishment" look of that decade.

Herman Bevis's sober dignity personified PW's reputation for integrity and superior service.

Bevis debates "Accounting and Auditing Comparability" with Arthur Andersen's Leonard Spacek in 1966.

PW's John Biegler greets colleagues at an American Accounting Association meeting in 1978. *Source:* AICPA Library, New York.

Joseph Connor introduced a strategic approach to the challenges of the 1980s.

The envelope please: In a production number at the 1983 Oscar awards ceremony, movie theatre ushers and usherettes introduce PW with a tap dance. PW has tabulated the results for the Academy of Motion Picture Arts and Sciences since 1935.

Shaun O'Malley is guiding PW into its second century.

conditions improve noticeably after the wage and price controls were lifted, for rates could not be raised rapidly enough to recover lost profits.[21]

Public opinion saw a direct relationship between business failure and inept accounting, and a flood of litigation threatened to overwhelm accountants in the early 1970s, underscoring yet again the importance of the legal scene to the profession. Prior to the late 1960s, accountants had been relatively free of legal liability. When problems arose, they were handled mainly in the context of SEC administrative proceedings, because third parties generally were unable to recover from accountants for ordinary negligence following the 1931 *Ultramares* case. A number of important changes occurred in the 1960s, however. With the liberalization of the Federal Rules of Procedure, a single stockholder was permitted to bring a class-action lawsuit on behalf of others. At the same time, legal commentators began to attack the high substantive standard of *Ultramares*. As one observer noted in 1966: "The legal duties of an auditor ought to be coextensive with his professional pretensions. He aspires to be more than a rubber stamp for management, so his legal duties ought to go beyond that status."[22]

Expectations of what an audit could accomplish were changing. Although nineteenth-century accountants often were asked to check company books in order to protect owners against fraud by employees, their twentieth-century counterparts argued that their role was to judge the overall validity of the financial statements and denied that disclosure of fraud was the purpose of an audit. Nevertheless, as one study showed, "two-thirds of the investing public surveyed believed that the audit is conducted primarily to uncover fraud."[23] The expectation gap between the belief of accountants as to what audits should reveal and the conviction of angry litigants that audits should ensure against fraud increasingly widened. The litigation developments suggested the real possibility that plaintiffs would look to large accounting firms to assume the burden of damages because they were well insured rather than because they were culpable.[24]

A number of important decisions in the late 1960s gave practical effect to these new concerns.[25] In a 1967 case, for example, a company's financial statements had shown a profit only because fraudulent entries by company employees had concealed a loss. Peat, Marwick accountants were alleged to have failed to disclose their knowledge of these falsified transactions for several months after they were discovered. The court gave two reasons for refusing to dismiss the case. First, it expressed concern for the unnecessary harm to investors who had purchased stock after Peat, Marwick's discovery, thus suggesting that auditors have a common law duty to disclose false and misleading information that they subsequently discover in clients' financial statements that are being relied on by investors. Second, the court noted that such a disclosure obligation could also arise under the fraud provisions of Section 10(b)(5) of the 1934 Securities Exchange Act, because the representations were made in the performance of a "very specialized and well-defined task—to audit and certify financial statements for the protection of investors."[26]

In a ground-breaking 1968 case brought under Section 11 of the 1933 Securities Act, investors sued Peat, Marwick accountants for certifying financial statements that were materially misleading. Peat, Marwick, in its due diligence defense, argued that an accountant who has issued a report on financial statements included in a registration statement filed under the Securities Act could escape liability for misstatements if he had made a "reasonable" investigation. The court refused Peat, Marwick's request to dismiss the case, underscoring the need for auditors who are put on notice of irregularities to be careful to conduct a reasonable inquiry into the transaction involved in order to avoid Section 11 liability.[27]

An avalanche of cases followed, and all of the Big Eight firms were involved in lawsuits by 1972. Borrowing from the emphasis on consumer interests popular in other areas, plaintiffs argued that CPAs must try to uncover fraud and must disclose a finding that a company was fundamentally unsound. In order to avoid involvement in litigation, accountants had to be concerned about matters outside the scope of their traditional responsibilities.

In 1976, the tide seemed briefly to turn when the U.S. Supreme Court held that "scienter," or knowledge, must be pleaded to sustain civil liability under the Securities Exchange Act of 1934.[28] At trial, Ernst & Ernst auditors had been found liable for violating Section 10(b)(5) of the act for failing to detect and report a brokerage house's lack of adequate internal accounting controls. Although the appellate court decision affirmed that an auditor's liability for damages under Section 10(b)(5) could be based on negligent failure to comply with generally accepted auditing standards, the U.S. Supreme Court reversed the ruling. The high court's holding, however, did not affect actions filed under Section 11 of the 1933 Securities Act or under state securities laws.[29]

The government also took an interest in the financial statements of failed businesses and deeply shocked the accounting profession by initiating criminal proceedings against accountants and getting convictions. Two cases involving criminal prosecution of Big Eight partners received widespread attention. In the first case, an appellate court upheld a trial court's conviction of two Coopers & Lybrand partners and their associate for certifying a company's false and misleading financial statements. It found that the trial court had correctly instructed the jury that the "critical test" was not whether the accountants followed generally accepted accounting principles, but whether the financial statements, as a whole, "fairly presented the financial picture of the company."[30] In the second case, a Peat, Marwick partner and associate were convicted of criminal fraud in a case arising out of a bankruptcy. The jury found that the accountants had allowed the consummation of a merger transaction even though they were aware that prior published audited financial statements and other, unaudited, information sent to stockholders were erroneous. The judge's instructions to the jury acknowledged that, although under ordinary circumstances an accountant did not have a duty to investigate the fairness of unaudited statements, this duty did arise "where the surrounding circumstances are sufficiently suspicious."[31]

Some accountants of the period found these decisions "ominous" and a "gross injustice." As a new "heightened" duty-of-care evolved, owed "to all reasonably foreseeable persons who happen to receive the audited financial statements pursuant to a proper business purpose," much of the public believed that an accountant no longer merely "ameliorated the risks of financial misinformation" but served as a "guarantor of safety."[32] In addition to cases in which accountants were sued for failing to report false and misleading financial statements, litigation involving representations made by clients in statements other than financial statements also increased dramatically. As a result, audit partners more often sought legal advice from their internal counsel in completing their assignments. By 1974, the number of pending suits against Big Eight firms had reached two hundred, a hundredfold increase from 1962.[33]

PW, like the other large accounting firms, was increasingly sued after auditing the financial statements of companies that later found themselves in difficulty. Indeed, lawsuits against the firm multiplied exponentially throughout the 1970s. When Biegler began as senior partner, one small case was pending, and he knew of only three other suits in PW's entire history. By the mid-1970s, the firm was engaged in a large number of lawsuits and responding to litigation had become, in Biegler's words, "an industry."[34]

The lawsuits dismayed, shocked, and angered PW partners. Despite what they saw as unfair and, at times, ludicrous statements, they were continually forced to choose between expensive settlements or more costly litigation. One lawsuit they chose to fight was brought by a couple who read about Columbia Pictures in *The Wall Street Journal*'s "Heard on the Street" column while driving, stopped abruptly at a New York Thruway gas station, and called their broker to place an order. They had never seen PW's report on Columbia's financial statements; indeed, they had never seen the financial statements themselves. Later, when Columbia's stock fell, they sued PW, alleging that the firm was liable because *The Wall Street Journal* would have presented Columbia less favorably had the financial statements and opinion been accurate. Although the U.S. Supreme Court ultimately found these claims "not credible," PW spent hundreds of thousands of dollars defending itself in this suit. Despite cases like this, however, PW's legal advisers reported that the firm had significantly less litigation throughout this period than the norm for the major accounting firms.[35]

DEFINING NEW ROLES

The 1970s were a decade fraught with legal challenge. Although it was litigation that prompted the profession to a greater degree of circumspection, the courts were not the only arena in which accountants were under fire, for the SEC and Congress had trained their sights on them as well.

John C. Burton's appointment as the SEC's chief accountant in 1972 marked the end of an era: the retiring chief accountant, Andrew Barr, was the last appointee to the agency from the 1930s. Burton, at the age of 41, was plainly an accountant of another generation, who had served ten years as a professor of accounting and finance at Columbia University and four years as a staff accountant at Arthur Young. His stated mission during his six-year tenure was to make accounting more responsive to the needs of the public and accountants more aware of their professional responsibilities. On assuming office, he warned that "the SEC will be increasingly activist in the area of accounting principles."[36] This activism was almost immediately apparent; within a year, Burton surprised the profession with a torrent of Accounting Series Releases and proposed releases. Throughout his term, he pressed for greater disclosure and sharply questioned the profession's ability to regulate itself.[37]

Accountants became embroiled in SEC actions growing out of the political scandals of the second Nixon administration. In 1972, a special prosecutor investigating the illegal cash contributions made to the Nixon re-election campaign found that many corporations, in addition to making illegal domestic political contributions, had made questionable payments to foreign governments and politicians for the purpose of obtaining or retaining business. Continuing revelations of unrecorded slush funds, secret bank accounts, and other devices to hide foreign and domestic bribes shocked the nation. International Telephone & Telegraph (ITT), for example, was disgraced by evidence of its offer to contribute $1 million to prevent the election of Salvador Allende as president of Chile in order to retain effective control of the Chilean

Telephone Company. Gulf Oil, then a PW client, admitted to paying $10.3 million in corporate funds, much of it illegally, to American and foreign political figures between 1960 and 1973. Between 1974 and 1976, fourteen major corporations were sued by the SEC and found in violation of the securities laws. By 1978, more than 350 companies admitted that they made payments to intermediaries who passed the money on to officials in foreign governments. The number and seriousness of these offenses raised the question whether audits should be able to detect corporate illegality.[38]

These events had a direct effect on PW, especially after the CEO of the firm's client United Fruit, Eli Black, committed suicide. It was later learned that United Fruit had paid a million-dollar bribe to Honduran government officials. Shortly thereafter, when the SEC began an investigation into *Fortune* 500 companies that had allegedly bribed domestic and foreign political officials, a number of PW clients were implicated. "We had lawyers," recalled Biegler, "up to our ears!" The SEC, in his view, "was really turning the screws on everybody and wanted to put us in jail."[39]

The SEC was slow to develop standards in the area of foreign payments, but Biegler immediately took the position that when firm auditors uncovered an improper payment, the client had an obligation to consult with legal counsel to learn if the payment required disclosure. Unless this counsel advised against disclosure in writing, the firm would not sign the accounts. This position, a sharp departure from prevailing practice, "created a lot of fuss and feathers," noted the firm's outside counsel at Cravath, Swaine & Moore. "It was a very, very moral stand. As far as I know, it was the first major accounting firm that said, 'Damn it all, we're not going to sign the accounts if you won't play the game as it's happening now!'"[40]

Indeed, PW's reputation for probity meant that the firm began to be retained, in certain unusual cases, by a third party to determine whether a company had a problem of impropriety. In a throwback to its turn-of-the-century investigation work, the firm was hired by counsel for the SEC, for example, and paid by Mattel to investigate why Mattel's profits, and subsequently its stock, had fallen so precipitously. Similarly, when Northrop was involved in improper payment difficulties, PW was asked by the company's board of directors to participate in an investigation of the company's financial affairs being conducted by Ernst & Whinney, Northrop's accountants.[41]

Partly as a response to the corporate investigations, Congress enacted an antibribery law, the Foreign Corrupt Practices Act (FCPA), in 1978. The law's provisions covered essentially all American companies, public or private, as well as foreign companies filing with the SEC, and prohibited payments to foreign officials, political parties, and candidates for the purpose of obtaining or retaining business. The FCPA required companies to record transactions and the disposition of assets in reasonable detail and to create internal accounting systems sufficient to provide reasonable assurances of accountability. Its extremely harsh sanctions, coupled with the potential for civil actions, underscored the need for many companies to reconsider their accounting procedures.[42]

Revelations of illegal bribes by business people, questions raised by the diversity of accounting practices in the oil and gas industry, and concerns over accounting for public utilities led to three separate congressional inquiries into the profession during the 1970s. In 1975, as part of a larger congressional probe into the energy crisis, Representative John E. Moss of California and his House Committee on Oversight and Investigations took issue with the widely known lack of uniform reporting methods among major oil companies, which resulted in financial statements that were difficult to compare. The accounting profession avoided the full brunt of Moss's proposals for reform. His recommendation that the General Accounting Office (GAO) establish uniform accounting standards was never implemented, and the legislation he ultimately secured, requiring the SEC to regulate the establishment of uniform standards in oil company financial statements, had little practical effect.[43]

The Moss investigation was only the first skirmish in a long battle with Congress. In 1976, "precipitated by continual revelations of previously unreported wrongdoing by major corporations, as well as a series of corporate failures and financial difficulties which have come to light in recent years," a highly publicized investigation of the profession was initiated by Senator Lee Metcalf of Montana.[44] Head of the Senate Subcommittee on Reports, Accounting, and Management, Metcalf began his investigation by issuing a detailed questionnaire to entities within the accounting establishment, including the Big Eight accounting firms, the American Institute of Certified Public Accountants, the SEC, and the Financial Accounting Standards Board.

Metcalf's findings from these questionnaires, contained in a 1,760-page staff study released in December 1976, were that the SEC had "over-delegated authority" on accounting matters to the profession, which, in turn, had exhibited an "alarming lack of independence and lack of dedication to public protection."[45] This highly critical study summarized the previous decade of discontent with accountancy and served as a recitation of the profession's troubles in this period: the continued revelations of wrongdoing by corporations; the lack of effective reporting and disclosure by the profession; the business failures; the newly recognized importance of accounting practice to the larger public welfare; the deceptiveness of flexible accounting practices; the doubts over the profession's independence, reliability, and competence, and the erosion of public confidence.[46]

When PW first learned of the Metcalf investigation, Biegler told the Policy Committee that the investigation and its ramifications were "potentially the most important thing the firm has faced in my memory." The study identified PW as being in a class of its own as the most influential of the Big Eight firms, noting that it provided auditing and accounting services for clients that accounted for 24 percent of the sales and 28 percent of the earnings of the corporations listed on the New York Stock Exchange. At that time, PW had at least sixty-five corporate clients with annual sales of $1 billion or more. Of these, thirteen, including Exxon and four other of the nation's ten largest oil companies, had more than $5 billion in annual sales. As one partner noted, "When you were attacking the accounting establishment, you were attacking PW more than the others."[47]

Acting within the long tradition of professional leadership by PW's senior partners, Biegler argued for a forceful response to the Metcalf recommendations. Rather than stonewall, he believed that the firm needed "to face the problem and do something about it." His response was based on a long-standing fear that the profession would not act decisively in a crisis; as early as 1971, Biegler had warned his partners that he "would not sit by and watch the profession set minimum standards."[48]

To prevent "dangerous drifting" and to derail intervention by unfriendly legislators, Biegler developed a proposal to compel the profession's attention. After working for months with special counsel from the Washington, D.C., law firm of Arnold & Porter and with a PW partner assigned full-time to the problem, Biegler devised a three-pronged plan that he believed would force the profession to react. He proposed that CPA firms practicing before the SEC formally register with the agency, that they submit to a peer review every three years, and that they file annual financial statements.[49]

Like Biegler's earlier democratic reforms within the firm, this proposal represented a sophisticated appraisal of changing realities. Although greater regulation had always been opposed by the profession, he believed that it would surely be imposed, and perhaps in a draconian and punitive fashion, if accountants failed to show their willingness to adapt. By calling for a dramatic increase in regulatory oversight, Biegler hoped to show PW's good faith and thereby ease the profession's defensive posture.

Metcalf's subcommittee held hearings throughout May and June 1977 in which more than forty-four individuals, including the chairman of the FASB, most senior partners of the Big Eight firms, SEC and GAO officials, and other important financial executives, appeared to testify. PW senior MAS partner Henry Gunders attended a hearing, and noted that it was not a "decorous setting": "There was a lot of commotion—people walking around and whispering in ears and passing papers back and forth and the people in the audience were getting up and leaving." The mood in the hearing room changed dramatically when Metcalf called Biegler as a witness:

> John just looked up over his glasses, looked around for a minute and didn't say a word. Then he said, "My name is John Biegler. I am the senior partner at Price Waterhouse," and again he kept quiet. You could hear a pin drop all through his testimony. Hardly anybody got up and left and there wasn't any whispering. They really paid attention.[50]

Outside the hearing room, accountants objected vehemently to Biegler's three-part proposal, their reactions running the gamut from surprise and dismay to disdain and disgust and, finally, to outrage and alarm. As the managing director of another Big Eight firm noted, "It's ill-timed, ill-conceived, illogical, and if I could think of any other ills, I'd include them too." Within the AICPA, PW was "literally ostracized from the profession," according to the firm's representative on the SEC Practice Section executive committee. The press, by contrast, reported very favorably on Biegler's initiative. Noting the "sensation" Biegler had caused, the *New York Times* devoted an editorial to his "sensible suggestions," and later described his 126-page position paper as a "masterly performance: progressive, eminently reasonable, well-argued and smoothly written."[51]

In November 1977, the Metcalf subcommittee issued a final report summarizing the conclusions it had reached as a result of the hearings and ending with sixteen striking recommendations. Among the most noteworthy were: congressional oversight of accounting practices and rules; amendment of the securities laws to reverse a recent Supreme Court ruling and to allow individuals to sue auditors for negligence; establishment and enforcement of accounting rules by the GAO or a new federal board; abandonment of any rule-making by CPA firms, who would be limited to acting as guarantors that a corporation's financial statements were fair and accurate; investigation by the Department of Justice of possible antitrust violations by Big Eight firms; submission of annual reports by auditing firms; and a prohibition on providing management consulting services.[52]

On the last point, despite chief accountant Burton's activism, the Metcalf subcommittee singled out the SEC for its failure to regulate management consulting by large firms. Its staff study found that the SEC had "seriously failed to protect the public interest and to fulfill its public mandate" and that management consulting services were "particularly incompatible with the responsibility of independent auditors and should be prohibited by Federal standards of conduct."[53]

In 1978 and 1979, in response to continuing congressional pressure, the SEC issued two Accounting Series Releases deeply threatening to the profession. The first, ASR 250, required disclosure in a publicly held company's proxy statement of the types of nonaudit services performed by a registrant's principal accounting firm and of the size of nonaudit fees versus total fees. The second, ASR 264, advised accountants and clients that using an auditor for nonaudit services created an appearance that impaired independence. Amid the profession's strenuous protests, PW once again took a highly visible position. Appearing at the American Accounting Association annual meeting in 1978, Biegler criticized the SEC's failure to provide definitive guidance on ASR 264. The firm later published a paper arguing that development of information systems for audit clients and the marshaling and analyzing of specific information for management decisions were permissible activities for large accounting firms. The AICPA also protested ASR 264, on the grounds that its record-keeping requirements and the publicity now attached to using accounting firms' consulting services would have a "chilling and depressing effect" on MAS work. In fact, according to a PW MAS partner, this is just what happened: "CEOs and CFOs began to think that to have too much in the way of consulting fees just didn't look right."[54]

Despite fears, further congressional inquiry at the close of the decade did not produce much action. In January 1978, Congressman Moss revisited the controversies swirling about the profession. Describing himself as disappointed and dissatisfied with "the self-regulatory program of the AICPA" and with the "SEC's unconstrained 'wait and see' attitude," he proposed establishment of a federal accounting regulatory agency, the National Organization of SEC Accountancy. His bill, which died in Congress, would have required mandatory registration of accounting firms practicing before the SEC and quality reviews to ensure compliance with standards. Moss did not seek re-election and efforts to reintroduce his proposals never materialized. Following Senator Metcalf's death in 1977, his subcommittee disbanded, and the banner was passed to Senator Thomas Eagleton of Missouri. In 1979, Eagleton convened two days of hearings before the Subcommittee on Governmental Efficiency and the District of Columbia to evaluate the profession's compliance with the Metcalf recommendations. The subcommittee considered issues such as the liability of auditors for negligence, limitations on MAS by auditors, the duty of auditors to report criminal or illegal acts, and the SEC's oversight role in MAS work, but it never issued a report.[55]

ORGANIZED RESPONSES

To protect itself against any possibility of government intervention, the profession began to take steps toward policing itself. It appeared to be particularly vulnerable in the standard-setting arena, where the Accounting Principles Board had come under increasingly heavy attack from business, academia, and accountants themselves. To resolve this issue, representatives from twenty-one major accounting firms began meeting with the AICPA in 1970 and established two blue-ribbon groups. The Wheat Committee, chaired by Francis M. Wheat, partner in the major Los Angeles law firm of Gibson, Dunn & Crutcher and former SEC commissioner, was charged with studying ways to strengthen the APB. The Trueblood Committee, led by Robert Trueblood, senior partner at Touche Ross and former AICPA president, had the mission of restating the goals of financial reporting.[56]

In the course of its work, the Wheat Committee heard approximately one hundred presentations by representatives of various government agencies, financial executives, investment bankers, security analysts, economists, stock exchange officials, corporation lawyers, and academicians. Biegler, the only CPA and thus the profession's sole representative on the committee, reported to his partners that this work was the "single experience in my professional career that has made a far greater impression on me than any other."[57] He experienced firsthand the suspicion and even cynicism with which the public, government, and some business people had begun to view accountants. For Biegler, the key question to resolve was how accountants could fulfill their legal responsibility to protect the public interest and yet still serve their clients as auditors.[58]

In 1972, the Wheat Committee recommended the creation of the Financial Accounting Foundation, an independent foundation and standard-setting entity, sponsored by various organizations that had a strong interest in financial accounting and reporting. The foundation's operating arm, the Financial Accounting Standards Board, was to be staffed by seven full-time members who had no other business affiliations, thus avoiding the appearance of conflict that had dogged the APB. The membership would include four CPAs and three non–CPAs, in an attempt to create an impartial board dedicated to developing objective, practical standards and to serving the public interest. PW and Haskins & Sells were the first two Big Eight firms to pledge $200,000 per year for the first five years toward the $3 million the FASB would require to operate. The profession's new standard-setting process was a break with past practice because, for the first time since George O. May's work with the New York Stock Exchange in the 1920s, senior partners of the large firms, or their delegates, were not directly involved in promulgating accounting principles. They "suddenly found themselves on the 'outside' of standard-setting activity, together with their clients."[59]

Once in operation, the FASB was an improvement over its predecessor, although critics rather quickly targeted its slow pace. Its initial statement on "Conceptual Standards," the profession's third major attempt in fifteen years to develop a theoretical framework for accounting standards, was not issued until 1978. Complaints also arose concerning the FASB's inability to issue broad statements, citing its twenty-seven pronouncements on leases alone. In fact, the FASB was faced with difficult kinds of issues partly because the Committee on Accounting Procedure and the Accounting Principles Board had already resolved the easier problems. "All the rabbits have been hunted out of the woods," noted one PW partner who was also an APB member. "There's nothing left but boars and dragons."[60]

A good example of the quandaries that beset the FASB was the controversy sparked by its Statement of Financial Accounting Standards 8 (known as FASB–8). This ruling grew out of the expansion of international business activities and the extensive currency realignments that occurred during the 1970s. Before the ruling, companies had considerable leeway in calculating the effect of currency fluctuations on their overseas subsidiaries' financial statements. FASB–8, which took effect in January 1976, required that all large multinationals or companies having business abroad include in their financial statements, during the quarter in which they occurred, any gains or losses resulting from foreign currency fluctuations. Although they protested vigorously, virtually all companies with foreign operations had to alter their accounting practices significantly to do this. Once FASB–8 was implemented, business people complained that it increased the volatility of their reported profits and depressed stock prices. The furor made FASB–8 the most controversial accounting rule ever put into effect, and by 1979, it was being rethought.[61]

In 1974, the AICPA responded to the pressure to ensure greater reliability of financial statements by establishing the "Commission on Auditors' Responsibilities," known as the Cohen Commission. Staffed by Big Eight firms and led by former SEC chairman Manuel F. Cohen, its charter was to consider the gap between public expectations and what auditors could reasonably accomplish. In 1977, it made a series of wide-ranging recommendations to the AICPA, including the development of appropriate guidelines for management reports and for developing criteria for the evaluation of internal accounting controls.[62]

Accountants also sought to repair lost credibility by implementing internal reforms. In 1977, the AICPA created the SEC Practice Section, which was monitored by a Public Oversight Board of distinguished non–CPAs. The SEC Practice Section's initial objectives were to implement peer reviews among those firms practicing before the SEC and to require rotation of primary audit partners every five years—recommendations that Biegler had already made. Consistent with its Metcalf position and with its traditions, PW again surprised the profession by seeking to strengthen the Public Oversight Board's authority to impose sanctions and to approve standards for peer reviews.[63]

ESCALATING RIVALRY

The troubled economy of the 1970s forever altered the practice environment of large public accounting firms. As fewer new companies were formed, went public, and made stock offerings, the high-growth audit market of the 1960s slowed down. New rules issued by the AICPA and the FASB increasingly minimized choice in accounting methods, giving rise to the argument that a particular firm's work was not distinctive and that audit work was becoming a standard commodity. Client companies began to seek proposals from other accounting firms with lower fees. As a result, accounting firms were unable to raise fees at a time when spiraling inflation meant increased costs. When auditors did discount their fees, hoping to keep clients or to encourage stability, cost-conscious clients went fee-shopping and switched to still cheaper firms. This practice accelerated after the AICPA, under threat of antitrust prosecution by the Department of Justice, voted in 1972 to allow competitive bidding and, in 1979, to allow advertising and solicitation. By the end of the 1970s, fierce competition had become a business norm. Coopers & Lybrand, for example, began a price war within the profession when it started a deliberate rate-slashing strategy to attract new clients. "Coopers had a very definite program," noted one PW partner. It told its partners: "You will not increase your income for five years and we will invest that money in getting new clients." In addition, Peat, Marwick was rumored to be giving a $1,000 to $3,000 bonus to any staff member who brought in a new client, an offer that PW partners found unprofessional. These competitive strategies had an effect, and in the eighteen-month period ending in June 1974, the number of auditor changes listed with the SEC increased 70 percent. Coopers & Lybrand and Arthur Andersen gained more clients during that period than any other firms, thirty-one and twenty-seven clients, respectively, compared to seventeen by PW. The atmosphere had become more like "Macy's and Gimbels instead of professional firms trying to behave like professionals."[64]

Under these circumstances, the loss of each big client was a wrenching event. PW lost Gulf Oil in 1977, a valued client of more than forty years' standing. When Gulf had become embroiled in improper payments disclosures, PW had delivered a letter of resignation. Although Gulf had persuaded PW not to resign at that time, it later changed auditors, giving as the reason its desire to implement a rotation policy—notwithstanding its election of PW three times since the initial disclosure and despite an SEC finding that PW had not acted improperly. PW concluded that its "repeated refusal to become a contributing party to the settlement of the Gulf derivative shareholders' actions relating to its 'improper payments' disclosures" was the deciding factor.[65]

Massive proposals, costing thousands, or hundreds of thousands, of dollars and involving numerous meetings and site visits, became common. In 1978, after a six-month proposal process, the firm won the Hewlett-Packard audit, prevailing over eight other candidates, including the rest of the Big Eight and the company's own former auditor. This victory set a new standard for the time, intensity of effort, and international scope required in securing new clients; eventually the Hewlett-Packard proposal style became the norm. The experience was invaluable, for, as Biegler had predicted to the Policy Committee, the firm was asked to submit new proposals for several major clients in the following five years.[66]

Despite the challenges of this period, PW prospered, as Exhibit 6.2 and Exhibit 6.3 show. The firm remained exceptionally strong in its clientele, especially in comparison with other firms. In 1977, it claimed 153 of the top 1,000 international companies, while Arthur Andersen, in second place, had 79. As the Metcalf study found when examining the average client financial and employment data of the firm's New York and American stock exchange clientele, including sales, net income, income taxes, number of employees, and total assets, PW stood well above its professional counterparts.[67]

In order to attract new clients and to keep existing ones, PW and the other large firms increasingly sought to add value to their audit services by developing expertise in a particular industry's accounting and regulatory requirements. The growing complexity of financial reporting, tax requirements, and management needs led more than 70 percent of the

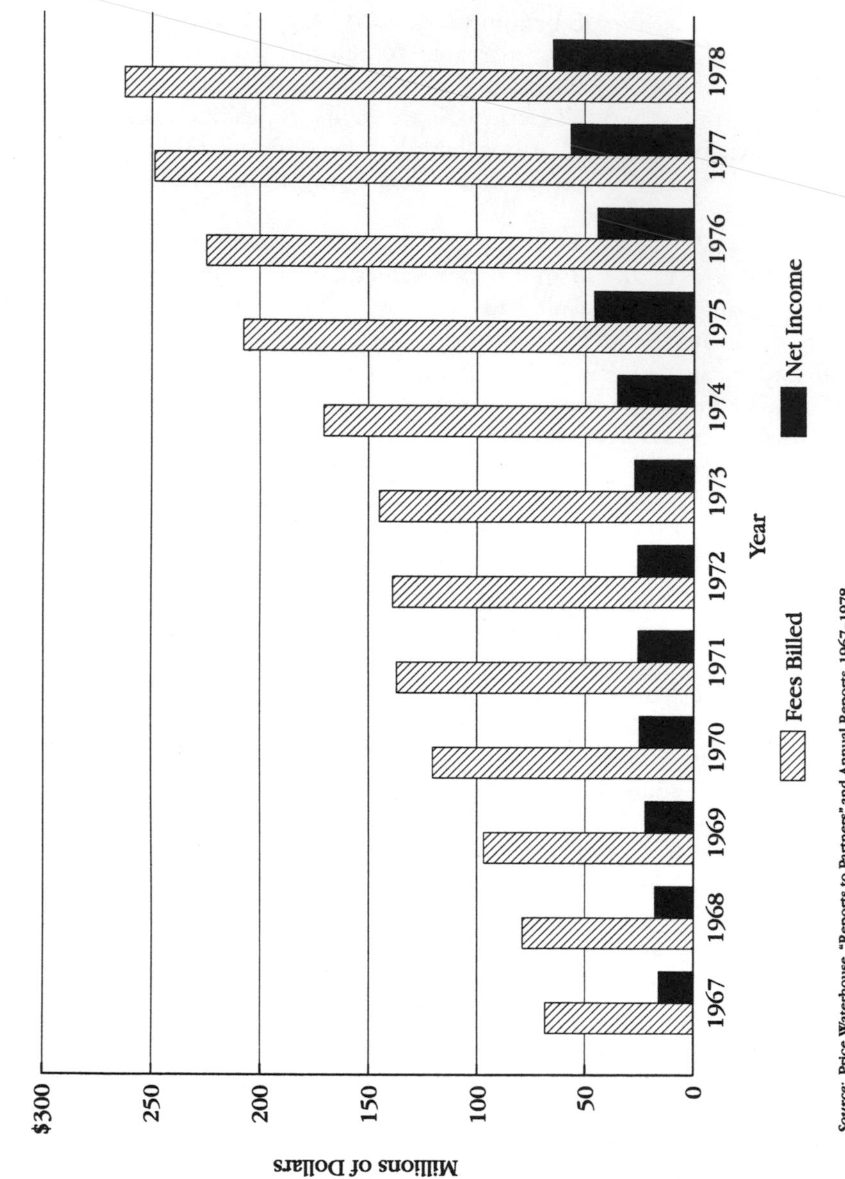

Source: Price Waterhouse, "Reports to Partners" and Annual Reports, 1967–1978, Office of the Firm Secretary, and National Information Center, National Office, New York.

EXHIBIT 6.2 Fees Billed and Net Income, 1967–1978

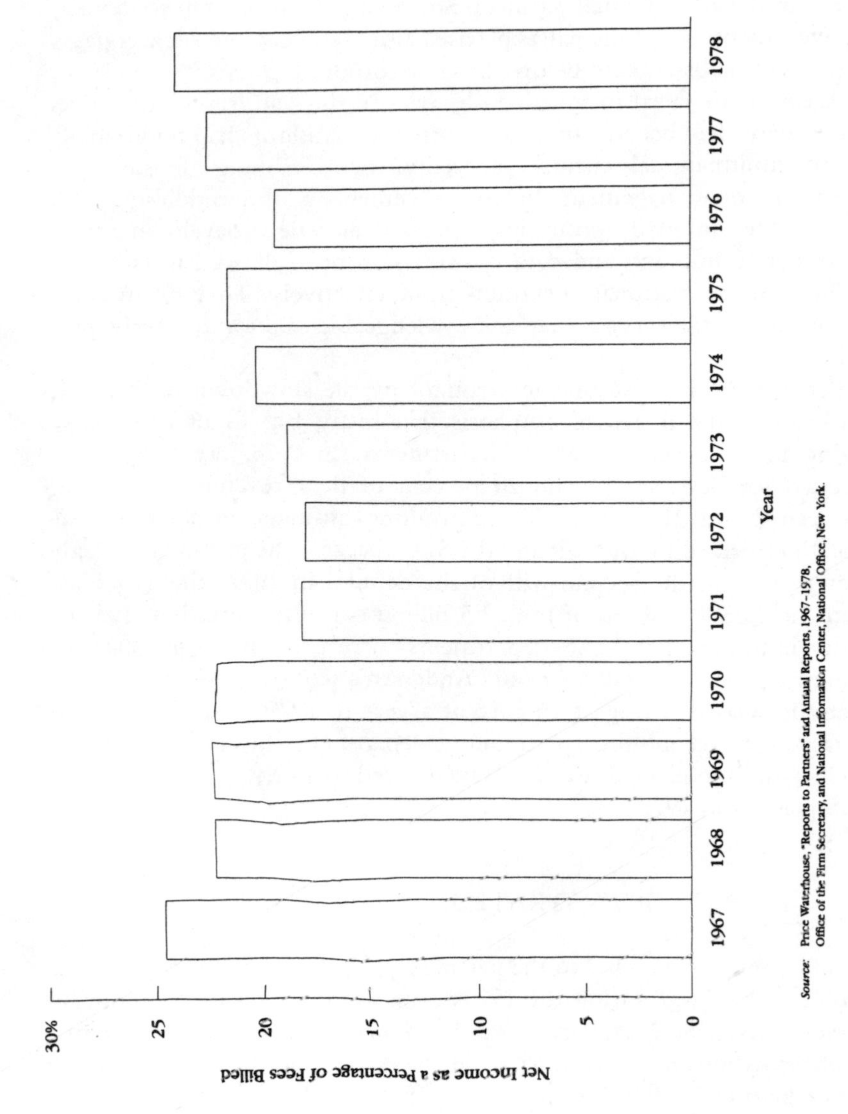

Source: Price Waterhouse, "Reports to Partners" and Annual Reports, 1967–1978, Office of the Firm Secretary, and National Information Center, National Office, New York.

EXHIBIT 6.3 Net Income as Percentage of Fees Billed, 1967–1978

...ntants responding to a 1977 AICPA survey to consider themselves ...ialists. Sole practitioners described themselves as specialists, pri...rily in the area of small business. Some large firms sought to develop government or municipal expertise, although fees for such engagements were substantially below those of corporate clients.[68]

Accountants faced formidable obstacles in their efforts to add value. Some clients had become more self-sufficient. Auditors had traditionally served multinational clients, especially their far-flung divisions, as extensions of management, but improvements at the middle-manager level, better internal accounting systems, and new developments in computer technology and data transmission now allowed head offices to monitor international operations more effectively. They thus needed less of the extra service that a knowledgeable auditor formerly provided.[69]

Perhaps the biggest change wrought by the slowdown in the audit market was the increased emphasis that many Big Eight firms were giving to their tax and MAS departments. In 1978, tax services accounted for between 14 and 20 percent of their revenues, and MAS between 7 and 21 percent. The consulting business, in particular, although criticized by Metcalf and the SEC, became the profession's high-growth area in the second half of the decade. In 1977, the Big Eight firms held $500 million of the $2.5 billion consulting market, and statistics indicated that MAS departments were growing faster than accounting firms overall. Arthur Andersen's consulting practice, for example, was growing at 15 percent a year in 1979, nearly four times as fast as its accounting and auditing department. Some 21 percent of its $546 million in 1979 revenues was derived from MAS work, up from 17.5 percent in 1972.[70]

PW'S STRATEGIC RESPONSE

Biegler's annual speeches to the partners not only described the practical problems he faced during the 1970s, but also revealed much about his personal style. Serious, earnest, and at times invoking the cadence of a minister exhorting his congregation, he directly addressed the difficult issues before the firm. Each year he pressed the partners to consult frequently with each other and to take advantage of research in difficult accounting areas. He also urged them to support industry specialization and practice development, to pay greater attention to small business, and to become more entrepreneurial. Biegler set goals for ten million chargeable hours by the 1979 fiscal year and for an expanded and strengthened International Firm.

Although he never developed an overall "super strategy," Biegler's "number one objective" during this tumultuous period was "to guard the firm's reputation for professional excellence."[71] Under his leadership, PW made a significant start at developing an integrated, broader range of services to clients. The Policy Committee approved a number of important moves in this direction, such as opening the Office of Federal Services (OFS), enhancing public relations, and providing vastly expanded continuing education. Existing functions, like industry specialization, practice development, and the International Firm, were reinvigorated.[72]

An important opportunity for the MAS practice arose out of the firm's Office of Federal Services, established in the early 1970s in order to enlarge PW's public-sector consulting work. For the previous twenty-five years, PW's government consulting had been minimal. The firm's prevailing belief during the period had been that consulting for the federal government was unprofitable. A secondary concern had been a perception, developed since May's active years, of a conflict between PW's role as defender of private business interests against government and service for the government.[73]

The opening of the OFS as part of the Washington practice office represented a departure from this long-standing policy. The Washington practice office had already developed a consultancy in federal tax, centered around securing advance rulings on tax issues for firm clients and getting informal opinions from the Internal Revenue Service. Roscoe Egger, whose work heading up this area had exposed him to the immense field of opportunity in the federal government, argued informally for the need to develop this practice. Biegler and Gunders, the MAS vice chairman, encouraged him to develop the idea in terms of another specialty that was part of the National Office.

In 1973, Biegler named Egger partner-in-charge of the OFS and charged it with "increasing timely and effective response to client problems with the federal government" and with "promoting business for the firm, either directly with the government or with other entities through government spending projects."[74] Egger brought the well-identified federal tax practice into the OFS, but the consulting practice was not clearly thought out at the time. Although it performed a number of small consulting engagements, the OFS did not do well in its first few years.[75]

The OFS consulting practice got its break when the general counsel of the U.S. Department of Transportation called Biegler to ask if PW would, on a pro bono basis, provide some railroad experts for a complicated problem. This work generated valuable goodwill. When the proposal to prepare the preliminary financial plan for what would later become Conrail was officially publicized, the OFS got the job. Egger recalls that it was a "psychological shot in the arm" that "gave the folks within the group a lot of hope and expectation that they could do the same thing in other ways."[76] At about the same time, OFS broadened its mandate by bringing in specialists in state, local, and foreign governments and, in 1976, re-named itself the Office of Government Services (OGS). Riding on the success of its Conrail work, OGS was able to secure other major assignments, such as an automated payroll accounting and personnel system for the U.S. Post Office, the largest nonmilitary employer in the United States. It later replicated this job, "a bell-wether for federal agencies," for the U.S. Army and the Treasury. At the end of the decade, OGS embarked on another major consulting project to develop a worldwide accounting system for the State Department. Ten years after beginning operation in 1974, the federal consulting practice had grown into the largest MAS department of any PW office in the country.[77]

Under Biegler, PW also made its first concerted public relations push, a tremendous departure from past practice for a firm that had always prided itself on having "the lowest of low profiles," in deference, perhaps, to its British heritage. White papers, such as that prepared by Bevis on deferred taxes, had been issued only sporadically and were directed to the business community and the partnership. In the 1970s, however, with the entire profession receiving greater public attention, Biegler sought to raise PW's profile. He hired external public relations counselors and assigned partner and former APB member Robert Hampton III to work full time on firm publications. In 1974, PW published the first edition of *Accounting Events and Trends*, a newsletter of opinions and comment "designed to be a forum from which PW could sound off on a number of topics for the edification of their clients." It was very well received, reaching a circulation of 25,000–30,000 by the end of the decade. Another, less universally popular public relations effort was the publication of the firm's Annual Report, which was printed throughout most of the 1970s, until a significant number of partners felt it unnecessary. Publication was then discontinued.[78]

PW's practice development had an uneven history. As Biegler noted, developing new work was not a continuous process, but rather something that the firm "started enthusiastically and then it would fall of its own dead weight and then it would start up again." He believed that one problem with the Business Research Committee of the 1950s, the firm's first organized effort at practice development, was that it had not been "diplomatic" and had irritated people, "creating resistance rather than results."[79] The marketing function did not become an operating unit within PW at that time. Later, although the formal position of director of practice development was created, it was occasionally left vacant. By the 1970s, however, PW's leadership was ready to address the problem of attracting new business.

In 1972, the Policy Committee, on Ganner's recommendation, formed a nine-member Practice Development Task Force (PDTF). This team of "heavy hitters and business developers" was charged with establishing a program to improve skills in attracting new clients. The PDTF took a grass roots approach by visiting practice offices and encouraging their efforts to develop new business. "We started off and dropped some bombshells," recalled a PDTF member. "We told each office that we'd come around to see them and they had to have a whole program worked up to show us what they'd done, what they were doing in the community."[80] After putting out guidelines, the PDTF teams checked to see if offices were implementing them.[81]

The PDTF encouraged each office to designate a partner to oversee practice development, and certain team members made themselves available to help with client proposals. It published an internal practice development manual and laid the foundation for later videotapes such as one entitled "Marketing of Professional Services." In addition, the PDTF prepared extensive statistical data showing, for example, that many companies that had been PW clients ten years earlier were no longer with the firm; for the most part, they had been acquired by other companies. These data encouraged partners to realize the importance of building new business and of helping present clients grow and prosper.[82]

One clever marketing device was a watch that the chairman of the PDTF, Frederick M. Werblow, had specially designed with the PW logo. Each year, he gave all new partners watches and a speech exhorting them never to forget that "every hour of every day," they must be doing something, either to assist existing clients or to develop new business. Today, over three-quarters of the partners have these watches.[83]

Committing to firmwide marketing goals was difficult in a partnership as autonomous as PW. Despite the support of the firm's leadership for the PDTF, a number of partners resisted its efforts. Some PDTF members and partners complained that PW was not moving quickly enough, noting that "it was like pulling teeth to get partners to do business development." Others protested that they did not have enough time to seek new business, and still others seemed to feel no urgency for the task. The PDTF worked hard for five years, until its functions were assumed by a national director of industry specialization. Overall, the PDTF's most significant accomplishments were a general re-evaluation of views on practice development and a raised level of consciousness about building the business.[84]

To support all of these initiatives, PW continually improved its internal systems. Partly as a result of the barrage of lawsuits against many other large firms arising out of business failures and the improper payments scandals, the firm re-examined its auditing procedures and was the first of the Big Eight to submit voluntarily to an in-depth peer review. Although PW had been involved in close exchanges of information regarding practices and procedures with the other national accounting firms since the 1950s, peer review was a dramatic departure from past practice. Allowing another firm to study thoroughly its techniques was risking a disclosure of the firm's "trade secrets" and "unique methodology."[85]

As its "auditor," PW chose Haskins & Sells because of a strong cultural affinity. "They were our kind of people," Biegler recalled. "We liked their style and had admiration for them. We thought their professional style was like ours."[86] Over six months in 1974, at a cost of more than $1 million, Haskins & Sells thoroughly reviewed the firm's personnel policies, staff training, and client work papers, and approved its system of audit control as "suitably designed to achieve its objectives" and as "operating effectively."[87]

However, Haskins & Sells sparked much controversy by recommending that a second partner be assigned to review each audit for compliance with professional requirements, an idea incompatible with the PW philosophy that "a partner was a partner was a partner and he wasn't supposed to have anybody looking over his shoulder on professional matters."[88] Biegler, however, was very pleased with this recommendation and thought it was a "tremendous idea, once again from a management point of view." He felt that it dealt with his concern of "How can I be sure that somebody isn't running off on his own?"[89] Biegler informed the partners that the involvement of a second partner was not designed to limit their freedom, but to bolster the functional abilities of autonomous partners. Other factors, however, including the increasing audit risks and the continuing decline in average age and experience of engagement partners, increased the need for a second partner. In addition, second-partner reviews were already standard with all other Big Eight firms.[90]

Another critical area of concern to Biegler was industry specialization. Although all the large partnerships had specialties that had evolved naturally out of their long-time client base (PW's traditional strengths in the steel and oil industries were perhaps the best-known examples), by the 1970s, the term "industry specialization" not only identified a firm's historical strengths, but was also an important marketing technique. Although PW had had an industry specialization program since the 1950s, its performance had been uneven. The firm prided itself on the generalist orientation of its partners, and it was difficult to get them to commit to a specialty. "Partners didn't want to be pigeon-holed," recalled one partner. "It didn't give them enough freedom or flexibility or room to let their imagination roam."[91] In addition, partners strongly believed that involvement in diverse industries gave them a more advantageous business perspective. Nonetheless, industry specialization gained priority in 1971, when Biegler appointed Robert Field, national director for manpower and special services, to lead the first firmwide initiative on specialization. The amount of time spent by professional staff on writing articles for trade journals, serving on industry-related committees in the AICPA, and attending industry conferences more than doubled in the next two years. Although specializing in one area was still a part-time pursuit in 1972, the Policy Committee planned to have thirty partners and fifty-five managers devoted fulltime to their specialized field within four years.[92]

PW made important progress toward greater specialization throughout the decade. It identified industries and functional areas with unique features, and designated lead specialists to develop and implement programs dealing with their industry's problems. As the program became more refined, the firm placed lead specialists in practice offices with significant client responsibility and encouraged them to concentrate on commitments only within their specialty. By 1977, PW had designated seventy-four specialists to cover twenty areas, including banks, hospital and medical services, insurance, and entertainment.[93]

One very successful and unique specialty that burgeoned during this period was PW's law firm expertise. Pioneered by Herman Bevis, who began a statistical survey for a number of law firms in the late 1950s, it was taken over by Biegler and the SEC Department in the 1960s. The survey work generated financial statistics to assist law firms in managing their practices and led to a large number of law firm consulting engagements concerning management practices, partnership arrangements, and financial reporting and control. PW experts maintained close relations with the national and local bar associations, participated in legal conferences, and obtained wide recognition for their articles, papers, and "law firm know-how." The law firm specialty became immensely successful—more than 1,000 law firms were part of the survey by the end of the 1980s.[94]

As often occurred in any area of practice development, problems arose with specialization. For example, offices receiving inquiries in a particular industry or specialty would sometimes propose to do the work themselves, without involving the firm's specialist. For Biegler, this was a source of continuing frustration. Although he had made industry specialization his "number one deployment priority" in the later years of his administration, looking back, he considered it a major intractable area of his tenure as senior partner.[95]

THREE PRACTICES IN TRANSITION

All three PW practice areas underwent dramatic changes in the 1970s. From an administrative perspective, they were all reorganized, with support functions led by national directors located in the National Office. Each practice was substantively shaped by the changing business environment, the strategic requirements of the firm, and the continuing evolution in services, as well as by the demands growing out of the unique function of the PW partner.

Improving Audit Support

Within the audit and accounting practice, a massive effort was made to improve support materials and to assist partners in the field. In 1972, three years after being named national director of the newly created Accounting and Auditing Services Department, Henry Hill oversaw a headquarters staff of forty to fifty people providing technical support to the practice offices. At this point, the professional audit group numbered 2,834, including 170 partners, 493 managers, 823 seniors, and 1,348 staff accountants and interns. A sophisticated audit and accounting support system had become essential when the extraordinary pace of developments made it "almost impossible for a practicing accountant to keep up," Hill noted at the time, adding that "accounting has changed so fast in recent years that it is doubtful that anyone who has been away for more than a year or two would even recognize the climate in which we are operating."[96] He saw his task as providing three important services: general reference information, advice on active problems, and performance checks on the offices.[97]

Despite the press of day-to-day problems he encountered as A&AS partner, Hill quickly became involved in developing the firm's accounting research material. Historically, the Research Department had grown by taking calls from partners on difficult problems. Unlike partners in other Big Eight firms, PW's engagement partners were known for their ability to commit the firm in discussions with their clients, without consulting the National Office. The Research Department sought to preserve and enhance the competitive advantage that PW had in this respect. Hill's plan was to develop the research function's capacity to generate material to support the engagement partner in the field. He pointed out that changing times had made the old system obsolete. As he noted,

> You couldn't run the firm by telephone. If a partner in St. Louis or Minneapolis couldn't get the Research Department, he'd call the SEC Department. Each one of these guys had built up a farm team, or kind of a list of patrons who would call him. You never knew whether this guy in the SEC Department was giving the same answer as this guy in the Research Department.[98]

An enhanced Research Department meant that, initially, Hill walked a fine line between establishing greater uniformity and infringing on the partners' personal freedom to act. "It took a little while to get through to them that we were not trying to take their prerogatives away, but to make them bigger and stronger in dealing with their clients." His intent was to allow a partner to project confidence and autonomy, because he believed it was very damaging, both to the individual engagement partner and to the firm generally, for a partner to say to a client, "I agree with you, but I'll have to check with headquarters to see if it's all right." By creating an authoritative reference source and by clarifying the lines of authority between offices and the Research Department, Hill sought to give engagement partners the best technical support possible.[99]

As a first step, Hill assigned a young colleague to consolidate the Research Department's existing twenty-volume looseleaf *Accounting and Auditing Service* into a single publication, serving as a basic reference source for partners and staff. Containing authoritative material unavailable elsewhere, including PW's own interpretations of accounting rules, and a roadmap showing where an auditor could find information, the revised *Accounting and Auditing Service* was first published in 1971 and subsequently updated annually.[100]

Hill also worked with the audit research partner to strengthen the office reviews that had been ongoing since the late 1950s. New, better organized "auditing standards review" teams, drawn from outside the particular office under scrutiny, visited once every three years, promoting improved audit techniques and working papers throughout the firm, greater involvement in planning, and better understanding of the mechanics of other offices.[101]

A Tax Partner in Every Office

Improving support functions was also important in the tax area, although lack of personnel was its most serious problem. By the early 1970s, the Tax Department had become a significant part of the firm's total business. Composed of 51 partners, 183 managers, and 349 seniors and staff in 1972, it accounted for 16.5 percent of total billing value and 15 percent of the total hours of the U.S. offices for that year. William Miller's election as the first tax partner to sit on the Policy Committee underscored the new importance of the tax area within PW. Miller used his position to promote the importance of placing a tax partner in every office; "The philosophy I had was that the people really had to give the service at the partner level. Clients wanted to talk to the top people, they didn't want to talk to somebody down the line."[102] His personal approach, developed in the Los Angeles office, was partly responsible for his success in recruiting new staff and in selling his ideas to the partnership. Many offices lacked tax partners when Miller began; by the time he retired in 1978, most had at least one.[103]

Albert Cohen, then partner-in-charge of the New York tax practice, succeeded Miller on the Policy Committee and later as vice chairman, heading the Tax Department. Cohen saw computerization as a primary need for the tax practice. At this time, many individual tax returns were being sent to an outside agency for processing, although a number of computer initiatives flowed up from the practice offices. The Chicago office, for example, sought to develop applications of computer software to solve international corporate tax problems; when its requests for budget support from the National Office and for freedom to pursue this research were granted, it produced important and highly marketable programs. These and other software programs established PW as a leader in computerized solutions to complex tax problems. The Tax Department prospered; by the end of the 1970s, the New York tax practice had doubled in size, and San Francisco's tax office had grown to be the firm's second largest.[104]

Crisis in Consulting

Though the unpredictable business environment had some impact on the tax practice in the 1970s, it was the firm's management consultants who were most adversely affected. Although the practice rebounded by the end of the decade, the early 1970s were years of crisis and turmoil. The MAS Department, headed by Arthur Toan, began the decade with an unbroken record of increases in chargeable hours and staff. It had a professional staff of 460, including twenty partners. It did its own recruiting, training, and research, had a large government practice, and did work for many nonaudit clients. MAS personnel had broadly based skills in data processing, accounting systems, industrial engineering, mathematical modeling, and marketing. By the 1970s, the MAS Department was creating and merchandising on a significant scale computer packages containing well-developed and documented EDP programs and procedures suitable for installation in a variety of situations with only minor modifications. Toan's 1970 "Report of the MAS Department to the Executive Committee" highlighted the success of seven such packages, including a financial reporting system that maintained a general ledger and could be used to prepare a set of financial reports.[105]

The scope of services offered by PW's MAS Department was deliberately rather narrow compared to that of similar departments in other accounting firms. After the late 1960s, the firm's policy was to concentrate on organizational structures, systems, procedures, and information, rather than to provide advice on strategic management decisions. The department worked to offset the fears of a number of audit partners who believed that MAS work could jeopardize their client relationships. Some MAS consultants chafed at these restrictions and noted that the Canadian firm had actually spun off its consulting practice into "PW Associates." In a 1970 speech, Toan rejected such a solution for the firm's American practice. Acknowledging the fears of audit partners concerning MAS, he nevertheless called for an expanded scope of services as well as the freedom to solicit assignments from, and to work for, nonaudit clients. He urged the partners

> to forget that we are an auditing firm and set for ourselves a larger and broader goal—to be a "*full*-service firm"—in which all of the departments of the firm—audit, tax and MAS and other specialist groups—act in an equally supportive role of something bigger than any one of us.[106]

Toan's comments might have found greater favor throughout the firm but for the economic contraction of 1970–1971 and the wage-price freeze, both of which had a serious effect on the MAS Department's profitability. Two-thirds of its business was nonrepetitive, and new requests dropped to "virtually zero overnight," where they remained. Although severe staff cutbacks were required, the department was locked into contracts with its managers (50 percent of the staff) that required a year's notice for layoffs. These budget problems were exacerbated by substantial salary increases that had just been made to offset inflation.

Even after the MAS Department had cut its staff in half, it continued to operate at a considerable loss. In fiscal 1972, it posted a 20 percent decline in chargeable hours and in number of staff from 1970. As the consulting practice's profits and standing plummeted, Toan and his successor, Gunders, were asked to study the organization, operation, and scope of MAS activities within PW. They recommended the reduction of the MAS staff to 330 (it eventually fell to 275) and further restriction of the scope of services in comparison with those offered by other accounting firms. The Policy Committee, forced to take strong action, accepted these recommendations.[107]

Eventually, however, the department's fortunes improved. Once price controls were removed in 1972, MAS business recovered and additional work flowed in. By 1974, chargeable hours were up 17 percent from the year before, as the upswing in the economic cycle leveled out the substantial declines of 1971 and 1972. Although another recession pulled growth down to 2.2 percent in 1975, the consulting practice was growing again by the next fiscal year.

All management consulting performed by accounting firms was condemned by the Metcalf subcommittee in 1977, but this criticism was soon forgotten. Two years of steady growth in fiscal years 1978 and 1979 allowed PW's MAS Department to surpass its previous record for chargeable hours. The consulting practice survived, although its scope remained relatively constrained because of the events of the 1970s. Comparative statistics for 1977 showed PW's consulting practice at 6 percent of revenues (with audit 76 percent, tax 16 percent, and other 2 percent), with only Haskins & Sells having a smaller share for its consulting practice, only 5 percent. As a percentage of revenues, Arthur Andersen's MAS practice was nearly three times as large as that of PW, and those of Arthur Young and Touche Ross were both more than twice the size.[108]

ADJUSTMENTS TO A WORLD OF DIVERSITY

If some internal areas proved difficult to change or resolve, Biegler made a great deal of progress in his plans for reorganization and development of PW's international organization during the 1970s. As part of the firm's long-standing international approach, the partnerships around the world had developed and refined their first International Firm structure in a creative burst beginning in 1946 and ending in the early 1950s. The agreement drawn up at that time recognized the American, British, Canadian, continental European, South American, and Australian firms and allowed them the irrevocable use of the PW name in their respective areas.

In the early 1970s, this overall structure was still in place although the International Firm had grown from 146 offices in forty-seven countries in 1960 to 230 offices in seventy-four countries by 1973. It was run by committees composed of representatives from each top firm. In addition to promoting and arranging exchanges of people, the International Firm took on the major substantive task of developing and monitoring accounting and auditing standards. The American, British, and Canadian firms collaborated in producing, in 1973, *Accounting Principles and Reporting Practices: A Survey in 38 Countries*, which listed 233 accounting principles and practices and recorded "the degree of conformity with each principle and practice by the business community and the accounting profession" in each country. The *Survey*, widely distributed outside the firm, was subsequently updated twice to cover conditions in more than sixty-four countries.[109]

Although its 1946 charter gave it the appearance of a coordinating body, until the early 1970s, the International Firm was never more than a conglomerate of separate, autonomous firms around the world, all practicing with the name PW. Aside from work like the *Surveys*, the yearly committee meetings, with participants drawn from all the member firms, were its only concrete manifestation. Throughout the 1950s and 1960s, the committees provided the forum for the individual partnerships to talk with each other, articulate International Firm policy, and make International Firm decisions.

When Biegler became senior partner, he carried on his earlier role as representative of the U.S. firm to the International Firm and, in doing so, became increasingly aware of its limitations. It "wasn't accomplishing anything," he recalled. "It was just limping along." Meanwhile Arthur Andersen was proclaiming to international businesses that "PW was just a loose federation of disparate firms, whereas we at AA are one firm, one standard, one discipline. You hire us to do your worldwide audit and you'll get the same quality of work done everywhere in the world."[110] As business and competition continued to assume a more global character, PW, long the leading international firm, began to see other firms strengthening their practice overseas.[111]

To respond to the growing threat of international competition, Biegler and Stanley Duncan, senior partner of the British partnership, improved the International Firm organization in 1971. All partners around the world were united as a single entity that operated through a General Council composed of the senior partner and other representatives of the eighteen constituent firms. Representation on the General Council was based largely on the numerical strength of each national partnership. A Policy Committee of six to eight senior partners was also created. Within this umbrella structure, PW could legitimately state that its newly renamed firm, "PW International" was a "one world partnership" that could introduce global planning, develop worldwide standards of client service, and monitor the performance of all firms bearing its name. These changes were made without sacrificing what many saw as the International Firm's great virtue; in true PW fashion, it was governed by consent, rather than by a centralized authority, and it retained the strong national base of the member PW firms. During its first year, Duncan served as senior partner of PW International only part time, supported by a full-time executive partner. In the next few years, funded by regular levies from member firms, Duncan added a headquarters staff in London composed of partners from member firms responsible for monitoring audit quality control and developing staffing procedures and principles.[112]

As it began to get off the ground, the restructured PW International was caught up in the wave of anti-American sentiment of the 1970s. Countries in which PW International had a practice were becoming more and more nationalistic. Though some only threatened to enact legislation restricting the practice rights of American accounting firms, the Mexican PW firm was in fact "Mexicanized" in 1972. Foreign practices without national or indigenous ownership had a long tradition of second-class status and had been run exclusively by British or American accountants. Nationals, who usually could aspire only to local partner status, were permitted to attend American manager, but not partner, meetings. Biegler rejected the second-class status as inappropriate for the 1970s, and he sought to localize these partnerships as independent firms as soon as they were capable of supporting themselves. In July 1973, a "Middle Americas" firm was formed to foster coordination and integration of the Central American, Colombian, Ecuadorian, Panamanian, and Venezuelan offices. All existing partners in those practices were made partners in the new firm, which was managed by an Executive Committee reporting to the U.S. Policy Committee. The Middle Americas firm marked the official recognition of the autonomy and importance of the foreign offices. The Japanese firm soon followed suit, gaining its "independence" in 1975.[113]

In the United States at this time, the outlook of people working in accounting firms was also changing. More people than ever before were entering the profession. Twice as many undergraduate and graduate degrees in accounting were awarded in 1977 as at the beginning of the decade. These new accountants, however, were quite different from those of the preceding generation. Surveys taken in 1965 and 1970 showed a growing gap between the values and ideals held by partners and those held by entry-level accountants. New staff placed less emphasis than their predecessors on organizational issues such as deference to administrators, loyalty to the firm, adherence to the firm's rules and procedures, and work standardization, and they gave greater importance to egalitarian work relationships and increased involvement in work-related decisions. The availability of consulting work was also a strong factor in attracting young people to the profession.[114]

The ethnic and gender composition of the profession also began to change. In the 1960s, minority representation in the accounting profession was very small—much less, for instance, than in the legal or medical professions. The federal Civil Rights and Fair Employment Acts, passed in 1964, seemed at first to have little effect on accounting employment. However, as amendments, regulations, and Executive Orders amplified the acts' coverage, more women and minorities became accountants. Even so, the absolute numbers were small. In a survey of black accountants in the late 1960s, only 136 were identified out of more than 100,000 CPAs in the United States.[115]

From 1969 to 1975, the federal Equal Employment Opportunity Commission investigated PW for discrimination against minorities. While the firm's general counsel reported that "these investigations resulted in no significant adverse determinations," the inquiry spurred the partnership to implement affirmative action programs in all offices by 1973.[116]

The late 1970s were a "growth period for women in public accounting," however, progress in hiring women was uneven within the profession. According to one contemporary study, the problems of integrating women and minorities were greatest in the large accounting firms. Although women made up almost 13 percent of Big Eight staff by 1977, advancement was difficult. In 1978, the Big Eight's 4,448 partners included only seventeen women and fewer than fifteen blacks; these figures increased over the next decade.[117]

PW's efforts to hire more women and minorities followed these trends. Its first partner who was a woman, an international tax specialist, was admitted in 1973. By 1978, PW had 6 senior managers, 46 managers, 170 senior accountants, and 425 staff accountants who were women. A dozen years later, in 1990, 35 percent of the firm's total professional staff was female, including 34 partners, 770 contract staff (managers and senior managers), 1,042 senior accountants, and 1,144 staff accountants. The firm's attempts to hire minorities were more disappointing, reflecting, in part, the intense competition for the relatively few minority accounting graduates at this time. As of 1975, the firm still had no partners who were members of minority groups, and only 2 managers, 28 senior accountants, and 91 staff accountants. These numbers increased by 1990, when the firm had 26 partners, 217 contract staff, 229 senior accountants, and 247 staff accountants who were members of minority groups.[118]

PW had other personnel problems that were a legacy of its planned growth strategy of the 1960s. Despite a relatively large increase in partners and staff during the 1970s, the firm still suffered from a chronic and sometimes desperate shortage of partners. Filling vacancies left by retirement was less a problem than finding the right people with the necessary skills for the new offices that became critically important as the firm expanded into new specialties and geographic areas. Throughout Biegler's tenure, the Policy Committee was directly involved in extensive re-arrangement of partner resources, and eventually its members spent more time on partner transfers than any other issue.[119]

The decreasing age and experience of personnel was another important issue. The recession had forced PW to cut back on staff and, as a result, lower-level employees were being promoted more rapidly than they had been in the past, and no one expected "any reversal in this trend."[120]

As managers became partners at a younger age, increased emphasis on professional development became essential. Albert Cohen, the national director of professional development, sought to improve audit education by requiring an extensive change in the course programming. The audit department had a thorough introductory course for new college graduates but only a series of yearly meetings for seniors and managers. Moreover, the meetings were heavily social in purpose and content, featuring golf and other recreational activities as well as professional improvement.[121]

Cohen attacked the problem by enriching the content of programs. Courses that sought to coordinate what had previously been only departmental continuing education efforts were developed by a rotating group of managers assigned by the National Office. They were taught by a mix of partners, managers, and outside experts, and in this way reflected PW's view that its personnel should be exposed to the broadest possible experience in order to give good client service. By imparting a broad scope to continuing education, Cohen was not contradicting the need for specialization, but rather buttressing PW's commitment to being a full-service firm in which each department acted in a supportive role toward others.

Knowledge was shared across departments through education, and by adding tax and MAS material to audit continuing education and vice versa. These changes in professional development were timely, for many states were then passing measures requiring forty hours of continuing education to enhance professional ability. In 1975, the Policy Committee made this standard a minimum requirement. By the mid-1970s, the firm was spending over $4 million each year in out-of-pocket costs on the development and presentation of programs. This large expenditure of resources reflected the growing realization that on-the-job training was no longer enough, and that the stream of highly technical FASB pronouncements now made extensive classroom work necessary. It was also important for PW to match the programs provided by other firms in order to continue to attract high-quality applicants.[122]

In the meantime, having redesigned PW's leadership shortly after taking office, Biegler again reorganized the firm in 1976. The old system, in which all sixty partners-in-charge reported directly to him, had become impractical, so he limited his direct reports to five vice chairmen—of Accounting and Auditing Services, Tax Services, MAS, and International—and the vice chairman/deputy senior partner for U.S. operations.[123] These partners were based in the National Office and provided support services to the partners-in-charge. Exhibit 6.4 shows the firm organization near the end of Biegler's tenure.

Biegler further restructured PW into four geographical regions, each supervised by a regional managing partner (RMP) drawn from the Policy Committee. These positions provided national responsibility to four more Policy Committee members who were viewed as candidates to succeed Biegler. Together with the deputy senior partner, the RMPs formed an operating committee responsible for operations and finance, administration, and management of the firm, and they made recommendations for action to the Policy Committee. Under the new system, partners-in-charge reported to RMPs, and RMPs were given executive responsibility for practice office operations in each of the four regions. RMPs visited offices and inquired about progress and problems. Although the regional system was needed to simplify reporting, to divide the firm into more manageable sections, and to improve the monitoring of the firm's overall performance, creating the RMP positions was "very sensitive" because, historically, each partner had a direct line to the senior partner. However, RMPs were only a half-step toward greater centralization and supervision; they lacked personal decision-making power, reserved for the whole Policy Committee and the senior partner, over partner admissions, assignments, retirements, transfers, and compensation. Under these circumstances, RMPs found it difficult to assert authority over partners.[124]

Biegler continued to publicize information about partnership compensation throughout his tenure. During the Metcalf proceedings, he released written information about his own income and shares, as well as about the total number of shares owned by the Policy Committee and top management. By the end of his term, he had implemented another refinement to the partner compensation plan that measured work at three performance levels. In the retirement area, he moved to correct the imbalances that had developed over many years and to promote greater equity between working and retired partners by lowering the ceiling on the number of shares that could be owned by a

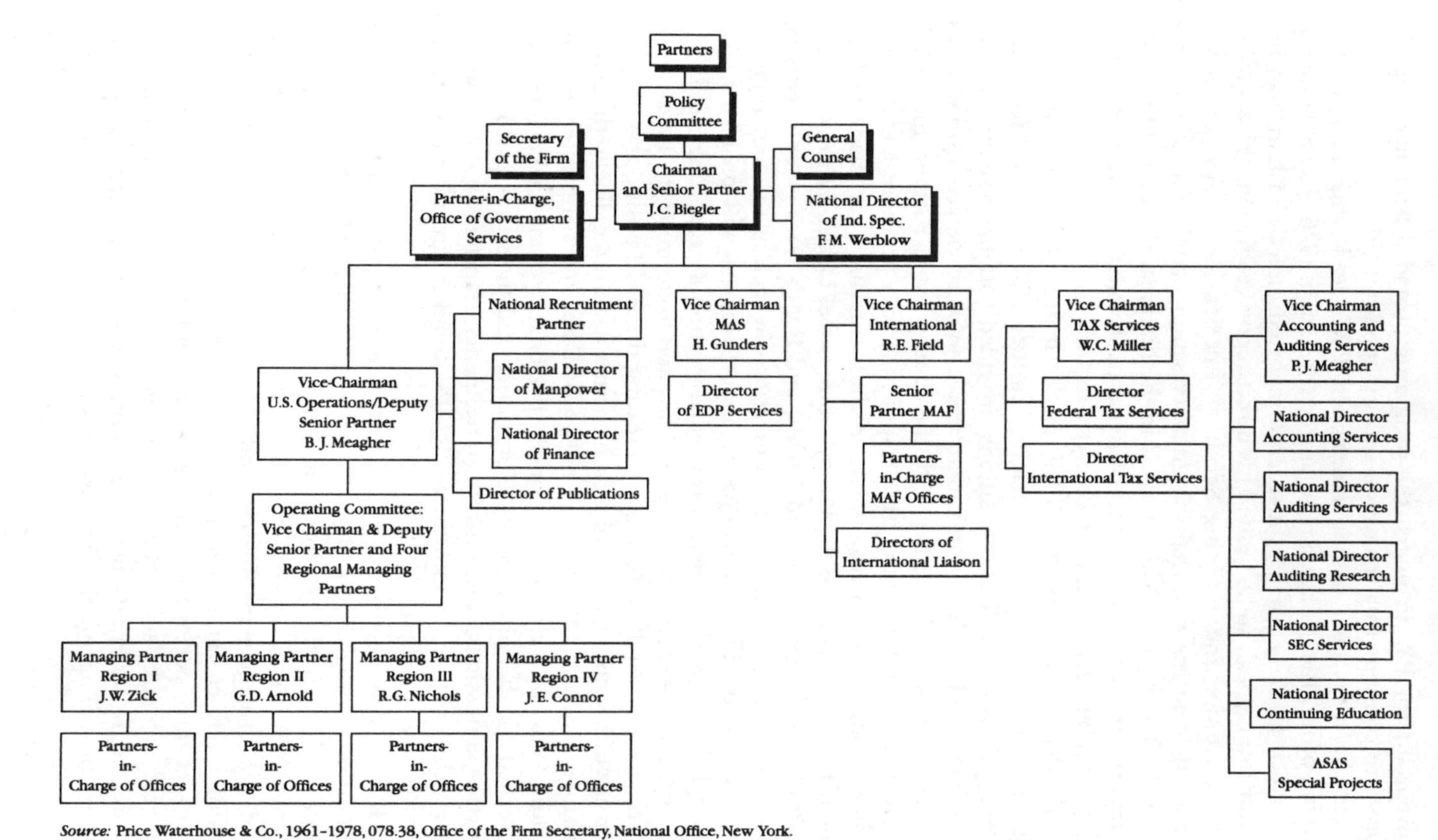

Source: Price Waterhouse & Co., 1961–1978, 078.38, Office of the Firm Secretary, National Office, New York.

EXHIBIT 6.4 U.S. Firm Organization Chart, July 1977

retired partner. He also changed the firm's mandatory retirement provisions, allowing for early retirement at age 55 with no penalty.[125]

As John Biegler's years as senior partner drew to a close, PW continued to face fierce competition, a volatile economy, and an increased litigation burden, as well as widespread public skepticism about the effectiveness of the profession's role. The Metcalf investigation, in particular, seemed a climax to the decade's events. "When the long history of the firm and the profession is written, the past twelve months will merit being singled out as representing a very critical turning point for us," Biegler told the partners in 1977. "Never has there been a year of greater challenge or perhaps, for some, even greater personal trial." Although he still had one year remaining in his second five-year term, Biegler retired early to assume the chairmanship of the International Firm. In October 1978, Biegler was succeeded as senior partner of PW in the United States by Joseph Connor.[126]

Despite the turbulent environment of the 1970s, Biegler had helped PW steer a steady course. Although the firm had struggled, along with the rest of the Big Eight, with a desultory economy, severe competition, and hostile publicity, it rose to meet these challenges, ultimately because of its willingness to adopt democratic processes, professionalize the practice, forthrightly respond to its critics, and market its business. Having opened up its voting procedures for the Policy Committee and senior partner, reformed its retirement system, and disclosed more information about partner compensation, PW made important steps in the 1970s toward becoming a more democratic organization. The firm had professionalized its practice in a number of important ways, such as by promoting specialization, strengthening audit review procedures, and enlarging support functions for each of the practice areas. It was the first of the Big Eight to undergo a peer review, and it chose to respond directly and openly to the Metcalf investigation and the illegal payments scandal. Finally, the firm took an important step in creating new business opportunities by establishing the Office of Federal Services, improving its public relations, and enhancing its practice development. PW's willingness to make these changes helped position the firm to greet the dilemmas and new opportunities of the 1980s.

CHAPTER 7

New Directions, 1978–1988

During the 1970s, changes had swept through the accounting world. Congressional investigations, an explosion of litigation, stiff competition within the profession, and innovation in its standard-setting process violently disturbed almost forty years of relative calm. Disruptive as they were, these events were merely a prelude to the 1980s, when it became clear that the traditional practice of large firms, as established by the securities legislation of the 1930s, was breaking down.

Three significant trends emerged in the business environment of the 1980s, each with enormous implications for the future of the accounting profession. First, the ongoing revolutions in information and communication technologies wrought a fundamental change in the ways in which accountants performed their work, creating new opportunities in consulting, tax, and other specialties. Second, the 1980s saw widespread restructuring of American-based businesses, including accounting firms. These were years of turmoil and upheaval in American industry, as many proud companies struggled and some disappeared. All the Big Eight firms wrestled with the implications of these changes. Although each pursued its own individual strategy, a common pattern emerged of a strong turn toward specialization in every area, as well as an effort to join forces through acquisition and merger. Finally, the rapid globalization of the American economy made it increasingly important for major firms to strengthen an international presence and to speed the harmonization of worldwide standards.[1]

During his senior partnership, Joseph E. Connor led a number of critical changes in Price Waterhouse's management and organization to meet these challenges, in some cases clearly breaking with traditions long a part of the firm's history. Perhaps the most visible example of his strong leadership was his ability to marshal the partners to support a merger with a major rival. Like many of his predecessors, Connor assumed a leading role as a spokesman for the accounting profession.

The 1980s saw the establishment of the PW World Firm and the beginnings of management and integration of the business on a global scale. Internally, PW continued its crucial shift from a generalist to a specialist orientation. This change of focus was assisted by adopting a strategic direction that reinforced the independence of its partners, one of the firm's oldest traditions. Another important change was PW's fresh enthusiasm for marketing; not since Arthur Lowes Dickinson's day had a senior partner personified so completely what current senior partner Shaun F. O'Malley has called "market consciousness."[2] Throughout all the turmoil, as it introduced new strategies and successfully tackled its problems, the firm maintained its premier reputation. By the end of the decade, PW had developed an extraordinary dynamism, having grown and changed more dramatically in this period than ever before in its history.[3]

RESTRUCTURING AT THE TOP

Connor described his early career path at PW as fairly traditional. After graduating from the University of Pittsburgh, he went to the business school at Columbia University, where he received his MBA. In 1956, he joined PW in New York as a staff accountant and, in 1961, began two years in New York's small business department. When he resumed work with the general staff, he became lead manager on the Exxon audit and, after admission to the partnership in 1967, continued with Exxon. In 1973, he left New York to head the firm's Los Angeles office. A year later, he was elected to the Policy Committee, and in 1976, he became regional managing partner for the western United States.[4]

The process, initiated during Biegler's term, that led to Connor's election as senior partner marked a departure from PW's own past practice and was unusual for any major accounting firm. The choice took place among candidates who were members of the Policy Committee and who were known to the partners on a national, rather than a regional, basis. The identification of a prospective senior partner was done by a nominating committee selected by noneligible members of the Policy Committee and approved by the full committee as well as elected by the partnership as a whole. In its search for a new senior partner, members of the nominating committee canvassed each partner and then reached a consensus.[5] The committee nominated Connor, who was then voted on, in a secret ballot, by all the partners.

Connor was, in the eyes of many partners, just what the firm needed—a more aggressive, less traditionalist leader known for his pragmatic, hard-driving, "let's get things done even if we make mistakes" approach. Early in 1978, he was appointed deputy senior partner when Biegler decided to leave the U.S. firm early in order to serve as chairman of PW International. Connor assumed his new duties as senior partner in the fall of that year.[6]

Connor initiated immediate organizational changes. He described the management structure he inherited as fragmented, with sixty-two geographic offices and four regional managing partners who had no direct line authority over the practice offices. His first step was to install an expanded top management structure. He instituted an office of the chairman consisting of the senior partner and two deputy senior partners and co-chairmen, John W. Zick for operations and Robert G. Nichols for practice planning and support. (Zick was succeeded by Thomas L. Raleigh, Jr., and Nichols first by Henry Gunders and then by Burnell H. DeVos, Jr.) Under this arrangement, the four regional managing partners reported to the co-chairman of operations, as did the national directors of manpower and of finance. The vice chairmen of Tax, MAS, and Accounting and Auditing Services, and the national directors of industry specialization, practice development, services marketing, and continuing education reported to the co-chairman of practice planning and support. This delegation of responsibility left Connor free to think in terms of long-range strategies and public issues.[7]

Connor also reorganized PW's committee structure. In July 1979, the Policy Committee was expanded from twelve to sixteen members and renamed the Policy Board. Day-to-day operations and administrative responsibilities were handled, within policy guidelines, by a ten-person Management Committee, created in 1978, and composed of the chairman, the two co-chairmen, the three vice chairmen, and the four regional managing partners. Like a board of directors, the Policy Board provided oversight to this Management Committee.[8] Exhibit 7.1 shows the firm's organization following these changes.

In addition, Connor set the tone for firmwide, rather than officewide initiatives. The firm's "Audit of the 1990s" initiative, which built on the Audit Guide series that had been developed by the firm in the 1970s, envisaged that, within a decade, all of PW would have a common audit philosophy, method, and software. He indicated that he wanted to be involved in all major proposals, and he let the partners know that clients

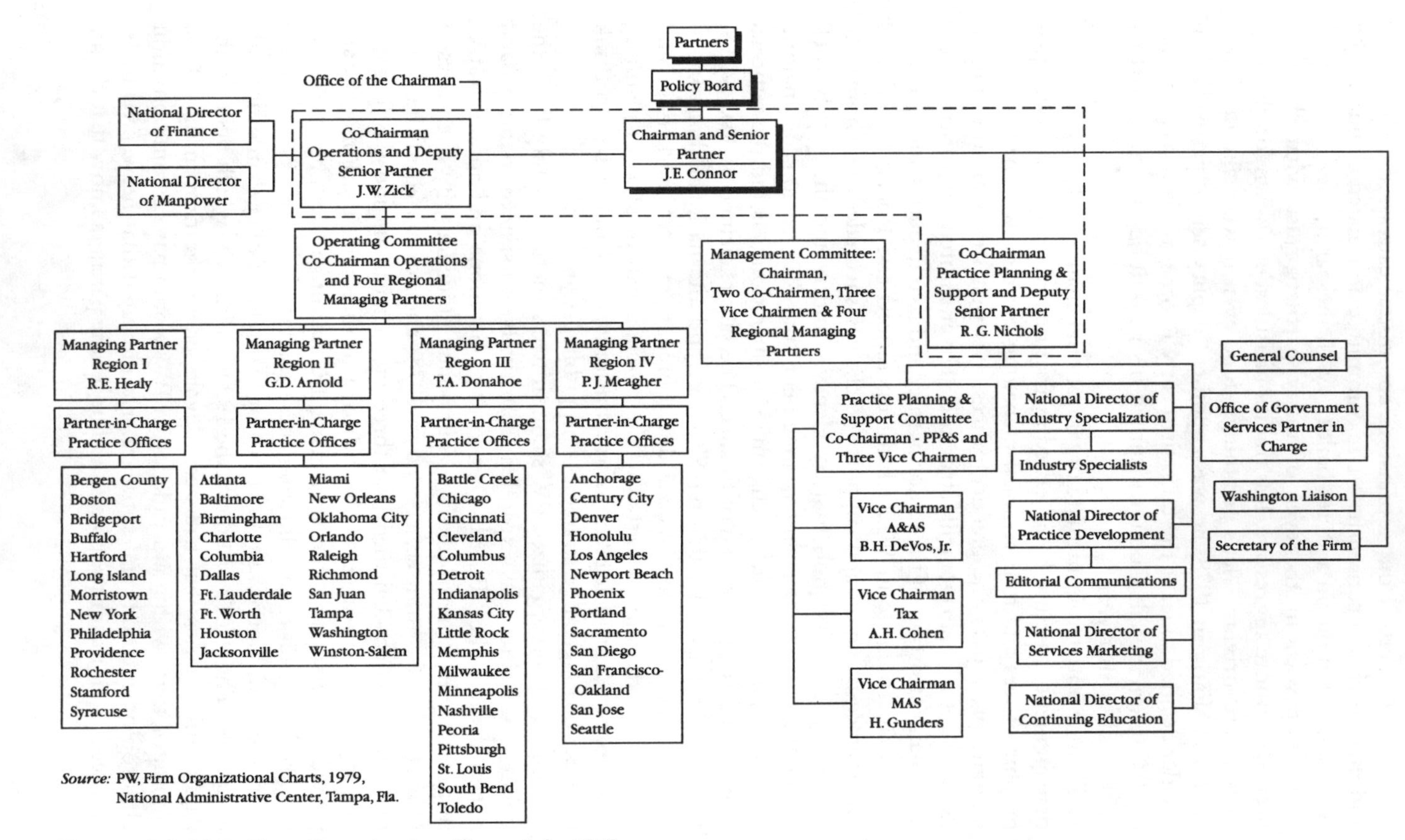

Source: PW, Firm Organizational Charts, 1979, National Administrative Center, Tampa, Fla.

EXHIBIT 7.1 U.S. Firm Organization Chart, July 1979

were the firm's top priority. "He'd upset the schedules of 20 other people to deal with a client," noted one of his deputy senior partners.[9]

Connor also acted decisively to maintain PW's role as a leader on issues of importance to the profession and to the business community generally. Facing an ever-mounting number of laws, regulations, and accounting rules, he told partners that

> [I do] not intend to sit at my desk for appreciable periods of time. I see my role clearly as the spokesman for the firm. I believe it is necessary for our positive public image that we be seen as a firm with ideas and a public interest.[10]

In the months preceding his first partners' meeting as senior partner, he met with the chairmen of twenty-one key clients, held five press interviews, and talked with senators, members of Congress, and members of the White House staff who dealt with the accounting profession.[11] Like other PW senior partners, he became a public spokesman for the firm, and addressed scores of diverse audiences on a variety of subjects "regardless of inherent controversy," making PW's views "clearly known, and contributing substantively to the public dialogue."[12] Connor spoke out on timely subjects, such as inflation accounting and international trade issues. He was often critical of the Financial Accounting Standards Board, taking issue, for example, with its position on pension accounting. On occasion, he put forward PW proposals for better internal financial controls in government and for a federal chief financial officer. This prominent role led one PW partner to note that "Joe speaks his mind and as a result, PW may on occasion march to its own drummer."[13]

Connor came to the senior partnership with a full appreciation of the changing competitive environment. In 1977, at a time of increasing demand by prospective, and even long-standing, clients for detailed and well-articulated proposals, he had been the manager of the major and successful effort for the Hewlett-Packard audit that set a precedent for the years ahead. Connor was prepared to make a major investment in specialization, arguing that in a "world increasingly becoming specialized, we were losing our advantage—which had always been to be everything to all people—a superbly trained generalist accountant."[14] He set an example in his own work with clients, such as the French company Pechiney, by emphasizing the importance of specialized experience. The company had turned to the U.S. firm because of PW's long-standing expertise in stock exchange and SEC matters.[15]

Connor and his new management team immediately affirmed a commitment to industry specialization. In certain lines of business, such as entertainment and petroleum, the firm had engaged in industry specialization for decades, but these early specialties had all been built around the accounting and audit relationship. The development of industry specialization in other areas had been slow, not only because of turf battles and a lack of clearcut objectives, but also because specialization had to take place within the firm's traditional generalist framework.

Under Connor, the Policy Board swiftly set a goal of identifying firm specialists, dipping into the ranks of the Tax and MAS departments to find them. In mid-1979, PW established continuing education courses and published brochures for its professionals working in key industries. A pilot program to enhance small business services called Comprehensive Professional Services was also started that year in several localities; by 1990, this client segment accounted for a significant part of the firm's annual growth. PW also developed incentives to encourage specialization such as compensation premiums and assurances to recruits that specialized work would not be a barrier when they became candidates for partnership in PW.[16]

To be successful, all of these initiatives needed to be integrated in an overall strategic direction, as the practice was changing quickly and posing dramatic challenges to the profession.

THE BREAKDOWN OF TRADITIONAL PRACTICE

During the 1980s, several factors, including new information technologies, a fresh stream of litigation, and public inquiry into the performance of American corporations led the large accounting firms to reassess the nature of their services. These factors converged around the audit, the source of most of the profession's revenues and profits since the 1930s.

When electronic data processing was first introduced to the business world during the 1950s and 1960s, most Big Eight firms were quick to embrace it. By the late 1970s, however, technological innovations took computing power out of the hands of programmers and consultants and into the hands of users; microcomputers developed and proliferated. As electronic spreadsheet software became readily available, accountants and auditors were increasingly forced to rely on electronic records. In addition, the historical distinction between MAS and audit expertise began to erode, as auditors needed to know much more about computer technology and its applications, which were formerly the exclusive preserve of MAS consultants, and as consultants became more knowledgeable about the auditing procedure.[17]

The increased speed and reliability of computers also led to greater pressure to provide more complete and meaningful attestations. Over time, automated workpaper packages and statistical sampling programs were developed to meet these needs. As the pace of automated audit tasks accelerated, the auditor's focus changed as well, with greater emphasis placed on systematic risk analysis and analytical review. The growing sophistication of computer technology and its applications called for a new mix of audit personnel and for greater allocation of manager and partner time to an assignment. Moreover, as more accounting and auditing systems became computerized, questions arose. Were auditing techniques suitable for a manual environment adequate for testing a complex computerized system? How could integrity, basic controls, completeness, and accuracy be ensured? Accountants sought to address these questions throughout the 1980s.[18]

The use of microcomputers for auditing procedures also made it easier for the auditor to perform tests that might lead to the discovery of fraud. In addition, data manipulation provided more opportunities to pass on additional information of greater value to the client. Developments that permitted an enhanced audit were critically important in the 1980s, when audit work was declining as a percentage of total business.[19]

The question of whether the audit was a commodity, "a fungible good" that was "acquired based solely on price," had been discussed in the 1970s. A number of factors combined to make the issue more pressing a decade later. Lifting the ban on advertising by accountants intensified the competitive environment, and fees were cut even as costs rose. At the same time, inflation and cost-cutting by clients continued to squeeze profit margins. In some cases, firms reduced the audit to a more routine, even minimal, amount of service. Clients had become much more self-sufficient, and their in-house accounting and auditing skills had increased dramatically. In addition, accounting standards had proliferated. Originally justified by the goal of maintaining high quality and assuring consistency, the increase in rules was also perceived to reduce an audit's unique quality. This impression was reinforced by the decline in the average number of years of experience of accountants engaged in audits, although the quality of the individual from a technical or educational standpoint was often superior. Those clients willing to believe the worst felt that there was nothing unique about an audit by a Big Eight firm.[20]

Insistence that the audit was simply a commodity gave rise to the practice of clients' shopping for the cheapest price. By the 1980s, this became a serious concern; in 1984, for example, some 450 public companies, many of them small, changed auditors, more than in any recent year and nearly double the number in 1981. According to filings with the SEC, "cost savings" and "service" were the main reasons for these changes, although nearly 20 percent of the firms were dropped by clients because the accountants had submitted a qualified or dissenting opinion on financial statements.[21]

Accountants found alarming the suggestion that the audit was a commodity. They profoundly disagreed with a notion whose implications threatened the very foundation of their profession. Not only did it create a sense of unpredictability, but it also threatened to lead to difficulty attracting to the profession talented young people, who were not enchanted by the thought that auditing was merely a "compliance" function and that much of it was routine work suitable for junior staff. That accounting work was being perceived to be less interesting or attractive by college students seemed to be confirmed by the statistics: during the 1970s, the number of accounting graduates with bachelor's degrees doubled, increasing from 23,800 to 49,870; during the 1980s, the figure rose slightly, and then fell to 1977 levels.[22]

Over time, client desires for more experienced accountants, staff interest in more rewarding work, and the general cost-cutting climate of the 1980s led to a dramatic change in audit working patterns. The typical "pyramid" in an auditing assignment of the 1960s had been composed of one partner and approximately fifteen staff members. By the 1980s, although the partner and managers remained, the number of seniors and staff accountants had declined. This trend continued, forcing PW and the accounting firms to pay closer attention to recruiting, developing, and keeping their staff. In late 1987, PW eliminated overtime pay, boosted its entry-level salaries by as much as a third, and increased vacation time in order to continue to attract the highest-quality accounting graduates.[23]

Critics highlighted anachronisms in accounting standards that encouraged, they argued, a short-term orientation by some business leaders. Periodic financial statements, prepared pursuant to generally accepted accounting principles, could show increased profits even when the long-term economic health of an enterprise was in jeopardy, and this fact was a source of great concern to outside users of these statements. As limitations in financial statements became clear, new, more relevant accounting models were sought that could deal with uncertainty and day-to-day change. Some analysts called for more extensive use of nonfinancial indicators.[24]

These criticisms, in conjunction with the revolution in information technology, accelerated a growing interest in soft data. First encouraged by the SEC and the FASB in the late 1970s, soft data comprised financial information that in many cases could be neither exactly determined nor effectively verified by auditors. Such information was often presented outside the body of basic financial statements and was not audited or reported on directly by the auditor. To understand and convey this information effectively, CPAs had to become increasingly involved with less objective, and less auditable, data than those underpinning basic financial statements.[25]

Financial forecasting was one kind of soft data that became increasingly popular. With the rapid inflation of the 1970s and 1980s making it increasingly difficult for investors to predict a company's financial future, the SEC decided in 1978 to encourage forecasting. This decision spurred a demand by investors for supplemental information about companies' physical plants, present and prospective products, personnel, operating and planning systems, and strategies. When asked to compare the usefulness of quantitative measures included in financial statements with other financial information, two-thirds of the respondents in a 1985 Harris poll indicated that "quantitative information presented outside the financial statements, such as management observations, strategic plans and goals, market growth, etc., often can be more useful than quantitative measures included in the financial statements."[26]

The concept of "continuous auditing," to accompany the constant flow of financial information, considered by many as the wave of the future, was another innovation growing out of the instantaneous nature of computer-generated information. Use of accounting software to analyze, sample, and test the correct functioning of client systems gave auditors the opportunity to access, test, and sample systems. Continuous auditing permitted a moving picture instead of the old snapshot. Although investors traditionally waited until the end of each quarter for financial results, within "ten to fifteen years," predicted some experts in the mid-1980s, "corporate financial statements will be supplanted by a steady flow of computer-generated information."[27]

Faced with the possibility that their work might be superseded, treated as a commodity, or lose its significance, CPAs responded by defining their audit work more expansively, as just one part of a continuum of services. One suggestion for a value-added service was based on expanding the auditor's responsibility for detecting fraud.[28]

A Looming Liability Crisis

During the early 1980s, the accounting profession faced a rising tide of litigation as business failures growing out of the recession of this period led to a marked increase in lawsuits.[29]

One explanation for the upswing in litigation involving accountants was the evolution of legal doctrine, for courts continued to extend the responsibility for product liability to accountants. By the 1980s, there was a broadening of the parties who had a cause of action on the grounds that they had relied on an accountant's report. Although most courts held that a party's reliance on the financial statements or other information supplied by the accountant had to be either known or actually foreseen by the accountant, others promulgated an unrestricted foreseeability rule, making an accountant liable for ordinary negligence to anyone "whom the accountant could have reasonably foreseen would rely on his financial report."[30] Moreover, in a decision eroding the privity doctrine and enlarging negligence liability, New Jersey's highest court expressly assumed the availability of insurance coverage for accountants, when in fact, by the mid-1980s, it had become painfully apparent that no such stable pool of insurance existed. Big Eight accountants felt that they were being pinned under a "crushing burden of limitless liability" and had become the "insurers for all business failures."[31] Their firms had paid close to $180 million in damages in audit-related settlements between 1980 and 1985, with Arthur Andersen having paid out $137.1 million, Peat, Marwick $19.4 million, Ernst & Whinney $6.0 million, Deloitte, Haskins & Sells $5.0 million, Coopers & Lybrand $4.4 million, PW $3.5 million, Touche Ross $2.3 million, and Arthur Young $1.5 million.[32]

Accountants took heart when New York's highest court, in 1985, upheld the classic rule on privity, which stated that the profession generally could not be held liable for negligence to third parties, a rule first enunciated in the *Ultramares* case fifty years earlier. The inability of courts and juries to distinguish between "audit failure" and "business failure," however, was demonstrated in its most extreme form in 1983, when one federal appeals court decision upheld the application of the RICO (Racketeer-Influenced and Corrupt Organization) statute to an accounting firm.[33]

Accountants were also in retreat in cases alleging fraud under the federal securities laws. A number of courts had relaxed the requirement that to sue an accountant plaintiffs must have relied on his or her alleged misrepresentations. However, in a 1982 federal court case that went well for the profession, the jury found that an accounting firm could not be sued by client management for failing to detect or report a $25 million inventory fraud involving at least two of the client's corporate officers. The court of appeals affirmed the jury verdict and drew a distinction between fraud on behalf of the company, such as by management, and fraud against the company by a single employee. Although auditors must investigate if they suspect fraud, the court held that auditors "are not detectives to ferret out fraud" and noted that the management had made fraud impossible to detect in this case because they had turned the company "into an engine of theft against outsiders." Thereafter, the accounting firm was permitted to sue the company to retrieve the $3.5 million that the firm had paid to the client's shareholders in a 1980 class-action suit.[34]

Litigation was yet another pressure brought to bear on the audit. It increased the need to search for fraud and lent credence to the argument that such an inquiry should be made a standard part of the audit. Commentators noted that the threat of expanded liability of auditors for detecting fraud brought higher costs to an already tight pricing market.[35]

Pressure for a More Effective Audit

The reforms of the 1970s, including the peer reviews required by the AICPA's SEC Practice Section and the wider participation in setting accounting standards permitted by the FASB, enabled the profession to make significant strides toward continued self-regulation. Ongoing problems with the FASB's effectiveness and another congressional investigation into accounting firms and their activities, however, appeared to signal the need for further government intervention. In the end, the demands of clients and the public for a more effective audit meshed well with the profession's own needs to enhance and supplement its services.

Observers of the FASB encouraged the perception that the profession needed more oversight. The standard-setting board was often criticized for being out of touch with its constituency. It had become embroiled in a series of controversies, most notably over accounting practices for pensions and inflation. Moreover, it was making very slow progress toward establishing a conceptual framework for future decisions.[36]

Some of the FASB's problems were structural, having arisen out of changes in the process of standard setting. Under the FASB's predecessors, the Committee on Accounting Procedure and the Accounting Principles Board, the profession had recommended initiatives in proposed accounting standards and sought the SEC's reaction. By the 1980s, the SEC had begun to take an increasingly active role in the standard-setting process, and its input was given great weight. In accounting for inflation and in accounting for oil and gas companies, "it was not unusual for the SEC to propose new standards and for the professional institutions, led by the FASB, to implement the changes."[37] The FASB's absolute mandate seemed less clear. In addition, it was criticized for its slow and cumbersome decision-making process, as well as for creating a standards overload.[38]

As the FASB struggled with these issues, accountants came under fire for their role in the banking scandals of the early 1980s. The failures of Penn Square Bank and Continental Illinois National Bank and Trust gave rise to public concern about the efficacy of audits and about the auditor's responsibility to search for fraud. Because these banks had been given "clean opinions," critics identified their business failures as "audit failures" and, rather than examining the cause of the business failure, contended that the profession's self-regulation process was inadequate. Public outcry increased when federal officials closed down the Beverly Hills Savings & Loan in 1985. That this bank had employed three different accounting firms in ninety days was seen as a perfect, if egregious, example of shopping for a clean opinion.[39]

Prompted by these developments, Michigan congressman John D. Dingell, chairman of the House Energy and Commerce Oversight and Investigations Committee, convened an investigation into the accounting profession and the SEC in February 1985. He opened the hearings with the stern warning that the profession was facing its "last opportunity to regulate itself." Comparing independent public accountants to "sorcerers," he declared that "it is impossible to understand the auditors themselves since all we know is the little they choose to tell us." Aside from the ineffectiveness of the profession's self-regulatory structure, Dingell considered a wide range of issues, including proposals to prohibit accounting firms from providing management or tax consulting services to audit clients, to require that accounting firms publish annual reports giving the same information that companies disclose, to require that auditors assume responsibility for preparing financial statements and disclose that responsibility in their report, and to require that the SEC assign auditors to publicly held companies and rotate the appointments periodically.[40]

Testimony at early hearings was given by, among others, an SEC commissioner, the AICPA president, and the chairman of the FASB, as well as by accounting professors and leaders of the large firms, including Joseph Connor of PW. Connor's testimony drew on a PW white paper that reviewed the recent history of the accounting profession and recommended actions to bolster accountants' declining stature and remedies to contain the mounting liability crisis.[41]

Connor explained that concern focused on three issues: public misunderstandings and unrealistic expectations of what an audit can and should accomplish, competitive pressures on the audit that could undermine its quality and independence, and inadequate oversight in the peer-review process, which appeared "too secretive, too self-contained, and too hesitant in punishing substandard audit performance and practice." In addition, he also focused on the liability crisis, which posed financial burdens "of unprecedented magnitude" on the profession.

Connor proposed that the profession seize the initiative by calling for expanded auditing standards, enhanced self-regulation, and equity in civil liability. He spoke out for reports that covered both the financial position and the financial condition of companies. With such information, he argued, the public would be better informed of "expectations as to the prospective realization of assets, occurrence of liabilities, and cash flows" within a company's operating environment. He also suggested new standards, requiring an auditor to review and evaluate management controls, and to identify red flags that would indicate a higher risk of fraud or an intentional misstatement of financial records. Connor did not believe that these procedures would detect all instances of material fraud, or that the auditor should accept responsibility for doing so, but he felt that they would help substantially to reduce the risk that fraud would go undetected.[42]

Connor also argued that simply fine tuning the current system would be inadequate to improve the peer-review process. Rather than continue with the SEC's informal oversight, PW's solution was to create a self-regulating organization under the Securities Exchange Act of 1934 that would incorporate the substance of the SEC Practice Section program with several improvements. These included mandatory membership of all firms and individuals who were auditors of SEC registrants, creation of a governing board that represented the profession, business, and the public interest, and greater oversight by the SEC on rule making, disciplinary procedures, membership, and administration. Although the proposed agency featured "governmentally supervised self-regulation, not direct SEC regulation," it would not have auditing or accounting standard-setting authority, which would remain with the Auditing Standards Board and the FASB.

Connor recommended that the profession seek self-help measures such as the establishment of professional corporations to protect the personal assets of partners from vicarious liability. He also urged the profession to work to secure both legislative and judicial remedies at the state and federal levels. "If the accounting profession is to sustain the public's faith and confidence in our role and ultimately in the financial reporting system," he noted, "we cannot stubbornly refuse" to accept change in current auditing standards and peer review. Nor can the profession "stand by and allow civil liability to undermine our viability."[43]

PW used the forum provided by the congressional hearings as an opportunity to identify a more sharply defined contribution that an audit might make to the business world. The firm acknowledged the public's interest in guarding against fraud by suggesting that the focus of the audit be broadened and that auditors accept the responsibility for searching for management fraud that might be detected in the examination of financial statements. PW auditors prided themselves on their "business" approach to auditing, which they viewed as an art not a science, and believed that they could add value using audit work as a base. Connor's proposals laid the foundation for an enhanced, value-added audit.[44]

Although the AICPA and other accounting firm leaders reacted negatively to Connor's suggestions, his proposals anticipated a parallel development in another quarter. In 1985, in reaction to the commencement of the congressional hearings, the AICPA, the American Accounting Association, the Financial Executives Institute, and the Institute of Internal Auditors convened the Treadway Commission to look into the question of fraud. Chaired by former SEC commissioner James C. Treadway, the Commission on Fraudulent Financial Reporting consulted with all parties to the problem, including the reporting entities, the regulatory apparatus, and the accounting firms. Completing its work in early 1987, the Treadway Commission concluded that the auditor's report "suffers from substantial shortcomings" and recommended that it be revised to communicate the auditor's role and responsibility more effectively, particularly regarding fraud detection.[45]

Overall, congressional attitudes toward the profession had moderated since the 1970s, and, despite his tough talk, Dingell was seeking answers rather than searching for scapegoats. Criticism of accountants in these hearings took a less vitriolic and accusatory cast than it had in the past. Nevertheless, by the mid-1980s, it was clear that changes in audit standards would further expand the scope of an auditor's work and responsibility. This process had already begun with the 1982 revision of the AICPA's auditing standards to state that "an auditor has responsibility to search for material errors or irregularities and must audit with professional skepticism and awareness that fraud might occur." This statement was quite a change from earlier pronouncements, which merely insisted that an audit was not designed to uncover fraud and could not be relied on as a guarantee against it.[46]

The Diversification of Services

As growth in audit work leveled off, consulting practices within major accounting firms expanded dramatically. Information technology was a significant part of this expansion, for although it had always been the foundation of the profession's consulting work, the complexity and applications of information technology to business had grown exponentially. For many companies, computer systems had become fundamental to their operations, and to stay competitive, they had to take advantage of new developments in this field:

> Information technology is no longer restricted to automating back office functions. It is creating new manufacturing methodologies that outstrip the old, it is generating entirely new classes of products and services, it is bringing new levels of internal cooperation to nationwide and worldwide organizations, and it is opening up important ways of buying and selling.[47]

Clients increasingly asked accountants how to make use of financial information for their business advantage. As a result, the scope of accountants' services expanded and diversified. Market research showed that the wider the range of assistance that an accounting and management consulting firm supplied, the greater the client's perception of the quality of services received. This finding dovetailed perfectly with client demands for a package of services with specialized functions and with the Big Eight's need to diversify.[48]

As technological systems became more sophisticated, however, so too did the knowledge required to master them. To provide these higher-value services and to advise clients on important financial and information matters, accountants needed a good understanding of information technology and its applications to individual industries.[49] To be successful, accounting firms had to become familiar with each client's total environment. Companies demanded that their financial advisers have professionals dedicated to the study of the industries to which the companies belonged. These experts were expected to monitor industry developments, to understand the impact of technology on the industry, to be able to advise on technological innovations, and to be knowledgeable about the dynamics of profit-and-loss and business strategies. The largest accounting firms focused on improving and broadening their services to major companies. Multinationals, in particular, required a wide range of sophisticated services in many countries with a variety of government regulations, management styles, and currency and taxation regulations, all demanding specialized skills.[50]

Companies struggling to control rising expenditures for communications, document production and reproduction, and information retrieval often suffered from a lack of integration among their different technological systems. Accounting firms began to help clients design, organize, and monitor these systems. Among the important consulting areas spawned by information technology was systems integration, which involved the design and installation of multifaceted client computer systems.[51]

Systems integration and other management consulting work had a significant impact on accounting firms' income, as management consulting services became an ever-larger portion of the Big Eight's revenues. In 1987, consulting averaged 21 percent of total fees or chargeable hours of the biggest American accounting firms, compared with only 12 percent a decade earlier. Five of the ten top management consulting firms in the nation were accounting firms, with Arthur Andersen in first place and Peat, Marwick, Price Waterhouse, Ernst & Whinney, and Coopers & Lybrand in fifth, eighth, ninth, and tenth place, respectively. Andersen's consulting practice amounted to 33 percent of the firm's almost $2 billion in worldwide revenues in 1987 and involved primarily the design of computer systems. Consulting revenues at all the major firms were growing at an average of 30 percent annually, almost double the growth of auditing and tax revenues.[52]

The lucrative consulting opportunities offered by technological advances were not unalloyed blessings. New technology allowed banks, lawyers, and financial planners to provide services traditionally offered by accounting firms. Many of them, as well as consulting firms, law firms providing tax services, and large information systems companies, now competed with accountants in these new areas. Consulting had become a battlefield, and the weapons were well-trained specialists, sophisticated software systems, and the ability to "interface" with a client.[53]

THE PROFESSIONAL ENVIRONMENT

In view of the changes in direction of traditional practice, PW decided on a comprehensive re-examination of the firm's strategy and management. The firm had not formally re-assessed its direction since the 1960s, when Herman Bevis had implemented his program of planned growth. With so many changes affecting the profession, it now seemed appropriate to reconsider basic questions about the business. The consensus of the Policy Committee in the late 1970s was that PW did not really have an integrated and well-articulated strategy responsive to the current and expected economic forces of the time.

In April 1979, the firm engaged the management consulting firm McKinsey & Company to assess its strategic position. Inviting those from outside the profession to examine the firm would have been unthinkable a decade earlier, and even in 1979, some partners looked askance at the prospect. McKinsey's first mission was to assist the partners in determining the significance of the audit in an increasingly competitive world, as well as the possibility of developing a distinctive PW audit. The McKinsey team undertook an extensive fact-gathering project, followed by an analysis of the three practice areas. It also studied the firm's client base, identified client needs, and analyzed industry specialization.

In March 1980, McKinsey began a series of discussions, stretching over the next two years, on issues identified as important to PW's overall strategy. In May 1981, it presented the Policy Board with a plan for an integrated approach, bringing together its studies of the three practice areas. McKinsey concluded its investigation in February 1982. Throughout the whole process, and consistent with PW's traditions, all reports and recommendations were extensively reviewed and discussed by the partners in sectional meetings.[54] These discussions led to revisions in area geography, stimulated new initiatives, and reinforced changes in emphasis already undertaken. The McKinsey study clarified two core principles as the basis for a strategic direction. The first of these was that the engagement partner remained the "fundamental, [professionally] autonomous, self-motivated decision maker" within PW. The second emphasized that the firm's "primary focus" should be the rendering of "superior and distinctive client services."

The notion of a professionally autonomous engagement partner confirmed a long-standing tradition and emphasized the responsibilities, and the opportunities, of the partner in developing and managing the practice. The engagement partner had full authority to make decisions on client service and to speak for PW in matters related to the client, but effective decision making also required consultation with other partners and use of information gathered by the firm's support resources.

To implement the second core principle, and to ensure that the focus of the partnership was in the rendering of superior and distinctive client services, changes were necessary. The engagement partner had to provide more services tailored to individual client needs; all partners and managers had to communicate more effectively with clients; new products had to be developed continually to meet new needs; and better techniques had to be established for rendering existing services.[55]

Once it was affirmed that the professional autonomy of partners was not only the "keystone" of PW but also a distinctive competitive advantage, the question remained of how to capitalize on this asset. Ultimately, the partners decided that specialization was the answer. PW's new strategy represented a shift to a market-driven organization that sought out opportunities as demands for new services developed.

During the McKinsey study, it became clear that market opportunities outstripped PW's ability to pursue them simultaneously, especially since the firm was grappling with a serious personnel shortage. Although PW had experienced this problem in earlier decades, the 1980s presented a wider range of opportunities in which to deploy a larger, but still limited, pool of human resources. Under these circumstances, the firm had to make hard choices about how to position its people and its financial resources. Any new strategic emphasis had to rely heavily on ongoing efforts to build specialties such as the specialized practice units (SPUs) established in 1983, which had been developed from within the audit, tax, and consulting practices. These leading-edge units were growing rapidly and often hired outsiders who provided high visibility in certain industries.[56]

The success of the SPUs highlighted some deep-rooted structural obstacles to firmwide specialization. Recruitment of experienced professionals for SPUs was hampered by the firm's bias against direct admission to the partnership, which made it particularly difficult to hire non–CPAs at high levels. In addition, at least three other factors constrained the development of firmwide industry specialization. The first constraint was internal cultural resistance, based on PW's generalist tradition. It was still largely true that most firm members who were hired and trained as generalists resisted being channeled. This was partly because specialist assignments garnered less prestige for the assigned partner, yet the work involved required extensive travel, entailed significant writing and other demands, and provided few benchmarks to measure performance.[57]

The second constraint was the difficulty of developing enough specialized practitioners quickly, especially because of the way in which these were selected. Industry specialists typically arose from within the partnership and expanded their expertise and recognition after working with a leading client. One vice chairman noted that industry specialization was a bootstrap operation in which

> You became an industry specialist the way I did: You did three or four engagements and if you did enough of them, you became a specialist. The problem was that very few of these people were dedicated, so what we called an industry specialist was maybe spending fifty per cent of his time.[58]

Finally, even after industry specialists were expressly dedicated to particular activities, they still operated within the local practice office and were still assigned to the partner-in-charge. There were no barriers erected around professionals in SPUs, so local practice partners could "borrow" them quite easily for their own projects. As Connor noted regarding these local arrangements, "It was an organization that had served us well for too long and was focused almost totally on 'what opportunities do I have that I can see out of the corner of my window, down the street?'"[59]

Initiatives proceeded slowly. By 1981, the drive for industry specialization had lost some of its early momentum. PW's structure made it difficult to assign tour-of-duty managers to some specialties. In addition, partners-in-charge of specialties were unable to obtain needed personnel. Specialist morale was "fair at best."[60] For industry specialization to work, important changes were still needed. Among the most valuable results of the McKinsey study had been the recognition of the need to undertake ongoing strategic planning. In 1983, PW formalized its first in-house strategic planning function, committing partners and managers to the area full time. With the planning group's guidance, the firm began to move toward a new, strengthened area structure a year later.[61] (The firm's increased size had required the reorganization of the line structure in 1981, and the four existing regions were expanded into six practice areas: Metropolitan New York, New England and Upstate New York, Mid-Atlantic, Midwest, Far West, and Southwest as shown in Exhibit 7.2.) Ultimately, however, it took a much larger event—the merger discussions with Deloitte, Haskins & Sells—to galvanize the firm into decisive action.

The Restructuring of Corporate America

During the late 1970s and early 1980s, the competitive environment for American-based corporations changed dramatically. Until the late 1970s, high inflation and a weak dollar had protected many manufacturers from foreign competition, but with the disinflation that followed, manufacturers could no longer raise prices to recover cost increases. In addition, a sharp rise in the dollar's value made foreign products less expensive for Americans and American products more costly to foreigners. More important, a revolution in the organization and technology of manufacturing operations was occurring in Japanese and some European companies, putting American producers in an even more precarious competitive position.[62]

Although America still led the world in productivity, its economy was growing neither as fast as it had in the past nor as fast as the economies of other countries. Environmental factors such as the high cost of capital and the large and increasing share of business capital controlled by institutions pushed many American companies to manage for short-term results. Trade and regulatory conditions also played a significant role in investment decisions. Moreover, recurring weaknesses appeared in production technology and process improvement. In product quality, service to customers, and speed of product development, many American companies were no longer seen as world leaders.[63]

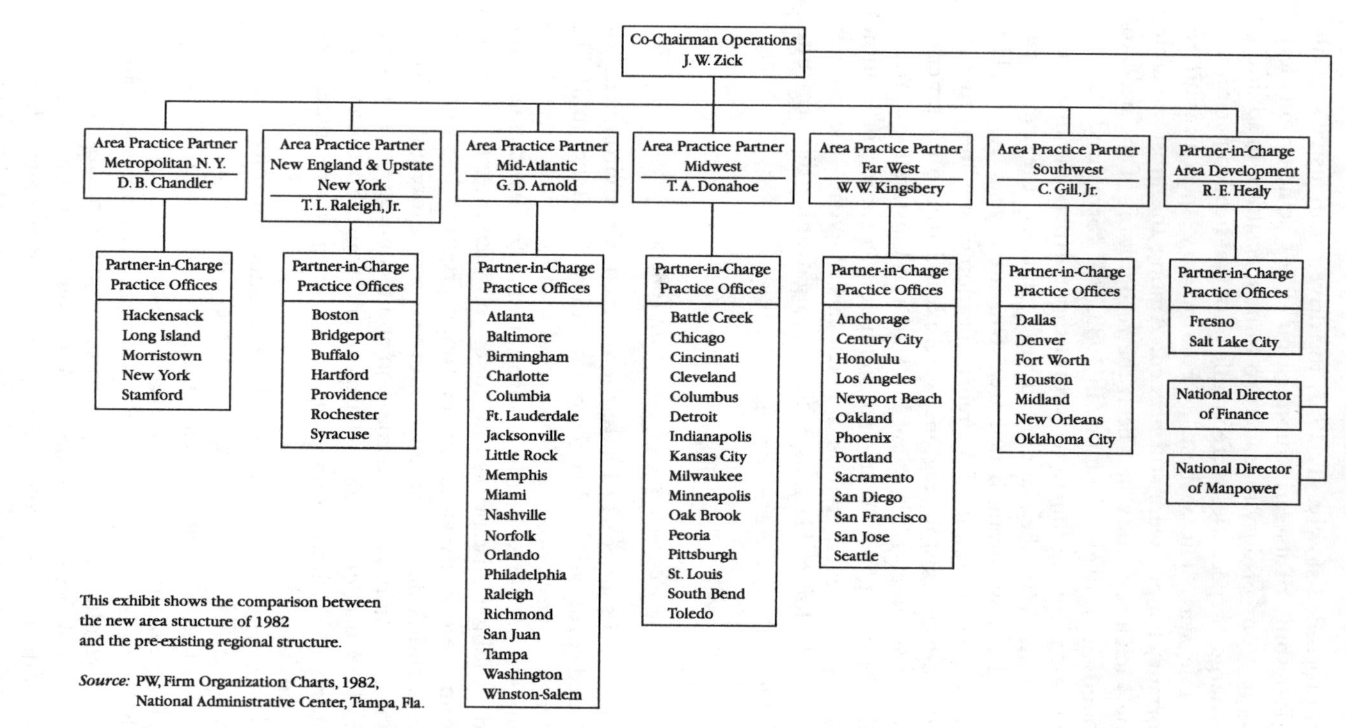

This exhibit shows the comparison between the new area structure of 1982 and the pre-existing regional structure.

Source: PW, Firm Organization Charts, 1982, National Administrative Center, Tampa, Fla.

EXHIBIT 7.2 U.S. Firm Organization Chart, Operating Line Organization, March 1982

In addition, a wave of takeovers, mergers, and acquisitions distracted corporate management from production concerns. In the eighteen months from January 1984 to June 1985, for example, nearly 400 of the 850 largest corporations underwent some type of restructuring or major portfolio change such as acquisition, divestiture, spin-off, or stock buy-back. From 1981 to 1986, the recorded number of large corporate acquisitions increased at a rate roughly double that of the 1970s, exceeding the pace of the conglomerate merger wave of the 1960s and reaching record highs in 1986. Although the 1980s merger boom included a smaller number of transactions than that of the 1960s, it was larger in terms of the gross sums involved and in the importance attached to it.[64]

The restructuring of corporate America had a number of important consequences for accountants. Firms lost clients and income, and competitive pressure on the profession intensified as a number of public companies left the scene. When General Foods merged with Philip Morris in November 1985, for example, PW lost General Foods to Coopers & Lybrand. Similarly, when General Electric acquired RCA, Peat, Marwick audited the newly merged company and Touche Ross lost RCA. Changes like these produced a net loss of audit dollars, for the audit fee of the newly merged entity averaged less than two-thirds of the combined audit fees of the two companies taken independently. On the other hand, the boom provided new business opportunities for accountants, and some firms, like Deloitte, Haskins & Sells and Touche Ross, began to emphasize consulting for investment bankers in mergers, reorganizations, and bankruptcies.[65]

PW sought to involve itself more deeply in the tax aspects of restructurings, mergers, and acquisitions. Although its specialists solved complicated tax problems and saved clients millions of dollars, the firm's late appearance in the process limited its ability to participate in restructurings and restricted fee revenues. Accordingly, PW decided to provide more than tax work for mergers and acquisitions so it would not be seen as simply "fixing up some technical issues." PW was the first of the Big Eight to register an investment adviser affiliate with the SEC. In doing so, the partnership sought to expand its services in the financial planning area. Partners contended that, whereas investment bankers were surrounded by the controversy growing out of their deals, independent CPAs could be depended on to give a more objective evaluation of financial information.[66]

Opportunistic versus Strategic Growth

Concerned about unfavorable business trends and the erosion of its traditional client base and apprehensive about how best to service an ever-widening array of client needs, PW began to look at more dramatic initiatives. When an opportunity suddenly arose to merge with Deloitte, Haskins & Sells, PW was attracted by the prospect, viewing it as a way to achieve growth on a grand scale overnight. As a result, Connor pursued the opportunity vigorously. To the PW leadership, the potential merger seemed to be a way to fulfill unmet needs quickly.

> We would have had twice as many people, and with the then-current resource shortages in the firm, it would give us a whole bunch of able people in a hurry. And that way we could blanket a huge market, which we weren't able to do with our own people.[67]

The prospect was also viewed with some concern. Such a merger, which would have been inconceivable a decade earlier, given the problems of mixing two disparate cultures, was seen by some as a "potentially divisive and destructive route to take."[68]

Talks between the two accounting giants began in the fall of 1984. Although there had been increased merger activity among smaller firms, this was the first hint of such changes among the Big Eight. Consolidating Deloitte's 103 American offices and 8,000 employees with PW's 90 American offices and 9,000 employees, and their comparable organizations overseas, would create the largest independent accounting firm in the world. Analysts of the profession generally stressed the positive sides of the merger, noting that it would result in a powerful consulting practice, stem the erosion of the audit business, and boost growth rates by realizing synergies from complementary client bases.[69]

The merger discussions, however, raised concern in the profession over economic concentration and potential antitrust implications. Members of smaller accounting firms noted that the Big Eight already audited 94 percent of the 1,536 companies listed on the New York Stock Exchange, and that a combined PW–Deloitte firm, plus Arthur Andersen, would audit almost half of those corporations. These critics also saw the merger as a potential threat to fast-growing areas such as consulting. They argued that the combined firm would be better able to invade the small business market, which previously had not been of much interest to the Big Eight. Congressman Dingell weighed in, as well, charging that the combination could have the "unintended and untoward result of setting off a merger wave among the Big Eight firms, resulting in the creation of the Big Four," which would lead to "unacceptable and inimical" competition. PW lawyers argued that the antitrust implications were remote because of the enormous amount of competition that existed outside the Big Eight, noting that barriers to entry in the profession were minimal. After review, the Department of Justice concluded that the proposed merger failed to pose "significant competitive concerns." At the same time, the British government gave its permission.[70]

Within PW, an elaborate system was established to seek partner comment and reaction. Both firms also sought the confidential reaction of selected clients. Since the transaction involved a combination of partnerships, rather than a merger of business units, it could not be completed without a very high level of support (above 75 percent in one case) from PW's four major national partnerships in the United States, the United Kingdom, Australia, and Canada. Although the American partners in both PW and Deloitte strongly supported the merger, they were keenly disappointed by the absence of agreement in "certain important countries" that made it necessary to terminate discussions.[71]

The proposed merger with Deloitte would have addressed PW's resource constraints and uneven position in some emerging markets, but it was not viewed as the way to implement specialized practices. Had the merger gone through, one of Connor's deputy senior partners observed,

> We probably would have gone ahead with specialization, but not with the same zest. . . . We'd have been big enough not to have to worry about specialization as the prime tool. We could have both generalization and specialization.[72]

When the merger had been voted down, PW was forced to make up its mind about industry specialization and the restructuring of the practice. Confronted with the choice of continuing to support a broad-based strategy or of initiating one that was market-driven and more venturesome, the partners chose the second course and sought to develop markets critical for the success of the new policy. Before a market-driven approach focusing on service and a strong commitment to specialization could succeed, however, the firm had to marshal its professional staff and its financial resources in order to develop key markets.[73]

The firm's strategic planning function gave form to the new initiative. The firm made a significant break with the past by instituting a matrix structure establishing the functional area, and not the geographic region or practice office, as the primary management unit of the firm. The specialized practice units were given a new emphasis within the areas and served as a counterweight to the traditional organizational structure.

The particular markets that partners chose to target for SPUs were not necessarily those in which PW was already strong, but rather those where the opportunities seemed brightest for the future. The partners realized that "we cannot be all things to all people in all places" and that efforts must be directed to "opportunities where we can make a significant difference."[74] In 1985, the firm identified eleven top industries as the basis for SPUs staffed by full-time specialists: financial institutions, health care, high technology, insurance, investment companies, law firms, nonprofit organizations, petroleum, public utilities, real estate, and retailing. Specialization suited the changing career aspirations of staffers as, by the 1980s, "a lot of younger people wanted to get hooked onto the specialties because it's easier to understand where you fit than to be left in the generalist pool."[75] By the end of Connor's second term, the number of areas had increased to eleven, as Exhibit 7.3 shows, and the number of SPUs had increased tenfold, approximately equivalent to the number of the firm's offices.[76]

Various kinds of SPU structures developed as the partners accepted the idea of meeting market needs and recognized that what was good for one office or area might not work in another. Some SPUs were self-contained within one office, whereas others covered a group of offices. Some units covered a whole region or combination of regions, and others were national in scope, reporting directly to the Tax or MAS (renamed MCS in 1984) vice chairman or to the national director of industry specialization.[77]

In addition, Connor and others worked to modify PW's historic predisposition against hiring outsiders. In so doing, the firm shifted from its "hire and grow" philosophy, first enunciated by George O. May seventy years earlier, to one that enabled the firm to "acquire and grow" when conditions warranted it. The firm began to admit a number of people directly, recalled one partner, "specialists in tax, specialists in MCS, in fact, occasionally a specialist in auditing, specialists in executive financial services, in executive compensation, in valuations," and in retailing.[78] The proportional increase in partners admitted to the firm's audit and nonaudit practice after 1960 is shown in Exhibit 7.4.

Freed from traditional constraints, PW merged with three relatively small entities in 1985. In March, it joined forces with Management Horizons, an Ohio-based international management consulting and market research organization that served retail businesses and consumer goods distribution industries. Six months later, the firm united with Computech Corporation, a Connecticut EDP software development and management services concern involved in the insurance industry. And in December, PW joined with the Massachusetts-based Consumer Financial Institute, a provider of personal financial plans that combined the use of computer systems with analysis to produce individualized reports for employees in company-sponsored financial planning programs.[79]

PW's new focus marked a major shift in orientation, as specialization became a "strategic imperative" rather than "a marketing gimmick."

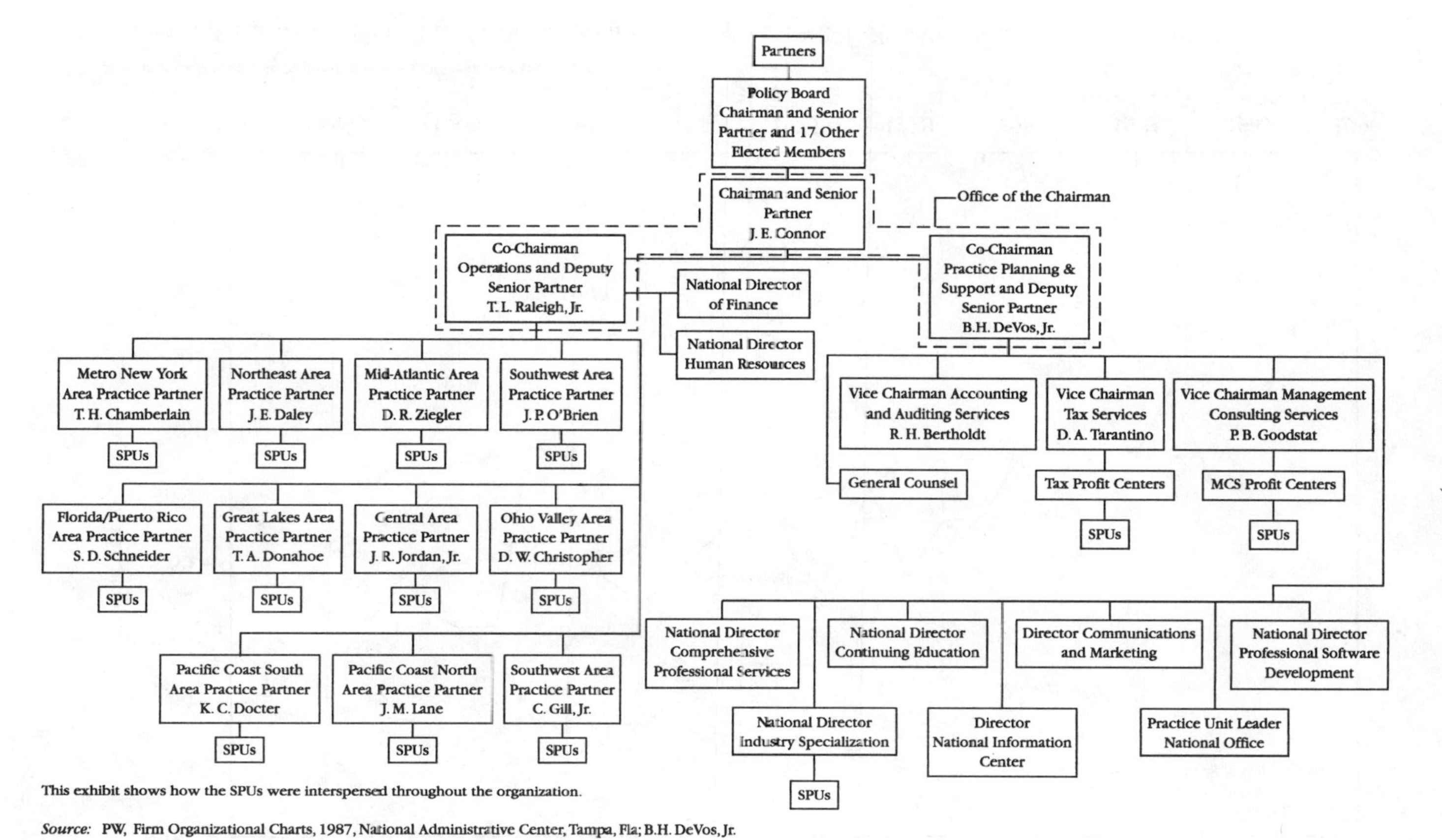

This exhibit shows how the SPUs were interspersed throughout the organization.

Source: PW, Firm Organizational Charts, 1987, National Administrative Center, Tampa, Fla; B.H. DeVos, Jr.

EXHIBIT 7.3 U.S. Firm Organization Chart, November 1987

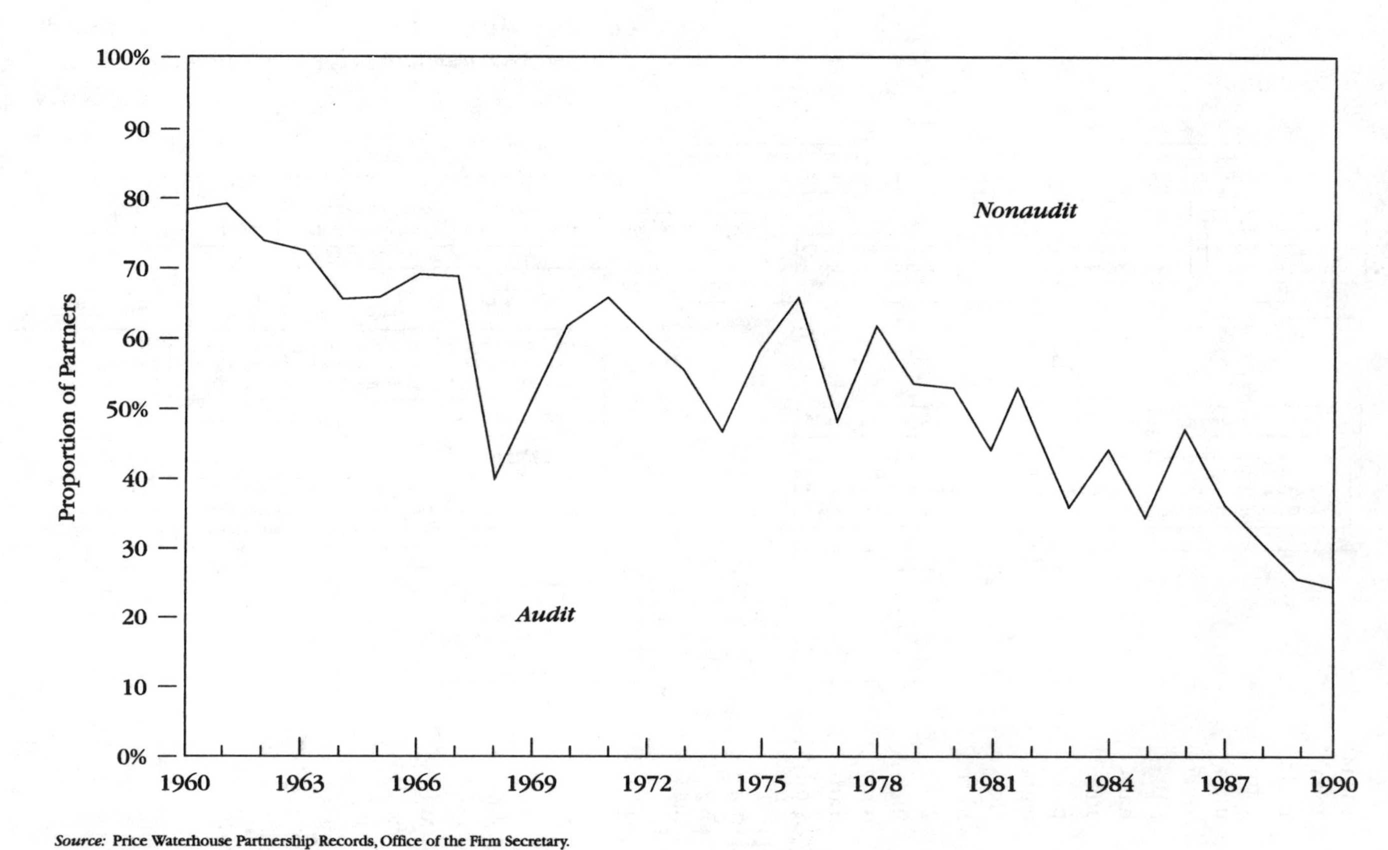

Source: Price Waterhouse Partnership Records, Office of the Firm Secretary.

EXHIBIT 7.4 Partners Admitted to Audit and Nonaudit Practices, 1960–1990

PW was moving away from simply providing excellent service in certain functional areas to seeking out market sectors that provided growth potential for the firm. Not only were there alterations in firm management, finance, and human resource policies, but there were also "significant attitudinal changes" as well. The SPU and area thrust was controversial because it contradicted the time-honored authority of the office partner-in-charge. Moreover, specialization ran directly counter to what Connor once described as PW's "fetish of generalization." The McKinsey study, augmented by the work of the firm's strategic planning group, had helped to prepare the partners to recognize that the practice had segmented into many different products and services and to see the need for more widespread specialization. In the end, the partners endorsed the goals of the new strategy.[80]

By 1986, PW had evolved to the point where its mission was to become nothing less than a "full-service business advisory firm." Other noteworthy departures from the firm's traditional approach were the imperative to provide increased consulting capability and the clear responsibility of every PW professional, rather than only partners, to "cross-sell" services across disciplines. Making this vision of the firm's future a reality, however, would depend not only on these changes in outlook, but on a dramatic expansion in the consulting and tax practices as well.[81]

Specialization within the Traditional Practice

The traditional practice areas of tax and consulting led the way in developing increasingly specialized services by tapping entirely new markets and industries. They thus underscored their growing independence from the audit practice, which was historically the source of most of the firm's business.

In the mid-1980s, tax services provided by the Big Eight constituted from 18 to 26 percent of their practices.[82] Although PW made a strong commitment to hiring specialists only in the early 1980s, the firm had implemented the practice in the tax area a few years earlier, following the passage of the Employee Retirement Income Security Act (ERISA) in 1974. PW's technical tax partner at the time viewed this as

> a watershed period for most tax practitioners, when those of us who thought we knew something about employee retirement plans and the complications in this area had to give up because ERISA was another world. It was like another Internal Revenue Code for the employee benefits area, and we were overwhelmed by it.[83]

An audit relationship with a prospective ERISA client was no longer a guarantee that tax work would also be forthcoming, because retirement plan work required specialized knowledge. In order to provide it, the Tax Department increasingly hired outside experts.

After 1980, as changes in the tax field gathered momentum, the firm became more active in tax policy matters in its Washington office. A tax partner attributed much of the growth to Congress, as the pace of tax legislation was far greater from 1981 to 1989 than ever before. Beginning with Ronald Reagan's administration, major tax laws were passed in seven out of nine years, and the legislation often left key elements to be defined in regulations promulgated much later. These circumstances endowed the Treasury Department, which would issue the regulations, with much broader authority and responsibility. Predictably, businesses became greatly concerned and sought more tax consultation in light of unforeseen and potentially harmful consequences. PW's Tax Department almost doubled in five years, from 850 professionals in 1978 to 1,600 in 1983.[84]

The tax area created several important specialties in this period, some developed with internal resources and others requiring outside expertise. In 1981, Bernard M. Shapiro was invited into the partnership to become PW's national director of tax policy, one of the first individuals admitted without previous experience with the firm. Shapiro had been chief of staff of the congressional Joint Committee on Internal Revenue Taxation. He was joined at PW two years later by his successor on the congressional committee staff. Over time, PW's national tax policy group grew from a four-person operation to one that employed over 120 professionals in 1990. The Washington national tax service (WNTS) focused on assisting partners and clients in their efforts to secure rulings from the IRS, providing information on legislative and regulatory activities, and dealing directly with the congressional Joint Committee on Internal Revenue Taxation on aspects of tax legislation. Another important growth area was international assignment tax services (IATS), which provided services to employees of multinational corporate clients and accounted for 15 percent of total tax revenues in the mid-1980s.[85]

Tax specialization led to increasingly sophisticated software products to assist clients in making complex tax planning computations. PW's CCATS group (corporate computer-assisted tax services), located in the Chicago office, converted comprehensive software developed by the firm for use in mainframe computers into modules for microcomputers. The program, named the international tax management system (ITMS) was released in 1985 and later expanded to address domestic and state needs under the umbrella name, tax management system (TMS). By 1990, TMS was contributing significantly to the firm's software sales;

its client base of nine hundred companies included 30 percent of the *Fortune* 500 list. Although audit clients like Amoco, Eastman Kodak, Turner Entertainment, and Westinghouse used TMS, 75 percent of TMS's users were nonaudit clients and included companies such as American Express, Time Warner, General Electric, Apple Computer, and RJR Nabisco.[86]

By the end of the decade, specialization in the tax area had progressed rapidly, and expansion, along product and service lines, proceeded more quickly than in any other practice of the firm. By 1989, 25 to 35 percent of the practice already reported to service-oriented profit centers rather than to an office partner-in-charge.[87]

Dramatic changes were also taking place in the firm's other nonaudit practice area, management consulting. Long a secondary focus within PW, consulting became an important line of business during the 1980s. The MAS Department posted significant gains during the late 1970s and early 1980s: partners increased from 33 in 1975 to 71 in 1980, and to 108 by 1985; staff increased in even greater proportions, from 337 to 1,300 (8.2 percent to 18 percent of total firm personnel) in the same period. In addition, the consulting practice's contribution to profit doubled, from 6.8 percent to 13.3 percent. Its dependency on work for audit clients declined at the same time, from 64 percent in 1975 to 26 percent by 1985, largely as a result of a rising volume of work from government organizations. The composition of MAS also changed. By 1988, only one out of four consultants were CPAs, compared with one out of two in 1974. In 1980, a milestone for the MAS Department was reached when one of its non–CPA partners, Paul Goodstat, began to serve on the Policy Board. Symbolic of all of these developments was the 1984 decision to rename this practice area Management Consulting Services.[88]

Despite its gains, MCS was constrained by its decentralized network scattered throughout many of the sixty-three local practice offices. Only sixteen offices had more than one MCS partner, and just six had more than three. "This fragmented resource position," noted the MCS vice chairman, "led to the evolution of many small, generalist consulting practices with a relatively low level of specialized service capability."[89] In 1985, MCS practice units were removed from the local offices and reorganized under the area structure. Consolidating MCS allowed more consultants to specialize and it reduced the tendency to view the practice office by office. Consulting services were redeployed to just twelve regional areas under the direction of regional MCS partners, rather than under partners-in-charge of local offices. It put the department on a different footing, allowing the firm to run MCS more as a distinct business. The change, however, was resisted strongly by some partners-in-charge of offices, who were accustomed to turning to the MCS partner in their own offices when they had a consulting assignment.[90]

During the 1980s, MCS developed business in information technology, uniform systems methodologies, and software sales. It made a major long-term investment in developing an information technology training program that focused on educating younger PW personnel. MCS made large strides in strategic systems planning, systems development, data security reviews, and computer installation effectiveness. With its creation of Systems Management Methodology (SMM), uniform standards for developing and executing consulting assignments worldwide were available; until that point, variation had been increasing, as more and more new people entered the firm and brought their own standards with them.[91]

The 1980s marked an important turning point for MCS, as it outgrew its traditional role as back-up to the audit. Connor told the Policy Board that MCS should never again be referred to as a "support function." By the end of the decade, there was a growing sense that in many ways PW's future would be closely tied to consulting.[92]

THE FIRM IN A SHRINKING WORLD

The 1980s were a watershed for the American economy. The relative position of the United States had declined, and the nation took its place with Japan and West Germany as one of several strong economies. During this period, the newly industrialized countries of the Pacific Rim and Latin America provided very competitive sources of labor, materials, and manufactured goods. For large American companies, interdependent, globalized markets and intense international competition were the hallmarks of the new era.[93]

For major accounting firms, a global presence became fundamental to ensuring future growth. In the past, PW had consistently served more of the top American multinationals than any of its competitors. In the 1980s, the firm continued to dominate these rankings, as Exhibit 7.5 shows.[94]

From the Big Eight to the Big Six

During the 1980s, the accounting profession's apparently stable configuration was shaken by mergers among the Big Eight firms. Although talks between PW and Deloitte fell through in 1984, other mergers were consummated. In 1986, Peat, Marwick united with Klynveld Main

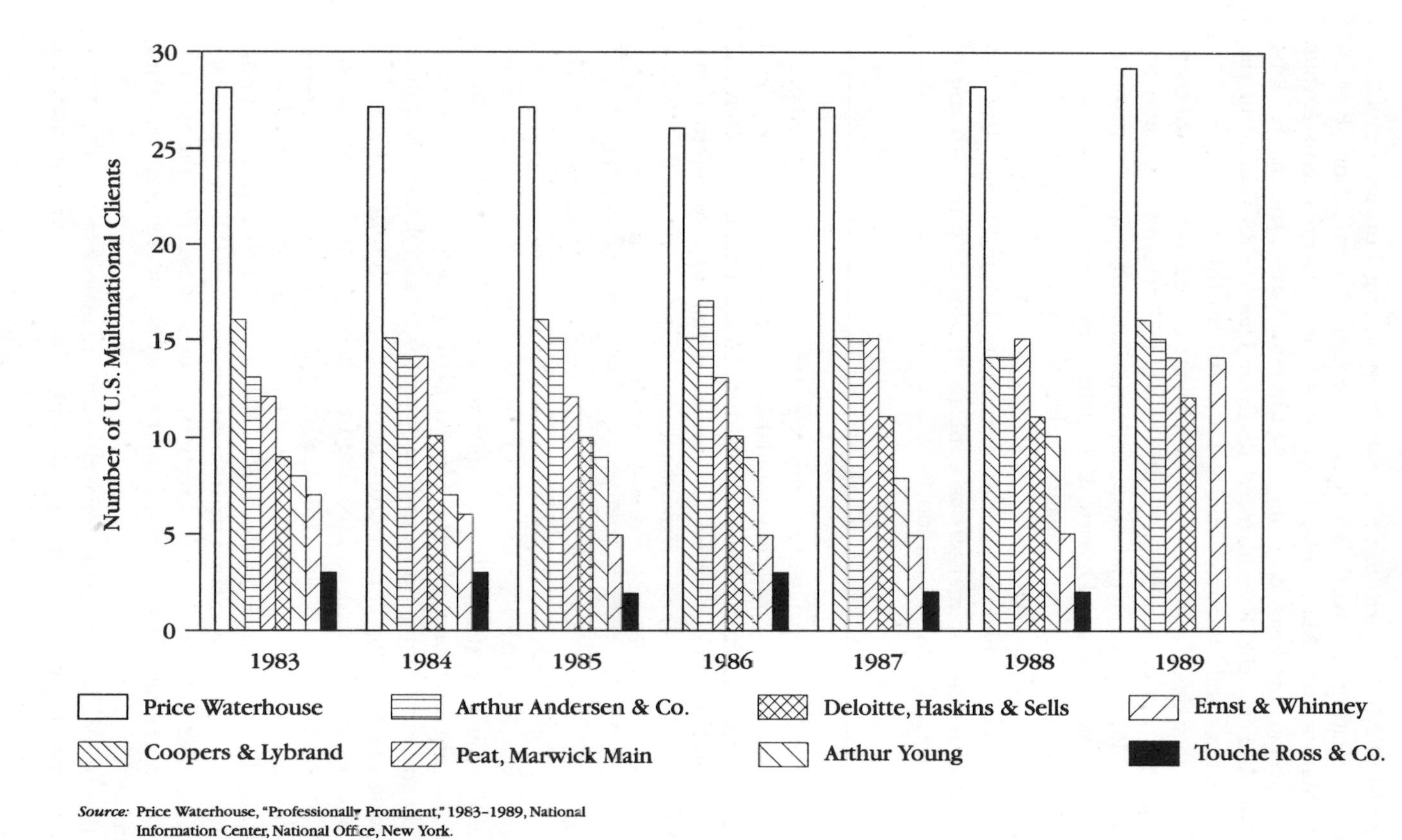

Source: Price Waterhouse, "Professionally Prominent," 1983–1989, National Information Center, National Office, New York.

EXHIBIT 7.5 Accounting Firms Serving *Forbes'* 100 Largest U.S. Multinational Companies, 1983–1989

Goerdler (KMG), a firm with an extremely strong European practice, thereby creating the world's largest accounting organization, KMG–Peat, Marwick. In May 1989, Ernst & Whinney merged with Arthur Young to become Ernst & Young. At the same time, Deloitte, Haskins & Sells and Touche Ross merged to form Deloitte & Touche in the United States and Deloitte, Ross & Tohmatsu worldwide.[95]

In the face of a flat domestic audit market, a need to rationalize costs to preserve profits, and the necessity of a global presence, all the firms chose to follow the strategies of specialization and strengthening through consolidation. The new Deloitte & Touche firm, for instance, provided the advantage of Touche's Japanese relationship. Likewise, Peat, Marwick's merger with KMG, with its strong West German presence, significantly strengthened the position of the new firm in Europe. PW also continued to consider mergers as a means of providing growth and of strengthening its global position.[96]

The World Firm

The growing interdependence within the global economy increased pressure to harmonize accounting standards. Accounting principles, legal requirements, and financial statements differed from country to country, and misunderstandings arose that impeded the flow of international investment. A number of international organizations have tried to reduce differences and to create a less diverse system of international accounting. In 1973, the International Accounting Standards Committee (IASC) was founded to promote worldwide acceptance of uniform accounting procedures. Unfortunately, its members, which were national accounting institutes, were unable to set or enforce standards in many countries where accounting standards were government controlled. Other international organizations, like the United Nations and the Organization for Economic Cooperation and Development (OECD), also sought to address the problem. The European Economic Community's (EEC) accounting standards committee, the first such body to have significant authority in the area of accounting principles, was the most successful in devising comparable standards as its members moved toward integrating their economies in the 1980s. PW, through its role as a special consultant to the U.S. State Department and through PW International's EEC Center in Brussels, was directly involved in assisting the international government organizations in their work on financial reporting standards.[97]

Before 1982, PW's international efforts were mainly technically driven rather than business or strategy driven. The needs of multinational companies, however, and the growth of international competition spurred PW to explore the commonality of interest of all its firms. The existing mind-set of a collection of local perspectives with an Anglo-Saxon overlay was abandoned in order to achieve a new involvement in the local environments of non–English speaking countries. PW accepted the notion that its pre-eminence was not just a function of high professionalism, but also a result of better business practice. Its partners argued that only those accounting firms that could make the transition from an amalgamation of national firms to an integrated world entity would remain significant players in the future.[98]

A supplementary McKinsey study of PW International had confirmed a loss of worldwide position by PW at a time of increasing challenge, a competitive weakness in countries that represented rising capital and business markets, and an inadequacy in selected service areas in some countries. With the increasing tension between the firm's disposition of its forces and the requirements of the marketplace, it was clear that the international network needed a tighter organization and clearer business objectives.[99]

In light of the McKinsey findings, the PW International Firm was reorganized into the PW World Firm, with the former senior partner of the UK firm, Michael Coates, as its first chairman. The new body was structured to create greater worldwide participation by both the national partnerships and their partners and to provide an increased focus on global strategy. It was managed by a Policy Committee, consisting of a chairman and eight senior partners of member national firms; a Council of Firms, comprising the chairman and senior partners of the nineteen council firms; and a Council of Partners, approximately one hundred engagement partners from various national firms, which served as an advisory body to assist the chairman in determining World Firm needs and strategies. For the first time, engagement partners, in addition to management partners, were directly connected with the international organization. A number of projects were initiated, including the development of distinctive auditing services and international marketing approaches, the strengthening of MCS practice worldwide, and the creation of stronger practices in European countries, the Far East, and the Middle East. In 1984, the World Firm created the firm's first technology center in Palo Alto, California, intended to identify future information technology and to assess its potential application for PW firms worldwide.[100]

In 1985, a joint study group composed of representatives from the American and British firms was appointed to discuss and make recommendations for a global strategy. In 1987, its recommendations were approved by the World Firm and endorsed by partners in the national firms. Thereafter, the World Firm set up working groups to develop more specific proposals. Their efforts produced a "Global Strategy" document that was adopted by the partners in 1988. It recommended the development of an effective management body to supervise the worldwide practices, to maintain greater parity of income among partners in the growth of worldwide practices, and to develop services and personnel throughout the world.

By 1988, when Connor succeeded Coates as the chairman of the World Firm, the PW organization consisted of some 40,000 individuals at 420 offices in 120 countries. He set a goal of greater uniformity in audit, tax, and consulting services as well as to encourage more industry-specific practices in PW firms throughout the world. Connor believed that the World Firm was well positioned to emphasize international and multinational services to clients of PW national firms. A global outlook was important for the U.S. firm at a time when so much of the American economy's growth was dependent on foreign investment, especially by Japanese companies. As one partner observed, PW's "strength in the United States is increasingly a function of our strength abroad."[101]

The new global strategy echoed the goals of the former PW International Firm, that "PW firms in every part of the world [should be] interconnected through mutual benefit arrangements geared at a common economic interest." The partners recognized that their worldwide firms shared both a common past and a common destiny.[102]

SUMMING UP

At the close of the 1980s, PW was a significantly different firm from the one Connor inherited. It had grown much tougher-minded about its business and had taken a number of aggressive steps to place itself at the forefront of change in the profession.

From a purely quantitative standpoint, the decade witnessed a series of impressive accomplishments. Over forty new offices were opened, increasing the total number by almost 50 percent, as Exhibit 7.6 shows. The partnership also increased from about five hundred partners to more than eight hundred (see Exhibit 5.3). Even more significant, the firm's chargeable hours rose 65 percent between 1978 and 1988, as Exhibit 7.7 shows.

Looking back on his tenure, Connor identified the institutionalization of strategic planning as the most important development during his term as senior partner, in part because it helped transform the firm's global

Year	Opening	Closing
1890-1899	2	0
1900-1909	6	0
1910-1919	4	0
1920-1929	6	0
1930-1939	3	1
1940-1949	2	0
1950-1959	17	0
1960-1969	23	2
1970-1979	15	5
1980-1990	47	10

Source: DeMond, *PW in America;* PW office directories, 1946-1990, National Information Center, National Office, New York.

EXHIBIT 7.6 Price Waterhouse U.S. Firm Office Openings and Closings, 1890–1990

involvement. Connor's efforts, and those of other firm leaders, helped to raise the partners' awareness that the rules had changed. By 1988, every partner recognized the imperative to understand market forces, to prospect constantly for new opportunities, and, in a world of increasingly scarce resources, to set priorities.[103]

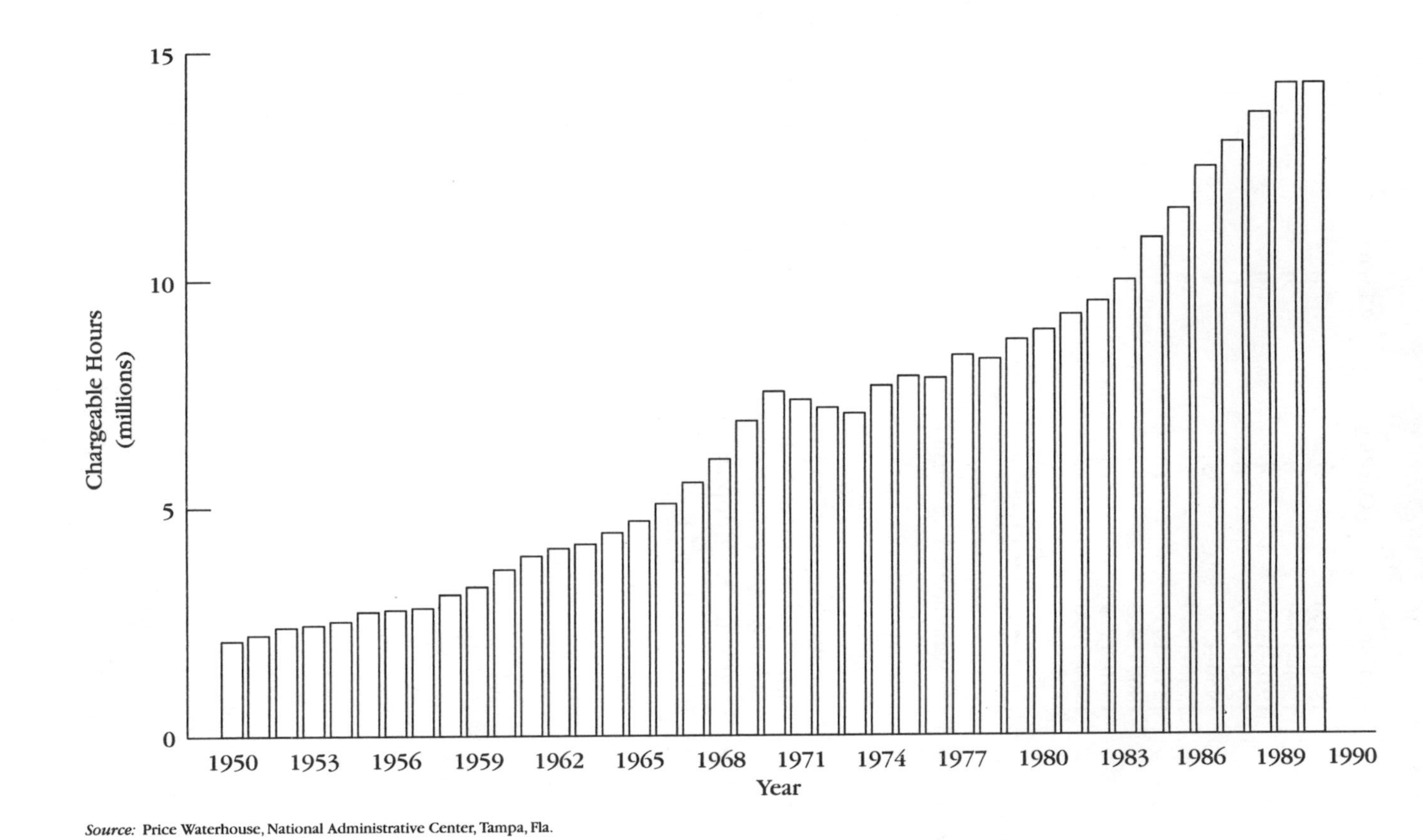

Source: Price Waterhouse, National Administrative Center, Tampa, Fla.

EXHIBIT 7.7 Growth of PW Chargeable Hours in the United States, 1950–1990

CHAPTER 8

BEGINNING A SECOND HUNDRED YEARS

Shaun F. O'Malley's election as Price Waterhouse senior partner in November 1987 initiated a searching re-evaluation of the firm's strategic direction. During the next several years, O'Malley presided over an important rededication of PW's purpose.

O'Malley's professional experience was broad and diverse. He had joined the Philadelphia office in 1959, and early in his career he served tours of duty in Tokyo and Osaka, providing technical support and client service for PW's fledgling practice in Japan. He also worked in the Accounting Research Department in New York, analyzing the impact of decisions of the Accounting Principles Board and writing case studies on "live client situations" for the firm's national continuing education curriculum. He was admitted to the partnership in 1970, and since 1980 he had been partner-in-charge of the Philadelphia office, where he had earned a reputation for stressing client service. He had been a member of the Policy Board since 1984, and his long-standing interest in international business also led to service on the World Firm's Council of Partners for five years, followed by a stint on its General Council.

On taking office, O'Malley made a number of important changes to the firm's management and line organization. By March 1988, he had appointed his executive staff, naming to the Office of the Chairman Dominic A. Tarantino as co-chairman, managing partner; and James E. Daley as co-chairman, operations. The two co-chairmen shared leadership with O'Malley and worked as a team to a greater extent than their predecessors under previous senior partners. Tarantino acted as senior partner in O'Malley's absence and was responsible for human resources and market and industry service development. Daley coordinated geographic practices and professional services, including auditing and accounting, tax, consulting, and firm finances.

O'Malley instituted key operational changes, some of which are shown in Exhibit 8.1. A more streamlined structure was created by collapsing the eleven area practices into five regions, each headed by a regional vice chair. Vice chairmen continued to head the services areas of accounting and auditing, tax, and MCS. Two new vice chair positions were created, one to oversee CPS, or comprehensive professional services (now called middle market and growing companies division, or MMG), and another to oversee industry specialization. In another important move, O'Malley restructured the practice units into six practice regions with twenty-five office groups.

O'Malley also reconstituted the Management Committee and the Policy Board. The mandate of the Management Committee, now consisting of the geographic and services vice chairmen and the members of the Office of the Chairman, was defined as developing and implementing a focused and effective firm strategy. A clear distinction between the Policy Board and the Management Committee was effected by excluding members of the committee from serving on the board, except for those included in the Office of the Chairman. The Policy Board thus could exercise an oversight role over the Management Committee, and ideas that came from the Management Committee could be "aired" by a "cross-section of non-management people." The board's principal concerns were defined as budgets, mergers, and partnership issues, including admissions.

Most important, O'Malley led the firm through a comprehensive strategic planning procedure. Soon after taking office, he initiated a strategic assessment process coordinated by the Management Committee. Out of these meetings came a focused three-part strategy: to provide the highest quality service, to exercise selectivity in markets and services, and to recruit and retain the "best and the brightest" talent. Over the next two and a half years, this strategy was communicated throughout the firm, ultimately leading to what is now known as the "Price Waterhouse Vision": to be the best professional services firm in the world. For O'Malley, the firm's future, its vision, is his "number one priority."

In limiting the vision to three broad points, PW partners sought to moderate the pace of change. The firm's leadership felt that the intense competitive pressures on accounting firms in the 1980s made them "continually expand, expand, expand—taking on new services, pursuing new client markets, and opening new offices at breakneck speed." As

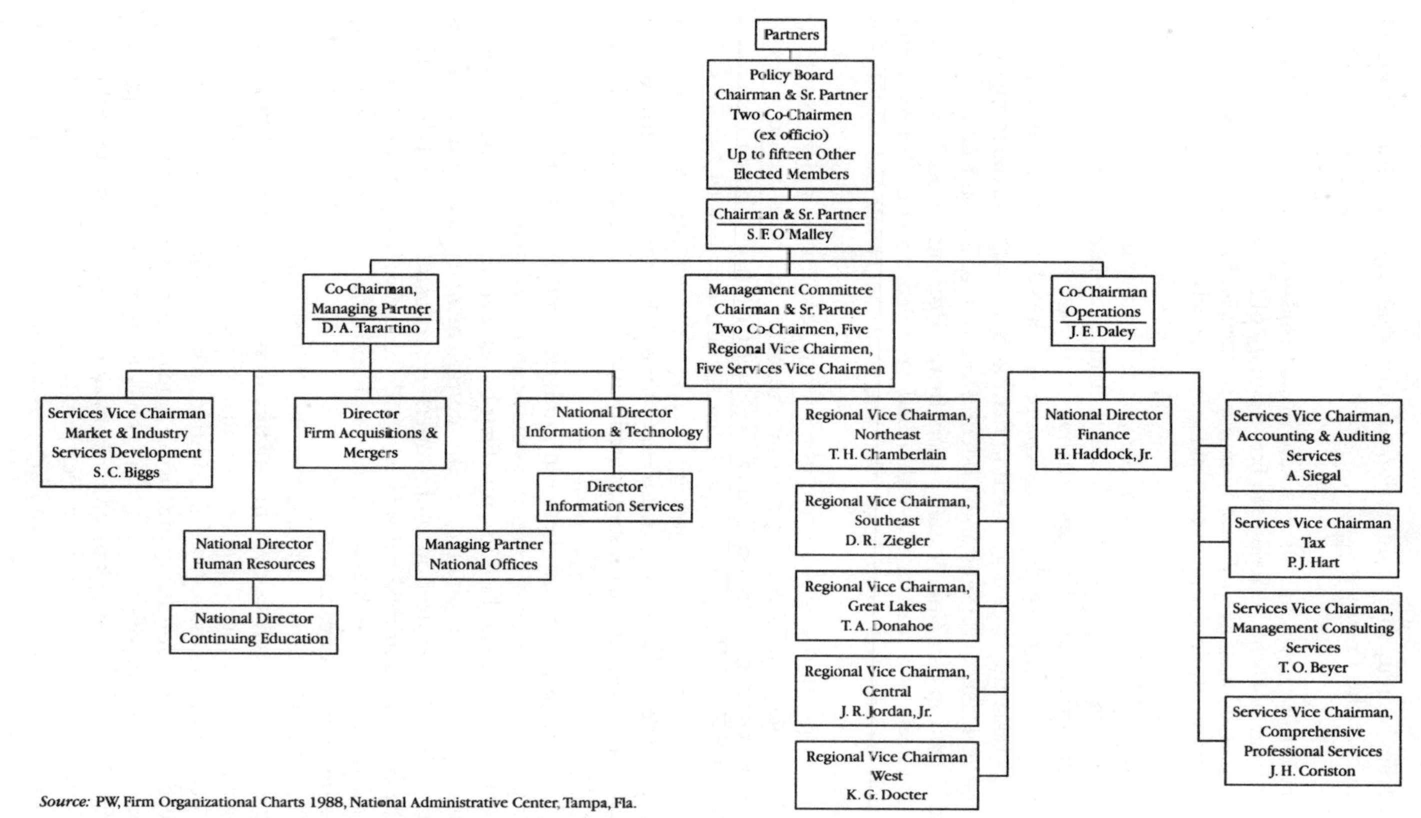

Source: PW, Firm Organizational Charts 1988, National Administrative Center, Tampa, Fla.

EXHIBIT 8.1 U.S. Firm Organization Chart, November 1988

O'Malley noted, the proliferation of offices and SPUs within PW had meant that the firm

> tried to be too many things to too many people—pursuing too broad a range of clients, offering too broad a range of services, and inflicting too broad a range of demands on our partners and staff. . . . And the pace has left little time to stop and assess our actions.

In mid-1989, a fresh burst of merger talks among the major accounting firms in the United States startled independent observers. In the most dramatic case, PW and Arthur Andersen gave notice of formal talks, to run for sixty days, to explore the possibility of a merger that would create the largest accounting firm in the world. At the same time, Deloitte, Haskins & Sells and Touche Ross & Co. announced that they had agreed in principle to unite their firms. Both announcements came on the heels of a merger wave that had involved Ernst & Whinney and Arthur Young & Co. in May 1989 and Peat, Marwick and KMG two years earlier.

Certainly all the major accounting firms recognized a clear competitive advantage in increasing their size in order to achieve economies of scale, to enter new markets, and to benefit from combined resources. Since the early 1980s, PW had given serious thought to mergers, including the possibility of joining forces with Deloitte. When news of the Andersen talks broke, it did not evoke the negative reaction within the PW partnership that it undoubtedly would have faced even five years earlier.

The proposed merger between Andersen and PW would transform the profession, as two longtime competitors, each with very different operational styles and important client bases, became one. The proposed unification could capitalize on the complementary strengths of PW's international organization and Andersen's consulting capability. That such an action could be considered at all was a sign of the changes afoot in the industry, as well as an indication that the firms were now, perhaps, less different than earlier.

Problems surfaced almost immediately in the talks, however, including serious differences over management and organization. Arthur Andersen had long been highly centralized, whereas PW prided itself on its decentralized orientation. In addition, a number of issues arose around the respective consulting practices. Andersen was concerned over the potential dilution of the voice of its consultants in a joint firm. In January 1989, Andersen had enhanced its consultants' position by reorganizing its management advisory services into a separate unit called Andersen Consulting. Andersen's consulting partners thereby gained a greater say in management and improved their profit-sharing arrangements. One result of the proposed merger, Andersen consultants feared, could be the loss of their new power and influence.

Engineering a fit between the two firms' consulting practices was also perceived as a problem. Only about 19 percent of PW's revenues came from consulting, compared to Andersen's 37 percent, a sizable portion of which stemmed from massive computer systems integration work. In a merger, PW's smaller consulting practice might be dominated by its new partners. On the other hand, although Andersen Consulting was large, recent defections, including that of its lead partner, left some doubt about its future course.

In addition, PW was concerned about the effect that such a merger might have on its important audit clients. PW partners believed that business ties with audit clients were prohibited by accountants' independence and also by relevant SEC rules. Andersen was involved in substantial consulting joint ventures with such PW audit clients as IBM and Hewlett-Packard. A choice would need to be made between the auditing and consulting relationships.

Although talks continued up to the initial 60-day deadline, and both parties agreed to extend them indefinitely, the discussions ended less than thirty days later. Differences in the way the firms funded their retirement plans surfaced in the press as the predominant reason for the termination of the talks but, according to O'Malley, other incompatibilities, particularly those involving business ties with audit clients and the dominant role of Andersen Consulting, proved more troublesome. In the end, he noted, the parties had only agreed to talk "to see whether it made sense to put the two firms together, and we concluded those talks and decided that it didn't make sense."

Like the breakdown of talks with Deloitte, the end of discussions with Andersen highlighted the choices facing PW as a stand-alone entity. Pressures to globalize were driving other accounting firm mergers, and failure to consummate a deal with Andersen strongly reinforced PW's commitment to its international practice, leading to the deployment of more people and resources to this area. Both sides, in fact, had gained from the talks. Andersen saw the value of PW's strong multinational practice and PW benefited from exposure to Andersen's industry focus.

The Andersen talks did not end PW's ongoing strategic assessment discussions, and the conclusion of the merger negotiations only reinforced the firm's intention to move ahead. Over the next two years, the Management Committee continued to communicate the three-part strategy, and the firm began to develop its vision of the future. The Management Committee next began an ambitious process to implement the vision that involved the partnership at all levels. In September 1991, with O'Malley noting a "sense of urgency," the partners began to evaluate the Management Committee's implementation plan. Over the course of discussions, it became clear that PW's vision was perhaps not altogether different from the strategic plans of the other large firms; only those firms that were effective in their implementation would succeed. Given PW's distinguished past and the strong traditions that surround the partnership, as well as the fierce present commitment to success, the firm will, according to O'Malley, "accept nothing less."

REFLECTIONS ON THE FIRST CENTURY

The hundred years that have passed since PW was first established in America divide into three periods, each characterized by its own problems and dilemmas. The first era, covering roughly 1890 to the late 1920s, saw the Americanization of the practice and the rise of the firm around professionally autonomous partners. The second era, from the early 1930s to the late 1960s, marked the dominance of PW in the regulated, monolithic environment in which the accounting profession then functioned. The third era, from the early 1970s through the early 1990s, saw the reformulation of the PW agenda in a period of radical change in both the marketplace and the profession.

The early years of PW's development shaped its subsequent success. The firm's strategy from the very beginning—which became its enduring trademark—was to focus on blue-chip clients, to do work of the highest quality, and to build a partnership organized around professionally autonomous partners. This positioned PW well for its success in the decades that followed.

The changes that occurred during the 1970s and 1980s in the U.S. economy, however, precipitated a breakdown in the monolithic structure of the accounting profession that had prevailed for more than fifty years. The steady absorption of the more successful local and regional practices into the Big Eight, and more recently, the Big Six firms, a phenomenon that started in the 1950s, has accelerated. These consolidations reflect ever-increasing innovation in technology, a shifting client base, changes in service mix, and adverse legal decisions. At the same time, greater competitiveness has led to the dismantling of earlier professional prohibitions against advertising and solicitation. Practice standards required by Congress and the SEC have resulted in sharp increases in overhead costs. All of these developments have not only affected the economics of individual large firms, but have also eroded the industry structure established in the 1930s.

These changes directly challenged PW, and the firm's management responded by instituting greater specialization and centralization. The fact that PW had been so successful for so long, however, made adjustment to the changes of the 1970s and 1980s difficult. The need for a more centralized firm clashed with the concept of the autonomous PW partner. Similarly, senior partner John Biegler's initial moves to emphasize specialization marked a departure from the firm's historical focus on generalists. PW's efforts to reorganize its partnership and reorient its strategy to meet future requirements and opportunities emerged from the resolution of these tensions.

PW has also built a broader client base at home and abroad and worked to provide a more extensive range of specialized services. The firm's ability to continue to provide a high-quality audit depends on its developing a wide range and mix of other professional skills.

PW's success over its first century was unquestionably linked to the decisions taken by partners in its early decades. The firm adopted, and then adhered to, a clear formula and, by the turn of the century, it had developed a practice in investigations for a client base that comprised the largest and best-known American companies and banking interests. Following passage of the securities laws in the 1930s, PW provided audit and accounting services to these large, blue-chip clients. The firm's British pedigree, and its senior partner, George O. May, who often represented the accounting profession to the world and who helped to shape the regulatory reforms of the 1930s and to promote generally accepted accounting principles, secured it an enduring leadership role. PW built a reputation for quality and high standards that differentiated it from its leading competitors.

Although the business environment changed a great deal over the century, PW's approach remained both stable and successful. The firm's strategy for expansion was to open offices near its clients or in major cities. It did not compete aggressively on price, because it did not need to, and the firm had long operated in a world in which such behavior in any profession was unseemly as well as unnecessary. PW led the accounting profession for decades, and as the years went by, its enduring high reputation reinforced its claim to leadership. Other large firms had never been able to make serious inroads into PW's select market so they responded by diversifying earlier into other professional services, by initiating price competition, or by seeking global or market dominance through sheer size. Although some rivals grew larger, PW remained prestigious and retained a disproportionally high number of elite clients.

The firm's culture developed in tandem with its reputation. A decentralized authority structure evolved because PW's rapid geographical expansion required partners in scattered locales to be virtually autonomous in their activities. Its partners had a reputation for being circumspect and scrupulous, willing to sacrifice monetary rewards for the sake of principle. In every decade, there were examples of PW partners, supported by their senior partners, who chose to lose clients rather than bow to pressures for improper accounting treatments.

PW was also known as a thoughtful and prudent firm. Its outstanding accountants, such as May and Paul Grady, brought a reflective, scholarly perspective to day-to-day accounting issues. Their advanced thinking and professional leadership did much to mold the collective self-image of PW. In addition, recruiting and training practices ensured that all partners would become acclimated to the organization's style. The firm's insistence on developing its own young accountants, rather than hiring laterally from other firms, served to perpetuate the PW culture.

PW's strategy reflected its considerable success. Until well into the late 1960s, the firm prospered in a structured environment. As corporations in the United States grew larger, it was imperative for the accounting firms that serviced these companies to expand as well. Passage of the securities laws in the 1930s requiring periodic financial reports of publicly traded companies encouraged the growth of the accounting profession, institutionalized the audit, and reinforced a trend toward a stable, uniform profession. There was a very close relationship between law and accounting. The securities laws underscored the legitimacy of large-scale public corporations in their time of greatest crisis and ensured a client base to the large accounting firms that served them. At the same time, government regulations raised standards of performance within the accounting profession. Gradually, accounting for large public corporations was provided by the handful of large firms able to service multinational operations and to provide the specialized expertise required by such clients as Standard Oil of New Jersey and U.S. Steel.

During this period, the prestige of the profession was high, and public accounting firms could count on a regular stream of high-quality recruits. The steady growth trends of the post–World War II era, manifested in the calm and prosperity of the 1950s and the booming economy of the 1960s, were reflected in the profitability of all the large accounting firms. As American corporations took their place as the world's richest and most powerful economic actors, PW and the rest of the profession rode the crest of this wave.

By the early 1970s, an unsettled world economy and the increasing threat of foreign competition spelled the end of the postwar boom. Within the accounting profession, the tumultuous events of the 1970s and 1980s ended the traditional industry structure and thoroughly transformed aspects of big-firm practice. For example, the profession's market structure changed dramatically. Price competition in audit work became common, leading to decreased profit margins and threatening the profession's traditional economics. Competition for "customers" also grew fierce; clients switched auditors more easily, and rivalry among firms became intense. Mergers reduced the client base of the major accounting firms. The economics of practice was further affected by an explosion of litigation that increased costs. As these factors changed, the business of accounting became increasingly transaction-oriented. In the 1960s, for example, it was not common for accounting firms to provide tax or MCS services to audit clients of other firms; by the late 1980s, this had become an everyday practice. Large accounting firms found it necessary to adjust to the expansion of competition on an international level; some firms sought to secure their market position by merging with others. In the 1980s, accounting firms also had to compete for personnel with more financially attractive opportunities outside the profession in investment banking and other fields.

Even the unique place that the profession had established for itself vis-à-vis its regulators over the course of a half-century was irrevocably changed. Caught up in the competitive and market changes of the 1960s and early 1970s, the accounting profession's rule-making body was no longer able to operate effectively. Problems had begun as early as the late 1950s, in the debate between Herman Bevis and Leonard Spacek over accounting principles and later, in the Accounting Principles Board's increasing inability to articulate a shared vision for the profession. Widespread criticism led to the creation of a full-time Financial Accounting Standards Board, a new standard-setting body not composed entirely of practicing accountants. The historically cooperative relationship between the profession and its regulators came under scrutiny as Congress and the SEC took a more distant, and at times adversarial, stance toward the accounting profession, instigating investigations, new disclosure requirements, and periodic efforts to restrict the scope of practice.

Technology was another destabilizing element. New products such as smaller, faster, and cheaper computers transformed financial reporting and forced changes in traditional audit work patterns. New information technologies supported the proliferation of ancillary services by accounting firms in the consulting and tax areas and lowered barriers to entry in many kinds of financial services.

All of these changes posed challenges for PW. First, its client base was especially hard hit. The firm had always had the largest collection of major industrial clients, which were precisely the companies most affected by the conglomerate merger movement of the late 1960s, the financial and energy crises of the early 1970s, and the global competition and restructuring activity of the 1980s. The health of these clients, long the center of PW's success, could no longer be taken for granted. Facing the prospect of a shrinking domestic client base, PW committed itself to further strengthening its focus on large multinationals. Other markets emerged, as well; high levels of foreign direct investment in the United States, particularly by Japan and Western Europe, resulted in important service opportunities.

The new environment required dramatic changes in PW's mix of services. The firm had always conceived of itself as the profession's foremost auditing and accounting firm. In the 1970s, the growing sense that the audit was becoming a commodity put pressure on PW, as it became more difficult for partners to assert that the firm's audit was distinctive. Efforts to overcome an identification with the audit posed risks, however, to a firm that had long based its reputation on its auditing skills and that had earned its greatest profits from that service. PW responded by developing its "Audit of the 1990s" and related initiatives to increase audit efficiency.

In the 1970s, as price pressure on audit services put all firms at a disadvantage, and as MCS and tax were perceived as more profitable growth areas, PW began the difficult process of redirecting partner resources and readjusting partner career expectations. Recognizing that the traditional philosophy of developing generalists and focusing on the audit prevented the rapid deployment of expertise elsewhere, the firm started to admit specialists and non–CPAs and merged with smaller businesses in areas such as financial services and management consulting.

During the 1980s, PW emphasized encouraging and training specialized nonaudit professionals and concentrated on targeting and developing markets involving multinationals, information technology, and financial services. The firm launched a federal government consulting practice in the 1970s, an area that became very successful, and continued to strengthen its worldwide organization to take advantage of emerging opportunities abroad.

The new environment also forced changes in the firm's traditional organizational structure. For two decades, beginning with Biegler's introduction of the regional managing partner position in the mid-1970s and continuing with the further division of the firm into areas and SPUs, PW steadily moved away from the collection of geographically dispersed autonomous fiefdoms that had served it well for so long. The matrix structure of the 1990s was oriented around services, specialties, and new markets.

It is too early to tell whether the firm's reorganization around a more focused and more profitable service mix will endure, although there is little doubt that the rapid development of innovative products to meet clients' changing needs is increasingly critical to long-term success. As have all accounting firms, PW has stressed that consulting work—which has existed throughout the firm's history, although not in today's specialized sense—is central to the firm's continued growth and profitability. It is also aware that the pace of change is rapid and that the firm's character will inexorably be altered as a result.

Among global accounting firms, size and resources are essential aspects of competitive life. PW, however, has never embraced the strategy, first debated during Herman Bevis's time, of aggressive growth. In the 1970s, the partners saw opportunities to deploy a larger pool of human resources, but the historically small partnership meant costly delays in opening offices and providing new services. By the 1980s, however, the firm was opening new offices at a record-breaking rate. The firm's current vision depends on expanding on the basis of quality clients and quality work, reminiscent of aspects of the planned growth model formulated in the 1960s by Herman Bevis and reflecting the continued strength of the firm's historical pattern.

As the firm faces future changes in the world economy, it intends to anticipate and selectively target appropriate markets. Its strategy of the early 1990s is to identify the economic potential of such markets and to develop a strong commitment to specialization in them.

By not merging with other firms in 1984 and 1989, PW may have missed opportunities to decrease costs and increase profitability, and it has emerged as one of the smallest of the large, worldwide accounting organizations. To succeed globally, the PW worldwide firm is positioning itself to provide services in those countries where capital formation is rising and business markets are growing. Even though PW is historically strong in a number of countries, the consolidation of PW Europe with PW–U.K. is an effort to establish a stronger position in the European Community. PW's recent joint venture in Japan will assist in building a more prominent position there and in other Pacific Rim countries. To bring organizational ties ever closer, executive leadership of the World Firm is now jointly held by the senior partners of the U.S. and U.K. firms.

Although the U.S. firm has expressly made its connection to the global PW organization an important part of its strategy for the future, a major banking scandal of the early 1990s suggests that there may be practical limits to such an approach—at least for the near future. In the fall of 1991, international banking regulators seized and closed the Bank of Credit and Commerce International (BCCI), asserting that the bank had engaged in fraud on a multimillion-dollar scale. Since that date, litigation has commenced against several accounting firms that audited BCCI, including PW's British firm, on behalf of BCCI's depositors worldwide. Although the outcome of these actions is indeterminate, early indications from official British inquiries appear to vindicate PW's role in the affair. Whatever its outcome, the controversy raises important issues about PW's evolution toward a global firm. In a statement on the BCCI matter, senior partner O'Malley identified one inherent limitation of a global organization in a world of separate nations. "As with other international accounting firms," he wrote in a letter to the *New York Times* in November 1991, "our business organization is dictated largely by the laws and professional requirements of the various jurisdictions in which the Price Waterhouse firms practice accounting." Given the differences among nations' laws and regulations, at present neither PW nor any other accounting firm can become a completely integrated international organization, certainly not in the legal sense.

Much of PW postwar history can be seen through the lens of its dominant role in the profession. Percy Brundage and John Inglis had no reason to question the firm's historically successful formula and made only minor adjustments to it such as the creation of a Systems Department to help clients with the new information-gathering technology. As the firm was successful in the 1960s, Herman Bevis had even less reason to question the partners' outlook, and he focused instead on positioning the partnership to meet future demands and on instituting critical internal management reforms. Even when external pressures intruded, such as those leading to the planned growth debate of the 1960s, they were not perceived as fundamentally at odds with the traditional PW pattern of a small partnership performing high-quality services for elite clients.

By the late 1970s, the firm's leadership recognized that changes were necessary. PW became more focused on the external environment and sought to make itself into a leaner, more entrepreneurial organization. John Biegler initiated this process by emphasizing specialization, reflecting his belief that the business environment of the time offered opportunities for innovative service areas. By the 1980s, Joseph Connor, building on Biegler's efforts, had articulated a clear strategic emphasis on specialization and away from a geographic organizational structure. Notwithstanding these changes, the firm's past conservatism and insistence on quality remained an asset. PW's careful client screening and other control policies allowed it to avoid many questionable enterprises, most notably the troubled savings and loan industry, whose problems created major difficulties for nearly all other large accounting firms.

As a result of its history and culture, PW faced special challenges in order to succeed in the global business environment of the 1990s. The new demands of the accounting business conflicted with the firm's traditional partnership structure modeled on its nineteenth-century British parent organization, which had led to semiautonomous offices distributed along geographical lines. The trend toward global competition challenged this approach, and functional and service divisions came to play the central role in the firm's structure. The sheer number of partners in the U.S. firm, more than nine hundred by the late 1980s, made it difficult to preserve traditional aspects of the PW culture, such as collegiality and the sense of being part of a small, elite organization. In the 1990s, PW found it necessary to adapt its partnership, by affirming the partner as the vital core of the firm, but acknowledging the need to modify the independence of partners in the working environment of the future.

The role of partners in the firm's culture was re-examined as part of the strategic assessment process that led to formulation of the PW vision. "On balance our culture is a strength, a strong, unifying sense of partnership bringing us together and impelling us to work together," O'Malley observed. In an increasingly market-driven world, however, the traditional "lionization of the generalist" within PW could be counterproductive. Professional autonomy had long been a PW strength, but O'Malley believed that it was necessary to rededicate the firm to a "collegiality . . . that minimized hierarchy, stressed our relationship as colleagues and fellow owners, and recognized the need to place the firm's needs above individual desires."

To some readers, it may appear that the partnership form itself is anachronistic—given that PW is now larger than many public corporations. Since the turn of the century, PW and other large accounting firms have been affected by regional laws governing the establishment of professional partnerships. These statutes distinguish between corporate business activities and those services in which medical, legal, and accounting professionals, among others, hold themselves out to the public on the basis of their character, reputation, and skill. Whereas corporation owners are immune from suit, these laws hold professional service providers responsible to their clients. The pressures of the 1970s and 1980s have led some partnerships, particularly in the investment banking and real estate areas, to restructure themselves as corporations in order to raise capital and to avail themselves of limited liability provisions. Given the current scale, scope, and diverse functions of an accounting firm like PW, a long-term question remains as to whether the partnership form will continue to be best suited to a truly global enterprise.

A recent and dramatic legal case underscored the problem of liability and raised again the issue of PW's ownership structure. The case involved Standard Chartered, PLC, a London-based international bank and its claim of alleged losses following its acquisition in 1987 and its divestiture in 1988 of United Bancorp of Arizona, a PW audit client.

Standard Chartered sued PW, saying it was misled by the firm's audits of United Bancorp. In May 1992, a jury in Arizona agreed, and ordered PW to pay Standard Chartered $338 million in damages. The firm loudly protested the verdict and planned a speedy appeal.

In PW's view, the jury's verdict was absurd and contrary to the evidence because the firm's audit met or exceeded professional standards. PW also pointed out that the amount of the verdict actually exceeded Standard Chartered's original investment in United Bancorp. It contended that Standard Chartered's losses were the result of its own business decision to sell the bank in a severely depressed market—independent of any information contained in PW's audits. With this suit, PW asserted, Standard Chartered sought to shift responsibility for its own error onto an accounting firm.

Although the eventual outcome of this case is unknown, it raises disturbing questions for PW and for all accounting partnerships. The sheer magnitude of the verdict, should it be upheld, would have a significant impact on the firm, but this case, together with the savings and loan cases and other litigation against other large firms, would undoubtedly force far-reaching and significant changes in the accounting industry and users of its services.

At the end of its first century, PW was generally regarded as the highest "quality" firm in the accounting profession. Its history endowed it with an outstanding client base, a reputation for probity and high principles, and a tradition of strong-minded, independent partners. This inheritance provided the base for a formidable strategy for the future, as the firm continues to be profitable and to grow throughout the United States.

The firm's historic strengths are very important. PW's widely known name and its blue-chip reputation are unique and valuable assets. In addition, its traditional position at the apex of the accounting profession allows PW senior partners to speak with authority on a variety of issues. John Biegler and Joseph Connor played prominent roles in shaping the modern profession's agenda, just as George O. May and Herman Bevis had in earlier periods. Another source of strength lies in the firm's selective partnership. PW's partners are accustomed to thinking and making decisions on their own, an advantage in a rapidly changing world.

Abundant experience in worldwide operations is another PW asset. The firm has long been a major presence abroad. The 1988 adoption of its global strategy suggests that the PW World Firm is determined to emphasize international services to clients of its member firms. As the U.S. firm and the European firm grow closer together as partners in a larger worldwide network, the history of PW can be seen as coming full circle.

During its first one hundred years, PW responded to a variety of challenges posed by the needs of its clients, the demands of the domestic and international economies, and the requirements of government. Choices that the partners' leadership made—to focus narrowly on the audit, to work for a specific customer base, and to rely on a reputation for high quality—have been adapted to address the new issues and requirements of the 1990s. During the 1980s, PW devoted a great deal of thought to its competitive strategy. It has prepared itself to confront the pressures of change by adapting its distinctive strengths and unique culture. Shaun F. O'Malley's job in 1990 was markedly different from that of Arthur Lowes Dickinson in 1905, or that of George O. May in 1925, or that of Herman W. Bevis in 1965. Given the pace of change, the day-to-day routine of the senior partner in 2025 is likely to be even more different. Undoubtedly, however, PW's strong culture and sense of history will serve as a source of strength and a solid basis for meeting the future's challenges.

APPENDIX

Price Waterhouse U.S. Firm Partners and Principals 1895–1992

Name	Year Admitted
William J. Caesar	1895
Sandys B. Foster	1895
Lewis D. Jones	1895
Henry W. Wilmot	1899
Arthur L. Dickinson	1901
Charles J. Marr	1902
George O. May	1902
William E. Seatree	1906
George R. Webster	1906
Joseph E. Sterrett	1907
Robert O. Berger	1911
Alexander B. Brodie	1911
John H. Bowman	1914
Charles P. Carruthers	1914

Sources: Chester W. DeMond, *Price, Waterhouse & Co. in America: A History of a Public Accounting Firm* (New York: Price Waterhouse, 1951); *Price Waterhouse Review*, 1955–1980; tables, memoranda, official firm correspondence, various firm sources; Partnership records, Office of the Secretary of the Firm, National Office, New York. (Service interruptions not shown.)

Name	Year Admitted
David L. Grey	1914
Joseph E. Masters	1914
Donald M. McClelland	1914
John Medlock	1914
John C. Scobie	1914
William B. Campbell	1917
William D. Bonthron	1918
Frank C. Belser	1920
Ismay G. Pattinson	1920
Harold West	1920
Donald Arthur	1924
Thomas Jackson	1924
Francis P. Byerly	1926
Geoffrey G. Rowbotham	1926
Ward B. Reynolds	1929
J. C. Moresby White	1929
Percival F. Brundage	1930
Arthur L. Brockway	1933
Einar C. Christensen	1933
John P. Dawson	1933
William W. Law	1933
Rodney F. Starkey	1933
William Charles	1934
Anthony Jaureguy	1934
Emile R. Niemela	1934
Hubert A. Stanley	1934
Robert W. Williams	1934
Archibald J. Bloodsworth	1936
Ernest O. Lothrop	1937
Percy Rappaport	1937
Hubert F. Ravenscroft	1937
Roy Andreae	1939
William L. Ashbaugh	1939
John B. Inglis	1939
O. Kenneth Pryor	1939
Chester W. DeMond	1940
Nicholas A. Leitner	1940
Alan P. L. Prest	1940
Alden C. Smith	1940
Thornton G. Douglas	1941

Name	Year Admitted
David F. Houlihan	1941
James W. Mathews	1941
John W. F. Neill	1941
Leland G. Sutherland	1941
Russell A. Zimmermann	1941
Donald R. Jennings	1943
John R. White	1943
Louis A. Wynhoff	1943
Andrew W. Barr	1944
Jonathan O. Dickinson	1944
Paul Grady	1944
William E. Wilkenloh	1945
Herman W. Bevis	1946
Edwin C. Chinlund	1946
Alphonsus T. Cummins	1946
Robert M. Griffiths	1946
Benjamin F. Jackson	1946
Joseph Pelej	1947
Royal C. Thurston	1947
William T. Hazelton	1949
Weston Rankin	1949
Gordon F. Gardner	1951
Raymond A. Hoffman	1951
Leslie Mills	1951
H. Dudley Murphy	1951
Walter M. Baird	1952
Maurice J. Dahlem	1952
Burnell H. DeVos	1952
Benjamin L. Enloe	1952
Horace S. Irving	1952
Robert H. Irving, Jr.	1952
John R. Jordan	1952
Paul E. Nye	1952
Edgar C. Suor	1952
Robert O. Berger, Jr.	1953
Hugh M. Campbell	1953
Richard S. Chamberlain	1953
Clark Sloat	1953
Charles A. Stewart	1953
Arthur B. Toan, Jr.	1953

NAME	YEAR ADMITTED
Frank M. Budik	1954
Theodore Herz	1954
George D. McCarthy	1954
Kallman Nashner	1954
Warde B. Ogden	1954
Theodore L. Wilkinson	1954
H. Edward Brunk, Jr.	1955
James W. Clark	1955
Emerson LeClercq	1955
John S. Darling	1955
Hugh M. Mercer	1955
Russell G. Rankin	1955
Adolph G. Schlossstein, Jr.	1955
Lawrence F. Shepack	1955
Stanley R. Thomas, Jr.	1955
Philo R. Zimmerman	1955
Clemens A. Erdahl	1956
Henry P. Hill	1956
William C. Miller	1956
C. Atwell Moore	1956
Fred G. Page	1956
Wyman G. Patten	1956
Joseph L. Roth	1956
B. Kenneth Sanden	1956
William A. Schan	1956
A. Carl Tietjen	1956
Owen Boal	1957
Francis C. Dykeman	1957
Hugh J. Fleming	1957
Charles E. Grenier, Jr.	1957
D. Ralph Malcolm, Jr.	1957
Gerald A. Maxfield	1957
Brendan J. Meagher	1957
Fred M. Rusk	1957
Paul C. Zaenglein	1957
John C. Biegler	1958
Joseph W. Brown	1958
Verden R. Draper	1958
Harry L. Freeman	1958
Thomas A. Ganner	1958

Name	Year Admitted
William F. Kewer	1958
Patrick J. Meagher	1958
John B. O'Hara	1958
Charles A. Utzinger	1958
George C. Watt	1958
Robert E. Field	1959
Eugene R. Mullins	1959
Edward H. Robertson	1959
Harry B. Sanders	1959
Ernest G. Weiss	1959
Harold J. Wolosin	1959
Wilbert W. Begeman	1960
Arthur Bettauer	1960
Otto P. Butterly	1960
Joseph D. Coughlan	1960
Ralph H. Franclemont	1960
Henry Gunders	1960
John P. Kelsey	1960
Herbert L. Koerner	1960
Harold R. Lammie	1960
Weldon B. Manwaring	1960
James G. Markezin	1960
Robert M. Maynard	1960
James J. McIntyre	1960
Charles K. Miller	1960
George S. Mottershead	1960
Leonard W. Raichle	1960
Leonard M. Savoie	1960
Arthur E. Surdam	1960
Ray B. Vaughters	1960
Edwin K. Walker	1960
John W. Zick	1960
G. Dewey Arnold	1961
Robert O. F. Bixby	1961
Robert P. Burns	1961
Earl P. Christensen	1961
Vincent Coe	1961
Albert H. Cohen	1961
Claude M. Cox	1961
Roscoe L. Egger, Jr.	1961

Name	Year Admitted
James Gibbons	1961
Wallace E. Giles	1961
Mark D. Larkin	1961
Richard E. Luhmann	1961
Clyde D. Mason	1961
John G. Peetz	1961
W. Arthur Stimpson	1961
Zach T. White	1961
Kenneth G. Cadematori	1962
Grant A. Fuller	1962
John D. Hannah	1962
Thomas J. Hayes, Jr.	1962
John G. Henderson	1962
Carl H. Hepp	1962
A. Dale Leighton	1962
Richard F. Luecht	1962
Clement L. Maher	1962
Aidan I. Mullett	1962
Guy R. Neely	1962
N. Clifford Nelson	1962
Ralph J. Nicholson	1962
Thomas L. Raleigh, Jr.	1962
Frank T. Rea	1962
Henry S. Sawin	1962
C. Robert Sturgis	1962
Gordon W. Tasker	1962
Wallace W. Willard	1962
Milton B. Basson	1963
John B. Farrell	1963
Richard D. Fitzgerald	1963
Howard L. Guyett	1963
Crawford C. Halsey	1963
H. Jackson Hendricks	1963
C. Paul Jannis	1963
Maurice E. Peloubet	1963
Percy W. Pogson	1963
Donald Rappaport	1963
William H. Shine	1963
Harold H. Shreckengast, Jr.	1963
Bruce F. Smith	1963

Name	Year Admitted
Frank E. Small	1963
Vance A. Wadhams	1963
Duane E. Watts	1963
Jack W. Wyker	1963
William Young	1963
Robert W. Ash	1964
James A. Dowsley	1964
Clyde H. Folley	1964
Robert H. Graves	1964
Paul A. Henschen	1964
Edward J. Lynott, Jr.	1964
Donald L. McIntosh	1964
Harry L. Morris	1964
Leon M. Nad	1964
John R. Purdy	1964
Donald H. Trautlein	1964
Charles E. Bradley	1965
Bertram A. Colbert	1965
Charles B. Daly	1965
Raymond J. Dubrowski	1965
Robert W. Ford	1965
John W. Gruber	1965
James E. Jensen	1965
Gifford E. Joseph	1965
Walton W. Kingsbery	1965
W. George Kramer, Jr.	1965
John M. Lane	1965
Raymond C. Lauver	1965
Paul B. Anderson	1966
John A. Carley	1966
David W. Christopher	1966
Burnell H. DeVos, Jr.	1966
J. Michael Farrell	1966
William R. Gifford	1966
Richard M. Hammer	1966
Robert E. Healy	1966
Richard J. Matteson	1966
V. Dennis McDade	1966
Sidney I. Oberman	1966
James M. Phillips	1966

Name	Year Admitted
Joseph J. Rigney, Jr.	1966
Frank M. Stotz	1966
Robert C. Thomas	1966
Donald K. Wilke	1966
Thomas Buck	1967
Thomas E. Byrne, Jr.	1967
Donald B. Chandler	1967
Joseph E. Connor	1967
Jack Farber	1967
Charlie Gill, Jr.	1967
Edward C. Harris, Jr.	1967
Robert V. W. Jahrling	1967
Richard N. Jensen	1967
Donald J. Kirk	1967
E. Keith Larson	1967
Frank N. Leitner	1967
Charles MacVeagh	1967
Robert C. Mann	1967
Donald F. Markstein	1967
Donald R. Mellert	1967
Robert G. Nichols	1967
Roger W. Nyquist	1967
Donald F. Schuppe	1967
Thomas R. Selby	1967
Dominic A. Tarantino	1967
Albert F. Zanger	1967
Donald R. Ziegler	1967
Jack B. Adams	1968
Richard H. Bertholdt	1968
William F. Clark	1968
Charles W. Elliott	1968
James J. Feeney	1968
Fred G. Frick	1968
Paul W. Hillier, Jr.	1968
Howard G. Johnson	1968
Michael F. Klein, Jr.	1968
John H. Kuckens, Jr.	1968
Phillip E. Lint	1968
Robert J. McDonald	1968
Charles J. O'Drobinak	1968

Name	Year Admitted
James W. Park	1968
Carl W. Ruppert	1968
Wade B. Salisbury	1968
Carl G. Ward	1968
James H. Weimer	1968
Fredrick M. Werblow	1968
John F. Williams	1968
Larimore Wright	1968
Richard G. Alfeld	1969
Karl W. Almquist	1969
Joseph V. Anania	1969
Robert L. Banks	1969
Ronald J. Bannister	1969
Vincent E. Benstead	1969
Thomas A. Brown	1969
Robert E. Conklin	1969
John A. Foppiano	1969
Raymond J. Gonzalez	1969
Malvern J. Gross	1969
William D. Hutchens	1969
Robert P. Kelly	1969
James J. Klink	1969
David M. Lang	1969
Norton R. Lowe	1969
Roger G. Marcellin	1969
Thomas M. McDonald	1969
James A. McMullen	1969
David P. Parker	1969
Walter D. Pugh	1969
Donald J. Reid	1969
Stanley I. Siegal	1969
William C. Smart	1969
Donald R. Smith	1969
Jay H. Anderson	1970
Robert J. Arndt	1970
John E. Buelt	1970
James J. Christensen	1970
Gerald F. Ciciola	1970
Charles J. Cook	1970
Ronald C. Crofton	1970

Name	Year Admitted
C. William Devaney	1970
Harold T. Dokupil	1970
Thomas A. Donahoe	1970
J. Garfield Donelson	1970
Ralph G. Egger	1970
Burton N. Forester	1970
James W. Gallagher	1970
Edward J. Haller	1970
Gayford L. Hinton	1970
Charles W. Hogue	1970
Jerrold A. Hunt	1970
Daniel W. Jerbasi	1970
John J. McAndrew	1970
Eugene L. Meyer	1970
James G. Nussbaum	1970
George M. Olson	1970
Shaun F. O'Malley	1970
Ira L. Paret	1970
Charles S. Schutte	1970
William Stoddart	1970
Daniel J. Sullivan	1970
Edward J. Taylor	1970
Benton B. Warder	1970
William Warshauer, Jr.	1970
William U. Westerfield	1970
Edward C. Arnold	1971
David A. Benner	1971
Roger S. Bruttomesso	1971
Thomas H. Chamberlain	1971
Thomas L. Curless	1971
Robert A. Dardenne	1971
Paul V. DeLomba	1971
R. Willis Faulk, Jr.	1971
James F. Hurley	1971
Ray H. Johnson	1971
John L. McDonough, Jr.	1971
Henry C. McPherson, Jr.	1971
Roger E. Miller	1971
James B. Swenson	1971
William A. White	1971

Name	Year Admitted
Paul E. Altig	1972
Thomas O. Beyer	1972
Sheridan C. Biggs, Jr.	1972
Walter R. Bogan	1972
Howard L. Braitman	1972
Joseph M. Buckheit	1972
Charles N. Coates	1972
James M. Costello	1972
Federico Davila	1972
Jerry D. Dingle	1972
Franklin R. Johnson	1972
John R. Jordan, Jr.	1972
James R. Keith	1972
Arthur Lindenauer	1972
J. Thomas Macy	1972
Timothy C. Mooney	1972
Lewis F. Nigh	1972
Robert C. Odmark	1972
Matthew J. O'Rourke	1972
John J. Pasteris	1972
Carl H. Poedtke, Jr.	1972
G. Edward Powell	1972
David C. Samuelson	1972
Dean H. Secord	1972
Arthur H. Siegel	1972
Norman Statland	1972
Richard H. Wheaton	1972
Raymond J. Worst	1972
Robert P. Albanesi	1973
J. Paul Breitbach	1973
Marianne Burge	1973
Craig D. Choate	1973
John W. Dillon	1973
Andrew L. DuBoff	1973
Jack W. Flamson	1973
Peter J. Gibbons	1973
Robert L. Gorvett	1973
T. Jarvis Greer	1973
Robert Hampton III	1973
Grant L. Hamrick	1973

Name	Year Admitted
Peter J. Hart	1973
Herbert P. Haschke, Jr.	1973
Norman F. Hollander	1973
Rollin P. Johnson	1973
Raymond J. Kosak	1973
Eugene I. Krieger	1973
Leonard E. Lofthus	1973
Joseph X. Loftus	1973
Richard P. Meehan	1973
Garry E. Moeller	1973
Clark M. Nelson	1973
Eldon Olson	1973
Thomas R. Orsi	1973
John P. Quinn	1973
Howard J. Sample	1973
Robert M. Sarsany	1973
George E. Schott	1973
James O. Stepp	1973
Michael J. Van Demark	1973
Robert F. Watson	1973
Peter G. Weiland	1973
Jeffrey W. Baus	1974
Merle D. Bird	1974
Robert D. Blair	1974
Duane C. Bojack	1974
Stanley H. Breitbard	1974
Edward L. Cameron	1974
Angel L. Castro	1974
L. Dale Crandall	1974
James G. Crump	1974
Daniel H. Cummings, Jr.	1974
D. Banks Currin	1974
James E. Daley	1974
Warren G. Davies	1974
Clifford T. Dirkes	1974
Mark W. DuMars	1974
William L. English	1974
James R. Fako	1974
Olaf M. Falkenhagen	1974
Richard E. Fogg	1974

Name	Year Admitted
David J. Fraboni	1974
Ralph P. Genovese	1974
Paul B. Goodstat	1974
Alan K. Greene	1974
Harold Haddock, Jr.	1974
John M. Hofmann	1974
Robert B. Hoover II	1974
James P. Huber	1974
George Jamieson, Jr.	1974
Bernard L. Johnson	1974
G. Hunter Jones	1974
Daniel P. Keegan	1974
Robert B. Kern	1974
Stephen H. Knowlton	1974
Yale Levin	1974
Thomas A. Marinkovich	1974
Robert S. McCoy, Jr.	1974
Peter B. McDowell	1974
James R. McKenzie	1974
Robert W. McMullen II	1974
Fred B. Miller	1974
James A. Miller	1974
Roger W. Peck	1974
Robert A. Petersen	1974
Robert E. Roth	1974
Arthur L. Ruffing, Jr.	1974
Robert P. Schmidt	1974
Sheldon D. Schneider	1974
R. Lawrence Soares	1974
James C. Stalder	1974
C. Dale Steinmetz	1974
Diedrich Von Soosten, Jr.	1974
J. Elwood Walker	1974
Joel Whitman	1974
John K. Wingfield	1974
H. William Acker	1975
John Bonacci, Jr.	1975
William R. Boothby	1975
Timothy M. Coffey	1975
James M. Coriston	1975

Name	Year Admitted
Arthur W. DeMelle	1975
Kenneth G. Docter	1975
Kenneth J. Doyle	1975
Peter S. Drotch	1975
John B. Esch	1975
Howard S. Frank	1975
Richard H. Gherst II	1975
Norman J. Ginstling	1975
John O. Hatab	1975
William G. Joyner	1975
William M. Keane	1975
James S. Kozera	1975
Lawrence F. Kunkler	1975
H. Gary Larson	1975
William J. Larson	1975
Donald T. Menovich	1975
Peter W. Minges	1975
R. Watson Moyers	1975
Robert A. Mulshine	1975
James M. Norman	1975
John P. O'Brien	1975
Michael J. Passeralla	1975
Paul O. Pederson	1975
Lawrence F. Portnoy	1975
John H. Reed, Jr.	1975
Christopher D. Simpson	1975
Richard J. Strowger	1975
John R. Walsh, Jr.	1975
W. James Whelan	1975
Martin J. Blumberg	1976
Frederic I. Bower III	1976
Abbott L. Brown	1976
William J. Driscoll, Jr.	1976
J. Stephen Enlow	1976
Lewis M. Gill, Jr.	1976
David W. Hamstead	1976
John H. Harrington	1976
Ralph A. Hoffman	1976
Arthur E. Jenks	1976
John W. Kercher III	1976

NAME	YEAR ADMITTED
Mark L. Klein	1976
Thomas D. Leddy	1976
John A. Leyes	1976
James R. Lovett	1976
John A. Lynn	1976
James L. McDonald	1976
Earle J. Milbery	1976
David W. Orange	1976
Thomas A. Porter	1976
James F. Rabenhorst	1976
Daniel C. Regis	1976
Thomas J. Scanlon	1976
Beuford T. Shirley, Jr.	1976
Gilbert Simonetti, Jr.	1976
John B. Singel, Jr.	1976
Ronald L. Skates	1976
Robert C. Thorell	1976
Douglas E. Van Scoy	1976
Bob W. Vick	1976
G. Thomas Willis	1976
Norman B. Adams	1977
William L. Bax	1977
John F. Bernier	1977
Paul C. Brou	1977
A. Bernarr Burke	1977
Kevin K. Carton	1977
Richard O. Connell	1977
Glenn E. Corlett	1977
F. George Drewry	1977
J. Rodney Felts	1977
Peter B. Frank	1977
John J. Gaffney	1977
Jonathan D. Harris	1977
F. William Hoffman	1977
Thomas L. Hoops	1977
Lawrence S. Kaplan	1977
Richard J. Kaplan	1977
Patrick M. Keller	1977
Anthony M. Komlyn	1977
Thomas W. Kuchta	1977

Name	Year Admitted
D. Leon Leonhardt	1977
Barry G. Lewis	1977
Dean J. Markezin	1977
Terence D. Martin	1977
John J. McCabe	1977
James P. McNally	1977
Edward F. Miller III	1977
Francisco J. Olazabal	1977
John D. Pastor	1977
Charles V. Ricks	1977
Glenn A. Rose	1977
Coleman D. Ross	1977
Steven M. Scheiner	1977
Richard E. Schreiber, Jr.	1977
Larry W. Shoultz	1977
Roger J. Steinbecker	1977
Robert W. Strickler	1977
Norman R. Walker	1977
William H. Walker	1977
W. Ronald Walton	1977
Joseph E. Warden	1977
William M. Wheeler II	1977
Neal W. Zimmerman	1977
Dean A. Adams	1978
Thomas E. Baker	1978
Donald C. Bamberger	1978
Douglas E. Bender	1978
Robert D. Biggs	1978
Paul R. Bjorn	1978
Jay D. Brodish	1978
Robert E. Butler	1978
Edward R. Cheramy, Jr.	1978
Edward H. Cichurski	1978
James Clancy	1978
John F. Connell	1978
J. Terry Eager	1978
David G. Efurd	1978
William F. Emswiler	1978
Lionel I. Endsley	1978
Donald Epelbaum	1978

NAME	YEAR ADMITTED
Jeffrey E. Ferries	1978
Antonio Ginorio	1978
Woodrin Grossman	1978
O. Bruce Gupton	1978
Rockell N. Hankin	1978
William R. Harlowe	1978
Richard S. Hirsh	1978
Robert A. Huber	1978
William F. Huber	1978
Edward G. Jepsen	1978
Robert R. Keenan	1978
Franklin H. Kelly	1978
James P. Kovacs	1978
Edward L. Krommer, Jr.	1978
Lewis J. Krulwich	1978
Suryanarayan Lakshmanan	1978
David R. Lawrence	1978
Ronald A. Leberfing	1978
Lennart S. Lindegren	1978
John H. MacKinnon	1978
Glenn W. Matthews	1978
John J. McGowen	1978
John J. McNally	1978
Jack P. McSherry	1978
Alan R. Miller	1978
Ernest J. Mortensen	1978
Thomas C. Musgrove	1978
L. Theodore Neighbors	1978
Donald T. Nicolaisen	1978
Bernard P. O'Hare	1978
Solomon Packer	1978
Jerome F. Peck	1978
Benjamin W. Perks	1978
John A. Roszak	1978
Ronald W. Ruppel	1978
Hans G. Schumacher	1978
J. Taylor Simonton	1978
C. Randolph Skidmore	1978
Joseph F. Spencer	1978
Terrance T. Stretch	1978

NAME	YEAR ADMITTED
Paul C. Sundeen	1978
Philip A. Tremonti	1978
Gerald E. Van Strydonck	1978
James G. Walls	1978
Kent D. Watson	1978
Douglas C. Younce	1978
Allen I. Young	1978
Thomas W. Baxter	1979
David L. Beasley	1979
Richard J. Behrens	1979
Jeffrey B. Bradford	1979
Robert W. Calcutt	1979
Douglas D. Calvin	1979
John L. Carroll	1979
Alan N. Certain	1979
Daniel P. Connealy	1979
Stewart R. Crane	1979
George F. Davin	1979
James M. Dewey	1979
H. John Dirks	1979
Wallace A. Ducayet	1979
John V. Ehmann	1979
Michael H. Francisco	1979
Eugene F. Gaughan	1979
William H. Giese	1979
James H. Hance, Jr.	1979
C. Scott Hartz	1979
Linda C. Heller	1979
John A. Hess	1979
A. Jackson Holt	1979
Glenn H. Johnson, Jr.	1979
Emory L. Kesteloot	1979
Robert D. Kittredge	1979
William D. Kramer	1979
Fredric L. Laughlin	1979
Thomas A. Leipzig	1979
Robert B. Lewis	1979
Robert J. Marzec	1979
Robert M. Mathis	1979
William T. Muir	1979

Name	Year Admitted
Lawrence G. Nardolillo	1979
Michael J. Quinn	1979
Michael R. Redemske	1979
James W. Schenold	1979
James J. Schiro	1979
Lester L. Shonto	1979
Kenton J. Sicchitano	1979
James A. Spielmann	1979
John R. Tennant	1979
Grady M. Townsend	1979
Thomas D. Trimmer	1979
Raymond S. Weinstein	1979
Alan S. Woodberry	1979
Martin F. Baumann	1980
Thomas E. Blythe	1980
Raymond J. Bromark	1980
Jeffrey F. Brugos	1980
Robert J. Burgess	1980
John H. Cary	1980
Ross C. Cramer	1980
J. Richard Dowell	1980
Craig P. Duncan	1980
Paul G. Flores	1980
G. Thomas Frankland	1980
Ronald J. Gibson	1980
Robert B. Glisson	1980
Oakley Hall	1980
Michael D. Hendrickson	1980
R. Braxton Hill, Jr.	1980
Creighton G. Hoffman	1980
Mark S. Housel	1980
James B. Hunt	1980
George H. Juetten	1980
Carl F. Kantner	1980
Eugene S. Katz	1980
Paul M. Kiffner	1980
Keith C. Klaver	1980
David F. Kleeman	1980
Kay M. Lindstrom	1980
Paul E. Lohneis	1980

Name	Year Admitted
Roland Maas	1980
Philip P. Mannino	1980
James J. Mogelnicki	1980
Joseph C. Murphy	1980
George J. Mutter	1980
Walter J. Pankiewicz	1980
J. David Parrish	1980
John J. Pauliny	1980
William M. Pfann	1980
Peter R. Powell	1980
Oz T. Scogna	1980
John M. Smartt, Jr.	1980
Richard R. Spears	1980
Lawrence A. Stoler	1980
Jack E. Sum	1980
Leslie J. Thomas	1980
Stanley V. Vogler	1980
Thomas W. Walsh	1980
Ronald F. Watts	1980
William H. Allen	1981
Carl B. Barnes	1981
William P. Batiste	1981
Ben I. Boldt, Jr.	1981
James A. Byrne	1981
Robin Callan	1981
Luther L. Campbell, Jr.	1981
Girard S. Clothier	1981
Brian L. Cornell	1981
Joseph D. Dionisio	1981
Gary F. Dornbush	1981
David J. Drury	1981
Robert G. Eiler	1981
Roger J. Guido	1981
Jay P. Hartig	1981
Eric G. Juline	1981
Steven Kramer	1981
Charles A. Lang	1981
Alan B. Lee	1981
William M. Lehman	1981
William A. Mooney, Jr.	1981

Name	Year Admitted
Joseph B. Moore	1981
Robert K. Neilson	1981
Jack R. Nicolai	1981
Harold J. O'Keefe	1981
Wayne H. Pace	1981
Vijay Raval	1981
James H. Rosenthall	1981
Raymond B. Ryan	1981
Bernard M. Shapiro	1981
Eric A. Simonsen	1981
J. Larry Stevens	1981
Harold J. Straka	1981
Mark L. Sullivan	1981
John B. Turner	1981
Paul E. Weaver	1981
Steven A. Wolf	1981
Lawrence M. Alleva	1982
Frank M. Alston	1982
William J. Bawden	1982
Michael J. Boberschmidt	1982
Michael Budnick	1982
Shirley J. Cheramy	1982
Barry R. Chernack	1982
Donald L. Crews	1982
G. William Dauphinais	1982
Stephen D. Desmond	1982
David A. Dresner	1982
James K. Edmund	1982
J. Christopher Everett	1982
Robert S. Falcone	1982
H. McDonald Felder	1982
John R. Fridley	1982
Reed S. Gardiner	1982
Kevin C. Gaynor	1982
Russell C. Gesme	1982
Walter K. Goletz	1982
James E. Goodwin, Jr.	1982
Thomas W. Green, Jr.	1982
Robert L. Haddad	1982
John M. Hillhouse	1982

Name	Year Admitted
Stephen F. Huggins	1982
Lawrence G. Hupka	1982
E. Joseph Kallas, Jr.	1982
James R. Kilzer	1982
Daniel A. Kubiak	1982
Michael D. Le Roy	1982
Daniel R. Lyle	1982
Thomas J. Madonna	1982
John S. McCormack	1982
Dennis L. Neider	1982
J. Michael Patterson	1982
Hugh R. Penny	1982
Barbara J. Pope	1982
L. Fred Pounds	1982
Robert R. Ross	1982
Edgar C. Shanks	1982
Stanley F. Shimohara	1982
Stephen P. Tacke	1982
Gerald M. Ward	1982
Brett D. Yacker	1982
Thomas T. Yamakawa	1982
Ranjit R. Advani	1983
Robert L. Anderson	1983
C. Michael Benston	1983
Richard J. Berry, Jr.	1983
Richard P. Boyatzi	1983
Willard W. Brittain	1983
Arden S. Bucher	1983
John J. Coneys, Jr.	1983
Duane C. Cutter	1983
Barry L. DeMartini	1983
P. Timothy Dietz	1983
Ronald Dobey	1983
Michael O. Gagnon	1983
David R. Hancock	1983
Marinus N. Henny	1983
Gregory P. Hickey	1983
Stephen D. Higgins	1983
Sam W. Hunsaker	1983
Donald L. Irving	1983

Name	Year Admitted
Chandler H. Joyner	1983
R. James Kelly, Jr.	1983
A. Lawrence Kikkert	1983
Montie F. Lee	1983
William A. Linnenbringer	1983
Henry W. H. Lum	1983
Mark D. Lutchen	1983
Rafael F. Martinez	1983
Michael J. Mayer	1983
Mark L. McConaghy	1983
Richard B. McKnight	1983
David L. Miller	1983
W. Frank Morgan, Jr.	1983
John B. Morse, Jr.	1983
Marc D. Oken	1983
Randall S. O'Hare	1983
Patrick J. O'Malley	1983
Stephen O. Pierce	1983
Fred U. Pshyk	1983
Ernest L. Puschaver	1983
Stanley H. Rose III	1983
Ralph A. Rouse	1983
James R. Sass	1983
Carl E. Schwab	1983
Richard B. Skor	1983
Aaron A. Smith	1983
Mordecai Soloff	1983
Jimmie T. Stark	1983
Terry L. Stevens	1983
Paul J. Sullivan	1983
David M. Todd	1983
John R. Waite	1983
Jonathan E. Wilfong	1983
Wesley W. Williams III	1983
William A. Wilson	1983
Patricia J. Bedinger	1984
Charles E. Berg	1984
Dennis Blanc	1984
William J. Butler	1984
K. Clark Childers	1984

Name	Year Admitted
William J. Chrnelich	1984
William J. Cleary	1984
Thomas P. Colberg	1984
W. Thomas Cross	1984
Carl M. Donnelly	1984
John S. Fowler	1984
James L. Gegg	1984
Patrick M. Gray	1984
Richard E. Hennessey	1984
Roger C. Hindman	1984
Robert L. Hoyer	1984
Thomas E. Johnson	1984
Scott W. Kaufman	1984
Richard P. Kearns	1984
Clifford T. Kernohan	1984
Richard R. Kilgust	1984
Ben B. Korbly	1984
W. Craig Kuhl	1984
Robert A. Lass	1984
Mark A. Lassiter	1984
Ruurd G. Leegstra	1984
Vanelli A. Lovisa	1984
Dennis J. Luboznyski	1984
Edward J. Mahoney	1984
Deirdre W. Marshall-Broom	1984
George E. Minnich	1984
Jerome T. Mullaney	1984
Jose A. Perez	1984
Francis A. Piantidosi	1984
Guy M. Piper II	1984
Bernard K. Plagman	1984
John J. Power, Jr.	1984
Kevin F. Roach	1984
Richard A. Rossi	1984
Michael Salzberg	1984
Dean P. Schuckman	1984
Kenneth G. Simpson	1984
Brian W. Smith	1984
Robert A. Smith	1984
Michael S. Steinberg	1984

Name	Year Admitted
Robert M. Tarola	1984
Frederick C. Tinsey III	1984
James T. Wheary	1984
John A. Witt	1984
William F. Wolf	1984
Alfred J. Amoroso	1985
Reinhard R. Augustin	1985
Jerome H. Bailey	1985
Martin R. Bailey	1985
Gregory E. Bardnell	1985
James M. Barrett	1985
Charles A. Bauer	1985
Barbara J. Bealer	1985
Michael D. Cannon	1985
Gary R. Cesnik	1985
James D. Cigler	1985
Michael S. Collins	1985
Thomas E. Darcy	1985
Darrell D. Dorrell	1985
Frances C. Engoron	1985
Osmund R. Fretz III	1985
Thomas H. Gibson	1985
Louis P. Goldsman	1985
Andrew P. Harwood	1985
Steven Heck	1985
Stephen N. Holland	1985
Edwin N. Homer	1985
Fernando Ibarguengoitia	1985
Thomas H. Insley	1985
W. Theodore Kresge, Jr.	1985
Stanley R. Kwiatkowski	1985
L. Michael Larrenaga	1985
Jan M. Larson	1985
David B. Lewis	1985
Ralph G. Loretta	1985
Daniel J. Maloney	1985
Richard A. Martin	1985
Joseph J. Marucci	1985
Michael K. Meredith	1985
Andrew M. Miller	1985

Name	Year Admitted
Paul J. Mooney	1985
Dennis D. Morrison	1985
Dennis M. Nally	1985
Karen A. Nold	1985
Gary L. O'Banion	1985
Ronald L. Padgett	1985
Daniel H. Pollock	1985
William O. Powell III	1985
Richard C. Ramsden	1985
Gary L. Rhea	1985
Charles J. Robel	1985
Lloyd J. Russell	1985
James M. Schneider	1985
E. Jan Smith	1985
Anthony P. Spohr	1985
Richard B. Spooner	1985
Richard B. Stanger	1985
John L. Steffan	1985
Daniel J. Sweeney	1985
Steven O. Swyers	1985
Guy M. Tufo	1985
Michael J. Wagner	1985
Steven A. Wagner	1985
John F. Walsh	1985
Cyrus C. Wilson	1985
John B. Woodlief	1985
W. Dale Young	1985
Howard H. Aycock	1986
George E. L. Barbee	1986
John H. Bell	1986
Robin D. Beran	1986
Francis N. Bonsignore	1986
Robert M. Bowlin	1986
Julian G. Buck	1986
Michael J. Byrne	1986
Nicholas Cammarano, Jr.	1986
Donald F. Caputo	1986
Robert H. Cawly	1986
James F. Chadbourne III	1986
Gary R. Claus	1986

NAME	YEAR ADMITTED
Kenneth L. Cooke	1986
Michael V. Costanzo	1986
Arthur B. Dana	1986
Larry L. Dildine	1986
Thomas J. Duvall	1986
Dieter W. Elsner	1986
Thomas M. Field	1986
J. Christopher Forhecz	1986
Michael E. Graves	1986
Richard D. Greaves	1986
Jorge A. Gross	1986
Richard C. Highberger	1986
Abram E. Hoffman	1986
Thomas E. Hoffmeister	1986
Wilbert H. Howey	1986
Ronald J. Hull	1986
Spencer C. Jones	1986
Harold D. Kahn	1986
E. Andrew Kaskiw	1986
Richard M. Kenyon	1986
Edward J. Kernan	1986
Allen Kirkpatrick IV	1986
John J. Korbel	1986
Sheldon J. Laube	1986
David L. Laudel	1986
C. Martin Leinwand	1986
Robert W. Linaberry	1986
Steven A. Lupinacci	1986
Edward W. Machir	1986
J. Robert Medlin, Jr.	1986
Brian J. Monbouquette	1986
Richard A. Muir	1986
Joseph P. Page	1986
Douglas L. Pinney	1986
Lee S. Piper	1986
David W. Pittman	1986
Stephen L. Powlesland	1986
Robert J. Price	1986
Larry B. Quimby	1986
Albert A. Remekis	1986

Name	Year Admitted
Barry P. Robbins	1986
Robert C. Russell	1986
Arnold Z. Segal	1986
Paul C. Seitz	1986
Mark B. Singer	1986
Catherine Z. Smith	1986
James L. Solley	1986
J. Richard Stamm	1986
John M. Tangney	1986
Gary A. Thalhuber	1986
Irene M. Thompson	1986
Joseph S. Tibbetts, Jr.	1986
Anthony D. Todd	1986
William F. Vieson	1986
D. L. Hughes Watler, Jr.	1986
Harold K. Wiebusch	1986
Keith S. Wishon	1986
John T. Zembron	1986
Juan C. Acebal	1987
Marta Acevedo	1987
Donald V. Almeida	1987
Joseph T. Anastasi, Jr.	1987
Lloyd G. Ator, Jr.	1987
Gary L. Bannon	1987
Christopher D. Barbee	1987
Robert R. Bench	1987
Peter S. Beveridge	1987
Mark J. Bonner	1987
Thomas R. Bretz	1987
Francis A. Brown	1987
Ryan D. Burdeno	1987
Victor P. Capadona	1987
William H. Carter	1987
John D. Cavanaugh	1987
Trent B. Chambers	1987
Christopher A. Cipriano	1987
John W. Copley	1987
Gail P. Cummins	1987
Stephen R. Darcy	1987
James H. Dezart	1987

Name	Year Admitted
Daniel V. Dooley	1987
Martin E. Doran	1987
Charles H. Eggleston	1987
James A. Eidam	1987
Scott B. Fabricant	1987
Gregory S. Farish	1987
Raymond L. Fiegel	1987
Robert S. Franco	1987
Keith J. Fulmer	1987
P. Gregory Garrison	1987
Warren H. Glettner	1987
A. Timothy Godwin	1987
William T. Gordon III	1987
Roger J. Grabowski	1987
John M. Hannon	1987
Raymond G. Harrier	1987
John G. Henderson, Jr.	1987
Glenn A. Hiraga	1987
Richard H. Holoman	1987
Richard H. Izumi	1987
Charles R. Jones	1987
David B. Kaplan	1987
Richard G. Kleiner	1987
Michael D. Lincoln	1987
Wayne B. Lippman	1987
Samuel J. Martin	1987
Donald A. McGovern	1987
Richard H. Miller	1987
Thomas M. Moore	1987
Maureen F. Morrison	1987
Brady W. Mullinax, Jr.	1987
Michael P. Nelligan	1987
Joseph A. Ness	1987
Ippei Okutake	1987
Joseph A. Osbourn	1987
Richard D. Paterson	1987
Gary R. Pell	1987
Robert E. Pound	1987
Michael L. Reidy	1987
Robert P. Roche	1987

Name	Year Admitted
Robert J. Rock	1987
Thomas I. Rubel	1987
B. Robert Rubin	1987
Carol M. Rutlen	1987
James R. Shanahan	1987
Timothy R. Slapnicka	1987
John B. Stine II	1987
Mark X. Stratman	1987
George G. Strong, Jr.	1987
John P. Surma	1987
Donald E. Thomas	1987
T. Craig True	1987
Lloyd E. Voneiff, Jr.	1987
Don L. Waters	1987
Richard A. Watts	1987
Sydelle B. Weinberger	1987
William T. Willis	1987
Michael R. Winter	1987
Peter R. Woolf	1987
Margaret M. Worthington	1987
Steven M. Abraham	1988
Gregg A. Agens	1988
Barnell Albers	1988
Mark A. Anderson	1988
Anthony J. Artabane	1988
Alan R. Augenstein	1988
Stephen G. Austin	1988
Mary Beth Backof	1988
Richard M. Bayersdorfer	1988
Mark S. Beery	1988
Jonathan P. Bellis	1988
John T. Bigalke	1988
Barrett L. Boehm	1988
Thomas M. Brantley	1988
Thomas W. Britton, Jr.	1988
Thomas P. Butler	1988
William M. Byerley	1988
John D. Caplan	1988
Elizabeth A. Case	1988
Timothy C. Clayton	1988

Name	Year Admitted
John J. Contini	1988
Michael G. Corrigan	1988
Thomas J. Craren	1988
William S. Crewe	1988
Michael F. Deniszczuk	1988
Dominic DiNapoli	1988
Carl W. Duyck	1988
J. Dennis Fennessey	1988
Craig L. Fitzgerald	1988
Robert M. Fitzgerald	1988
Robert A. Flaum	1988
James P. Gannon	1988
Gregory S. Garvey	1988
Cornelius A. Gaskin III	1988
Dale L. Gentsch	1988
Paul L. Gillis	1988
Jay B. Goldman	1988
Lawrence B. Gooch	1988
Patricia A. Hammer	1988
J. Richard Harvey, Jr.	1988
David Hodgson	1988
James M. Holec, Jr.	1988
Willis B. Jones	1988
John A. Kavka	1988
Francis J. King	1988
Jeffrey H. Kinrich	1988
Herbert J. Kleinberger	1988
Ronald C. Knecht, Jr.	1988
E. William Koons III	1988
Charles F. G. Kuyk	1988
Susan K. Leonard	1988
Rodney R. Litke	1988
Gregory N. Lubushkin	1988
Steven K. Lumpkin	1988
Thomas J. Marine	1988
Edward J. Matley	1988
D. Reed Maughan	1988
Thomas A. McSweeny	1988
Karl H. Moody, Jr.	1988
Stewart S. Morick	1988

Name	Year Admitted
Douglas R. Muir	1988
Jonathan H. Mullins	1988
Thomas M. Murnane	1988
Maryann E. Murphy	1988
Andrew E. Nolan	1988
William M. Noonan	1988
Peter B. O'Brien	1988
Norman K. Nystrom	1988
Peter B. O'Brien	1988
Stephen E. Odom	1988
Michael S. Olszewski	1988
Jeff C. Parmet	1988
Dominic C. Pino	1988
Judith A. Reach	1988
M. Freddie Reiss	1988
Kenneth M. Rem	1988
Howard V. Richardson	1988
Alan L. Ross	1988
Richard K. Roth	1988
M. Stan Royal	1988
Roberto E. Santa Maria	1988
John S. Scheid	1988
Herbert C. Schulken, Jr.	1988
Jim D. Schultz	1988
Nyles B. Schumaker	1988
L. Gregory Scott	1988
William R. Shipley	1988
Patrick J. Shouvlin	1988
Raymond S. Sims	1988
Robert S. Smith	1988
Roger C. Smith	1988
Thomas M. Sullivan	1988
David E. Sweet	1988
James D. Tapper	1988
Rajagopal S. Tatta	1988
Stephen A. Terry	1988
William D. Turner	1988
Michael van den Akker	1988
Peggy M. Vaughan	1988
Ronald G. Vollmar	1988

Name	Year Admitted
James A. Waddell	1988
Barry Wagenknecht	1988
Robert M. Wagman	1988
James R. Ziegelbauer, Jr.	1988
John E. Bachman	1989
Kevin M. Bacon	1989
Saul J. Berman	1989
James G. Bowers	1989
V. Walter Bratic	1989
J. Frank Brown	1989
Robert L. Brown	1989
Frederic C. Brussee	1989
Daniel W. Campbell	1989
Elaine K. Church	1989
Ira Cohen	1989
Larry R. Cosmo	1989
Bruce A. Daigh	1989
Douglas H. Dickey	1989
David J. Duray	1989
David A. Eisner	1989
James T. Elliott, Jr.	1989
Stephen G. Errico	1989
Roger A. Feusier	1989
George B. Forster	1989
Gregory M. Fowler	1989
Donard P. Gaynor	1989
Karl C. Gebert	1989
Dante H. Giannini	1989
Robert R. Glatz	1989
Susan A. Graham	1989
W. Reed Graves, Jr.	1989
Jay L. Henderson	1989
Henry P. Holland	1989
David B. Horner	1989
Peter N. James	1989
Mary E. Kearney	1989
Nevada A. Kent IV	1989
Harish Khanna	1989
Kenneth H. Kral	1989
Anthony M. Krizman	1989

Name	Year Admitted
Douglas F. Kunkel	1989
John K. Lane	1989
Patrick J. Leemputte	1989
Ed J. Lynch	1989
Kevin T. Maguire	1989
Robert T. McCahill	1989
Krishen Mehta	1989
Thomas P. Morgan	1989
Robert P. Muir	1989
Cathy J. Neuman	1989
Michael L. Pfeiffer	1989
Robert E. Pickering, Jr.	1989
J. Dale Ragone	1989
Lawrence F. Ranallo	1989
Gary W. Riley	1989
Joseph G. Roosevelt	1989
Rip A. Sanders	1989
Bruce A. Shepard	1989
Robert A. Sherwood	1989
Marc V. Simons	1989
John M. Simpson	1989
Brian J. Stief	1989
Matthew C. Stolte	1989
Jennifer Taylor	1989
David J. Trogan	1989
Mark A. Volker	1989
Herbert E. Walter II	1989
Wendell W. Weakley	1989
Frederick D. Wolf	1989
Elizabeth H. Yant	1989
Stephen J. Yarina	1989
Raymond F. Young	1989
Robert A. Zarzar	1989
Henry G. Adamany, Jr.	1990
Paula Alvary	1990
Michael E. Balk	1990
Edward H. Bastian	1990
Richard C. Beaumont	1990
Rodman W. Benedict	1990
Samuel E. Berger	1990

NAME	YEAR ADMITTED
Thomas G. Berkery	1990
Lawrence G. Bieniek	1990
John R. Blankinship	1990
Neil S. Blumenthal	1990
Jarrad L. Bunch	1990
Richard J. Calzaretta	1990
Glenn W. Carlson	1990
Carol R. Caruthers	1990
Michael P. Cenko	1990
Richard H. Colabella	1990
Stephen B. Cook	1990
Charles V. Dannewitz	1990
Jeremy R. Davies	1990
E. Wilson Davis	1990
John H. Deane	1990
Thomas C. Devlin	1990
Timothy J. Donnelly	1990
Cullen A. Duke	1990
Kristian D. Engh	1990
Frederick W. Fagerstrom	1990
Jeffrey Felton	1990
John K. Fletcher	1990
Richard A. Genovese	1990
George J. Gillen, Jr.	1990
Dennis J. Goginsky	1990
Edmund O. Goll	1990
Donald M. Haas	1990
Christopher A. Hamilos	1990
Michael J. Hamilton	1990
Philip G. Hirsch	1990
Daniel C. Hirschbuehler	1990
Wallace W. Hussey	1990
Timothy M. Inglis	1990
Robert L. Jerome	1990
Richard L. Johnson	1990
Thomas B. Joyce	1990
Edward W. Kay, Jr.	1990
Donald P. Keller	1990
Peter K. Kelly	1990
George L. Kennedy	1990

NAME	YEAR ADMITTED
Robert S. Knudsen	1990
Erman E. Lepley, Jr.	1990
Stephanie M. Manuel	1990
Marcia W. Marsh	1990
Franklin D. Marsteller	1990
James R. McCarthy	1990
Michael J. McColgan	1990
Vicki H. Wilson-McElreath	1990
Thomas A. Merritt	1990
Geoffrey W. Miller	1990
Timothy G. Morgan	1990
William R. Morris	1990
Patricia B. Norris	1990
Daniel J. O'Dea	1990
Mark J. Ondash	1990
Robert G. Page	1990
David J. Piper	1990
Richard A. Quimby	1990
Stephen F. Ralbovsky	1990
Frank J. Roney	1990
Randall C. Runk	1990
Arlene J. Sakatos	1990
Joseph Scirocco	1990
Joseph A. Smialowski	1990
Duaine D. Smith	1990
Judith Stoikov	1990
Karen L. Stuckey	1990
Raymond D. Trakimas	1990
Michael M. Wathen	1990
Melvin E. Weems	1990
Kenneth L. Wertz	1990
Bettina M. Whyte	1990
David W. Zechnich	1990
Peter N. Zolintakis	1990
Richie L. Zook	1990
Christopher C. Barry	1991
Bruce P. Benson	1991
Robert I. Biebel	1991
Stephen E. Buehler	1991
Vincent L. Burns	1991

Name	Year Admitted
Carl E. Calendar, Jr.	1991
Carol M. Calkins	1991
Richard M. Clark	1991
Kevin G. Connolly	1991
Barry L. Dennis	1991
R. Bruce Den Uyl	1991
Stephen M. Ditman	1991
Michael Donahue	1991
Carmen R. Eggleston	1991
Gregory A. Falk	1991
Daniel P. Feheley	1991
Vincent L. Flannery	1991
Mark C. Gasbarra	1991
Robert A. Golden	1991
Randy D. Gray	1991
Gail H. Hadley	1991
Mark W. Haller	1991
Ward R. Hamm III	1991
James H. Henry	1991
Mark E. Hoffman	1991
Ann B. Hopkins	1991
Paul J. Horowitz	1991
Cathleen G. Hylton	1991
R. Wayne Jackson	1991
Douglas I. Kalish	1991
J. Timothy Kelly	1991
John J. Kiely, Jr.	1991
John R. Kretchmer	1991
Francis J. Lattanzio	1991
Jeffrey R. Lehman	1991
Lawrence B. Leisure	1991
Albert P. Lilienfeld	1991
D. Lee McCreary	1991
Peter J. McIntosh	1991
Kevin R. Merkell	1991
Kurt R. Miller	1991
Brian A. Mitchell	1991
Marshall L. Mohr	1991
Cynthia R. Morris	1991
Curtis L. Muncy	1991

Name	Year Admitted
Steven R. Nameth	1991
Christian W. Nolet	1991
James J. O'Shaughnessy	1991
Robert J. Pachmayer	1991
Bruce B. Piper III	1991
Robert J. Puls	1991
John J. Reville	1991
Auguste E. Rimpel, Jr.	1991
Dean L. Ruehle	1991
Stephen M. Schlabs	1991
Michael J. Schroeck	1991
Mark C. Sheeran	1991
Michael B. Sirkin	1991
Christine G. Snyder	1991
Frank C. Steininger	1991
John R. Stubbs	1991
Phillip C. Surprenant	1991
Lawrence A. Thibodeau	1991
Robert L. Vallee	1991
Anthony C. Venezia	1991
Albert A. Vondra	1991
E. Steven White	1991
R. Michael Willis	1991
Paul M. Balas	1992
Wayne L. Bartel	1992
Simon J. Beaumont	1992
Michael A. Bell	1992
Spencer H. Clawson	1992
Denis J. Duncan	1992
Randall L. Edgar	1992
Donald P. Favre	1992
Yasuo Fukushima	1992
Glenn J. Galfond	1992
James S. Gonet	1992
Michael L. Herman	1992
H. Fletcher Homer III	1992
Frank E. Hydoski	1992
Kevin M. Kelleher	1992
William P. Kelleher	1992
H. Robert Kennedy	1992

NAME	YEAR ADMITTED
Dean M. Kern	1992
John J. Klee	1992
Michael J. Kliegman	1992
Martha E. M. Kopacz	1992
Charles E. Lambert	1992
Jeffrey M. Margolies	1992
Kiyoshi Matsuo	1992
Michael J. May	1992
William M. McGee	1992
Hugh A. Menown	1992
Jorge Morazzani	1992
Douglas E. Morgan	1992
James C. Palumbo	1992
Juan A. Pujadas	1992
William J. Ramsden	1992
R. Byron Ratliff	1992
Michael J. Reuschel	1992
David Y. Rogers	1992
Deborah L. Rogers	1992
Mark J. Rubash	1992
Timothy J. Sacheck	1992
Steven C. Schnoebelen	1992
Michael A. Sommer	1992
Roy E. Strowd, Jr.	1992
Robert P. Sullivan	1992
Keith R. Ugone	1992
Arthur A. Wachholz III	1992
Paul J. Weber	1992
David R. Williams	1992
Spencer M. Wong	1992
Philip M. Zinn	1992

NOTES

CHAPTER 1

1. G.E. Richards, *History of the Firm: The First Fifty Years, 1850–1900* ([London?]: [Price, Waterhouse & Company], 1950), 1.

2. Edgar Jones, *Accountancy and the British Economy, 1840–1980: The Evolution of Ernst & Whinney* (London: B.T. Batsford, 1981), 30, 32.

3. Ibid., 30, 45.

4. Richards, History of the Firm, 1; Jones, *Accountancy and the British Economy*, 32–33, 66–68. The Institute imposed a rigorous admission process of apprenticeship and examination.

5. Jones, *Accountancy and the British Economy*, 28–29.

6. Ibid.; Richards, *History of the Firm*, 1–2.

7. Jones, *Accountancy and the British Economy*, 29, 51–52.

8. Ibid., 47, 48–49, 50, 51–52, 99.

9. Ibid., 61, 98, 100.

10. Much of the factual account of the English firm and its founders that follows comes from Richards, *History of the Firm;* George O. May and Robert O. Berger, "History of Price, Waterhouse & Co. and Jones, Caesar & Co., 1890 to June 30, 1901" (in 17 chapters, typescript), n.d. [c. 1945], Cammarata Box, George O. May File Room, Price Waterhouse, National Information Center (NIC), New York, Chapter 1; and the recent research of Edgar Jones, who edited a selected version of the Edwin Waterhouse diaries, *The Memoirs of Edwin Waterhouse: A Founder of Price Waterhouse* (London: B.T. Batsford, 1988).

11. By about 1850, a Mr. Edwards, presumably William Edwards, formed a partnership with William Turquand which, with the amalgamation of two other firms, became Coleman, Turquand, Youngs & Co. in 1857. This is the firm that employed both Holyland and Waterhouse in the early 1860s. Jones, *Accountancy and the British Economy*, 20–21, 34.

12. On Waterhouse's severe manner, see the memoir of his son, Sir Nicholas E. Waterhouse, "Reminiscences, 1877–1960," typescript and bound, NIC, 90–92, 96.

13. Jones, ed., *The Memoirs of Edwin Waterhouse*, 26, 81.

14. The name remained Price, Waterhouse & Co. until 1940, after which time it was progressively shortened, finally becoming simply Price Waterhouse. According to Richards, the comma in the name of the English firm was removed in 1940, "somewhat of a war casualty, arising as it did when it became necessary to redesign the heading to fit a smaller sheet of note-paper[;] it was later considered to be more appropriate in that it correctly described Price Waterhouse as the entity it had become and not as the two original partners." *History of the Firm*, 5. A decade later the comma was deleted in the U.S. firm name. Executive Committee Minutes (November 21, 1950), 1, Office of the Secretary of the Firm, National Office, New York. For convenience, the firms are referred to as PW throughout the text that follows.

15. J.R. Edwards, "Edwin Waterhouse," in *Dictionary of Business Biography: A Biographical Dictionary of Business Leaders Active in Britain in the Period 1860–1980*, ed. David J. Jeremy et al., 5 vols. (London: Butterworth, 1984–1986), 5 (1986): 674–679.

16. Income for Professional Work, Summary and Estimates, PW Archives, 12/6, Price Waterhouse, Southwark Towers, London (hereafter PW archives, London). By the end of the century, the firm's fees began to rival those of Turquand, Youngs & Company, its oldest and most respected competitor. Jones, *Accountancy and the British Economy*, 45.

17. Price Waterhouse did, however, establish an agency in Melbourne, Australia, in 1896 with Davey Flack & Company, an Australian accounting firm. This agency continued until relatively modern times. Mary Murphy, "Draft History of Price Waterhouse," MS, c. late 1940s, Records Center, New York Practice Office, 229.

18. See, in general, P.L. Cottrell, *British Overseas Investment in the Nineteenth Century* (London: Macmillan, 1975), especially 20–22, 30, 34; Peter J. Buckley and Brian R. Roberts, *European Direct Investment in the U.S.A. before World War I* (New York: St. Martin's Press, 1982), 20–24.

19. On the investment climate of nineteenth-century Britain in the aftermath of the Industrial Revolution, see E.J. Hobsbawm's *Industry and Empire: An Economic History of Britain since 1750* (London: Weidenfeld and Nicolson, 1968), especially 1–9, 88–97, 124–126.

20. A.K. Cairncross, *Home and Foreign Investment, 1870–1913: Studies in Capital Accumulation* (Cambridge, England: Cambridge University Press, 1953), 84–85.

21. Hobsbawm, *Industry and Empire*, 126. Investment figures come from Cleona Lewis, *America's Stake in International Investments* (Washington, D.C.: Brookings Institution, 1938), 560, and are based on an extensive set of data presented in "Appendix B: Estimates of Foreign Investments in the United States," ibid., 517–560. From the data provided, British investment composed about 60 percent of the total in any given year. From 1865 to 1914, it has been estimated, as much as a third of Britain's overseas investment went to the United

States. During World War I, Britain liquidated perhaps as much as 70 percent of its American investment to finance its war effort and became heavily indebted to the United States. Michael Edelstein, *Overseas Investment in the Age of High Imperialism: The United Kingdom, 1850–1914* (New York: Columbia University Press, 1982), 39–40.

22. For a general discussion of these foreign-owned businesses, see Lewis, *America's Stake in International Investments*, 78–113; and Buckley and Roberts, *European Direct Investment in the U.S.A.*, 43–84.

23. Edelstein, *Overseas Investment in the Age of High Imperialism*, 60.

24. Buckley and Roberts, *European Direct Investment in the U.S.A.*, 53.

25. Ibid., 26–27. For changes in British foreign lending from 1860 to 1913, see Brinley Thomas, "Migration and International Investment," in *The Export of Capital from Britain, 1870–1914*, ed. A.R. Hall (London: Methuen, 1968), 45–47.

26. Cairncross, *Home and Foreign Investment*, 90, 101; Cottrell, *British Overseas Investment*, 30–31, 34.

27. On O'Hagan's life, see David T.A. Kynaston and R.P.T. Davenport-Hines, "Henry Osborne O'Hagan," in Jeremy et al., eds., *Dictionary of Business Biography*, 4 (1985): 479–483; and on his American ventures, see his *Leaves from My Life* (London: John Lane The Bodley Head, 1929), 2 vols., especially, 1: 294–324, 329–361, 376–382, 391–396, 401–408.

28. In 1890, Guthrie drew up the original agreement establishing the American agency, and he provided important legal counsel in the troubling 1890s. Cravath very kindly allowed the authors to review Guthrie's correspondence with O'Hagan during the 1880s, especially vols. 74–78 (September 27, 1889–June 14, 1890), which is bound in a long, continuous series of letter-press volumes.

29. O'Hagan, *Leaves from My Life*, 1: 295–296, 304, 308, 314–315, 329–331.

30. During the 1880s, PW also took on work in other parts of the world, including India and the West Indies. Richardson, *History of the Firm*, 5.

31. Jones, ed., *The Memoirs of Edwin Waterhouse*, 123.

32. James T. Anyon, "Early Days of American Accountancy," part II, *Journal of Accountancy* 39 (1925): 162–163, as cited in May and Berger, "History of Price, Waterhouse & Co.," Chapter I, 5.

33. May and Berger, "History of Price, Waterhouse & Co.," Chapter I, 6; O'Hagan, *Leaves from My Life*, 1: 295.

34. Agreement: Messrs. Price, Waterhouse & Co. with Mr. Lewis D. Jones, September 11, 1890, Uncatalogued Partners' Papers, G.O. May File Room.

35. May, Professional Training Classes, 1921, Introductory Lecture, 16.

36. Agreement, 1890, Sections 2–5.

37. Ibid., Sections 6–12. These provisions were modified slightly in early 1892 when it was agreed that Caesar would become the agency's representative in Chicago. Under the new terms, the basis for agency profit remained unchanged, although the proportion was increased to 37.5 percent, with 22.5 percent going to Jones and 15 percent to Caesar. The total minimum salary for the agency was increased to $7,500. Lewis D. Jones and W.J. Caesar to PW [London], February 27, 1892 (two letters, one including a copy of the original

agreement with Jones), Box C10, 1892/5, PW Archives, London. Reluctance to accept the work of American accountants may have reflected the lack of a certification process. New York promulgated the first CPA law in 1897.

38. This continued to be the headquarters of the New York office until May 1896, when it was moved to 54 Wall Street. May and Berger, "History of Price, Waterhouse & Co.," Chapter XV, 1.

39. Most of the agency's records, including bill books, letter books, journals, and time books, are housed in the Records Center of the New York Practice Office. James Alexander very kindly allowed the authors to examine these early records.

40. Lewis D. Jones to PW [London], December 12, 1890, Box C10, 1890/1; ibid., January 9, 1891; ibid., 1890/2; ibid., May 29, 1891, and PW [London] to [Jones], June 9, [18]91, Box 58/115 (Misc. Docs.), all PW Archives, London.

41. PW [London] to [Jones], June 9, [18]91, Box 58/115 (Misc. Docs.), PW Archives, London.

42. W.J. Caesar to PW [London], September 30, 1890, Box 10/38, PW Archives, London. Caesar's letter, written at a most propitious time, followed Caesar's visit to the firm's London office, where he sought a position.

43. May and Berger, "History of Price, Waterhouse & Co.," Chapter XIV, 1–3.

44. Ibid., Chapter II, 2–3.

45. Income for Professional Work, 12/6, PW Archives, London; New York Agency: Balance Sheet and Profit and Loss a/c, June 30, 1891, Box C10, 1891/1, PW Archives, London. Figures here and elsewhere are based on Price Waterhouse's fiscal year, which runs from July 1 through June 30.

46. The first reference to the Chicago office indicates that it was opened on May 1, 1892, and was located on the eighth floor of the Monadnock Building at 53 West Jackson Boulevard; it held the first lease taken out for space in that prominent structure. May and Berger, "History of Price, Waterhouse & Co.," Chapter XV, 1.

In that year, Sandys Birket Foster, a 22-year-old member of the Institute of Chartered Accountants, came to the American agency to work as a member of the Chicago staff. Three years later, in 1895, when Jones and Caesar were designated general partners, Foster was given a special junior partnership. In 1897, he resigned from the firm to work for a brewing company. Chester W. DeMond, *Price, Waterhouse & Co. in America: A History of a Public Accounting Firm* (1951; reprint ed., New York: Arno Press, 1980), 27.

47. Caesar to Fowler, July 26, 1892, Box C10, 1892/5, PW Archives, London.

48. Lewis D. Jones and W.J. Caesar to PW [London], Box 58/47, and reply, April 5, [189]2, Box 58/28, PW Archives, London.

49. The most notable of these British equity investments were Eastman Kodak Company of New York, Ingersoll Sargeant Drill Company (later Ingersoll Rand), Strattons Independent Gold Mine, and Horlicks Malted Milk, many of which were subsequently repurchased by American interests. May and Berger, "History of Price, Waterhouse & Co.," Chapter III.

50. Calculations of "London origin" and other work taken on by the American agency in the 1890s were made by May and Berger, and were based on a calendar rather than on the PW fiscal year. Although client work was not segregated in this manner in the records that they examined, their classifications seem sufficiently well founded. See ibid., Chapter III, 1–3, for important details.

51. Ibid., Chapter IV.

52. Other agencies, such as Deloitte's, also experienced a reversal of fortunes, and some of their staff sought employment elsewhere, including the Price Waterhouse agency. Price, Waterhouse & Co., American Agency, Accounts, June 30, 1893, C10, 1893/1; Jones to PW [London], August 25, 1893, Box 58/30; Caesar to Fowler, November 4, 1893, Box 58/33; Jones to Fowler, January 31, 1894, Box 58/35; Caesar to Fowler, February 14, 1894, Box 58/115; Fowler to Jones, August 30, [189]4, Box 58/110, PW Archives, London. The "vexed silver question" refers to the controversy surrounding the silver versus gold standard for currency, the fundamental issue in the 1896 presidential election.

53. PW [London] to Messrs. Winston and Meagher, January 2–3, 1894, Box 58/27; Winston and Meagher to PW [London], January 13, 1894, Box 58/83; PW [London] to Messrs. Winston & Meagher, January 31, [189]4, Box 58/99; Jones to Fowler, February 12, 1894, Box 58/98; Caesar to Fowler, February 14, 1894, Box 58/115; Fowler to Jones, February 26, [18]94, Box 58/97, PW Archives, London. The differences between Caesar and Meagher, partner in Winston & Meagher, a Chicago law firm with strong connections to PW clients in England, were apparently patched up in 1899, at the time of Jones's funeral. We "discussed our old troubles just as if they had been prehistoric matters, and wondered how we ever came to fall out." Caesar to A.W. Wyon, February 26, 1899, Box 58/107, ibid.

54. Caesar to Fowler, November 4, 1894, Box 58/33; Jones and Caesar to PW [London], January 27, 1894, Box 58/110; Jones to Fowler, January 31, 1894, Box 58/35; ibid., February 12, 1894, Box 58/98, PW Archives, London; Private (Very) Memorandum from Historian (Retired) London to Historian (Present) New York, July 14, 1950, 10/14, PW Archives, London.

55. Jones and Caesar to PW [London], January 27, 1894, Box 58/110, PW Archives, London.

56. Jones and Caesar to PW [London], January 27, 1894, Box 58/110, PW Archives, London. A few days later, Jones tempered this letter by writing that their proposal was "merely . . . a suggestion for your Consideration. What we are anxious to do is to devise some plan of securing new business without tampering the laws of professional Etiquette." Jones to Fowler, January 31, 1894, Box 58/35, PW Archives, London.

57. Jones and Caesar [Caesar] to PW [London], December 7, 1894, Box 58/110, PW Archives, London.

58. Caesar to Fowler, February 14, 1894, Box 58/115; PW [London] to Jones and Caesar, August 11, [189]4, Box 58/110, PW Archives, London. After the decision to close the agency was made, Fowler described how the London office had reflected upon the American situation following the previous August: "When your accounts for last year [i.e., the period ending on June 30, 1893, which

arrived two months later] came before us in a completed form, we decided at once that so far as we were concerned, we saw no advantage in continuing the Agency. So far as you and Caesar are concerned we thought that there was a nucleus of a business got together which it might be worth your while to get on with for a time on the hope that other business of a lucrative nature might follow in due course." Both sides apparently thought that the American agency should be abandoned, outright in the case of the firm, modified by reorganization, according to the agents. Fowler to Jones, August 30, [189]4, Box 58/110, ibid.

59. Jones to Fowler, August 20, 1894, Box 58/110; Fowler to Jones, August 30, [189]4, ibid.; Jones to Fowler, September 10, 1894, ibid., PW Archives, London.

60. Caesar to PW [London], September 26, 1894, Box 58/110, PW Archives, London.

61. PW [London] to [Jones and Caesar], October 10, 1894, Box 58/110, PW Archives, London.

62. Ibid. In the course of working out their new relationship with the London partners, Jones and Caesar were asked to abandon their solicitations to other British firms. [Jones, Caesar] to Messrs. Turquand, Youngs, Bishop & Clarke, November 7, 1894, Box 58/110, PW Archives, London.

63. Price, Waterhouse & Co. (American Agency), Trial Balance, June 30, 1895 (after closing entries), Box C10, 1895/10; Jones, Caesar & Co. to PW [London], July 23, 1895, ibid., 1895/1, PW Archives, London; Jones, Caesar & Co. to PW [London], July 8, 1896, Box C10, 1896/4; ibid., July 14, 1896, ibid.; Price, Waterhouse & Co. (American Agency), Trial Balance Sheet, June 30, 1896, Adjusted, C2/4th Box File, PW Archives, London; Price, Waterhouse & Co., American Agency, Trial Balance, June 30, 1897, Box C10, 1897/3; Jones, Caesar & Co. to PW [London], December 21, 1897, Box 58/108; Price, Waterhouse & Co., Closing Journal Entries, June 30, 1898, Trial Balance Sheet (before Closing), June 30, 1898, and Analysis of Expenses Year Ending June 30, 1898, Box C10, 1898/5, 14, 15, PW Archives, London. See also, Notes made by JGF [Joseph Gurney Fowler] during visit to New York in February 1898, Box C10, 1898/19; Jones and Caesar [Caesar] to PW [London], December 7, 1894, Box 58/110; Jones, Caesar & Co. to PW [London], December 21, 1897, Box 58/108, PW Archives, London.

64. Caesar to A.W. Wyon, June 12, 1896, Box C10, 1896/5; Jones, Caesar & Co. to PW [London], June 9, 1897, 1897/18, PW Archives, London.

65. Glenn Porter, *The Rise of Big Business, 1860–1910* (Arlington Heights, Ill.: AHM Publishing, 1973), 76.

66. May and Berger, "History of Price, Waterhouse & Co.," Chapter VI, 2.

67. The connection with Morgan apparently originated in 1896, when he asked the firm to examine the receivership account of the Northern Pacific Railroad Company. Caesar to Fowler, September 17, 1896, Box C10, 1896/5, PW Archives, London.

68. May and Berger, "History of Price, Waterhouse & Co.," Chapter VI, 1–8. The number of Jones, Caesar & Co. clients increased from 34 in 1894, when it was still the Price Waterhouse agency, to 55 in 1895, when it began to operate

on its own. Thereafter the number of clients increased almost yearly, accelerating after 1897. The following figures show the number of clients annually and the relatively declining number of London referrals in parentheses: 1895: 55 (33); 1896: 59 (29); 1897: 59 (30); 1898: 73 (33); 1899: 116 (34); 1900: 108 (30). Ibid., Chapter IX, 1.

69. For short biographies of these and other important early firm leaders, see Chapter 2.

70. Caesar to A.W. Wyon, January 20, 1899, C10, 1899/1, PW Archives, London.

71. May and Berger, "History of Price, Waterhouse & Co.," Chapter III, 6–8. The quotation is from Caesar to A.W. Wyon, June 12, 1896, Box C10, 1896/5, PW Archives, London.

72. PW [London] to Messrs. Jones, Caesar & Co., October 25, 1897, Copy, Box 58/57; Jones, Caesar & Co. to PW [London], November 5, 1897, Box 58/43; Jones, Caesar & Co. to PW [London], November 17, 1897, Box C10, 1897/18, PW Archives, London.

73. Jones, Caesar & Co. to PW [London], December 21, 1897, Box 58/108, PW Archives, London.

74. Jones, Caesar & Co. to PW [London], December 24, 1897, ibid., January 5, 1898 (2 letters); ibid., January 8, 1898; ibid., January 10, 1898; ibid., January 11, 1898, all Box 58/44, 100, 101, 108, PW Archives, London. The London partners may have surmised that profits of Jones and Caesar were now greatly in excess of their own work in the United States. This situation, if not dealt with in a new agreement, might lead to wider disparity and more difficulty in arranging a reorganization in the future. American Agency, Approximate Profit and Loss Accounts Jones, Caesar, C., June 30, 1898, extracted by JGF [Joseph Gurney Fowler], May [18]99, Box 58/70, ibid.

75. Caesar to Fowler, September 21, 1898, October 14, 1898, Box 58/103, PW Archives, London.

76. Jones, Caesar & Co. to PW [London], October 14, 1898; PW [London] to Messrs. Jones, Caesar & Co., November 12, 1898, Box 58/103, 104, PW Archives, London.

77. PW [New York] to PW [London], January 10, 1899, PW [London] to PW [New York], February 1, [18]99, C10, 1898/1, PW Archives, London.

78. Jones to Wyon, January 23, 1899, C10, 1899/1, PW Archives, London.

79. Caesar to PW [London], February 7, 1899, Caesar to A.W. Wyon, February 20, 1899, C10, 1899/1, PW Archives, London.

80. Caesar to A.W. Wyon, February 27, 1899, Box 58/106, PW Archives, London.

81. PW [London] to W.J. Caesar, March 24, [18]99, Box 58/105; Caesar to PW [London], April 6, 1899; Telegram, PW [New York] to PW [London] May 31, 1899; H.W. Wilmot to Caesar, June 3, 1899; Telegram, PW [London] to PW [New York], June 12, 1899, all Box C10, 1899/1, PW Archives, London.

82. Caesar to Fowler, May 14, 1899, Box C10, 1899/1, PW Archives, London.

83. American Agency, Heads for Articles of Partnership, prepared May 1899; telegram, PW [London] to PW [New York], May 15, 1899; Wilmot to Caesar,

June 3, 1899; Caesar to PW [London], September 8, 1899; ibid., September 10, 1899; PW [London] to Caesar, September 20, 1899 (two letters); ibid., October 12, 1899; Caesar to PW [London], October 23, 1899; Caesar to Fowler, October 29, 1899; PW [London] to Caesar, November 4, 1899; ibid., November 22, 1899, all Box C10, 1899/1, PW Archives, London.

84. PW [London] to Jones, Caesar & Co., June 17, 1899; Telegram, PW [London] to PW [New York], June 15, 1899; PW [London] to Wilmot, August 11, 1899; Wilmot to PW [London], August 21, 1899; PW [London] to Caesar, August 30, 1899; PW [London] to Wilmot, September 9, 1899, all Box C10, 1899/1, PW Archives, London.

85. Articles of Partnership, Messrs. Price Waterhouse & Co. with W.J. Caesar Esquire, December 22, 1899, Uncatalogued Partnership Papers, G.O. May File Room.

86. Jones, Caesar & Co. Analysis, Private Ledger, Year Ending June 30, 1900, Price Waterhouse & Co. Analysis, Private Ledger, Year Ending June 30, 1900, Box C2, Top Box File, PW Archives, London.

87. Caesar to Fowler, June 12, 1900, Box 58/60, PW Archives, London.

88. Ibid., August 1, 1900, Box 58/61, ibid., August 27, 1900, Box 58/59, PW Archives, London.

89. W.H. Winterbotham to Edwin Waterhouse, September 26, 1900, Box C10, 1900/4, PW Archives, London.

90. Caesar to Fowler, May 28, Fowler to PW [London], June 8, 1901, Box C10, 1901/3; American Agency, Accounts to June 30, 1901, Box C2, Top Box File, PW Archives, London; Dickinson to PW [London], July 9, 1901, Uncatalogued Partnership Papers, G.O. May File Room; Agreement, Messrs. Price, Waterhouse & Co. and another and Mr. William James Caesar, June 29, 1901, ibid. Caesar's final payment was substantially reduced from his own high estimate of about $150,000 to only one half of that amount.

91. Fowler to Caesar, August 16, 1900, Box 58/61; Caesar to PW [London], October 26, 1900, Box C10, 1900/4, PW Archives, London.

92. Caesar to PW [London], October 14, 1898, Caesar to Fowler, August 1, 1900, Box 58/103, 61, PW Archives, London.

93. May and Berger, "History of Price, Waterhouse & Co.," Chapter X, 12–13.

94. American Agency, Approximate Profits and Loss, Accounts Jones Caesar C., June 30, 1898, extracted by JGF, Box 58/70, PW Archives, London. Among those who resigned was John B. Niven, who had worked in the Chicago office from December 1897 to August 1900, after which time he helped form Touche, Niven & Co., later Touche Ross. May and Berger, "History of Price, Waterhouse & Co.," Chapter X, 12.

95. Dickinson to PW [London], December 7, 1901, Box C10, 1901/11, PW Archives, London.

CHAPTER 2

1. For further details on Dickinson's life prior to becoming senior partner in the United States, see Mary E. Murphy, "Arthur Lowes Dickinson, 1859–1935:

An International Accountant and the Progress of Accounting in His Time," typescript MS, [1947], in Cammarata Box, George O. May File Room, Price Waterhouse, NIC, New York; and J.R. Edwards, "Sir Arthur Lowes Dickinson," *Dictionary of Business Biography: A Biographical Dictionary of Business Leaders Active in Britain in the Period 1860–1980*, ed. David J. Jeremy et al., 5 vols. (London: Butterworth, 1984–1986), 2 (1984): 103–107.

2. Michael Chatfield, *A History of Accounting Thought* (Hinsdale, Ill.: Dryden Press, 1974), 274.

3. Dickinson to [Joseph Gurney] Fowler, October 14, 1902, Box C10, 1902, PW Archives, Price Waterhouse, Southwark Towers, London (hereafter PW Archives, London).

4. Dickinson to PW [London], December 7, 1901, Box C10, 1901, PW Archives, London.

5. W.J. Caesar to A.W. Wyon, January 20, 1899, Box C10, 1899, PW Archives, London. London, though not disapproving this course of action, wondered, for unexplained reasons, when the American firm would open an office in San Francisco. Wyon to Caesar, February 1, 1899, PW [London] to PW, November 25, 1901, Box C10, 1899, 1901, Edward Stanley to Dickinson, February 19, 1902, Box C10, 1902, PW Archives, London.

6. Unidentified newspaper clipping, ca. 1904, printed in Chester W. DeMond, *Price, Waterhouse & Co. in America: A History of a Public Accounting Firm* (New York: Price Waterhouse, 1951), 53–54.

7. Dickinson to PW [London], December 7, 1901, Box C10, 1901, PW Archives, London.

8. Dickinson to PW [London], April 30, 1901, Box 58/114, PW Archives, London. See also Caesar to Wyon, January 20, 1899, and Wyon to Caesar, February 1, 1899, Box C10, 1899, ibid.

9. Dickinson to PW [London], April 18, 1902, Box C10, 1902, PW Archives, London.

10. Alfred D. Chandler, Jr., and Richard S. Tedlow, "J. P. Morgan, 1837–1913," in *The Coming of Managerial Capitalism: A Casebook on the History of American Economic Institutions* (Homewood, Ill.: Richard D. Irwin, 1985), 257. For the most recent and authoritative treatment of the U.S. Steel consolidation, see Vincent P. Carosso, *The Morgans: Private International Bankers, 1854–1913* (Cambridge, Mass.: Harvard University Press, 1987), 466–474

11. Paul J. Miranti, Jr., "Associationalism, Statism, and Professional Regulation: Public Accountants and the Reform of Financial Markets, 1896–1940," *Business History Review* 60 (1986): 443.

12. Murphy, "Arthur Lowes Dickinson," 58. Besides setting up U.S. Steel's unique financial statements, Dickinson also wrote two pamphlets in order to influence the Interstate Commerce Commission's requirements for railroad depreciation. Paul J. Miranti, *Accountancy Comes of Age: The Development of an American Profession, 1886–1940* (Chapel Hill: University of North Carolina Press, 1990), 91–92.

13. For the ongoing significance of Price Waterhouse's annual reports for U.S. Steel over the years, and the firm's important accounting adaptations in those reports over time, see Richard Vangermeersch, ed., *Financial Accounting Milestones in the Annual Reports of the United States Steel Corporation: The First*

Seven Decades (New York: Garland Publishing, 1986), especially his introduction and the sources he cites. For an overview on the relationship between accounting and the needs of large-scale business in the early twentieth century, see H. Thomas Johnson, "The Role of Accounting History in the Study of Modern Business Enterprise," *Accounting Review* 50 (July 1975): 444–450, and H. Thomas Johnson and Robert S. Kaplan, *Relevance Lost: The Rise and Fall of Management Accounting* (Boston: Harvard Business School Press, 1987), especially 47–123.

14. "Annual Report of the United States Steel Trust," *Scientific American* 88, no. 16 (April 18, 1903): 294; James T. Anyon, "Early Days of American Accountancy," part III, *Journal of Accountancy* 39 (March 1925): 164; Dickinson, "Notes on Some Problems Relating to the Accounts of Holding Companies," ibid. 2 (April 1906); ibid., "Some Special Points in Accountancy Practice," *The Accountant* (April 22, 1905); Edwards, "Sir Arthur Lowes Dickinson," 104.

15. Dickinson to PW [London], with handwritten draft reply, April 18, 1902, Box C10, 1902, PW Archives, London; John G. Griffiths to PW [London], March 18, 1902, ibid. American advertising claims were occasionally the result of enthusiastic client endorsements. But when the St. Louis Mechanics' National Bank referred to Jones, Caesar & Co. as "the leading firm of expert accountants of the world," Dickinson found the encomium "a bit too much even for St Louis." Mechanics' National Bank circular, attached to Caesar to PW [London], February 8, 1902, ibid.

16. Dickinson to Fowler, October 14, PW to PW [London], October 31, 1902, ibid., November 7, 1902, Box C10, 1902, PW Archives, London.

17. PW to PW [London], October 23, 1907, Box C11/1907, PW Archives, London.

18. Dickinson to PW [London], April 30, Box 58/114, Dickinson to PW [London], May 16, 1901, Box C10, 1901, PW Archives, London.

19. PW [Dickinson] to PW [London], August 13, 1901, Box C10, 1901, PW Archives, London.

20. PW to PW [London], January 11, 1902, Box C10, 1901; ibid., March 4, ibid., November 17, Dickinson to PW [London], December 2, 1902, Box C10, 1902; Dickinson to Fowler, March 24, 1903, Box C11/1903, PW Archives, London.

21. [Dickinson], undated, unsigned Memorandum; Dickinson to Fowler, June 28, August 31, 1903; Dickinson to Edwin Waterhouse, September 5, 1903, Box C11/1903; Minutes of Discussions at Meeting of Partners and Managers at Niagara, Sunday, June 14, 1903, Box C2/3d Box File, PW Archives, London.

22. For financial information during these years, see Dickinson to Fowler, April 10, 1906, Box C11/1906; ibid., November 21, 1905 and appendix, Box C11/1905, PW Archives, London. Profit had risen from a little over $12,000 in 1898 to $35,000 the following year. In 1900 it reached $110,000, followed by a drop to $60,000. In Dickinson's first full year, the profit level remained about the same.

23. [Dickinson], Memorandum for Mr. Sneath on the Principal Points Discussed During His Visit to America, Dickinson to Fowler, September 23, 1904, Box C11/1904, PW Archives, London.

24. Dickinson to Fowler, April 10, 1906, Box C11/1906, PW Archives, London.

25. For a fuller account of the movement, see James H. Potts, "The Evolution of Municipal Accounting in the United States: 1900–1935," *Business History Review* 52 (1978): 518–536; and as a specific example, Richard K. Fleischman and R. Penny Marquette, "Municipal Accounting Reform c. 1900: Ohio's Progressive Accountants," *Accounting Historians' Journal* 14 (1987): 83–94.

26. "Municipal Accounting," *Commercial and Financial Chronicle*, November 7, 1903, 1723; "The Minneapolis System of Municipal Accounting," ibid., July 1, 1905, 9–7; H.W. Wilmot, "Municipal Accounting Reform. As Illustrated in the City of Minneapolis," *Journal of Accountancy* 2 (1906): 97–106.

27. Edward Stanley to H.W. Wilmot, September 26, October 14; [PW] to Edward Stanley, October 10, 1902[3], ibid. to W.J. Rodenbeck, October, 13, 15, ibid. to Harvey S. Chase, October 15; W.J. Filbert to C. Filbert, October 24, 1903; Fred C. Bean to Jones, Caesar, Dickinson, Wilmot & Co., August 5, 1905, Municipal File, Records Center, New York Practice Office.

28. Memorandum on Mr. Nasmyth's Visit to Rochester, Syracuse, Auburn and Seneca Falls, N.Y., February 28 to March 16, 1905; Memorandum on Mr. Nasmyth's Visit to Philadelphia, April 7, 1905, Records Center, New York Practice Office.

29. Minutes of Meeting of Partners and Managers Held at the Hotel Schenley, Pittsburg[h], Pa., Saturday, December 31, 1904, and Sunday, January 1, 1905, C2/3d Box File, PW Archives, London. Minutes of Meeting of Partners and Managers Held at 54 William Street, New York, on Saturday, November 20, 1909, Uncatalogued Partnership Papers File, G.O. May File Room.

30. On the early history of national accounting associations, see John L. Carey, *The Rise of the Accounting Profession, 1: From Technician to Professional* (New York: American Institute of Certified Public Accountants, 1968), 36–54, 108–128; Miranti, "Associationalism, Statism, and Professional Regulation," 441–442. Lewis Jones had helped found the Illinois Society and was its first president. George O. May and Robert O. Berger, "History of Price, Waterhouse & Co., and Jones, Caesar & Co., 1890 to June 30, 1901" (in 17 chapters, typescript), n.d. [c. 1945], Cammarata Box, G.O. May File Room, Chapter II, 2–3.

31. Dickinson, "The Duties and Responsibilities of the Public Accountant," typescript, Cammarata Box, G.O. May File Room; Papers and Correspondence, Committee for the St. Louis Convention [International Congress on Accounting], 1903–1904, Records Center, New York Practice Office. Dickinson's own publications are too numerous to list; he served as an exemplar for others in the firm at this time and throughout his career. He wrote an article for the inaugural issue of the *Journal of Accountancy* in 1904, and often presented papers at meetings of accounting and other professional groups. Much of this activity culminated with the publication of his *Accounting Practice and Procedure* in 1914. For his other writings, see the listing in Edwards, "Sir Arthur Lowes Dickinson," 105–107.

32. Dickinson to Fowler, September 23, 1904, Dickinson to PW [London] December 3, 1904, Box C11/1904; Minutes of Meeting of Partners and Managers, 1905, PW Archives, London.

33. PW to PW [London], June 19, 1905, Box C11/1905; Price, Waterhouse & Co., Jones, Caesar, Dickinson, Wilmot & Co., Consolidated Balance Sheet and Profit and Loss Account for the Year Ending June 30, 1906, C2/4th Box

File, PW Archives, London. The firm's profit after expenses reached a record $242,000 in June 1906. At this time, a large piece of work could cause a serious cash-flow problem because bills were sent only on the completion of an engagement, or after a year's work on a longer project. PW History Advisory Committee, November 27, 1990.

34. Professional Training Classes, 1921: Introductory Lecture (G.O. May), November 1, 1921, typescript, 16, Cammarata Box, G.O. May File Room.

35. The Equitable Life Assurance Society of the United States, Investigation by Public Accountants, 1905, Prepared from Draft of Mr. Dickinson, and Supplemental Reports, 1906 [Eight Reports, 1905–1906], Records Center, New York Practice Office.

36. Deloitte, Plender, Griffiths & Co. and Dickinson, Wilmot & Sterrett, Joint Commission of Congress On Business Methods of Post Office Department and Postal Service, Report of the Public Accountants, September 30, 1907, Box 1094, Records Center, New York Practice Office. For the full report, see, U.S. Congress, Joint House and Senate Committee, *Preliminary Report on Business Methods of the Post Office Department and Postal Service*, 60th Cong., 1st sess., 1908, Rep. 201.

37. Edgar Jones, *Accountancy and the British Economy, 1840–1980: The Evolution of Ernst & Whinney* (London: B.T. Batsford, 1981), 46–47, 98–99. It was widely acknowledged at the time that Americans were far ahead of the English in both cost accounting and systems work. See *Journal of Accounting* (March 1907), 388–393. During this period, Ernst & Whinney operated in England under the name of Whinney, Murray. Although this British firm had an informal relationship with the American practice of Ernst & Ernst (founded in Cleveland in 1915), its connection was not formalized until a merger in 1979.

38. [Frank W. Thornton], *Memorandum on Moving Picture Accounts, July 10, 1916* (New York: Price, Waterhouse & Co., 1916), which was "issued for the Private and Confidential Information of Members of the Staff Only." Thornton was a prolific writer, and PW published his accounting treatises on *Brewery Accounts* (1913), *Duties of a Junior Accountant* (1917), cowritten with Ward B. Reynolds, *Duties of a Senior Accountant* (1932), *Stock Brokerage and Investment House Accounting* (1930), and *Examination of Financial Statements by Independent Public Accountants* (1936).

39. Dickinson to Fowler, January 9, February 9, 1906, Cammarata Box, G.O. May File Room.

40. Dickinson to Fowler, April 10, 1906; H.W. Wilmot to PW [London], April 10, 1906, Box C11/1906, PW Archives, London; [George O. May], Memorandum Regarding Partnership History, December 1, 1919; Supplemental Memorandum, Dated October 15, 1923, Cammarata Box, G.O. May File Room.

41. May, Memo Regarding Partnership History.

42. Ibid.; Supplemental Memorandum, dated October 15, 1923.

43. J.E. Sterrett, "The Education and Training of a Certified Public Accountant," *Journal of Accountancy* 1, no. 1 (November 1905): 1–3, 14; "Professional Ethics," ibid. 4, no. 5 (October 1907):; and Franklin Butler Kirkbridge and J.E. Sterrett, *The Modern Trust Company: Its Functions and Organization* (New

York: Macmillan, 1905; 4th ed., rev., 1913), vii, ix, which also discusses the growing importance of CPAs in the banking industry, 246–248. See also, Miranti, *Accountancy Comes of Age*, 79–82.

44. PW to PW [London], November 1, 1907, Box C11/1907; ibid., March 24, 1909, Box C11/1909, PW Archives, London.

45. Price, Waterhouse & Co., Dickinson, Wilmot & Sterrett, Consolidated Balance Sheet and Profit and Loss Account, for the Year ending June 30, 1908, C2/4th Box File; Dickinson to George Sneath, Box C11/1908; Price, Waterhouse & Co., Dickinson, Wilmot & Sterrett, Consolidated Balance Sheet and Profit and Loss Account For the Year Ending June 30, 1909, Box C11/1909; PW to Fowler, December 24, 1909, ibid.; Profit and Loss Summary for the Year Ending June 30, 1910, C2/4th Box File, PW Archives, London.

46. Minutes of Meeting of Partners and Managers Held at 54 William Street, New York on Friday and Saturday, October 21st and 22d, 1910, Together with Reports of Committees, Box C2/3d Box File, PW Archives, London; New York Office Organization, c. December 1909, Uncatalogued Partnership Papers, G.O. May File Room.

47. Jones to PW [London], June 25, 1891.

48. Frank C. Belser, Itinerant Checker, 15, typescript copy, Early Partner Files, Transfile Boxes, Office of the Secretary of the Firm, National Office, New York.

49. Ibid., 7; Caesar to J. Gurney Fowler, November 4, 1893, Box 58/115, 33; Dickinson to PW [London], December 3, 1904, Box C11/1904, PW Archives, London.

50. F.G. Phillipps to PW [New York], April 27, 1906 (two letters), Box C11/1906, PW Archives, London.

51. Minutes of Meeting of Partners and Managers . . . 1904 . . . and 1905, C2/3d Box File, PW Archives, London.

52. PW Dinner Program, Hotel Astor, August 14, 1909; Complimentary Dinner to Mr. A.B. Brodie, April 8, 1911, Fort Pitt Hotel, Pittsburgh, Pa., Toasts and Speeches, Records Center, New York Practice Office.

53. William Charles, "St. Louis," *Price Waterhouse Review* 7, no. 4 (Winter 1962): 42–44.

54. Dickinson to PW, June 21, 1910; Wilmot to [PW Partners], December 23, 1910, Uncatalogued Partnership Papers, G.O. May File Room. Following his years in the United States, Dickinson was a partner in the London firm from 1913 to 1924, and he served as a director of numerous English companies and on the board of governors of the London School of Economics. Obituary, *New York Times*, March 2, 1935, 16.

55. Dickinson to PW [London], March 29, 1904, Box C11/1904, PW Archives, London.

56. May, Training Class Lecture, 3–4.

57. Glenn Porter, *The Rise of Big Business 1860–1910* (Arlington Heights, Ill.: AHM Publishing, 1973), 78–79.

58. PW to PW [London], November 12, 1901; PW [London] to PW, November 25, 1901, Box C10, 1901; PW to PW [London], November 4, 1907,

Box C11/1907, PW Archives, London; *Commercial and Financial Chronicle*, October 8, 1904, 1481; 1911 and 1920 Partnership Agreements.

59. Nicholas E. Waterhouse, "Reminiscences, 1877–1960," typescript, n.d., n.p., 104.

60. May to John B. Inglis, July 1, 1960, Price Waterhouse & Co. History, 1960 File, G.O. May File Room.

61. George O. May, *Memoirs and Accounting Thought of George O. May*, ed. Paul Grady (New York: Ronald Press, 1962), 42; May, "Methods of Taxing War Profits Compared," *New York Times*, August 28, 1917, "Method of English War Profits Tax," ibid., September 4, 1917.

62. For much of May's earlier experiences, see his autobiographical account in *Memoirs and Accounting Thought*, 7–52.

63. May, *Memoirs and Accounting Thought*, 12–14.

64. Ibid., 14–20.

65. Dickinson to Joseph Gurney Fowler, October 14, 1902, Box C10, 1902, PW Archives, London.

66. May, *Memoirs and Accounting Thought*, 27. May himself acknowledged a tendency toward "laziness" in his autobiography. See, for example, 12, 18.

67. May, "Proper Treatment of Premiums and Discounts on Bonds," *Journal of Accountancy* 2 (1906): 174–186; "Premiums and Discounts," ibid. 3 (1906): 32–33.

68. May, *Memoirs and Accounting Thought*, 34; Profit and Loss Summary for the Year Ending June 30, 1910, C2/4th Box File, Profit and Loss Summary, 1926–1930, Box 13, PW Archives, London.

69. Agreement: Messrs. Price, Waterhouse & Co. with Mr. Lewis D. Jones, September 11, 1890, Uncatalogued Partners' Papers, G.O. May File Room; Denis King and Donald Malpas, "Price Waterhouse in South America: The First Seventy Five Years, 1913–1988," typescript, 1988, 11–12.

70. May, *Memoirs and Accounting Thought*, 39; Nicholas Waterhouse to May, August 7, 1945, Price Waterhouse & Co., 1945, File, G.O. May File Room.

71. G.O. May, Remarks of Mr. May at the Dinner Held at the Union League Club on Monday Evening, April 13, 1914, On the Occasion of the Completion of Arrangements for the Admission to the Firm of Messrs. Bowman, Carruthers, Grey, Medlock, Masters, McClelland and Scobie, April 17, 1914, Uncatalogued Partnership Papers, G.O. May File Room.

72. May to Dickinson, January 23; Dickinson to May, February 5, 13, 1914, Box 3, PW Archives, London. By the 1930s the program had been expanded to an exchange between firms, providing an American tour of duty for British accountants that promoted mutual understanding. Thomas B. Robson, later the British firm's senior partner, sent instructive letters about the American practice to the English firm, as well as first-hand comments about Roosevelt's "Hundred Days" during his stay in the early 1930s. John E.R. Tull provided a useful comparison between American and English accountants shortly after his arrival several years later.

> I have come to the conclusion that the young accountant over here matures more quickly than we do, due mainly I imagine to the larger jobs that he

> undertakes and the greater ground he is able to cover as a direct result of his different legal status. On the other hand I feel that from our slower and more detailed early training we are quickly able to acquire his somewhat more broadened outlook and are yet able to bring a wider knowledge to bear on any problems that come along.

Robson to A[lfred] E. Jones, March 20, 1933, Tull to PW [London], April 2, 1938, Box 13, PW Archives, London.

73. Professional Training Classes, 1921: Introductory Lecture (G.O. May), November 1, 1921, typescript, 12; J.E. Sterrett to George O. May, August 18, 1926, Cammarata Box, G.O. May File Room.

74. May & Berger, "History of Price, Waterhouse & Co.," Part II, Chapter XII, 4.

75. Ibid., 4–5.

76. May, Remarks of Mr. May at the Dinner Held . . . April 13, 1914.

77. May, Professional Training Classes, 1921, 12. The staff training class that May addressed continued until 1925, when the emphasis changed to "on-the-job training which provided excellent experience under an experienced manager." John B. Inglis, *My Life and Times: An Autobiography* (Passaic, N.J.: George Dixon Press, 1974), 40.

78. Price Waterhouse, Policies and Administrative References: Background Material [PAR Background], 1968 ed., 640.11, Office of the Secretary of the Firm, National Office, New York.

79. May, *Memoirs and Accounting Thought*, 32, 37; May to Herbert C. Freeman, May 24, 1952, Letters, 1952 (1), May Papers; May, *Twenty-Five Years of Accounting Responsibility, 1911–1936*, ed. Bishop Carleton Hunt, 2 vols. (New York: Price Waterhouse & Co., 1936), 1: 237–246.

80. "Uniform Accounts," *Federal Reserve Bulletin* (April 1, 1917), 270–284; May, *Memoirs and Accounting Thought*, 36; Maurice Moonitz, "Three Contributions to the Development of Accounting Principles Prior to 1930," *Journal of Accounting Research* (Spring 1970), 145–155; "Verification of Financial Statements," *Journal of Accountancy*, (May 1929), 358–359; Miranti, "Associationalism, Statism, and Professional Regulation," 452.

81. May, *Memoirs and Accounting Thought*, 36–37; Sterrett obituary, *New York Times*, March 23, 1934, 23; *National Cyclopaedia of American Biography*, 37 (1937), 266–267.

82. May, *Memoirs and Accounting Thought*, 36–37; Unnamed Speech by May, post July 29, 1957, enclosed in May to Inglis, August 16, 1957, Price Waterhouse & Co. History File, 1957, G.O. May File Room.

83. Roy M. Sommerfeld and John E. Easton, "The CPA's Tax Practice Today—And How it Got That Way," *Journal of Accountancy* 163 (May 1987): 169–170; Maurice Austin, "Relations Between Lawyers and CPAs in Income Tax Practice," ibid. 91 (1951): 813.

84. "The Bar's Effort to Limit Tax Practice," *Journal of Accountancy* 85 (March 1948): 216; Sommerfeld and Easton, "The CPA's Tax Practice," 169–170; Austin, "Relations Between Lawyers and CPAs," 813. The provision allowing

accountants to perform this work was found in Section 3 of Treasury Circular 230, which read, in part:

> a) Persons of the following classes who are found, upon consideration of their applications, to possess the qualifications required by these regulations, may be admitted to practice before the Treasury Department as attorneys or agents, respectively:
> 1) [practice by attorneys]
> 2) Certified public accountants who have duly qualified to practice as certified public accountants in their own names, under the laws and regulations of the states, territories, or District of Columbia, in which they maintain offices, and who are lawfully engaged in active practice as certified public accountants. . . .

David F. Maxwell and William Charles, "National Conference of Lawyers and CPAs," ibid. 81 (February 1946): 120–121.

85. Belser, Itinerant Checker, 13, 17. On the practical and methodological difficulties of wartime tax law, see T.S. Adams, "Principles of Excess Profits Taxation," *Annals of the American Academy* 75 (January 1918): 147–158.

86. May, Training Course Lecture, 11.

87. Memorandum, George O. May to Members of the Staff, June 30, 1925, attached to Minutes of the Meeting of Partners Held at the New York Office June 4, 1925, Box 14, PW Archives, London.

88. For details, see DeMond's listing of early partners and their dates for joining the firm and becoming partner. DeMond, *PW in America*, 310–313.

89. Partners' Meeting Minutes, December 8, 1923, May 26, 1924, October 16, 1929, Box 14, PW Archives, London.

90. Partners' Meeting Minutes, December 8, 1923, PW Archives, London; *Price, Waterhouse & Co. Manual for Use of Office Managers* (N.p.: [Price Waterhouse], 1925); PAR Background, 380.10, 700.10.

91. For examples, see Memorandum for Mr. May and Partners: In Re Review of Files of Correspondence and Reports Relating to Work Taken Up By the New York Office in the 12 Months from September 1922 to August 1923, December 7, 1923; Memorandum for Mr. May: In Re Results Disclosed by the Review by our Various Offices of Their Practice in Regard to Arranging for Work and Reporting to Clients Upon the Scope of the Work and the Limitations Thereof in Connection with the Verification of Cash Transactions, Etc., May 21, 1924, Uncatalogued Partners' Papers, G.O. May File Room; Belser, Itinerant Checker, 11.

92. Partners' Meeting Minutes, December 8, 1923; Miranti, "Associationalism, Statism, and Professional Regulation," 456.

93. May, *Memoirs and Accounting Thought*, 46; J.E. Sterrett to G.O. May, August 18, 1926, typescript copy.

94. *National Cyclopaedia of American Biography*, 37 (1937), 266–267; "Germany Decorates Mr. and Mrs. J.E. Sterrett On Eve of His Quitting Dawes Committee," *New York Times*, January 12, 1927; "Financial Probe Is Completed by Experts," *Excelsior*, April 15, 1928, Box 13, PW Archives, London; Obituary, *New York Times*, March 23, 1934.

CHAPTER 3

1. "Certified Public Accountants," *Fortune* 5 (June 1932): 63–66, 95–96, 101–102.

2. Thomas K. McCraw, *Prophets of Regulation: Charles Francis Adams, Louis D. Brandeis, James M. Landis, Alfred E. Kahn* (Cambridge, Mass.: Harvard University Press, 1984), 191–192.

3. "Certified Public Accountants," 63–66, 95–96, 101–102.

4. Obituary, *New York Herald Tribune*, June 23, 1934; William B. Campbell, "Cooperation between Accountants and Bankers," *Journal of Accountancy* 45 (1928): 1–13; Chester W. DeMond, *Price, Waterhouse & Co. in America: A History of a Public Accounting Firm* (New York: Price Waterhouse, 1951), 131.

5. George O. May, *Memoirs and Accounting Thought of George O. May*, ed. Paul Grady (New York: Ronald Press, 1962), 47; Draft Partnership Meeting Minutes, November 12–13, 1926, William B. Campbell File; Partnership Share Participation, 1927–1935, John C. Scobie File, Early Partners' Files, Transfile Boxes, Office of the Secretary of the Firm, National Office, New York.

6. Partners' Meeting Minutes, April 18–19, October 16, 1929, Box 14, PW Archives, London; Price Waterhouse, Policies and Administrative References: Background Material (PAR Background), 1968 ed., 655.11, 690.11, 790.10, Office of the Secretary of the Firm, National Office, New York.

7. Henry P. Hill, Interview (July 19, 1988); Wyman Patten, Interview (June 2, 1989); Hugh M. Campbell/John B. Inglis, Interview (May 21, 1987), 79–80; William A. Schan, Interview (October 20, 1987), 23; Weston Rankin, Interview (January 21, 1988); Walter M. Baird, Interview (March 28, 1988); William C. Miller, Interview (July 8, 1987).

8. Richard D. Fitzgerald, Interview (June 9, 1989).

9. Ibid.

10. Fitzgerald and Baird interviews.

11. Profit and Loss Summary, 1926–1930, 1929–1934, 1934–1939, Box 13; Partners' Meeting Minutes, September 17–18, 1931, Box 14, PW Archives, Price Waterhouse, Southwark Towers, London.

12. Frank C. Belser, Itinerant Checker, 18, typescript copy, Early Partners Files, Transfile Boxes, Office of the Secretary of the Firm, National Office, New York. See also F.W. Thornton, Report and Accounts, June 30, 1935, Box 14, PW Archives, London.

13. Partners' Meeting Minutes, May 19–20, December 8–9, 1932, Box 14, PW Archives, London; Letters from the partners "To the Members of the Staff," November 18, 1931 and February 26, 1932. The authors are grateful to Robert G. Nichols for providing these documents.

14. McCraw, *Prophets of Regulation*, 167–168.

15. "Uniform Accounts," 272, 273; James J. Tucker III, "Government Oversight in 1917: The Shape of Things to Come," *Journal of Accountancy* 163 (1987): 73–74, 76; Sidney Davidson and George D. Anderson, "The Development of Accounting and Auditing Standards," ibid., 114.

16. Campbell, "Cooperation between Accountants and Bankers," 10–11.

17. William Z. Ripley, "From Main Street to Wall Street," *Atlantic Monthly* (January 1926), 94–108; Ripley, "Stop, Look, Listen! The Shareholder's Right

to Adequate Information," ibid. (September 1926), 380–393; Paul J. Miranti, *Accountancy Comes of Age: The Development of an American Profession, 1886–1940* (Chapel Hill: University of North Carolina Press, 1990), 136–137.

18. G.O. May, "Publicity of Accounts—Some of Professor Ripley's Positions Are Challenged," *New York Times*, August 30, 1926, 14.

19. Ibid., 14.

20. Paul J. Miranti, Jr., "Associationalism, Statism, and Professional Regulation: Public Accountants and the Reform of Financial Markets, 1896–1940," *Business History Review* 60 (1986): 457–459.

21. Stephen A. Zeff, "Chronology of Significant Developments in the Establishment of Accounting Principles in the United States," in *Financial Accounting Theory I: Issues and Controversies*, ed. Stephen A. Zeff and Thomas F. Keller (New York: McGraw-Hill, 1969), 39; DeMond, *PW in America*, 211–212.

22. G.O. May Draft, 2/13/51TB, 10.

23. McCraw, *Prophets of Regulation*, 163.

24. Ibid., 167; Zeff, "Chronology," 40–41.

25. Dale L. Flesher and Tonya K. Flesher, "Ivar Kreuger's Contribution to U.S. Financial Reporting," *Accounting Review* 61 (1986): 421.

26. "Informal Portraits, J.W.F. Neill," *PW Review* 7, no. 3 (Autumn 1962): 40.

27. George O. May to Roy E. Larsen, April 6, 1933, Price Waterhouse & Co. Clients, 1933 File, G.O. May File Room.

28. Flesher and Flesher, "Ivar Kreuger's Contribution," 421–434.

29. Miranti, "Associationalism, Statism, and Professional Regulation," 457–459.

30. Miranti, *Accountancy Comes of Age*, 145–150.

31. Ibid., 150–151.

32. Ibid., 151–152.

33. Miranti, "Associationalism, Statism, and Professional Regulation," 464–465.

34. Zeff, "Chronology," 39–40; Miranti, *Accountancy Comes of Age*, 153–155.

35. McCraw, *Prophets of Regulation*, 191, Miranti, *Accountancy Comes of Age*, 175.

36. Miranti, *Accountancy Comes of Age*, 168.

37. Stephen A. Zeff, "Leaders of the Accounting Profession: 14 Who Made a Difference," *Journal of Accountancy* 163 (May 1987): 52; Davidson and Anderson, "The Development of Accounting and Auditing Standards," 116; Kenneth S. Most, "The Great American Accounting Principles Controversy," *The Accountant* (March 23, 1968), 377–380. May recruited prominent academicians to serve as research advisers to the Committee. Miranti, *Accountancy Comes of Age*, 174.

38. Miranti, "Professionalism, Statism, and Professional Regulation," 451–452, 464–465; DeMond, *PW in America*, 209; Michael Chatfield, *A History of Accounting Thought* (Hinsdale, Ill.: Dryden Press, 1974), 284–287; G.O. May, "Authoritative Financial Accounting," *Journal of Accountancy* 82 (1946): 103–104. For a documentary account of May's efforts with the Stock Exchange, see *Memoirs and Accounting Thought*, 57–74.

39. Stephen A. Zeff, "A First Guide to the Accounting Literature," in Zeff and Keller, eds., *Financial Accounting Theory I*, 5.

40. "Professional Training Classes," 1921: Introductory Lecture (G.O. May), November 1, 1921, 13, typescript, Cammarata Box, G.O. May File Room; Miranti, *Accountancy Comes of Age*, 173–177.

41. The breadth of May's interests and expertise can be seen by a review of headlines from this period. "May Testifies at Kreuger & Toll Hearing," *New York Times*, January 12, 1933, 1; Editorial on May's Testimony, ibid., January 13, 1933, 14. On the wide press coverage he received in light of his testimony on the tax bill, see Turner Catledge, "Tax Bill Unsound and Not Needed, Expert Testifies," and "Statement on Taxes by George O. May Before Senate Finance Committee," ibid., May 7, 1936, 5; Catledge, "Public Opinion Wins a Victory in Tax Debate, ibid., May 10, 1936, Sec. 4, 3; "Taxation: May Over Morgenthau," *Time*, May 18, 1936, 13–14.

42. "A Talk with George O. May," *Journal of Accountancy* (June 1955): 40. See also, "Chronological List of Published Articles by George O. May," *Memoirs and Accounting Thought*, 299–304; May, "Uniformity in Accounting," *Harvard Business Review* 17 (Autumn 1938): 1–8; "[May] Sees Broad Concepts Replacing Formulae," *New York Times*, October 8, 1940, 44; May, *Financial Accounting: A Distillation of Experience* (New York: Macmillan, 1943), 4.

43. Partners' Meeting Minutes, May 19–20, December 8–9, 1932, Box 14, PW Archives, London.

44. Belser, Itinerant Checker, 21; May to John B. Inglis, January 21, 1960; Price, Waterhouse & Co. History, 1960, File, G.O. May Papers; DeMond, *PW in America*, 235–236; May to C.P. Carruthers, July 13, 1934, Copy, Charles P. Carruthers File, Early Partners' Files, Transfile Boxes, Office of the Secretary of the Firm, National Office, New York.

45. Belser, Itinerant Checker, 21–22.

46. DeMond, *PW in America*, 243; Partners' Meeting Minutes, May 6–7, November 19–20, 1936, May 18–19, 1937, Box 14, PW Archives, London.

47. E.g., Partners' Meeting Minutes, November 19, 1930, May 13–14, September 17–18, 1931, November 14–15, 1935, Box 14, PW Archives, London.

48. Andrew Barr and Irving J. Galpeer, "McKesson & Robbins," *Journal of Accountancy* 163 (May 1987): 160.

49. For a more detailed account of the scandal, see "McKesson & Robbins: Its Fall and Rise," *Fortune* 21 (March 1940): 72–75, 120, 123–126, 128, 130–131.

50. Ibid., 123.

51. Ibid., 124.

52. Ibid.; "Accounting for McKesson-Robbins," *Business Week* (December 17, 1938), 15–16; DeMond, *PW in America*, 261.

53. "McKesson & Robbins," 120; Miranti, *Accountancy Comes of Age*, 175–176.

54. Chatfield, *A History of Accounting Thought*, 136.

55. "Findings and Opinions," *Journal of Accountancy* 72 (July 1942): 95.

56. Chatfield, *A History of Accounting Thought*, 136–138; Barr and Galpeer, "McKesson & Robbins," 160–161. SEC hearing testimony was published in the *Journal of Accountancy* 67 (April 1939): 199–203, (May 1939), 279–281, (June

1939), 350–363, exposing the issues raised by the controversy to a wider professional audience.

57. "Findings and Opinions," 90–95; "Special Report on McKesson & Robbins," ibid., 71 (January 1941): 90–94.

58. For May's views, see his correspondence with J.M.B. Hoxsey, February 3 through March 13, 1939, Securities and Exchange Commission File, 1939 (1); and to Arthur M. Cannon, December 21, 1955, Accountancy File, 1955, G.O. May File Room. See also, "McKesson & Robbins," 123.

59. Miranti, *Accountancy Comes of Age*, 177.

60. Ibid., 175; "Accounting Activities of the SEC: Securities and Exchange Commission Tenth Annual Report, fiscal year ended June 30, 1944," reprinted in part in "Official Releases," *Journal of Accountancy* 79 (June 1945): 501.

61. Chatfield, *A History of Accounting Thought*, 136–139; Miranti, *Accountancy Comes of Age*, 176–177.

62. Miranti, *Accountancy Comes of Age*, 176.

63. Chatfield, *A History of Accounting Thought*, 137.

64. Ibid., 139.

65. Partnership Agreement, July 1, 1939, PW Files, Cravath, Swaine & Moore, New York. The authors are grateful to Cravath for providing access to this document.

66. Scobie to PW [London], March 20, 1903, Box 58/86, PW Archives, London; Obituary, *New York Times*, August 1, 1944, 15; DeMond, *PW in America*, 311.

67. Belser, Itinerant Checker, 22.

68. Ibid., 23.

69. Ibid.; John B. Inglis, *My Life and Times: An Autobiography* (Passaic, N.J.: George Dixon Press, 1974), 83; Partners' Meeting Minutes, May 21, 1940, Box 14, PW Archives, London; Interviews, J. Robert White (July 9, 1987), William C. Miller (July 8, 1987), Walter Baird (March 28, 1988).

70. Mary Murphy, MS "Draft History of Price Waterhouse," c. late 1940s, Records Center, New York Practice Office, 722–723, 731–735, 749.

71. Belser, Itinerant Checker, 21–22.

72. Murphy, "Draft History," 773, 775.

73. Belser, Itinerant Checker, 11; Price, Waterhouse & Co. All Offices, Staff by Months for Year Ending June 30, 1938, McKesson & Robbins Case Records, Box 7, Cravath, Swaine & Moore, New York. The authors are grateful to Cravath for allowing access to these records.

74. Robert K. Elliott and Peter D. Jacobsen, "Audit Technology: A Heritage and a Promise," *Journal of Accountancy* 163 (May 1987): 209; Victor H. Stempf, "Auditing Under War and Postwar Conditions," ibid. 77 (January 1944): 18; Samuel J. Broad, "The Progress of Auditing," ibid. 100 (November 1955): 38–39; Alvin R. Jennings, "An Analysis of Current Developments in Auditing Standards," ibid. 90 (September 1950): 191–192; Arthur Andersen & Co., *The First Sixty Years: Arthur Andersen, 1913–1973* (Chicago: Arthur Andersen & Co., 1974), 62–63; "Informal Portrait," *Price Waterhouse Review* 15, no. 3 (Autumn 1970): 49.

75. Benjamin F. Jackson, Interview (July 28, 1987).

76. John B. Inglis, "Master Copy," February 27, 1973, typescript, 2; Chester W. DeMond, *Price, Waterhouse & Co. in America: A History of a Public Accounting Firm* (1951; reprint ed., New York: Arno Press, 1980), 293–295; Inglis, *My Life and Times*, 115, 118. One hundred and one women ultimately participated in Price Waterhouse's program. Richard Donham, "Price Waterhouse & Co.: Summary of Girls in Scholarship Training Programs," May 7, 1946, typescript, Misc. Firm Documents Box, c. 1930–1960, Office of the Secretary of the Firm, National Office, New York (offsite), 1.

77. Shari H. Westcott and Robert E. Seiler, *Women in the Accounting Profession* (New York: Marcus Wiener Publishing, 1986), 53; Glenda Reid, Brenda T. Acken, and Elise Jancura, "An Historical Perspective on Women in Accounting," *Journal of Accountancy* 163 (May 1987): 343.

78. Richard Donham, "Memorandum on Girl Trainees," typescript, May 8, 1946, Misc. Firm Documents Box, c. 1930–1960, Office of the Secretary of the Firm, National Office, New York, 1.

79. DeMond, *PW in America* (reprint ed.), 295; Eugenia Kaledin, *Mothers and More: American Women in the 1950s* (Boston: Twayne Publishers, 1984), 61. Some of these women went on to become managers by the mid-1950s. Robert Hampton III, Interview (May 31, 1989).

CHAPTER 4

1. Robert E. Field, Interview (January 27, 1988).

2. Louis Galambos and Joseph Pratt, *The Rise of the Corporate Commonwealth: United States Business and Public Policy in the 20th Century* (New York: Basic Books, 1988), 131–132.

3. Harold Vatter, *The United States Economy in the 1950s* (New York: W.W. Norton, 1963), 29–35, 45, 150–190; Alvin H. Hansen, *Economic Issues of the 1960s* (New York: McGraw-Hill, 1960), vii; Arthur M. Johnson, *The American Economy: An Historical Introduction to the Problems of the 1960s* (New York: Free Press, 1974), 60–61; Harry N. Scheiber, Harold G. Vatter, and Harold U. Faulkner, *American Economic History*, 9th ed. (New York: Harper & Row, 1976), 422–423; John K. Galbraith, *American Capitalism: The Concept of Countervailing Power* (Boston: Houghton Mifflin, 1952), 5; Galambos and Pratt, *The Rise of the Corporate Commonwealth*, 135, 141–142.

4. Scheiber, Vatter, and Faulkner, *American Economic History*, 425; Vatter, *U.S. Economy in the 1950s*, 7–8, 98–120; Arthur M. Johnson, "Economy Since 1914," in *Encyclopedia of Economic History*, ed. Glenn Porter (New York: Scribner's, 1980), 120. See also William L. O'Neill, *American High: The Years of Confidence, 1945–1960* (New York: Free Press, 1986), 288; John P. Diggins, *The Proud Decades: America in War and Peace, 1941–1961* (New York: W.W. Norton, 1988), 181; John K. Galbraith, *The Affluent Society* (Boston: Houghton Mifflin, 1958).

5. Arthur Andersen & Co., *The First Sixty Years: Arthur Andersen, 1913–1973* (Chicago: Arthur Andersen & Co., 1974), 62–63.

6. Herman W. Bevis, "The CPA's Changing Practice," *Journal of Accountancy* 100 (November 1955): 34; George R. Catlett, "New Demands on the Accounting Profession," ibid. 104 (July 1957): 25; Ronald V. Hartley, "Operations Research and its Implications for the Accounting Profession," *Accounting Review* 43 (April 1968): 321–322; Robert M. Trueblood, "Auditing and Statistical Sampling," *Journal of Accountancy* 103 (April 1957): 49–51, 57; Broad, "The Progress of Auditing," 39. See also, Henry P. Hill, "An Accountant Looks at Statistics," ibid. 105 (April 1958): 65; Alvin Jennings, "An Analysis of Current Developments in Auditing Procedures and Standards," ibid. 90 (September 1950): 191–192; Joseph Pelej, "Budgeting and the Corresponding Modernization of Accounting," ibid. 105 (June 1958): 65–68; Robert Trueblood, "Accounting and New Management Attitudes," ibid. 106 (October 1958): 37–39; Mary Murphy, "Effect on Financial Reporting of Law, Research, and Public Opinion in Britain and America," ibid. 93 (September 1952): 333; "The Auditor's Role in a Company Report," *Fortune* 57 (January 1958): 119.

7. Vatter, *U.S. Economy in the 1950s*, 10–12; Joseph Pelej, "How Will Business Electronics Affect Auditor's Work," *Journal of Accountancy* 98 (July 1954): 36; Edmund L. Van Deusen, "The Coming Victory over Paper," *Fortune* 52 (October 1955): 131–132; "Office Robots," ibid. 45 (January 1952): 82–83.

8. "New Survey Reveals Hiring Intentions of Major Accounting Employers," *Journal of Accountancy* 91 (March 1951): 289. See also, Trueblood, "Accounting and New Management Attitudes," 37–39; Edward B. Wilcox, "Social and Economic Trends Affecting Accounting," ibid. 80 (September 1945): 179; Bevis, "The CPA's Changing Practice," ibid. 34; Donald M. Shonting and Leo D. Stone, "Audit Techniques for Electronic Systems," ibid. 106 (October 1955): 54–61; Goodrich F. Cleaver, "Auditing and Electronic Data Processing," ibid. 106 (November 1958): 48–54; Joseph Pelej's article, "How Will Business Electronics Affect Auditor's Work," ibid. 98 (July 1954): 36, 44, was the first major discussion of how business electronics could affect the work of internal auditors. See generally, Arthur Toan, "Auditing, Control and Electronics" ibid. 99 (May 1955): 40–45; Catlett, "New Demands on the Accounting Profession," 25; Robert Sobel, *The Age of Giant Corporations: A Microeconomic History of American Business, 1914–1970* (Westport, Conn.: Greenwood Press, 1972), 229; "Office Robots," 82; Cleaver, "Auditing and Electronic Data Processing," 48, 52; "More Midnight Oil for CPAs," *Business Week* (September 29, 1951), 86; Pelej, "Budgeting and the Corresponding Modernization of Accounting," 64.

For a sociological perspective on the development of "information professionals" after World War II, see Andrew Abbott, *The System of Professions: An Essay on the Division of Expert Labor* (Chicago: University of Chicago Press, 1988), 236–246.

9. "More Midnight Oil," 84; Jennings, "An Analysis of Current Developments in Auditing Procedures and Standards," 190; "New Survey Reveals Hiring Intentions of Major Accounting Employers," 289.

10. Edward B. Wilcox, "The Role of Accountancy in Prosperity and Peace," *Journal of Accountancy* 84 (October 1947): 281.

11. Wilcox, "Social and Economic Trends Affecting Accountancy," 184. See also Arthur M. Cannon, "Accounting as a Social Force," *Journal of Accountancy* 99 (March 1955): 60.

12. Samuel J. Broad, "Why Do We Need Accountants?" *Journal of Accountancy* 80 (October 1945): 268.

13. Editorial, "Accounting at the Half Century Mark," *Journal of Accountancy* 91 (January 1951): 65–66.

14. Ibid. G.O. May quote is from Wilcox, "Social and Economic Trends Affecting Accounting," 180. Herman Bevis, who looked to George O. May as a "mentor," would later discuss corporate financial reporting in the same elevated terms: "a high quality of corporate financial reporting may be looked upon as a manifestation of, and an inspiration to, higher ethics in our society." Herman Bevis, *Corporate Financial Reporting in a Competitive Economy* (New York: Columbia University Press, 1965), 19.

15. John C. Biegler, Interview, Part 1 (October 18, 1987); John W. Zick, Interview (January 26, 1988); Field Interview; John B. Inglis, *My Life and Times: An Autobiography* (Passaic, N.J.: George Dixon Press, 1974), 117, 129–30; Weston Rankin, Interview (January 21, 1988); Russell Zimmermann, Interview (July 29, 1987); "Report of the U.S. Firm for the Year Ending June 30, 1950," Appendix C, 7, typescript (title varies), Office of the Secretary of the Firm, National Office, New York. The reports of the American firm were sent at the close of each fiscal year to the International Firm. All subsequent references are cited as: "Report of the U.S. Firm," with year and page notations. See also John B. Inglis, "Master Copy," February 27, 1973, typescript, draft chapter, 26. The authors are grateful to John B. Inglis for providing this and several other draft chapters including "Mergers in the United States," "Foreign Offices," and two other, untitled pieces composed by Inglis for a proposed Price Waterhouse history.

16. "Percival F. Brundage: Director of the Budget," *PW Review* 2, no. 2 (1955), 58–59; "A Tribute to Percy Brundage," ibid. 25, no. 2 (1980), 37; Price Waterhouse, Executive Committee Minutes, Office of the Secretary of the Firm, National Office, New York (April 15, 1943), (August 2, 1944); Inglis, *My Life and Times*, 116; Herman W. Bevis, Interview (September 1, 1987).

17. Field and Baird interviews; Arthur Andersen, *The First Sixty Years*, 100; Inglis, *My Life and Times*, 118; Bevis Interview; Richard Donham, "Memorandum: Relations with Colleges and Universities," May 9, 1946, typescript, Misc. Firm Documents Box, c. 1930–1960, Office of the Secretary of the Firm, National Office, New York, 1–2; Inglis, "Master Copy," 14–14A.

18. Bevis Interview; Rankin Interview; Richard Donham, "Memorandum: Accountants' Training-on-the-Job for Veterans," December 6, 1945, typescript, Misc. Firm Documents Box, c. 1930–1960, 1–3; Field Interview; J. Robert White, Interview (July 9, 1987); Inglis, "Master Copy," 3.

19. Rankin Interview.

20. George C. Watt, "A Story Written Expressly for the PW History," MS, June 6, 1989, 4–5. The authors are grateful to Mr. Watt for providing his written observations.

21. George C. Watt, "Staff Training in the 1950s," MS, June 7, 1989, 1.

22. Ibid.

23. Exec. Comm. Min. (October 9–10, 1947), 1; "Biography: Informal Portraits," *PW Review* 7, no. 1 (1961): 53; "Report of the U.S. Firm," 1952, Appendix C, 1; Exec. Comm. Min. (March 1–4, 1959), 2; Inglis, "Master Copy," 28–29.

24. Inglis, "Master Copy," 13–15.

25. Price Waterhouse, "Policies and Administrative References: Background Material [PAR Background]," 1958–1970, typescript, 064.11; 069.10, Office of the Secretary of the Firm, National Office, New York.

26. PAR Background, 064.15; Exec. Comm. Min. (May 15–16, 18, 20, 1958), 11; (January 9–11, 1958), 9–11.

27. PAR Background, 069.12–16.

28. By the early 1970s, the New York office had 1.2 million chargeable hours as compared with Chicago's 200,000. Zick and Larkin interviews; Robert Hampton III, Interview (May 31, 1989).

29. PAR Background, 069.11; Gunders, Part 1, Zick and Biegler, Part 1, interviews. Although Brundage had come from Boston to New York, he was most closely identified with the New York office.

30. In keeping with the British tradition, George O. May addressed his partners by their last names. May to Inglis, July 3, 1956, "Dear Inglis;" May to Grady, October 11, 1944, "Dear Grady." Cammarata Box, George O. May File Room, NIC, New York.

31. Inglis, "Master Copy," 3; Field Interview; Inglis, *My Life and Times*, 107.

32. Baird Interview.

33. Mark D. Larkin, Interview (October 29, 1987); Zimmermann Interview.

34. Inglis, "Master Copy," 4; Bevis and Zick interviews; Inglis, "Master Copy," 11. At this time, Executive Committee meetings were also moved to Seaview and expanded to two to three days, again with whole afternoons or mornings devoted to golf. The last New York City fall dinner-dance was in 1958. Inglis, *My Life and Times*, 107; Price Waterhouse History Advisory Committee (September 14, 1989).

35. Zick and White interviews; Wyman Patten Interview (June 2, 1989).

36. Bevis Interview; Inglis, "Master Copy," 30. Three of these new partners were tax specialists, two were from the MAS Department, and another from personnel. Rankin Interview; "PW Partners 1895–1986," tables, memoranda, official firm correspondence. The authors are grateful to Mark Larkin for providing these documents.

37. Chester W. DeMond, *Price, Waterhouse & Co. in America: A History of a Public Accounting Firm* (1951; reprint ed., New York: Arno Press, 1980), 301–304. At the time, practices were established in twenty-one countries. Robert E. Field, "Development of Our International Organization," in "Price Waterhouse: A Retrospective Look," typescript, June 29, 1982, NIC, New York, 1.

38. Draft Statement on Price Waterhouse World Firm, June 19, 1987, 5. The authors are grateful to John R. Jordan, Jr., for this document. See also, John L. Carey, *The Rise of the Accounting Profession* (New York: AICPA, 1970), 2: 369; DeMond, *PW in America*, 304; *Career Opportunities in Public Accounting with Price Waterhouse & Co: An Introduction to One of America's Largest Firms*, 1959, Files, "Price Waterhouse & Co.," NIC, New York, 15. The South African firm reported to the International Firm through the London firm. DeMond, *PW in America*, 307–308. See also "Price Waterhouse & Co. International Organization Charts, November 1954–September 1969," Files, "Price Waterhouse & Co.," NIC, New York. See generally, John B. Inglis, "Foreign Offices," undated typescript; John B. Inglis, untitled typescript concerning the International Firm, 3; "Report of the U.S. Firm," 1950, Appendix C, 6.

39. DeMond, *PW in America*, 305–306; *Career Opportunities in Public Accounting*, 15; Price Waterhouse & Co. (International Firm), Minutes of Meeting, September 24–28, 1948, attached to "Report of the U.S. Firm," 1948.

40. Henry S. Sawin, "Where Have We Been 1946–1980," typescript outline of a speech delivered to Region III MAS partners and managers, 4. The authors are grateful to Donald Markstein for providing this document. See also Zick Interview; Exec. Comm. Min., May 14, 1946, 4; Inglis, "Master Copy," 8–9; "Informal Portrait," *PW Review* 15, no. 3 (1970): 46–51; "Partners Retiring," ibid. 5, no. 2 (1960): 29–30; White Interview. Throughout the text, the terms "Systems," "MAS," and then in the 1980s, "MCS" are used. All terms refer to the same department.

41. Arthur B. Toan, "MAS: Some Observations and Reminiscences," MS., c. January 1989, 8–9. The authors are grateful to Mr. Toan for taking the time to put his recollections into writing. Inglis, "Master Copy," 18; Dykeman Interview; Exec. Comm. Min. (September 21, 1946), 3.

42. Toan, "Reminiscences," 9–10; Exec. Comm. Min. (April 23, 1947), 3; ibid. (August 22–23, 1949), 6; See also Inglis, "Master Copy," 10; Sawin speech, 5–7.

43. Services of the System Department, January 6, 1953, "Price Waterhouse & Co." Files, NIC, New York, 1.

44. Sawin speech, 9.

45. Exec. Comm. Min. (June 11, 1946), 2; Toan, "Reminiscences," 11; Sawin Speech, 9–12; "Report of the U.S. Firm," 1953, 6; Inglis, "Master Copy," 10; Exec. Comm. Min. (March 29–30, 1950), 5; (January 26–27, 1953), 6–7; (April 7–10, 1952), Appendix 2.

46. "Report of the U.S. Firm," 1954, 13; 1955, 13.

47. Ibid., 1956, 9.

48. Sawin speech, 11; "Report of the U.S. Firm," 1957, 11; Services of the Systems Department, 1–2; "Report of the U.S. Firm," 1954, 13.

49. Toan, "Reminiscences," 12–15; "Report of the U.S. Firm," 1956, 9.

50. Arthur Toan, Interview (September 27, 1988); Toan, "Reminiscences," 7, 10; Sawin speech, 3; "Annual Meeting of the MAS Group of the U.S. Firm, New York, February 28 and March 1, 1957," bound typescript, 1. The authors are grateful to Henry Gunders for supplying this document.

51. According to the minutes, the brochure bore the label "for use of the staff of Price Waterhouse & Co." Exec. Comm. Min. (January 10–11, 1955), 6; (May 15–17, 19, 23, 1957), 6–7.

52. Exec. Comm. Min. (May 16–20, 22, 24, 1956), 8; Price Waterhouse Advisory Committee, (March 6–7, 1990); Minutes of Meeting of Management Advisory Services Committee Held on September 30 and October 1, 1954 in Board Room of 56 Pine Street, New York, typescript, "Price Waterhouse & Co.," Files, NIC, New York, 16.

53. Inglis, *My Life and Times*, 38–52.

54. Ibid., 129; Price Waterhouse & Co. (International Firm), Minutes of Meeting, July 16–19, 1951, attached to "Report of the U.S. Firm," 1951; Herman Bevis, "Mr. Inglis Retires," *PW Review* 6, no. 2 (1961): 62.

55. Inglis, *My Life and Times*, 114–116, 134; "J.B. Inglis Named Head of NAA," *PW Review* 3, no. 2 (1958): 73; John L. Carey, *The Rise of the Accounting Profession to Responsibility and Authority, 1937–1969* (New York: AICPA, 1970), 1: 343–344.

56. Inglis, *My Life and Times*, 111; Richard Vangermeersch, ed., *Financial Accounting Milestones in the Annual Reports of the United States Steel Corporation, The First Seven Decades* (New York: Garland Publishing, 1986), Introduction, 6.

57. Rankin, Larkin, Hampton, Baird, and White interviews; Carl A. Tietjen, Interview (July 29, 1988).

58. Inglis, *My Life and Times*, 130.

59. Bevis, Baird, Zick, Field, and Meagher interviews; Inglis, *My Life and Times*, 130, 132–133.

60. Inglis, *My Life and Times*, 132; Exec. Comm. Min. (March 1–4, 1959), 1–2.

61. Inglis, *My Life and Times*, 132; Exec. Comm. Min. (April 24, 1948), 1; Baird, Inglis/Campbell, and Zick Interviews; Inglis, "Master Copy," 15, 23; Exec. Comm. Min. (October 14, 1954), 1; "Report of the U.S. Firm," 1955, 2; 1951, Appendix C, 1; Exec. Comm. Min. (May 23, 1954), 8; *Career Opportunities in Public Accounting*; Rankin Interview.

62. "Report of the U.S. Firm," 1951, Appendix C, 2; 1958, 3, 5; 1957, 5; 1954, 4; 1955, 3.

63. Inglis, *My Life and Times*, 130–131; Exec. Comm. Min. (March 1–4, 1959), 2, 13; "Report of the U.S. Firm," 1954, 2.

64. Roy M. Sommerfeld and John E. Easton, "The CPA's Tax Practice Today—And How it Got That Way," *Journal of Accountancy* 163 (May 1987): 169. This clash between lawyers and tax accountants is viewed by one sociologist as an effort by two different segments of a larger "information profession" to stake out their unique territory. See Abbott, *The System of Professions*, 233.

65. Dwight T. Williams, "Accounting and the National Economy," *Journal of Accountancy* 82 (September 1946): 193.

66. Sommerfeld and Easton, "The CPA's Tax Practice," 170.

67. James E. Hammond, "Statistics on the Accounting Profession," *Journal of Accountancy* 104 (November 1957): 44–45. See generally, Thomas H. Sanders, "An Analysis of the Forces Which Are Shaping the Future of Accountancy," ibid. 90 (October 1950): 282–289; Austin, "Relations Between Lawyers and

CPAs in Income Tax Practice," 805–815; Erwin N. Griswold, "The Tax Problem I: A Further Look at Lawyers and Accountants," *Journal of Accountancy* 100 (December 1955): 29–35; William J. Jameson, "Cooperation between the Legal and Accounting Professions," 101 (November 1956): 42–45; "Joint Report of the Special Commission," ibid. 103 (January 1957): 53–54.

68. Saul Levy, "The Scope and Limitation of Accountants' Practice in Federal Income Taxation," *Journal of Accountancy* 89 (June 1950): 470–471; Maxwell and Charles, "National Conference of Lawyers and Public Accountants," 120; Louis S. Goldberg, "A Plague on Both Their Houses: The Accountant-Lawyer Differences in Tax Practice," *Journal of Accountancy* 84 (September 1947): 188–195; Austin, "Relations Between Lawyers and CPAs," 805.

69. Editorial, "What Does the *Bercu* Decision Mean?" *Journal of Accountancy* 88 (September 1949): 185.

70. Levy, "Scope and Limitation," 470–471, 473; Austin, "Relations Between Lawyers and CPAs," 814. See New York County Lawyers Association v. Bercu, 273 App. Div. 524, 78 N.Y.S. 2d 209, *aff'd*, 299 N.Y. 728; 87 N.E.2d 451 (1949); Boris I. Bittker, "Does Tax Practice by Accountants Constitute Unauthorized Practice of Law?" *Journal of Taxation* 25 (September 1966): 185. See also, John C. Gardner and G.A. Swanson, "Legal Landmarks in the Development of Tax Practice," *Journal of Accountancy* 163 (May 1987): 190–192. John W. Queenan, "Lawyers and CPAs," ibid. 102 (November 1956): 47; Mark E. Richardson, "The Accountant's Position in the Field of Taxation," ibid. 98 (August 1954): 169–170; Goldberg, "A Plague on Both Their Houses," 194.

71. Goldberg, "A Plague on Both Their Houses," 188–194; Austin, "Relations Between Lawyers and CPAs," 814; Griswold, "The Tax Problem," 30; Queenan, "Lawyers and CPAs," 47.

72. Agran v. Shapiro, 127 Cal. App. 2d 807, 273 P2d 619 (1954); Marquis G. Eaton, "What Did Mr. Agran Do?" *Journal of Accountancy* 99 (June 1955): 33–38; Editorial, "The *Agran* Case in Perspective," ibid. 102 (December 1956): 29–31; Queenan, "Lawyers and CPAs," ibid. 47–48. See, e.g., Lowell Bar Association v. Loeb (Mass., 1943), Gardner v. Conway, 234 Minn. 468, 48 NW2d 788 (1950); In Re Kearney, 63 So. 2d. 630 (Fla. 1953).

73. Maurice H. Stans, "The Tax Problem II: A Proposed Solution to the Controversy," *Journal of Accountancy* 100 (December 1955): 36.

74. Queenan, "Lawyers and CPAs," 47–48; "The *Agran* Case in Perspective," 29; Albert H. Cohen, "Professional Conduct in Taxes," *Journal of Accountancy* 101 (January 1956): 35.

75. Queenan, "Lawyers and CPAs," 48.

76. "Joint Report of Special Committee on Professional Relations of American Bar Association and Committee on Relations with Bar of American Institute of Accountants," *Journal of Accountancy* 103 (January 1957): 53; Queenan, "Lawyers and CPAs," 48–49; T.T. Shaw, "Scope and Limitation of Tax Practice," ibid. 104 (August 1957): 37–41; "The *Agran* Case in Perspective," 29–31; Jameson, "Cooperation between the Legal and Accounting Professions," 42–45; "Joint Statement Relating to Practice in the Field of Taxation," *Journal of Accountancy* 107 (March 1959): 75–76.

77. 373 U.S. 379 (1963). Bittker, "Does Tax Practice by Accountants Constitute Unauthorized Practice of Law?" 184–187.

78. On the dual practice question, see W.D. Sprague and Arthur J. Levy, "Accounting and the Law: Is Dual Practice in the Public Interest?" *Journal of Accountancy* 122 (December 1966): 45–52; Phillip D. Brent, "Accountancy and Law: Concurrent Practice Is in the Public Interest," ibid. 123 (March 1967): 38–46; "Tax Advice by CPA Not 'Unauthorized Practice' Under Malpractice Policy," *Journal of Taxation* 19 (September 1963): 172.

79. Baird Interview.

80. "Report of the Tax Committee," typescript, April 1955, "Price Waterhouse & Co.," Files, NIC, 1, 3; William A. Schan, Interview (October 20, 1987).

81. Larkin, Cohen, and Miller interviews.

82. "Biography. Meet the Partners," *PW Review* 2, no. 4 (December 1957): 50; Miller Interview; "Report of the U.S. Firm," 1951, Appendix C, 1; Inglis, "Master Copy," 30; Inglis, *My Life and Times*, 115; Cohen Interview; "Report of the U.S. Firm," 1954, 3.

83. Exec. Comm. Min. (May 18–20, 22, 24, 1955), 6; Schan Interview; "Report of the U.S. Firm," 1959, 16. The reference file also contained information on "firm policies and practices . . . on preparation of returns and documents, publication of articles and preparation in technical meetings." Report of the Tax Committee, May 1954, "Price Waterhouse & Co." Files, NIC, New York, 2; Cohen Interview; "Report of the U.S. Firm," 1956, 2.

84. Field Interview.

85. "Report of the U.S. Firm," 1954, 3; ibid., 1960, 1; Raymond Lauver, Interview (June 1, 1989); Field and Rankin interviews; Inglis, *My Life and Times*, 115; Stephen A. Zeff, "Overview: The Past and its Leaders. Leaders of the Accounting Profession: 14 Who Made a Difference," *Journal of Accountancy* 163 (May 1987): 60–61; "Mr. Paul Grady Elected to Accounting Hall of Fame," *PW Review*, 9, no. 4 (1964): 51; "Biography: Meet the Partners," ibid. 3, no. 3 (1958): 64–65; "Paul Grady Receives Institute's Outstanding Service Award for Distinguished Contribution to Profession," ibid. 4 (1959), 46; Paul Grady, "The Increasing Emphasis on Accounting as a Social Force," *Significant Accounting Essays*, ed. Maurice Moonitz and A.C. Littleton (Englewood Cliffs, N.J.: Prentice-Hall, 1965), 38; "Report of the U.S. Firm," 1963, 12.

86. Field, Meagher, Miller, and Biegler, Part I, interviews.

87. "Report of the U.S. Firm," 1956, 2; Tietjen and Lauver interviews; Inglis, "Master Copy," 8. The other two obligatory volumes were AICPA reference works. "Report of the U.S. Firm," 1955, 19; ibid., 1957, 16; ibid., 1958, 13, 15; Biegler, Part I, and Rankin interviews; "Report of the U.S. Firm," 1960, 1.

88. "Report of the U.S. Firm," 1955, 13; Exec Comm. Min. (October 8–9, 1957), 5; Inglis, "Memo on Research Department," 2; Hampton Interview.

89. "Report of the U.S. Firm," 1959, 14; Lauver, Tietjen, Jackson interviews; John B. Inglis, "Memorandum on Research Department," typescript, February 7, 1958, 1. The authors are grateful to Carl Tietjen for supplying this document. Hampton Interview; "Research Department Index of Projects," October 26, 1960, "Price Waterhouse & Co." Files, NIC, New York.

90. Teitjen, Lauver interviews. The firm also sought consistency and centralization in other practice areas. Having been criticized by the SEC for lack of firmwide uniformity in filings, the firm created a SEC Department in 1952. Biegler Interview, Part 1; Inglis, "Master Copy," 27–28.

91. "Report of the U.S. Firm," 1950, Appendix C, 7; Price Waterhouse & Co. (International Firm), Minutes of Meeting, July 14–16, 1953, attached to "Report of the U.S. Firm," 1953; 1959, 14–15; 1954, 18; 1958, 16. See Exec. Comm. Min. (November 24–25, 1952), 1.

92. Hill and Hampton interviews; Exec. Comm. Min. (August 8–9, 1955); "Report of the U.S. Firm," 1958, 15, 17; ibid., 1959, 15; John B. Inglis, undated typescript concerning publications by firm partners, 2. Walter Baird, Interview (March 28, 1988). The royalties from *Sampling in Auditing* were generated for the Price Waterhouse Foundation, a nonprofit entity incorporated in 1956 "to make donations to educational and other institutions, particularly those engaged in teaching accounting." Hill Interview; "Report of the U.S. Firm," 1957, 20. The Foundation's income derived, for the first ten years, from contributions of individual partners, but later the firm itself became a major contributor. Inglis, *My Life and Times*, 133.

93. Arthur Andersen, *The First Sixty Years*, 64–67.

94. Ibid.

95. Andersen, *The First Sixty Years*, 36; Theodor Swanson, *Touche Ross: A Biography* (New York: Touche Ross, 1972), 17; Price Waterhouse & Co., "List of Offices and Representatives with Addresses as of Nov. 15, 1947," bound typescript, Price Waterhouse & Co. files, NIC, 1; T.A. Wise, *Peat, Marwick, Mitchell & Co.: 85 Years* (New York: Peat, Marwick, Mitchell & Co., 1982), 44–45.

96. Wise, *Peat, Marwick, Mitchell*, 45, 47–51; James Don Edwards, *A History of Public Accounting in the United States* (East Lansing, Mich.: Michigan State University Press, 1960), 217–218.

97. "Report of the U.S. Firm," 1953, App. C, 4; Maurice J. Dahlem, Interview (July 10, 1987); Henry Gunders, Interview, Part I (July 15, 1987); Exec. Comm. Min. (September 28, 1958), 5; (January 12–14, 1959), 10–12; Zick Interview; Joseph E. Connor, Interview, Part I (May 16, 1988); "Report of the Business Research Committee," 1953–1958, typescript; Dahlem Interview, 48. The authors are grateful to Maurice Dahlem for supplying these and other BRC documents referred to below. Exec. Comm. Min. (May 25, 1954), 9; (January 9–11, 1957), 3; "Answers to Questionnaire of Business Research Committee Prepared for Its Visit," September 8, 1955, typescript, 14–22.

98. Meagher Interview; Exec. Comm. Min. (January 12–14, 1959), 10; (May 13–15, 19, 1959), 12; (August 19–20, 1957), 6. Inglis himself saw public relations as useful only to combat bad publicity, rather than as an active, positive method of image enhancement. He questioned a proposal to create an in-house public relations function in 1960, although the Executive Committee voted to create it. Ibid., "Special Action" (January 1960), 1; (March 2–4, 1960), Appendix, 10, 12.

99. Baird Interview.

100. Exec. Comm. Min. (August 16–17, 1956).

101. Hampton and Larkin interviews; "A Statistical Summary of the Inquiries Received for the Year Ending March 31, 1953," typescript, Misc. Firm Documents Box, c. 1930–1960, Office of the Secretary of the Firm, National Office, New York, 1.

102. Rankin, Meagher, Zimmermann, and Baird interviews; T.A. Wise, "Part I: The Auditors Have Arrived," *Fortune* 62 (November 1960): 152; Reed Braithwaite, assistant vice president, Carnation, to William Murray, Price Waterhouse, January 4, 1963, letter and attachment. The authors are grateful to Olaf Falkenhagen for providing this document.

103. Bevis, Baird, Gunders, Part I, Meagher interviews.

104. The mergers were triggered by the success of Price Waterhouse's merger with Stagg, Mather and Hough in the West Indies. Inglis, "Mergers in the United States," 1. The other mergers during this period were with Butterly & Burrus, Denver, Colo., 1955; Vernon Maxfield, Seattle, Wash., 1956; Jackson & Zanglien, Rochester, N.Y., 1957; Amen Surdam & Co., Buffalo, N.Y., 1960. Several others occurred in the first year of the Bevis administration: Neely & Harrison, Phoenix, Ariz., 1962; Webster, Blanchard & Willard, Hartford, Conn., 1962. "Report of the U.S. Firm," 1960, 2; Inglis, "Mergers in the United States," 5–6. This period reflected the firm's historical high point for mergers until 1983–1987. Eleanor C. Mertson to Joseph E. Connor, "Phoenix Speech Material," September 2, 1987, typescript memorandum. The authors are grateful to Kathleen Gaffney, Office of the Secretary of the Firm, National Office, New York, for supplying this document.

105. Bevis, White, Baird, and Biegler, Part I, interviews. The U.S. Firm informed its international associates that "Haskins & Sells, Peat, Marwick, and Arthur Young have acquired the practices of many small firms during the last few years. Partly to set up new locations, partly for general expansion." "Report of the U.S. Firm," 1956, 1, 6; PW History Advisory Committee (March 6–7, 1990); Inglis/Campbell interviews; John B. Inglis, "Mergers in the United States," typescript, undated, 1–9. The authors are grateful to Mr. Inglis for supplying this document.

106. "Report of the U.S. Firm," 1957, 17; 1958, 18; 1959, 16–17. Around the same period, the American firm's foreign offices begin to mention foreign competition for the first time. For example, the Caracas, Venezuela, office, which served large oil companies, first noted the presence of Haskins & Sells and Arthur Young in 1957, and did so for each year thereafter until the end of the decade. Similar experiences were reported in Colombia and Mexico. Ibid., 1957, 12; 1959, 11; 1960, 10–11.

107. Gunders Interview, Part I; see also Wise, "The Auditors Have Arrived," 152; Larkin, Meagher, and Lauver interviews.

CHAPTER 5

1. Arthur Okun, *The Political Economy of Prosperity* (Washington, D.C.: Brookings Institution, 1970), 44–50; Arthur M. Johnson, ed., *The American*

Economy: An Historical Introduction to the Problems of the 1970s (New York: Free Press, 1974), 8–10; Herman Bevis, Interview (September 1, 1987).

2. Louis Galambos and Joseph Pratt, *The Rise of the Corporate Commonwealth: United States Business and Public Policy in the 20th Century* (New York: Basic Books, 1988), 129; 158–159, 161, 166–167, 170, 181–182; Ellis W. Hawley, "Challenges to the Mixed Economy: The State and Private Enterprise," in *American Choices: Social Dilemmas and Public Policy since 1960*, ed. Robert H. Bremner, Gary W. Reichard, and Richard J. Hopkins (Columbus, Ohio: Ohio State University Press, 1986), 159; Thomas Cochran, *American Business in the Twentieth Century* (Cambridge, Mass.: Harvard University Press, 1972), 208; Mira Wilkins, *The Maturing of Multinational Enterprise: American Business Abroad from 1914 to 1970* (Cambridge, Mass.: Harvard University Press, 1974), 287–291, 300–310, 374–375, 405, 427, 429, 431; Raymond Vernon, *Sovereignty at Bay: The Multinational Spread of U.S. Enterprises* (New York: Basic Books, 1971), 86–87, 309.

3. Cochran, *American Business in the Twentieth Century*, 208–210; Galambos and Pratt, *The Rise of the Corporate Commonwealth*, 164–165.

4. John Brooks, *The Go-Go Years* (New York: Weybridge and Talley, 1973), 154; "Report on the U.S. Firm for the Year Ending June 30, 1968," 17, typescript (title varies), Office of the Secretary of the Firm, National Office, New York. (All subsequent references are cited as: "Report of the U.S. Firm" with year and page notations.) Ibid., 1969, 20.

5. Galambos and Pratt, *The Rise of the Corporate Commonwealth*, 171–172; George Hafner, "Auditing EDP," *Accounting Review* 39 (October 1964): 979.

6. Edwin T. Boyle, "What the Computer Means to the Accounting Profession," *Journal of Accountancy* 121 (January 1966): 56–57; Howard F. Stettler, "CPAs/Auditing/2000," ibid. 125 (May 1968): 55–60; David F. Linowes, "The Future of the Accounting Profession," *Accounting Review* 40 (January 1965): 102; Arthur B. Toan, "Data Processing, Accounting and Business Accounting," *Journal of Accountancy* 114 (November 1962): 49; William L. Campfield, "Critical Paths for Professional Accountants During the New Managerial Revolution," *Accounting Review* 38 (July 1963): 522; Joseph W. Dodwell, "Operational Auditing: A Part of the Basic Audit," *Journal of Accountancy* 121 (June 1966): 31–39; W. Thomas Porter, "Evaluating Internal Controls in EDP Systems," ibid. 118 (August 1964): 34; Hafner, "Auditing EDP," 982.

7. Thomas W. McRae, "The Decline and Fall of the Accounting Profession," *Journal of Accountancy* 113 (June 1962): 66–67; see Boyle, "What the Computer Means to the Accounting Profession," 56; David F. Linowes, "Professional Organization and Growth," *Journal of Accountancy* 120 (July 1965): 24–29; Linowes, "The Future of the Accounting Profession," 103; Maurice B. T. Davies, "Impact of EDP on Relations Between Banks and CPAs," *Journal of Accountancy* 120 (July 1965): 60–61.

8. Robert K. Elliott and Peter D. Jacobsen, "Audit Technology: A Heritage and a Promise," *Journal of Accountancy* 163 (May 1987): 210; Porter, "Evaluating Internal Controls," 35; Brendan J. Meagher, Interview (January 28, 1988); Irving J. Sandler, "Plain Talk About Auditing in an ADPS Environment," *Journal of Accountancy* 125 (April 1968): 43–47.

9. "Accounting: A Crisis over Fuller Disclosure," *Business Week* (April 22, 1972), 57; "Report of the U.S. Firm," 1966, 15; Ed Cony, "CPA Invasion: Accounting Firms Push Deeper into General Management Consulting," *The Wall Street Journal*, October 30, 1961, 1.

10. Bevis Interview.

11. Ibid.

12. "Report of the U.S. Firm," 1956, 4. See ibid., 1956, 8; ibid., 1955, 8; ibid., 1958, 19; ibid., 1960, 21; ibid., 1957, 20; Richard Fitzgerald, Interview (June 9, 1989); Walter M. Baird, Interview (March 28, 1988); "Mr. Bevis Retires," *PW Review* 14, no. 2 (1969): 6–7; Bevis Interview. For general information on the committee, see, AICPA: Long Range Objectives Committee, 1956–1965: Historical Record of Committee Activities, NIC, New York.

13. John C. Biegler, Interview, Part I (October 19, 1987); Baird Interview.

14. Bevis Interview.

15. "Report of the U.S. Firm," 1960, 2–3; Bevis Interview; William C. Miller, Interview (July 8, 1987); "Policies and Administrative References: Background Material," 1961–1978 (several editions), typescript and bound, Office of the Secretary of the Firm, National Office, New York (hereafter referred to as PAR Background); sections 035.10–035.11, 064.35; Brendan J. Meagher, Interview; Weston Rankin, Interview (January 21, 1988).

16. Russell A. Zimmermann, Interview (July 29, 1987); "Retirement," *PW Review* 9, no. 2 (1964): 13; "Mr. O. Kenneth Pryor Named Managing Partner in Firm Administration," ibid. 6, no. 4 (1961): 7; "Report of the U.S. Firm," 1964, 1. Nye later served as the firm's secretary from 1969 until his retirement in 1971. "Retirement," *PW Review* 16, no. 2 (1971): 43.

17. Price Waterhouse, Executive Committee Minutes (March 14–16, 1962) 1 and Appendices, typescript, Office of the Secretary of the Firm, National Office, New York; Baird Interview.

18. Bevis Interview.

19. Bevis Interview; R.E. Field, T. Herz, B.F. Jackson, J.B. O'Hara, H.B. Sanders, L.A. Wynhof, Memorandum, Tenure of Membership on the Executive Committee and Methods of Election and Reelection Thereto, typescript, April 9, 1964, 2. The authors are grateful to Henry Gunders for supplying this document. Exec. Comm. Min. (October 15–17, 1962), 3 and Appendix A; Zimmermann Interview.

20. "Report of the U.S. Firm," 1966, 4.

21. Albert Cohen, Interview (March 15, 1989).

22. Ibid.

23. "Report of the U.S. Firm," 1961, 17; 1962, 21–22.

24. PAR Background, 075.12–13; Exec. Comm. Min. (August 7–11, 1967), 4.

25. Bevis Interview; Weston Rankin, Interview; PW History Advisory Committee (March 6–7, 1990).

26. PW History Advisory Committee (March 6–7, 1990); Meagher and Rankin interviews.

27. Robert E. Field, Interview (January 27, 1988); Baird, Zimmermann interviews.

28. Zimmermann, Baird, Zick, Bevis, Meagher interviews.

29. Baird Interview; Mark Larkin, Interview (October 29, 1987); Raymond Lauver, Interview (June 1, 1989).

30. Thomas J. Graves, "The Future of Tax Practice," *Journal of Accountancy* 118 (December 1964): 53, 55; Cohen Interview; "Report of the U.S. Firm," 1964, 16.

31. "Report of the U.S. Firm," 1964, 16; 1969, 30.

32. Ibid.

33. Cohen Interview.

34. Arthur B. Toan, "MAS: Some Observations and Reminiscences," MS, 43.

35. Ibid., 43.

36. "Report of the U.S. Firm," 1969, 22; 1968, 23; Toan, "Reminiscences," 18–20. For a sociologist's discussion of the origins of management advisory services and its development into a separate profession, see Andrew Abbott, *The System of Professions: An Essay on the Division of Expert Labor* (Chicago: University of Chicago Press, 1988), 240–246.

37. Despite staff shortages, the MAS Department had an impressive list of bank, utilities, insurance companies, government agencies, chemical companies, and oil company clients. Toan, "Reminiscences," 15–16, 43–44; "Report of the U.S. Firm," 1965, 16; Henry Gunders, "MAS Men As Professionals," typescript speech, June 28, 1966, "Price Waterhouse & Co." Files, NIC, New York, 1; "Report of the U.S. Firm," 1963, 1.

38. Toan, "Reminiscences," 21–23, 29–30.

39. "Report of the U.S. Firm," 1969, 23; Toan, "Reminiscences," 17, 28–29; "Report of the U.S. Firm," 1966, 18.

40. Toan, "Reminiscences," 24–26, 31–32; "Report of the U.S. Firm," 1969, 24–25; 1968, 23–25; 1963, 3.

41. "Report of the U.S. Firm," 1965, 16; 1968, 22.

42. Francis Dykeman Interview (March 24, 1988); Note, "The Worth of a Man: A Study of Reasonable Compensation in Close Corporations," *Southern California Law Review* 38, no. 2 (1965): 280–282; Dykeman, "The Impact of Expert Testimony in a Court of Law," *PW Review* 10, no. 2 (1965): 38–42; Larkin Interview; "Report of the U.S. Firm," 1967, 14.

43. Price Waterhouse, Files of the Research Department, Records Center, New York Practice Office, Hudson Street Warehouse, Box PA 110.

44. "Report of the U.S. Firm," 1965, 18.

45. "MAS Celebrates Twenty Years," *PW Review* 11, no. 3 (1966): 34–37; "Report of the U.S. Firm," 1948, 19; 1966, 15; 1965, 18.

46. Exec. Comm. Min. (March 10–14, 1969), 8.

47. Toan, "Reminiscences," 16, 21; Henry S. Sawin, "Where Have We Been, 1946–1980," typescript, outline of a speech delivered to Region III MAS planners and managers, 19. The authors are grateful to Donald Markstein for providing this document.

48. "Report of the U.S. Firm," 1968, 3. In 1969, these different functions were consolidated for the first time under the national director of Accounting and Auditing Services. See, e.g., Exec. Comm. Min. (August 12–14, 1969), 8.

See "Report of the U.S. Firm," 1954, 3; Wyman Patten, Interview (June 2, 1989); Biegler Interview, Part I.

49. "Report of the U.S. Firm," 1961, 12–13.

50. Ibid., 13.

51. Ibid., 1963, 12; 1964, 20; 1965, 23; 1967, 24.

52. George C. Watt, "Firsts (Opportunities)," in "PW History," June 14, 1989, MS, 3. The authors are grateful to Mr. Watt for putting his recollections into writing.

53. "Report of the U.S. Firm," 1961, 12.

54. Ibid., 1963, 12; 1964, 20.

55. "Report of the U.S. Firm," 1961, 12; 1967, 34; 1968, 33.

56. Richard D. Fitzgerald, Letter to Kathleen McDermott, February 1991.

57. "Report of the U.S. Firm," 1970, 25–26; 1971, 22. The Audit Guides were revived in the Connor era, and eventually published under the title *Guide to Accounting Controls* in 1979, with updates through 1986. Richard Fitzgerald letter to Kathleen McDermott, February 1991.

58. "Report of the U.S. Firm," 1965, 23; 1968, 32; 1969, 38.

59. Patten Interview; "Report of the U.S. Firm," 1969, 38–39; 1966, 23; 1967, 24.

60. George C. Watt, Transmittal Number 23 (January 30, 1990); Watt, Transmittal Number 24 (January 31, 1990).

61. "Report of the U.S. Firm," 1962, 16.

62. "Report of the U.S. Firm," 1960, 10; Richard M. Hammer, "U.S. Firm International Tax Practice: Where We Were—Where We Are!!! A Historical Perspective," draft speech, typescript, 1. The authors are grateful to Dominic Tarantino for providing this document; "Report of the U.S. Firm," 1962, 14, 16; 1961, 10–11; Fitzgerald Interview; Price Waterhouse, Report of Acquisitions and Merger Specialists (August 19, 1968), typescript memorandum, 2. The authors are grateful to George Watt for providing this document.

63. "Report of the U.S. Firm," 1961, 11; Cohen Interview.

64. Richard Fitzgerald telecon with Kathleen McDermott, January 1991.

65. Price Waterhouse & Co., Memorandum for Standard Oil of New Jersey, 8.

66. Fitzgerald Interview.

67. Price Waterhouse & Co., Memorandum for Standard Oil of New Jersey, 13–14; Chester DeMond, *Price, Waterhouse & Co. in America: A History of a Public Accounting Firm* (1951; reprint ed., New York, Arno Press, 1980), 205, 304.

68. Price Waterhouse & Co., Memorandum for Standard Oil of New Jersey, 19.

69. Ibid., 18.

70. Ibid., 27, 19.

71. "Report of the U.S. Firm," 1960, 17.

72. Lauver and Fitzgerald interviews; "Report of the U.S. Firm," 1961, 14; Richard D. Fitzgerald, "Council of Partners' Meeting," April 25–27, 1983, typescript speech, 1. The authors are grateful to Richard Fitzgerald for providing this document.

73. "Report of the U.S. Firm," 1962, 18; 1964, 21, 23–24; 1965, 24; 1968, 33; 1969, 39; 1957, 16; 1959, 15; Fitzgerald letter, February 1991.

74. "Report of the U.S. Firm," 1967, 25.

75. Robert Sobel, *The Age of Giant Corporations: A Microeconomic History of American Business* (Westport, Conn.: Greenwood Press, 1972), 195, 208. See also, Okun, *The Political Economy of Prosperity*, 62–99; Johnson, *The American Economy*, 10–11, 160–161; Hawley, "Challenges to the Mixed Economy," 165; Brooks, *The Go-Go Years*, 4, 153, 156; Cochran, *American Business in the Twentieth Century*, 173–174; Harry N. Scheiber, Harold G. Vatter, and Harold U. Faulkner, *American Economic History*, 9th ed. (New York: Harper & Row, 1976), 161; Leslie Hannah, "Mergers," in *Encyclopedia of Economic History*, ed. Glenn Porter (New York: Scribner's, 1980) 2: 640.

76. Baird and Field interviews; "Report of the U.S. Firm," 1965, 8. Other, similar evidence accumulated from both domestic and international sources showed that in 1967, Ernst & Ernst seemed to be Price Waterhouse's second most important competitor after Arthur Andersen. Peat, Marwick appeared to hold that position the following year. Ibid., 1967, 11; ibid., 1968, 15; Biegler Interview, Part I; Exec. Comm. Min. (March 16–19, 1965), Appendix M.

77. "Report of the U.S. Firm," 1968, 15.

78. Rankin Interview; Letter [Price Waterhouse & Co.] to A.E. Andersen, February 19, 1912 (The authors are grateful to Harold Haddock for supplying this document); Arthur Andersen & Co., *The First Sixty Years: 1913–1973* (Chicago: Arthur Andersen & Co., 1974), 2–9.

79. Baird Interview. See also Zimmermann interviews; Benjamin F. Jackson, Interview (July 28, 1987).

80. Robert Hampton III, Interview (May 31, 1989).

81. "Report of the U.S. Firm," 1962, 23; Bevis Interview.

82. Lauver Interview; PW History Advisory Committee (May 7, 1991).

83. Baird Interview; "Report of the U.S. Firm," 1965, 9.

84. Larkin, Meagher, and Biegler, Part I, interviews.

85. Zick Interview.

86. Brooks, *The Go-Go Years*, 154; Zick Interview; Price Waterhouse & Co., Memorandum for the Special Committee on the Firm of Price Waterhouse & Co. and Its Responsibilities and Functions Relative to the Jersey Engagement, September 16, 1965, bound typescript, 2. The authors are grateful to George Watt for providing this document. Exec. Comm. Min. (May 11–14, 18, 20, 1965), 1; (January 18–20, 1965), 1; "Report of the U.S. Firm," 1965, 8; Meagher and Baird interviews; Price Waterhouse & Co., Memorandum for Standard Oil of New Jersey, 3; "Report of the U.S. Firm," 1968, 19; 1967, 15.

87. "Charles E. Bradley, New Partner," *PW Review* 10, no. 2 (1965): 2, 7; Exec. Comm. Min. (January 10–12, 1962), 2; (March 8–10, 1961), 9; (May 12–15, 19, 21, 1964), 9; Gunders, Part I, and Bevis interviews.

88. Lawrence Aragon, "Profile: Matthew O'Rourke, A Career Shaped by Commitments to Faith, Family, and Hard Work," *The Business Journal*, April 24, 1989, 12; Price Waterhouse & Co., Memorandum for Standard Oil of New Jersey, 10; Hampton Interview.

89. John B. O'Hara, Interview (July 12, 1989); John B. O'Hara, "Partner Activities Report of John B. O'Hara," c. 1977–1978, typescript, 4. The authors are grateful to Mr. O'Hara for providing this document.

90. Aragon, "Matthew O'Rourke," 12; Matthew J. Culligan, *The Curtis-Culligan Story: From Cyrus to Horace to Joe* (New York: Crown Publishers, 1971), 74.

91. Editorial, *New York Times*, "Public Laws and Private Purposes," October 27, 1967, 16.

92. Price Waterhouse sought a ruling declaring that either the board's rule on temporary certificates was invalid as applied to Price Waterhouse, or that the firm could continue its public accounting practice in Florida as long as it did not hold itself out to the public as a firm of Florida public accountants. Bevis Interview; Exec. Comm. Min. (May 10–13, 17, 18, 1966), 7; (January 16–19, 1968), 2; (October 7–9, 1968), 6; (January 18–20, 1965), 2; "Report of the U.S. Firm," 1968, 35; 1969, 43; Stewart Bross and John Hupper, Interview (June 8, 1989).

93. Bross/Hupper Interview.

94. Bevis, Baird interviews; Henry Gunders, Interview, Part I (July 15, 1987).

95. Field, Bevis, Gunders, Part I, Beigler, Part I interviews.

96. Data on Touche Ross indicate that its partnership increased at least fourfold between 1960 and 1970, while Price Waterhouse only doubled. Theodor Swanson, *Touche Ross: A Biography* (New York: Touche Ross & Co, 1972), 19. For data on other firms see, T.A. Wise, *Peat, Marwick, Mitchell & Co.—85 Years* (New York: Peat, Marwick, Mitchell & Co., 1982), 50; "Report of the U.S. Firm," 1961, 3; 1968, 5; Biegler Interview, Part I; Bevis, Baird, Meagher, Cohen interviews; Herman W. Bevis, Memorandum, Planned Growth for the Firm, September 12, 1968, 2, 4–5. The authors are grateful to Henry Gunders for supplying this document. See also number of PW "new hires," Exec. Comm. Min. (October 24–26, 1966), 6; (October 20–22, 1969), 4.

97. Bevis, Planned Growth, September 12, 1968, 5.

98. Ibid., 1, 4; Appendices; Bevis Interview; Exec. Comm. Min. (January 13–15, 1969), 4.

99. Fitzgerald Interview.

100. Bevis Interview.

101. Fitzgerald Interview.

102. Herman W. Bevis, Memorandum to the Partners: Planned Growth for the Firm, typescript memorandum, October 20, 1968, 2. The authors are grateful to Henry Gunders for supplying this document.

103. Bevis, Planned Growth, September 12, 1968, 2; Henry Hill, Interview (July 19, 1988); "Report of the U.S. Firm," 1969, 6; Fitzgerald, Baird, Larkin interviews; Bevis, Memorandum to the Partners, October 20, 1968, 1–2; Price Waterhouse & Co., *Annual Report of the United States Firm*, 1978 (title varies), 30. These published *Annual Reports* are distinct from those "Reports" prepared by the U.S. firm for the International Firm. The *Annual Reports* were published at the close of each fiscal year from 1973 to 1980 and are cited as *Annual Report*, with year and page notations.

For discussion of a similar debate within a large regional law firm, see Kenneth J. Lipartito and Joseph A. Pratt, *Baker & Botts in the Development of Modern Houston* (Austin: University of Texas Press, 1991), 182–202.

104. "Report of the U.S. Firm," 1962, 2–3; 1967, 6; Exec. Comm. Min. (August 7–11, 1967), 11; Hugh Campbell/John Inglis, Interview (May 21, 1987); Miller and Hill interviews.

105. Exec. Comm. Min. (March 10–14, 1969), 4; Bevis, "Planned Growth," 2.

106. Baird Interview; "Report of the U.S. Firm," 1964, 2. During the time of senior partner John Biegler, the firm voted to limit re-election to five-year terms.

107. Stephen A. Zeff, "1926 to 1972 Chronology of Significant Developments in the Establishment of Accounting Principles in the United States," in *Financial Accounting Theory I: Issues and Controversies*, ed. Stephen A. Zeff and Thomas F. Keller (New York: McGraw-Hill, 1969), 39–42; "A Matter of Principle Splits CPAs," *Business Week* (January 26, 1963), 57; Zeff, "Some Junctures," 457; Henry P. Hill, Interview (July 19, 1988); Gary J. Previts and Barbara D. Merino, *A History of Accounting in America: An Historical Interpretation of the Cultural Significance of Accounting* (New York: John Wiley and Sons, 1979), 285.

108. Previts and Merino, *A History of Accounting in America*, 285; "Report of the U.S. Firm," 1957, 19.

109. Wise, "Part II: The Auditors Have Arrived," 145; Clifford V. Heimbucher, "Current Developments at the Accounting Principles Board," *Journal of Accountancy* 121 (February 1966): 47–48; G. Edward Phillips, "The Revolution in Accounting Theory," *Accounting Review*, 38 (October 1963): 697.

110. Previts and Merino, *A History of Accounting in America*, 286; "A Matter of Principle Splits CPAs," 57–60.

111. Stephen A. Zeff, "Impact of Changes in the Profession on the Debate over Accounting Principles," Jesse H. Jones Graduate School of Administration, Rice University, typescript, revised October 1985, 12; Leonard Spacek, "Are Accounting Principles Generally Accepted?" *Journal of Accountancy* 111 (April 1961): 41–46; Spacek, "Challenge to Public Accounting," *Harvard Business Review*, 36 (May 1958): 116–124; Spacek, "The Need for An Accounting Court," *Accounting Review* 33 (July 1958): 368–379; Spacek, "Can We Define Generally Accepted Accounting Principles?" *Journal of Accountancy* 106 (December 1958): 40–47. See also Arthur Andersen & Co., *The First 60 Years*, 112–113.

112. "A Matter of Principle Splits CPAs," 56.

113. Wise, "Part II: The Auditors Have Arrived," 145; Spacek, "Challenge to Public Accounting," 117; Spacek, "Need for an Accounting Court," 370–377. See also Maurice E. Peloubet, "Is Further Uniformity Desirable or Possible?" *Journal of Accountancy* 111 (April 1961): 35–46; Barbara D. Merino and Teddy L. Coe, "Uniformity in Accounting: A Historical Perspective," ibid. 156 (August 1978): 67; Zick Interview.

114. G.O. May quote from T.A. Wise, "Part II: The Auditors Have Arrived," 145.

115. George C. Watt, Interview (July 13, 1989).

116. May was skeptical of reform and, along with Grady, was the intellectual force inspiring Bevis's position. Biegler Interview, Part II (January 27, 1988); See also Previts and Merino, *A History of Accounting in America*, 287.

117. Herman Bevis, "Riding Herd on Accounting Standards," *Accounting Review* 36 (January 1961): 9–16; Bevis, "The CPA's Attest Function in Modern Society," *Journal of Accountancy* 113 (February 1962): 28–35; Bevis, "The Accounting Function in Economic Progress," ibid. 106 (August 1958): 27–34; and his *Corporate Financial Reporting in a Competitive Economy* (New York: Columbia University Press, 1965). The two "white papers" issued by the firm during Bevis's term were "Is Generally Accepted Accounting for Income Taxes Possibly Misleading Investors? A Statement of Position on Income Tax Allocation," July 1967, bound, typescript, NIC, New York, and "Problems Facing the Public Accounting Profession Today (white paper)," 1967, bound, typescript, NIC, New York.

118. Price Waterhouse & Co., "Problems Facing the Public Accounting Profession Today (white paper)," 8–9; Bevis, "Riding Herd on Accounting Standards," 10–12, 14. See also, Leonard Savoie, "Accounting Improvements: How Fast, How Far?" *Harvard Business Review* 41 (July 1963): 144–160.

119. Bevis, *Corporate Financial Reporting*, 199–201.

120. Watt Interview; Raymond Lauver, Interview (June 1, 1989).

121. Merino and Cox, "Uniformity in Accounting," 69.

122. Hill Interview. See also, Zeff, "Impact of Changes in the Profession," 13; Previts and Merino, *A History of Accounting in America*, 286, 291.

123. "A Matter of Principle Splits CPAs," 43, 50–51, 55, 57; "CPAs Churn New Rules," 70; G. Edward Phillips, "The Revolution in Accounting Theory," *Accountancy Review* 38 (October 1963): 697; "Accountants Modify Position on Investment Tax Credit Treatment," *The Wall Street Journal*, March 18, 1964, 2; Lee Silberman, "Officials of Big 8 Accounting Firms Split over Treatment of Investment Tax Credit," ibid., December 18, 1962, 32; Zeff, "Chronology of Significant Developments," 43; Lane A. Daley and Terry Tranter, "Limitations on the Value of the Conceptual Framework in Evaluating Extant Accounting Standards," *Accounting Horizons* 4 (March 1990): 21; Previts and Merino, *A History of Accounting in America*, 290–291.

124. Wallace E. Olson, *The Accounting Profession: Years of Trial, 1969–1980* (New York: AICPA, 1982), 61–62; Zeff, "Chronology of Significant Developments," 44; Hill Interview.

125. Price Waterhouse & Co., "Is Generally Accepted Accounting for Income Taxes Possibly Misleading Investors? A Statement of Position on Income Tax Allocation"; Price Waterhouse & Co., "Problems Facing the Public Accounting Profession Today," 10–11; "Tax Report: A Special Summary and Forecast of Federal and State Tax Developments," *The Wall Street Journal*, July 26, 1967, 1; Zeff, "Chronology of Significant Developments," 45; Zeff, "Some Junctures," 462–463.

126. Daley and Tranter, "Limitations on Conceptual Framework," 23–24.

127. Zeff, "Some Junctures," 458–462; Charles C. Hornbostel, "Financial Challenges in a Regulatory Environment," *Financial Executive* 40 (December 1972): 25; Olson, *Years of Trial*, 3; Henry Hill, *Accounting Principles for the*

Autonomous Corporate Entity (Westport, Conn.: Quorum Books, 1987), 116; Howard O. Rockness and Larry A. Nikolai, "An Assessment of APB Voting Patterns," *Journal of Accounting Research* 15, no. 1 (Spring 1977): 155.

128. Lauver Interview.

129. Hampton Interview.

130. George C. Watt, Richard Hammer, and Marianne Burge, *Accounting for the Multinational Corporation* (Homewood, Ill.: Dow Jones–Irwin, 1977), 346–347; Andrew Barr, *Written Contributions of Selected Accounting Practitioners*, (Urbana-Champaign: University of Illinois Press, 1979), 3: 593; Olson, *Years of Trial*, 62–63; Johnson, *The American Economy,* 161; Sobel, *The Age of Giant Corporations*, 206–209; Zeff, "Some Junctures," 463; Zeff, "Chronology of Significant Developments," 46; Hill, *Accounting Principles for the Autonomous Corporate Entity*, x; George C. Watt, Shareholders' Report, Year Ended June 30, 1973, Long Range Research, typescript memorandum, 2.

For the press's perspective, see "Accountants Turn Tougher," *Business Week* (October 18, 1969), 124; "Why Accountants Need to Tell a Fuller Story," ibid. (February 6, 1971), 86; Brooks, *The Go-Go Years*, 4, 159, 163. See also, "Why Everybody's Jumping on the Accountants These Days," *Forbes* 119 (March 15, 1977): 39; Herbert G. Lawson and Norman Pearlstein, "New Jolt for Accountants: Westec's Trustee Set to Sue its Auditor, Ernst & Ernst, on Negligence Charges," *The Wall Street Journal*, August 22, 1968, 26; Robert Metz, "Accounting Profession, Vexed by Lawsuits, Weighs Response to Shareholders," *New York Times*, November 20, 1966, D1, 14.

131. "Report of the U.S. Firm," 1969, 43; Maurice Dahlem, Interview (July 10, 1987).

CHAPTER 6

1. "Why Everybody's Jumping on the Accountants These Days," *Forbes* 119 (March 15, 1977): 37; Steven S. Anreder, "Called to Account," *Barron's* 52 (October 2, 1972): 3; Senate Committee on Governmental Operations, Subcommittee on Reports, Accounting, and Management, *The Accounting Establishment: A Staff Study*, 94th Cong., 2d sess., 1976, 2; Stanley R. Klion, "MAS Practice: Are the Critics Justified?" *Journal of Accountancy* 145 (June 1978): 72; John Brooks, *The Go-Go Years* (New York: Weybridge and Talley, 1973).

2. John Biegler, Interview, Part I (October 19, 1987).

3. Wyman Patten, Interview (June 2, 1989); "New Senior Partner," *PW Review* 14, no. 2 (1969): 4; Price Waterhouse & Co.—International Firm, "Report of the United States Firm for the Year ending June 30, 1968," typescript, Office of the Secretary of the Firm, National Office, New York, 5. See Biegler Interview, Part I; Price Waterhouse Executive Committee Minutes, (March 10–14, 1969), 18, Office of the Secretary of the Firm, National Office, New York. The Executive Committee changed its name to the Policy Committee in 1971. John C. Biegler, "Accounting Standards and Business Ethics: A Personal Perspective," *National Journal* 9 (1977): 448.

4. "New Senior Partner," *PW Review*, 4; "Policies and Administrative References: Background Material," 1961–1978 (several editions), typescript and bound, Office of the Firm Secretary, National Office, New York, 069.17, 069.19; Biegler Interview, Part I; Henry Gunders, Interview, Part I (July 15, 1987); Pol. Comm. Min. (July 26–27, 1971), 1; Price Waterhouse, *Annual Report to the Partners (Private) June 30, 1971* (title varies), 10. John Zick, Interview (January 26, 1988).

5. Gunders Interview, Part I; Biegler Interview, Part I; Pol. Comm. Min. (March 10–13, 1971), 5; Brendan Meagher, Interview (January 28, 1988); *Annual Report*, 1973, 11.

6. Meagher Interview; Biegler Interview, Part I and Part II (January 27, 1988); PAR Background, 075.12, 075.14; Pol. Comm. Min. (August 7–8, 1972), 9.

7. Biegler Interview, Part II.

8. Biegler Interview, Part I. See also, Herman W. Bevis, Speech, "An Opening Talk: Price Waterhouse and the Pursuit of Excellence," August 2, 1961, "Price Waterhouse & Co." Files, National Information Center (NIC), New York; Henry P. Hill, Interview (July 19, 1988).

9. *Annual Report*, 1971, 41; 1972, 7, 51; Pol. Comm. Min. (May 3–5, 1971), 7–8; Hill Interview; "PAR Background," 078.20.

10. Pol. Comm. Min. (August 12–14, 1969), 3. Although the National Office moved to the Exxon Building at 1251 Avenue of the Americas in 1971, the New York office remained behind at 60 Broad Street. In 1978, it moved to the Citicorp Building, 153 East 53rd Street. "A New Home for the Firm's Oldest Office," *Price Waterhouse Staff News* (March 1978), 6; "The Move to Citicorp Center," *Price Waterhouse New York Office News* 3, no. 2 (February 28, 1977): 1; Albert Cohen, Interview (March 15, 1989).

11. Biegler Interview, Part I.

12. *Annual Report*, 1972, 9; Zick Interview.

13. John Biegler telecon with Kathleen McDermott, January 10, 1991; PW History Advisory Committee (November 28, 1990).

14. Biegler Interview, Part I.

15. Godfrey Hodgkins, *America in Our Time: From World War II to Nixon, What Happened and Why* (New York: Vintage, 1978); Marshall Armstrong, "An Auditor for the Seventies," *Journal of Accountancy* 141 (April 1972): 57; Brooks, *The Go-Go Years*, 167, 281, 298; Carleton H. Griffin, "The Beleaguered Accountants: A Defendant's Viewpoint," reprinted from *American Bar Association Journal* (June 1976) in *Journal of Accountancy* 143 (January 1977): 82.

16. "Why Everybody's Jumping on the Accountants These Days," 37; Kenneth I. Solomons, Charles Chazen, and Barry S. Augenbraun, "Who Judges the Auditor and How?" *Journal of Accountancy* 142 (August 1976): 72; Griffin, "The Beleaguered Accountants: A Defendant's Viewpoint," ibid., 82; Brooks, *The Go-Go Years*, 161–162, 304; *The Accounting Establishment*, 7; "How to Keep from Being Taken," *Forbes* 105 (May 15 1970): 222; Harold M. Williams, "Financial Reporting in a Changing Economic Environment," *Management Accounting* 61 (September 1979): 14; Wallace Olson, "Is Professionalism Dead?" *Journal of Accountancy* 146 (July 1978): 79–80; Prem Prakash and Alfred Rappaport, "The

Feedback Effects of Accounting," *Business Week* (January 12, 1976), 12; David Solomons, "The Politicization of Accounting," *Journal of Accountancy* 146 (November 1978): 67; Lee J. Seidler, "Accountant: Account for Thyself," 135 (June 1973): 38; Norton M. Bedford, "Corporate Accountability," *Management Accounting* 55 (November 1973): 41–44.

17. Arthur M. Okun, *The Political Economy of Prosperity* (Washington, D.C.: Brookings Institution, 1970), 44–50, 62–99; Arthur M. Johnson, ed. *The American Economy: An Historical Introduction to the Problems of the 1970s* (New York: Free Press, 1974), 8–11; "Red Ink, Black Ink," *Forbes* 117 (January 1, 1976): 39.

18. Williams, "Financial Reporting in a Changing Environment," 14. See also, "Accountants Grapple with Inflation," *Forbes* 113 (March 1, 1974): 49–50; Henry C. Wallich and Mable I. Wallich, "Profits Aren't as Good as They Look," *Fortune* 89 (March 1974): 127; "A Controversial Method of Allowing for Inflation," *Business Week* (September 14, 1974), 91; "How to Report Results in Real Dollars," ibid. (May 5, 1975), 72; Robert Mims, "More Realism in Inflation Accounting," ibid. (January 19, 1976), 26; "Red Ink, Black Ink," 39; "Numbers Game: Waist Deep in Big Muddy," ibid. 117 (March 15, 1976): 92; Lawrence Revsine and Jerry J. Weygandt, "Accounting for Inflation: The Controversy," *Journal of Accountancy* 138 (October 1974): 72–78. Price-level adjusted statements are currently used in Europe and other parts of the world because they are thought to be more useful in evaluating long-term assets.

19. Richard Fitzgerald, letter to Kathleen McDermott, February 1991.

20. Gunders Interview, Part I.

21. Gunders Interview, Part I; Pol. Comm. Min. (January 7–9, 1970), 5; (March 10–13, 1971), 3; "Report of the U.S. Firm," 1971, 23; Zick Interview.

22. Harris J. Amhowitz, "The Accounting Profession and the Law: The Misunderstood Victim," *Journal of Accountancy* 163 (May 1987): 363. See also John G. Gillis, "Accountants Under Siege," *Financial Analysts' Journal* 29 (September 1973): 18, noting, for example, McKesson & Robbins, Inc., 3 CCH Fed. Sec. L. Rep. par. 72,020 (December 5, 1940) and *Touche, Niven, Bailey & Smart*, ibid., par. 72,100 (March 25, 1957). Ultramares v. Touche, 255 N.Y. 170, 174 N.E. 441 (1931) held that an accountant was ordinarily liable for negligent misrepresentation solely to his client or to the primary beneficiary of the financial information. Third-party liability was possible, but only if an accountant's conduct was fraudulent or so grossly negligent as to amount to fraud. A third-party plaintiff seeking to invoke statutory rights under the securities laws would also be barred, for such suits required such a plaintiff to assume the uncertainty and risk of pioneering in the interpretation of these statutes. Given this legal background, third-party actions against accountants generally failed.

23. Solomons, Chazen, and Augenbraun, "Who Judges the Auditors, and How?" 68.

24. Stewart Bross and John Hupper, Interview (June 8, 1989); Armstrong, "An Auditor for the Seventies," 57; C. Davis Baron et al., "Uncovering Corporate Irregularities: Are We Closing the Expectation Gap?" ibid. 144 (October 1977): 56.

25. Amhowitz, "The Accounting Profession and the Law," 359; "Numbers Game: Everybody Picks on Us," *Forbes* 113 (April 1, 1974): 54.

26. Fischer v. Kletz (more commonly known by the company name "Yale Express"), 266 F. Supp. 80 (S.D.N.Y. 1967) at 194. See also *Fischer* generally, and Note, "Accountants' Liabilities for False and Misleading Financial Statements," *Columbia Law Review* 67 (1967): 1444; Henry B. Reiling and Russell A. Taussig, "Recent Liability Cases—Implications for Accountants," *Journal of Accountancy* 130 (September 1970): 40; Gillis, "Accountants Under Siege," 18; Comment, "Auditors' Responsibility for Misrepresentation: Inadequate Protection for Users of Financial Statements," *Washington Law Review* 44 (1969): 173.

27. Escott v. Bar Chris Construction Corp., 283 F. Supp. 543 (S.D.N.Y. 1968); Comment, "Auditors' Responsibilities," 164; Reiling and Taussig, "Recent Liability Cases," 40; Gillis, "Accountants Under Siege," 19.

28. Ernst & Ernst v. Hochfelder, 425 U.S. 1851 (1976); Allen Kramer, "The Significance of the *Hochfelder* Decision," *CPA Journal* 46 (August 1976): 11–14; J. Jay Hampson, "Accountants Liability: The Significance of *Hochfelder*," *Journal of Accountancy* 142 (December 1976): 69–74; Amhowitz, "The Accounting Profession and the Law," 363. The picture did not improve appreciably by the 1980s, when commentators noted the continuing "general confusion about the extent of [accountants'] liability." Newton H. Minow, "Accountants' Liability and the Litigation Explosion," *Journal of Accountancy* 158 (September 1984): 80; Andrew H. Barnett and F. Fulton Galer, "Scienter Since Hochfelder," *CPA Journal* 52 (November 1982): 42; Bross and Hupper Interview.

29. T.A. Wise, *Peat, Marwick, Mitchell, & Co.—85 Years* (New York: Peat, Marwick, Mitchell, & Co., 1982), 55; "Accounting: A Crisis over Fuller Disclosure," *Business Week* (April 22, 1972), 57–58; Eldon Olson telecon with Kathleen McDermott, 1989; Solomons, Chazen, and Augenbraun, "Who Judges Auditors, and How?" 69; Victor M. Earle, III, "Accountants on Trial in the Theatre of the Absurd," *Fortune* 85 (May 1972): 227; Amhowitz, "The Accounting Profession and the Law," 359.

30. U.S. v. Simon ("Continental Vending"), 425 F. 2d 706 (2d Cir. 1969), *cert. denied* 397 U.S. 1006 (1970); Gillis, "Accountants Under Siege," 22; David B. Isbell, "The Continental Vending Case: Lessons for the Profession," *Journal of Accountancy* 130 (August 1970): 33–40.

31. Wallace E. Olson, *The Accounting Profession. Years of Trial: 1969–1980* (New York: AICPA, 1982), 19–20; Wise, *Peat, Marwick, Mitchell*, 62.

32. Amhowitz, "The Accounting Profession and the Law," 364.

33. Gillis, "Accountants Under Siege," 22; Solomon, Chazen, and Augenbraun, "Who Judges the Auditor, and How?" 71; Amhowitz, "The Accounting Profession and the Law," 363–364, citing Rosenblum v. Adler, 93 N.J. 138, 461 A.2d 138 (1983); *Annual Report*, 1973, 60–61; Reiling and Taussig, "Recent Liability Cases," 40.

34. Biegler Interview, Part I; Eldon Olson telecon, 1989.

35. Price Waterhouse v. Panzirer, 459 U.S. 1027 (1982); Zick Interview. This impression was confirmed by Price Waterhouse's outside counsel at Cravath, Swaine, & Moore. Bross and Hupper Interview.

36. William C. Norby, "SEC Adopts an Activist Role in Accounting," *Financial Analysts Journal* 28 (November 1972): 96.

37. Stephen A. Zeff, "1926–1972 Chronology of Significant Developments in the Establishment of Accounting Principles in the United States," *Financial Accounting Theory I: Issues and Controversies*, ed. Stephen Zeff and Thomas Keller (New York: McGraw Hill, 1969), 49; Steven S. Anreder, "Advise and Consent: How the SEC's Chief Accountant Sees His Job," *Barron's* 55 (September 15, 1975), 3; Gary Previts and Barbara Merino, *A History of Accounting in America: An Historical Interpretation of the Cultural Significance of Accounting* (New York: John Wiley and Sons, 1979), 317; "Numbers Game: An Active Autumn," *Forbes* 112 (October 15, 1973): 81; "New Rules Keep Investors in the Know," *Business Week* (January 15, 1974), 47; Olson, "Is Professionalism Dead?" 80.

38. George C. Greanias and Duane Windsor, *The Foreign Corrupt Practices Act* (Lexington, Mass.: D.C. Heath & Company, 1982), 17–19; Olson, "Is Professionalism Dead?" 80; Olson, *Years of Trial*, 40; Brooks, *The Go-Go Years*, 179; "Gulf Oil Inquiry Leads IRS to Seek Order for Auditor's Data," *The Wall Street Journal*, September 9, 1975, 38; William Proxmire, "The Foreign Payoff Law Is a Necessity," *New York Times*, February 5, 1978, 16F; D.R. Carmichael, "Corporate Accountability and Illegal Acts," *Journal of Accountancy* 143 (January 1977): 77–78; Thomas E. McKee, "Auditing under the Foreign Corrupt Practices Act," *CPA Journal* 49 (August 1979): 31.

39. Biegler Interview, Part I; Eleanor Johnson Tracy, Peter J. Schuyter, and John F. Ince, "Accountants are Slugging it Out," *Fortune* 95 (June 1977): 40. According to reporter Frederick Andrews, Price Waterhouse had known of United Fruit's payment, but had decided to keep it secret because its disclosure would "hurt the company." "Price Waterhouse Knew United Brands Paid Bribe but Didn't Require Disclosure," *The Wall Street Journal*, April 11, 1975, 4. According to this report, Price Waterhouse had checked its decision beforehand with the SEC, which raised no objection.

40. Bross and Hupper Interview. See also Biegler, Part I and Zick interviews.

41. B.H. DeVos, Jr., telecon with Kathleen McDermott, June 1991.

42. James J. Benjamin, Paul E. Dascher, and Robert G. Morgan, "How Corporate Controllers View the Foreign Corrupt Practices Act," *Management Accounting* 60 (June 1979): 43–49; Olson, *Years of Trial*, 41.

43. "Why Everybody's Jumping on the Accountants These Days," 37; Olson, "Is Professionalism Dead?" 80; Olson, *Years of Trial*, 36; PW History Advisory Committee (May 3–4, 1990).

44. "The Accounting Establishment," iii.

45. Ibid., v. In focusing on the SEC, the Metcalf Report echoed the Moss Subcommittee on Oversight and Investigations Report of 1976. Moss had investigated nine federal regulatory agencies, and although the report ranked the SEC first, it was sharply critical of the SEC's oversight of the accounting profession. Olson, *Years of Trial*, v, 36, 75.

46. "The CPAs Get Another Lashing," *Business Week*, (January 31, 1977), 76; "The Accounting Establishment," *Management Accounting* 58 (April 1977), 51; *The Accounting Establishment*, 25–69.

47. Hill Interview. See also Pol. Comm. Min. (April 14–15, 1976), 5; (February 2–3. 1976), 15; *The Accounting Establishment*, 5, 40; Frederick

Andrews, "An Upstaged Witness at Metcalf Inquiry," *New York Times*, May 24, 1977, 51.

48. John C. Biegler, "In Closing . . . Being a Collection by John C. Biegler during his Tenure as Senior Partner of Price Waterhouse 1969–1978 and as Chairman of Price Waterhouse International 1978–1982," bound volume, compiled by Martha Loden, 14. The authors are grateful to Mr. Biegler for supplying this book.

49. Biegler Interview, Parts I and II; Hill Interview; Pol. Comm. Min. (January 18–19, 1977), 11; Olson, *Years of Trial*, 49; Gunders Interview, Part I.

50. Gunders Interview, Part I.

51. Editorial, "Accountant, Heal Thyself," *New York Times*, May 19, 1977, 22. See also Zick Interview; Olson, *Years of Trial*, 49; Tracy, Schuyter, and Ince, "The Accountants are Slugging it Out," 40; Biegler Interview, Part I; Andrews, "An Upstaged Witness at Metcalf Inquiry," 51.

52. "Improving the Accountability of Publicly-owned Corporations and their Auditors—Report of the Subcommittee on Reports, Accounting and Management of the Committee on Governmental Affairs of the United States Senate," *Journal of Accountancy* 145 (January 1978): 88–96; Olson, *Years of Trial*, 20–24, 51–52; "CPAs Get Another Lashing," 76; "The Accounting Establishment," 52–54.

53. *The Accounting Establishment*, 173; "The Accounting Establishment: A Staff Study," *Journal of Accountancy* 143 (March 1977): 119.

54. Henry Gunders, Interview, Part II (September 2, 1987). See also, *The Accounting Establishment*, 173; "The Accounting Establishment: A Staff Study," 119; Olson, *Years of Trial*, 215, 217, 220; Bob Tamarkin, "Calling the SEC's Bluff," *Forbes* (December 10, 1979): 122–124; Lee Berton, "Self Regulation, Economic Impact Are Topics at AAA's Denver Meeting," *Journal of Accountancy* 146 (October 1978): 67.

55. "The Hill's New Assault on CPAs," *Business Week* (August 7, 1978), 89; "Moss Plans to Introduce Regulatory Legislation," *Journal of Accountancy* 145 (April 1978): 7; Olson, *Years of Trial*, 55, 57, 219; Daniel M. Hrisak, "Eagleton Hearings Focus on Independence, SEC Oversight, MAS and Governmental Accounting," *Journal of Accountancy* 148 (September 1979): 68.

56. "Why Accountants Need to Tell a Fuller Story," *Business Week* (February 6, 1971), 86; Zeff, "Evolution of Accounting Principles," 464. The Trueblood Committee worked for more than two years and issued its noncontroversial report, *Objectives of Financial Statements*, in October 1973. It identified the users of financial statements and their needs and was ultimately used in a later effort to develop standards. Olson, *Years of Trial*, 66–67; "Price Waterhouse Backs Revamping Rules Board for Accounting Field," *The Wall Street Journal*, April 5, 1972, 4.

57. Biegler, "In Closing," 12.

58. Olson, *Years of Trial*, 66–67; Biegler, "In Closing," 12–14.

59. Stephen A. Zeff, "Impact of Changes in the Profession on the Debate over Accounting Principles" Jesse H. Jones Graduate School of Administration, Rice University, typescript, revised October 1985, 19. See also "Why Accountants Need to Tell a Fuller Story," 87; "Accounting: A Crisis over Fuller Dis-

closure," 55; Sidney Davidsen and George Andersen, "The Development of Accounting and Auditing Standards," *Journal of Accountancy* 163 (May 1987): 122; "The Wheat Committee," ibid., 134.

While the FASB provided authoritative technical guidance, and promulgated generally accepted accounting principles (GAAP), the AICPA's Accounting Standards Executive Committee issued "Statements of Position" (SOPs) on a variety of accounting issues that the FASB could not consider because of budget constraints. Many of the SOPs were eventually incorporated into GAAP.

60. Robert Hampton III, Interview (May 31, 1989). See also, "Why Everyone's Jumping on the Accountants These Days," 38; Alfred Rappaport, "Economic Impact of Accounting Standards—Implications for the FASB," *Journal of Accountancy* 143 (May 1977): 92; "The Conceptual Framework Project," excerpt from FASB's Annual Report, 1975, 7–8, in *CPA Journal* 46 (July 1976): 69; "FASB Conceptual Framework," excerpt from Haskins & Sells's *The Week in Review* (December 10, 1976), in *CPA Journal* 47 (March 1977): 63. The conceptual framework study had its origins in the Trueblood Committee. Olson, *Years of Trial*, 66; Hill Interview; Zeff, "Impact of Changes in the Profession on the Debate over Accounting Principles," 18.

61. "Statement of Financial Accounting Standards No. 8—Accounting for the Translation of Foreign Currency Transactions and Foreign Currency Financial Statements," *Journal of Accountancy* 140 (December 1975): 78; Linda Snyder, "Have the Accountants Really Hurt the Multinationals?" *Fortune* 95 (February 1977): 85; R.M. Blieberg, "FASB–8—Catch 22 in the Foreign Money Game," *Barron's* 56 (November 1, 1976): 7; A. Merjos, "Lost in Translation: The Effects of FASB–8 Are Rippling Far and Wide," ibid. 56 (December 6, 1976): 11; "Ways Out of the Currency Translation Mess," *Business Week* (August 6, 1979), 80; "Are There Gnomes in Connecticut?" *Forbes* 123 (March 3, 1979): 104–105.

Attempts during the 1980s to remedy FASB–8 resulted in even greater furor. "History and Background of FASB and International Standards," *CPA Journal* 51 (June 1981): 78; "International Accounting Standards," ibid. (August 1981): 70; John N. Turner, "International Harmonization, A Professional Goal," *Journal of Accountancy* 155 (January 1983): 62; Larry D. Horner, "International Accounting Standards," *CPA Journal* 56 (April 1986): 6–7. See also, "Accounting Firms Shift Direction," ibid. 57 (February 1987): 8.

62. "A Sharper Definition of the Auditor's Job," *Business Week* (March 28, 1977), 55; Mark Stevens, *The Big Eight* (New York: Collier, 1984), 6. But while reforms like the Cohen Commission were well received by accountants, they were not taken as seriously outside the profession. For example, the SEC, having been the first to suggest the implementation of a peer review process by large firms back in 1971, heartily endorsed the firms' early reviews of each other. But hostile outside observers saw peer reviews as less than impartial and even collusive. Lee Berton, "Self-Regulation, Economic Impact Are Topics at AAA's Denver Meeting," *Journal of Accountancy* 146 (October 1978): 67; J. Michael Cook and Haldon G. Robinson, "Peer Review: The Accounting Profession's Program," *CPA Journal* 49 (March 1979): 11–12.

63. "Too Little and Too Late? U.S. Plan to Reform from Within," *Accountancy* 88 (November 1977): 13; "SEC Practice Section, Self-Regulation and Public

Credibility," excerpt from *Events and Trends*, Price Waterhouse & Co, August 1978, reprinted in *CPA Journal* 48 (December 1978): 8; Cook and Robinson, "Peer Review: The Accounting Profession's Program," 12.

64. Hampton Interview. See also Peter W. Bernstein, "Competition Comes to Accounting," *Fortune* 98 (July 17, 1978): 89; Olson, *Years of Trial*, 112; Bob Tamarkin, "The New Champion: Coopers & Lybrand," *Forbes* 122 (November 27, 1978): 37–38; Pol. Comm. Min. (January 20–21, 1975), 2; (May 6–7, 1975), 2; Zick, Meagher, Hampton interviews; Mark Larkin, Interview (October 29, 1987); Pol. Comm. Min. (January 20–21, 1975), 2. "Peat, Marwick makes it a matter of policy to weigh PD [practice development] efforts in determining compensation and promotion." Bernstein, "Competition Comes to Accounting," 91.

65. Price Waterhouse Press Release, December 14, 1977; Letter, from Price Waterhouse to the Chairman of the Board and the Members of the Audit Committee of the Board of Directors, November 29, 1977. The authors are grateful to Robert G. Nichols for providing these documents. See also, "Gulf Oil Board Votes to Replace Outside Auditors," *The Wall Street Journal*, December 14, 1977, 2; Bernstein, "Competition Comes to Accounting," 89–90.

66. Larkin Interview; Pol. Comm. Min. (October 11, 1977), 2.

67. *The Accounting Establishment*, Appendix B, 415; Peter Granger, "Services and the Market Place," in "Price Waterhouse: A Retrospective Look," June 29, 1982, typescript, bound volume, NIC, New York, 20, and attachment.

68. Gary Siegel, "Specialization and Segmentation in the Accounting Profession," *Journal of Accountancy* 144 (November 1977): 74–75; Bernstein, "Competition Comes to Accounting," 92; Brian McGlynn, "Excess Capacity," *Forbes* 123 (June 25, 1979): 76.

69. Draft Statement on Price Waterhouse World Firm, June 19, 1989, 7. The authors are grateful to John R. Jordan, Jr., for providing this document.

70. "Should CPAs Be Management Consultants?" *Business Week* (April 18, 1977), 70; Bernstein, "Competition Comes to Accounting," 92; Robert M. Smith, ed., "Nationwide MAS Surveys," *Journal of Accountancy* 139 (March 1975): 87; Tamarkin, "Calling the SEC's Bluff," 122–123; "Accounting: A Crisis over Fuller Disclosure," 54. Fees from Peat, Marwick's MAS department amounted to 12 percent of the firm's $674 million in worldwide fees. Tamarkin, "Calling the SEC's Bluff," 124.

71. Biegler, "In Closing," 19–20, 29–36, 50, 61–67; Biegler Interview, Part I.

72. Ibid.

73. Gunders Interview, Part I; Biegler Interview, Part I; Arthur B. Toan, Interview (September 27, 1988); Roscoe L. Egger, Interview (July 18, 1989).

74. Pol. Comm. Min. (November 24–26, 1973), 2.

75. Biegler Interview, Part I, Gunders Interview, Part I, Egger Interview.

76. Egger Interview.

77. Egger Interview; Pol. Comm. Min. (May 5–7, 1976), 18; (May 6–8, 1974), 6; Gunders Interview, Part I; Biegler Interview, Part I.

78. Price Waterhouse first retained the public relations firm of Kekst & Co. in 1974. Pol. Comm. Min. (May 15–17, 1974), 2; Hampton Interview.

79. Biegler Interview, Part I.

80. Larkin Interview.

81. Pol. Comm. Min. (September 21–23, 1972), 2; PW History Advisory Committee (May 3–4, 1990).

82. Pol. Comm. Min. (May 6–7, 1975), 2–3; (August 15–16, 1974), 1–2; Meagher Interview; PW History Advisory Committee (May 3–4, 1990).

83. Frederick M. Werblow, letter to Kathleen McDermott, April 9, 1991.

84. Larkin Interview; Pol. Comm. Min. (February 2–3, 1976), 1.

85. "Report of the U.S. Firm," 1960, 20.

86. Biegler Interview, Part II.

87. *Annual Report*, 1977, 15.

88. Biegler Interview, Part I.

89. Ibid.

90. Biegler Interview, Parts I and II; Biegler, "In Closing," 41–44, 48; Pol. Comm. Min. (December 16, 1976), 3; Meagher Interview.

91. Field Interview.

92. Richard D. Fitzgerald, "The Firm's Program of Industry Specialization," May 15, 1967, typescript speech, 2; Field Interview; Zick Interview; *Annual Report*, 1971, 44; 1973, 44; Pol. Comm. Min. (March 17–18, 1977), 8.

93. *Annual Report*, 1974, 20; 1977, 20.

94. Fitzgerald Interview; Fitzgerald, "Industry Specialization," 4, 8.

95. Francis C. Dykeman, Interview (March 24, 1988); Biegler Interview, Part I; Pol. Comm. Min. (November 21, 1978), 5.

96. Ibid., 1971, 11.

97. *Annual Report*, 1973, 29.

98. Hill Interview.

99. Letter, Henry P. Hill to Kathleen McDermott, January 23, 1990; Hill Interview.

100. "Report of the U.S. Firm," 1971, 19; Hill Interview; Henry Hill, "Accounting and Auditing Service/1971," c. 1971 in Preface, 1, attachment to Watt, "PW History," submission 9A, July 13, 1989; Hill letter, January 23, 1990.

101. Richard D. Fitzgerald, "Report on Results of Auditing Standards Review," c. 1973, typescript, speech, 1; Fitzgerald, "New Partners' Meeting," June 26, 1974, typescript, speech, 1; Hill Interview; Fitzgerald, "Report on Results of Auditing Standards Review," September 30–October 3, 1974, typescript, speech, 1. The authors are grateful to Mr. Fitzgerald for providing these documents.

102. Miller Interview.

103. Although the Tax Department's fortunes regularly rose and fell with the economy (for example, tax chargeable hours were up in 1974, fell in 1975, and rose again in 1977), its swings were not so extreme as those affecting MAS. *Annual Report*, 1974, 24; 1975, 23; 1976, 25; 1977, 38; 1972, 20; William C. Miller, Interview (July 8, 1987).

104. Miller, Larkin, Cohen interviews.

105. Arthur B. Toan, "MAS: Some Observations and Reminiscences," MS, 33. Arthur B. Toan, Memorandum, "Report of the MAS Department, July 22, 1970," in "MAS Policy Matters," 4–5.

106. Toan, "Reminiscences," 33–34; Arthur B. Toan, Memorandum, "Price Waterhouse Associates," 2, in MAS Policy Matters, 2; "Dilemmas and Problems in MAS," 10–12, in "MAS Policy Matters."

107. Toan, "Reminiscences," 21, 34, 40–41; *Annual Report*, 1972, 24. Arthur Toan and Henry Gunders, Memorandum, To the Members of the Policy Committee, November 24, 1971, typescript, Scope, II 5, 6; Economic Results, III C 2–4. The MAS Department's work in marketing, industrial engineering, and other skills that support the development of information systems was restricted. *Annual Report*, 1972, 24; Henry S. Sawin, "Where Have We Been, 1946–1980" (June 6, 1980) typescript, speech, 19; Toan and Gunders, memorandum, Scope, II, 5.

108. Toan, "Reminiscences," 34; *Annual Report*, 1974, 23; 1975, 20; 1977, 38. Arthur B. Toan [and Henry Gunders ?], Tables, Monthly MAS Chg. Hours (Average) including Middle Americas and Japan and Monthly MAS Chg. Hours including Mexico (through 6/72), Japan, and Central America, in Statistics (initiated by Art Toan and continued through Fiscal 1979) Monthly Chargeable Hours and Related Statistics–U.S. Offices only and U.S. Firm–Fiscal 1964 through Fiscal 1979), typescript compilation. See also "Should CPAs Be Management Consultants?" *Business Week*, April 18, 1977, 73.

109. Field Interview; Field, "Development of Our International Organization," in "Price Waterhouse: A Retrospective Look," 2. The associated firms were Bahamas, Jamaica, Japan, Trinidad, India, Middle East, Singapore/Malaysia/Thailand, and Southern Africa. Colin Brown, "People and Places," in "Price Waterhouse: A Retrospective Look," 10, and attachment; Biegler Interview, Part I.

The American firm also had a strong international practice and its own publications, including its *Guides to Doing Business Abroad, Information Guide Series*, and *Guides for the Reader of Foreign Financial Statements*. George C. Watt, "Efforts to Harmonize Accounting Principles and Reporting Practices Worldwide," MS, June 9, 1989, 1–3; Watt, Guide for Reader of Foreign Financial Statements ("Reader"), Price Waterhouse & Co., U.S.A., typescript, draft letter, c. 1974, 1. The authors are grateful to Mr. Watt for putting his recollections in writing, and for providing this and other documents. "Report of the U.S. Firm," 1971, 19. The Survey on Accounting Principles was updated in 1975 to forty-eight countries and in 1979 to sixty-four. NIC, New York.

110. Biegler Interview, Part I.

111. Biegler Interview, Part I; Biegler, "In Closing," 138; Field, "Development of Our International Organization," 3.

112. Price Waterhouse International, *Report to the Partners, 1973*, NIC, National Office, New York, 7–13 (hereafter cited as *PWI Report*); Partnership Agreement, Price Waterhouse International, January 10, 1973, World Firm Office, Southwark Towers, London, 3; *Annual Report*, 1973, 41; Biegler Interview, Part I; Hampton Interview.

113. "Report of the U.S. Firm," 1971, 24; Alphonsus T. Cummins, Interview (July 7, 1987); Biegler Interview, Part I; Field Interview; *Annual Report*, 1973, 15; 1975, 11.

114. Lawrence Minard and Brian McGlynn, "The U.S.'s Newest Glamour Job," *Forbes* 120 (September 1, 1977): 32; Klion, "MAS Practice: Are the Critics Justified?" *Journal of Accountancy*, 76; James E. Sorenson, John Grant Rhode, and Edward E. Lawler III, "The Generation Gap in Public Accounting," *Journal of Accountancy* 136 (December 1973): 42–46.

115. Quiester Craig, "Toward Integration of the Accounting Profession," *Journal of Accountancy* 163 (May 1987): 257; Glenda Ried, Brenda T. Acken, and Elise G. Jancura, "An Historical Perspective on Women in Accounting," ibid. 163 (May 1987): 344–345; Cynthia Fuchs Epstein, *Women in Law* (New York: Basic Books, 1981), 94; L. Gayle Rayburn, "Recruitment of Women Accountants," *Journal of Accountancy* 132 (November 1971): 57; William Aiken, "The Black Experience in Large Public Accounting Firms," ibid. 134 (August 1972): 60; Bert N. Mitchell, "The Black Minority in the CPA Profession," ibid. 128 (October 1969): 41.

116. *Annual Report*, 1973, 36–37.

117. Pol. Comm. Min. (May 14–17, 21, 1968), 11; (January 20–21, 1975), 7; *Annual Report*, 1973, 36–37; Ried, Acken, and Jancura, "An Historical Perspective on Women in Accounting," 345, 353; Shari H. Westcott and Robert E. Seiler, *Women in the Accounting Profession* (New York: Markus Weiner Publishing, 1986), 123, 125; Minard and McGlynn, "The U.S.'s Newest Glamour Job," 34; *Annual Report*, 1978, 39. See also, Richard M. Hammer, "U.S. Firm International Tax Practice: Where We Were—Where We Are!!! A Historical Perspective," draft speech, typescript, 2; *Price Waterhouse Quarterly* [British Firm], 6, no. 4 (1973): 5.

118. *Annual Report*, 1975, 11; 1978, 39. The figures for 1978 can be compared against the summary of the total professional staff in the practice offices in 1990: 422 partners, 325 senior managers, 756 managers, 1,354 seniors and consultants, and 1,959 staff accountants. Price Waterhouse, The 1990 Retired Partners' Meeting, October 22–23, 1990, remarks of D.A. Tarantino, Office of the Secretary of the Firm, National Office, New York, 89. Statistical information on women and minorities in the 1990s provided by National Human Resources, National Office, New York. The authors are grateful to Marybeth Capron for providing this information.

119. Biegler Interview, Parts I and II; Cohen Interview; Meagher Interview.

120. Richard D. Fitzgerald, "New Partners' Meeting," June 26, 1974, typescript speech, 7. The authors are grateful to Richard Fitzgerald for providing this and other documents. Professional staff turnover, especially at the senior level, became a serious problem that approached 26 percent in 1971. A turnover task force was appointed by the mid-1970s to address these concerns. Pol. Comm. Min. (January 24–26, 1972), 4; *Annual Report*, 1974, 12; 1975, 12.

121. Biegler Interview, Part I; Cohen Interview.

122. Biegler, "In Closing," 64; Arthur B. Toan, Memorandum, "Some Dilemmas and Problems in MAS," in "MAS Policy Matters to be Discussed at Executive Committee Meeting, August 12, 1970," typescript, 12. The authors are grateful to Henry Gunders for supplying this and other documents. "Report of the U.S. Firm," 1973, 10; Donald F. Markstein telecon with Kathleen McDermott, June 1989; Pol. Comm. Min. (January 20–21, 1975), 10; *Annual Report*, 1975, 15; Biegler Interview, Part I. Out-of-pocket costs of developing and presenting programs did not include the compensation of the partners and managers involved. Albert Cohen telecon with Kathleen McDermott, February 1992.

123. *Annual Report*, 1977, 15; PAR Background, 078.38; Pol. Comm. Min. (October 23, 1975), 6.

124. Pol. Comm. Min. (October 24, 1975), 6; Meagher Interview; *Annual Report*, 1976, 11; Biegler Interview, Part I; Meagher Interview; Biegler, "In Closing," 48; Walter M. Baird, Interview (March 28, 1988).

125. Biegler telecon, January 10, 1991; PW History Advisory Committee (November 28, 1990).

126. Biegler, "In Closing," 59; *Annual Report*, 1978, 5.

CHAPTER 7

1. Price Waterhouse World Firm, *Global Strategy for the 1990s: A Call for Action* (London: Price Waterhouse World Firm), 9.

2. Shaun F. O'Malley, Dominic A. Tarantino, and James E. Daley, Interview (December 18, 1989).

3. Price Waterhouse, Policy Board Minutes (June 23, 26, 1985), 1, Office of the Secretary of the Firm, National Office, New York.

4. Joseph Connor, Interview, Part I (May 16, 1988).

5. Burnell H. DeVos, Jr., Interview (April 25, 1988).

6. Ibid.

7. Connor Interview, Part I; Pol. Comm. Min. (January 17–18, 1978), 6–7; Joseph E. Connor, Memorandum to Partners, April 25, 1978 re: Plan for the Organizational and Professional Operations of the Firm, Effective October 1, 1978, PW Policies and Administrative References: Background Material [PAR Background], 1968 ed., 1978 revisions, 078.38, Office of the Secretary of the Firm, National Office, New York.

8. The regional managing partner positions were changed in 1981 to area practice partner positions when the four geographic regions were converted into six practice areas.

9. DeVos Interview. See also Pol. Bd. Min. (June 16, 19, 1981), 3; Joseph Connor Interview, Part II (June 10, 1988); Pol. Bd. Min. (August 9–10, 1979), 9.

10. Minutes of the Partners' Meeting, September 5–7, 1979, Office of the Secretary of the Firm, National Office, New York.

11. Ibid.

12. Price Waterhouse, *Annual Report*, 1979, 11–12.

13. Lee Berton, "Price Waterhouse, Deloitte Merger Talks Worry Some Accounting Competitors," *The Wall Street Journal*, September 13, 1984, 7, citing an unidentified PW partner. See also *Annual Report*, 1979, 24. For examples of his public statements, see, Connor, "The Foreign Corrupt Practices Act: Implications for Directors" (1979), "Testimony of Joseph E. Connor . . . before the Joint Economic Committee, 96th Congress, 2d. Session," reprint (1980); "Taxpayers Expect Greater Accountability from Their Governments" (1980); "Facing the Winds of Change" (1984); "Financial Reporting Realism" (1987), all published by Price Waterhouse, New York; Statement of Joseph E. Connor . . . in Association with Citizens Against Government Waste . . . Concerning Financial Management Reorganization and Cost Control Act, Senate Committee on Gov-

ernmental Affairs, May 13, 1986; Connor, "We Need a Federal CFO," *CFO* 3 (January 1981): 7–8.

14. Connor Interview, Part I.

15. Pol. Comm. Min. (January 17–18, 1978), 6–7; Connor Interview, Part I.

16. Pol. Bd. Min. (October 24, 1978), 5 (November 21, 1978), 5; (July 24, 25, 1979), 3; *Annual Report*, 1979, 11.

17. Theodore Levitt, "The Globalization of Markets," *Harvard Business Review* 61 (May–June 1983): 93; Dwight Wainman, "What's IT All About," *CA Magazine* 119 (August 1986): 36; F. Warren McFarlan, "Information Technology Changes the Way You Compete," *Harvard Business Review* 62 (May–June 1984): 98; Lee Berton, "Accounting Firms Get New Auditors' Tool: The Microcomputer," *The Wall Street Journal*, January 23, 1984, 37; Robert Roussey, "Microcomputers and the Auditor," *Journal of Accountancy* 156 (December 1983): 106–107.

18. Abe Akresh, "Accounting Profession Discards 'Number Crunching' Image: Today's Auditors are Creative Problem Solvers," *CPA Journal* 56 (October 1986): 4; "Auditing in the 1980s," ibid. 50 (April 1980): 93; Alfred M. King, ed., "Who'll Audit the Computer Systems?" *Management Accounting* 66 (June 1985): 16; "Computer Processing: Effects of Computer Processing on Financial Statement Examination is Subject of SAS," *Journal of Accountancy* 158 (August 1984): 34.

19. Berton, "Accounting Firms Get New Tool," 37.

20. Mary Ellen Oliverio, "The Audit—Is It a Commodity?" *CPA Journal* 56 (June 1986): 124, quoting Joseph Connor, 25; Fred L. Tepperman, "The Attest Function: Challenge of the Eighties," ibid. 51 (December 1981): 17; David Mosso, "Standards Overload, No Simple Solution," ibid. 156 (November 1983): 120; Christopher Power, "Canned Accountants," *Forbes* 133 (January 16, 1986): 123.

21. "A Solution to the Shopping Problem," *Journal of Accountancy* 161 (June 86): 105; "Saying No to Shopping for Yes-Man CPAs," *Business Week* (May 13, 1985), 130; Power, "Canned Accountants," 123. See also, Richard Greene, "If I Don't Cross the T," *Forbes* 135 (February 11, 1985): 134.

22. Oliverio, "The Audit—Is It a Commodity," 124–25; "Saying No to Shopping," 130; Emerson, *Emerson Report*, 6; Geoffrey Smith, "Toward a More Perfect Market," *Forbes* 134 (December 17, 1984): 73; Lewis J. Krulwich, Interview (1987); William S. Kanaga, "Self-Regulation in Accounting, Role of AICPA," *Journal of Accountancy* 152 (November 1981): 52; Richard Greene, "Blood on the Ledger," *Forbes* 139 (May 18, 1987): 204; "Accounting Profession Discards Image," 4; "The Supply of Accounting Graduates and the Demand for Public Accounting Recruits, 1989," brochure prepared by Mary Lou Walsh and Mary McInnes, New York: AICPA, 1989, Table 19.

23. Lee Berton, "Price Waterhouse Lifts Entry-Level Pay 20 Per Cent to 35 Per Cent for Accounting Graduates," *The Wall Street Journal*, October 13, 1987, 12. Changing perceptions about the Price Waterhouse partnership came to a legal test in the 1980s in a case involving a former Price Waterhouse manager who sued the firm, alleging that it had discriminated against her on the basis of sex during her review for partnership. She argued that Price Waterhouse's

position was based on sexual stereotypes of appropriate women's behavior in an administrative capacity and that such qualities in a man's personality would not have denied him admission to the partnership. "Price Waterhouse Appeal," ibid., March 8, 1988; Michael J. McCarthy, "Supreme Court to Rule on Sex-Bias Case," ibid., June 4, 1988, 37. After a trip to the Supreme Court to define the legal standards under Title VII, the federal district court, on remand, ordered Price Waterhouse to admit the manager as a partner. The manager has since been admitted to the firm. Ulric Sullivan, telecons with Kathleen McDermott, October 29, 1990, April 12, 1991.

24. Business school professors H. Thomas Johnson and Robert S. Kaplan contended in their history of the changes in cost accounting that "both historical cost accounting procedures and generally accepted accounting principles provided ample opportunity for executives to manage their income and investment measures." Johnson and Kaplan, *Relevance Lost: The Rise and Fall of Management Accounting* (Boston: Harvard Business School Press, 1987), 3, 197, 259; Robert K. Elliott, "Dinosaurs, Passenger Pigeons and Financial Accountants," *CPA Journal* 57 (January 1987): 4.

25. C. Wayne Alderman, Glenn E. Sumners, and Mary Jeanne Welsh, "The Trend Toward Soft Data in Accounting," *Management Accounting* 65 (December 1983): 34–35.

26. Robert Mednick, "The Auditor's Role in Society: A New Approach to Solving the Perception Gap," *Journal of Accountancy* 161 (February 1986): 71–72. See also Thomas Baker, "Relativity Comes to Accounting," *Forbes* 125 (June 23, 1980): 113; Elliott, "Dinosaurs, Passenger Pigeons and Financial Accountants," 4–10.

27. Baker, "Relativity Comes to Accounting," 113; Ruth Simon, "Wait and See," *Forbes* 135 (February 11, 1985): 135.

28. Smith, "Toward a More Perfect Market," 73. See also Joseph E. Connor, "Enhancing Public Confidence in the Accounting Profession," *Journal of Accountancy* 162 (July 1986): 76.

29. Paul Hooper and John Page, "The Legal Environment of Public Accounting," *CPA Journal* 54 (June 1984): 36; Newton N. Minow, "Accountants' Liability and the Litigation Explosion," *Journal of Accountancy* 158 (September 1984): 70; Stephen H. Collins, "Professional Liability, the Situation Worsens," ibid. 160 (November 1985): 57.

30. Dan L. Goldwasser, "Another Look at Accountants' Liability—Part I," *CPA Journal* 55 (August 1985): 22.

31. Minow, "Accountants and Litigation Explosion," 80.

32. Goldwasser, "Another Look at Accountants' Liability," 22, 28 (discussing H. Rosenblum v. Adler); Jill Andresky, "A Matter of Privity," *Forbes* 136 (September 23, 1985): 122; Catherine Yang, "Watching Pinocchio's Nose," ibid. (November 4, 1985), 73; Bill Densmore, "Court Decision Limits Accountants' Liability," *Business Insurance* 16 (April 12, 1982): 3; "Two Jury Verdicts Limit Accountants' Liability," 12; Greene, "Blood on the Ledger," 202.

33. Minow, "Accountants and Litigation Explosion," 76; see, e.g., Spherex, Inc. v. Alexander Grant, 122 N.H. 898, 451 A.2d 1308 (1982); Goldwasser,

"Another Look at Accountants' Liability," 22; see, e.g., H. Rosenblum v. Adler, 93 N.J. 324, 461 A.2d 138 (1983) and Citizens' State Bank v. Timm, Schmidt and Co., 113 Wis. 2d 376, 335 N.W.2d 361 (1983); Credit Alliance v. Arthur Andersen, 493 N.Y.S.2d 435, 65 N.Y.2d 536, 483 N.E.2d 110 (1985); Ultramares Corp. v. Touche, 225 N.Y. 170; 174 N.E. 441 (1931). Racketeering is defined as "any two instances of a variety of offenses, including securities fraud and mail fraud." Minow, "Accountants and Litigation Explosion," 78. See also, Chris Monical, "Caution: RICO Can Hurt You," *Management Accounting* 66 (April 1985): 62.

34. Minow, "Accountants and Litigation Explosion," 76; Cenco Inc. v. Seidman & Seidman, 686 F.2d 449 (1982), *cert. denied*, 459 U.S. 880 (1982); Densmore, "Court Decision Limits Liability," 3; "Two Jury Verdicts Limit Accountants' Liability in Respect to Negligence," *Journal of Accountancy* 153 (May 1982): 12.

35. Yang, "Pinocchio's Nose," 73.

36. "The FASB's Conceptual Framework Project: A Critique," *CPA Journal* 52 (December 1982): 76; Connor Interview, Part II; A. Clarence Sampson, "A Regulator's View of the FASB: The First Ten Years and After," *Journal of Accountancy* 156 (August 1983): 45–56; Walter B. Wriston "Financial Information: Have We Reached the Saturation Point?" ibid. 156 (September 1983): 127–128.

37. Mark Moran and Gary John Previts, "The SEC and the Profession, 1934–84: The Realities of Self-Regulation," *Journal of Accountancy* 158 (July 1984): 78.

38. Ibid.; Ronald S. Hertz, "Standards Overload: A Euphemism," *CPA Journal* 53 (October 1983): 24; Gerald W. Hepp and Thomas MacRae, "Standards Overload: Relief Is Needed," *Journal of Accountancy* 153 (May 1982): 52; "Standards Overload Relief Requires Top Priority, Says AICPA Committee Report," ibid. 155 (May 1983): 18.

39. Marshall B. Romney, W. Steve Albrecht, and David J. Cherrington, "Auditors and the Detection of Fraud," *Journal of Accountancy* 149 (May 1980): 63; Editorial, "The Elephant Is Twitchy," *California Magazine* 118 (June 1985): 3; "Auditing the Auditors: Why Congress May Tighten Up," *Business Week* (December 12, 1983), 130; Les Campbell, "Dingell—Will the U.S. Profession Emerge Unscathed?" *Accountancy* 96 (May 1985): 12; "Accountants Must Clean Up Their Act: Rep. John Dingell Speaks Out," *Management Accounting* 66 (May 1985): 21; "Saying No to Shopping," 128.

40. "Congress Looks at Accounting Practices," *Healthcare Financial Management* 39 (April 1985): 7; Campbell, "Will the Profession Emerge Unscathed?" 12.

41. "Congressional Subcommittee Convenes Hearings into SEC, Accounting Profession," *Journal of Accountancy* 159 (April 1985): 12–22; "Accountants Must Clean Up: Dingell Speaks," 21.

42. Joseph E. Connor, "Strengthening Public Confidence in the Accounting Profession," *Price Waterhouse Review* (1986), 2–5. Connor's white paper was published as *Challenge and Opportunity for the Accounting Profession: Strengthening the Public's Confidence, The Price Waterhouse Proposals* ([New York]: Price Waterhouse, 1985).

43. Connor, "Strengthening Public Confidence in the Accounting Profession," 5–8; "Statement of Joseph E. Connor, Chairman, Price Waterhouse, Before Subcommittee on Oversight and Investigations of the Committee on Energy and Commerce, U.S. House of Representatives, June 19, 1986," repr. (New York: Price Waterhouse, 1986).

44. Oliverio, "The Audit—Is It a Commodity?" 124–125; O'Malley, Daley, and Tarantino Interview.

45. Don W. Baker, "The Treadway Commission: Its Initial Conclusions," *Management Accounting* 68 (December 1986): 12. See also Lee Berton, "Price Waterhouse Urging Formation," *The Wall Street Journal*, November 29, 1985, 10; "AICPA President Responds to Plan for a New Oversight Group," *Journal of Accountancy* 161 (February 1986): 14; Baker, "The Treadway Commission," 6; "Fraudulent Financial Reporting and the Public Accountant—Update on Treadway," *CPA Journal* 57 (February 1987): 10; "Congress Looks at Accounting Practices," 7.

46. John A. Byrne, "Deep Pockets," *Forbes* 130 (November 8, 1982): 174. See also Richard H. Bertholdt, "Public Expectations—Meeting the Challenge," *CPA Journal* 56 (August 1986): 10; "Liability Lawsuits: The Profession Fights Back," *Journal of Accountancy* 155 (May 1983): 131.

47. Price Waterhouse, *Global Strategy*, 26.

48. Moran and Previts, "The SEC and the Profession," 78.

49. Emerson, *Emerson Report*, 7–8, quoting an MIT report on technology; O'Malley, Daley, and Tarantino Interview.

50. "Accounting Firms Shift Direction," 8; Emerson, *Emerson Report*, 5–6; Price Waterhouse, *Global Strategy*, 26.

51. Lee Berton, "Arthur Andersen Unveils Software to Aid Companies in Designing Own Program," *The Wall Street Journal*, April 1, 1988, 14; Wainman, "What's IT All About," 36.

52. Phillip M.J. Reckers and A.J. Stagliano, "The CPA's Non-Audit Services," *CPA Journal* 50 (February 1980): 28; John S.R. Shad, "The SEC's View of the Profession's Self-Regulatory Efforts," *Journal of Accountancy* 152 (November 1981): 43; Berton, "Consulting for Audit Clients," 18; John W. Buckley and Marline H. Buckley, *The Accounting Profession* (Los Angeles: Melville, 1974), 54; Lee Berton, "Cutting the Pie: Major Accounting Firms Face a Deepening Division over Consultants' Pay," *The Wall Street Journal*, July 26, 1988, 1, 14.

53. Price Waterhouse, *Global Strategy*, 19; Greene, "Blood on the Ledger," 206.

54. Pol. Bd. Min. (March 25–26, 1980), 4; (April 3, 1980), 5; (May 2, 1980), 2; (May 4–6, 1981), 13–16; (August 12–13, 1981), 4.

55. Joseph E. Connor, "The Strategy of Price Waterhouse," *PW Review*, 27, no. 1 (1983): 3, 4–5. Connor's statement was based on drafts of a long and detailed firm "Strategy Guide," completed in February 1982, and entitled "The Strategy of Price Waterhouse (United States)," Appendix to Pol. Bd. Min. (February 24–25), 1982. See also *Price Waterhouse Reports: The Changing World of International Business* (New York: Price Waterhouse, 1981), 17. See, "As Many of the Big Eight Centralize, Price Waterhouse Bucks the Trend," *Business Week* (October 24, 1983), 83–84.

56. Pol. Bd. Min. (July 19–20, 1983), 11.

57. Ibid.; Kenton Sicchitano, Interview (June 25, 1990).

58. Paul Goodstat Interview (November 9, 1989).

59. Connor Interview, Part II. See also Pol. Bd. Min. (July 19–20, 1984), 11; Sicchitano and Goodstat interviews.

60. Pol. Bd. Min. (December 3–4, 1981), 5; (September 13, 1981), 3; DeVos Interview.

61. Connor Interview, Part I; Pol. Bd. Min. (October 30, 1984), 1; (March 14, 1984), 3; (July 19–20, 1983), 11; (July 17–18, 1984), 16.

62. Johnson and Kaplan, *Relevance Lost*, 210.

63. C. Fred Bergsten, *America in the World Economy: A Strategy for the 1990s* (Washington, D.C.: Institute for International Economics, 1988), 36–41, 56–57, 97–98, 150–151; Cuomo Commission on Trade and Competitiveness, *The Cuomo Commission Report: A New American Formula for a Strong Economy* (New York: Simon & Schuster, 1988), 10–12; Robert H. Hayes and William J. Abernathy, "Managing Our Way to Economic Decline," *Harvard Business Review* (July–August 1980) 67; Johnson and Kaplan, *Relevance Lost*, 197; Michael L. Dertouzos, et al., *Made in America: Regaining the Productive Edge* (Cambridge, Mass.: MIT Press, 1989), 40–78.

64. Murray Weidenbaum, *Rendezvous with Reality: The American Economy after Reagan* (New York: Basic Books, 1988), 158–159; Abernathy and Hayes, "Managing Our Way to Decline," 75; John Brooks, *The Takeover Game* (New York: E.P. Dutton, 1988), 175; Michael C. Jensen, "Takeovers: Folklore and Science," *Harvard Business Review* 62 (November–December 1984): 109.

65. Greene, "Blood on the Ledger," 204; Lee Berton, "Consulting for Audit Clients: A Conflict of Interest," *The Wall Street Journal*, July 8, 1987, 18; see also, Lee Berton, "Accountants Struggle as Marketers," ibid., July 10, 1989, B1.

66. Tarantino Interview; Barbara Rosewicz and Bruce Ingersoll, "PW Will Be the First to File Affiliate as Investment Advisor with SEC," *The Wall Street Journal*, September 30, 1987, 40; Connor Interview, Part I.

67. DeVos Interview.

68. Connor, Interview, Part I; DeVos Interview.

69. Lee Berton, "Deloitte Haskins and Price Waterhouse Weigh Merger, Sources at the Firms Say," *The Wall Street Journal*, September 10, 1984, 2; "Price Waterhouse, Deloitte Tell Staffs of Possible Merger," ibid., September 12, 1984, 6; "The Big Eight Could Soon Be the Big Seven," *Business Week* (September 24, 1984), 37–38.

70. Lee Berton, "Merger Issue Is Dividing CPA Firms," *The Wall Street Journal*, October 16, 1984, 31. See also Berton, "Price Waterhouse, Deloitte Merger Talks Worrying Some Accounting Competitors," 7; "A Bid to Stop Big Eight Firms from Getting Bigger," *Business Week* (November 19, 1984), 49; Stewart Bross and John Hupper, Interview (June 8, 1989).

71. "Price Waterhouse Tie to Deloitte Haskins Is Approved by U.S.," *The Wall Street Journal*, November 12, 1984, 11; "Price Waterhouse Chief Would Head New Firm Formed by Deloitte Link," ibid., September 14, 1984, 7; "Price Waterhouse–Deloitte Combination Stalls; Other Firms Seen Mulling Merger,"

ibid., November 26, 1984, 32; "Price Waterhouse, Deloitte End Plans to Merge as Some Partners Veto Move," ibid., December 19, 1984, 2; Connor Interview, Part I.

72. DeVos Interview.

73. Ibid.; Pol. Bd. Min. (Jan. 14–15, 1985), 27; (February 20–21, 1985), 12; Sicchitano Interview.

74. DeVos Interview.

75. Ibid.

76. Price Waterhouse, Price Waterhouse Business Strategy and Directions, March 18, 1985, typescript (memorandum to the partners). The authors are grateful to Mr. Sicchitano for providing a copy of this document. DeVos Interview; Pol. Bd. Min. (July 16–17, 1985), 1, 3; Connor Interview, Part II; Sicchitano Interview.

77. Sicchitano Interview.

78. Dominic A. Tarantino, Interview (December 18, 1989). See also Connor Interview, Part II.

79. Pol. Bd. Min. (March 14, 1985), 6; (September 17, 1985), 6; (December 5, 1985), 7; "About Management Horizons," in William R. Davidson, Cyrus C. Wilson, and Daniel J. Sweeney, "Winning Retailers and How They Do It," *PW Review* 30, no. 1 (1986), 13; "About the Consumer Financial Institute," in George E.L. Barbee, "Downsizing with Dignity: Trends in Employee Reelection Programs," ibid., no. 3 (1986), 14–15; O'Malley, Daley, and Tarantino Interview.

80. Goodstat Interview; Henry Gunders Interview, Part I (July 15, 1987); Pol. Bd. Min. (July 17–18, 1984), 3.

81. Price Waterhouse, Videotape, "Firm Services Opportunities," presentations at the 1986 Annual Partners' Meeting by Burnell H. DeVos, Jr., Dominic A. Tarantino, and Paul B. Goodstat. The authors wish to thank Mr. DeVos for providing this material.

82. The breakdown was Price Waterhouse, 20 percent; Arthur Young, 26 percent; KMG/Peat Marwick, 25 percent; Coopers & Lybrand, 21 percent; Arthur Andersen, Ernst & Whinney, 20 percent, Touche Ross, 19 percent; Deloitte, Haskins & Sells, 18 percent. "Blood on the Ledger," 204.

83. Tarantino Interview.

84. Reckers and Stagliano, "CPA's Non-Audit Services," 25–28; "Help Wanted: Tax Experts Proliferate as Tax Laws Grow More Complex," *The Wall Street Journal*, September 21, 1983, A1; Sanford L. Jacobs, "Accountants Are Bracing for Tax Season That Many Say Will Be the Worst Ever," ibid., December 31, 1987, 9.

As tax accountants became more successful, they once again clashed with lawyers. See David Bucholz and Joseph Moraglio, "IRS Access to Workpapers: The Supreme Court Decision," *Journal of Accountancy* 158 (September 1984): 91. In March 1984, the United States Supreme Court decided in U.S. v. Arthur Young, 465 U.S. 805 (1984), that auditors' tax accrual work papers were relevant to an IRS audit of tax refund and were not protected from disclosure in response to an IRS summons. The Court's reasoning was that, unlike lawyers, accountants have a public duty that transcends their employment relationship with a client. This controversy was resolved by IRS Commissioner Roscoe Egger, who announced that the IRS would not capriciously ask to see an accountant's work papers on every examination, but only in rare and unusual cases. Tarantino Interview; "Help Wanted: Tax Experts Proliferate," A1.

85. Pol. Bd. Min. (February 24–26, 1981), 11; (July 17–18, 1984), 7; (March 14, 1985), 3.

86. Price Waterhouse, History of the Technical Tax Group, December 19, 1990. The authors are grateful to Robert Nichols and Stacy Collett for providing this document.

87. Tarantino Interview; Peter Hart Interview (November 29, 1989); Pol. Bd. Min. (February 24–26, 1981), 11; "Accounting Concerns Assume Burgeoning Role as Lobbyists, Often Outshoot Federal Bureaucrats," *The Wall Street Journal*, March 7, 1989, A26; Goodstat Interview.

88. Pol. Bd. Min. (May 8–9, 1984), 13.

89. Goodstat Interview.

90. Paul Goodstat, "Making It Happen," Speech Delivered at the 1985 MCS Management Group Seminar, July 8–9, 1985. The authors are grateful to Mr. Goodstat for providing a copy of this speech. Price Waterhouse, Price Waterhouse Business Strategy and Directions (March 18, 1985), 22–24; Goodstat Interview.

91. Goodstat Interview.

92. Ibid.

93. Price Waterhouse, *Global Strategy*, 9.

94. DeVos Interview; Pol. Bd. Min. (March 14, 1985), 6, 8; (June 23, 26, 1985), 1; Linda Grant Martin, "The 500: A Report on Two Decades," *Fortune* (May 1975): 238.

95. Emerson, *Emerson Report,* 4–5; Lee Berton, "Peat–KMG Merger Proposal Strained as Units in Some Countries Drop Out," *The Wall Street Journal*, January 6, 1987, 7; Connor Interview, Part I; Lee Berton, "Talk of Merger Sweeps through Accounting Field," *The Wall Street Journal*, June 19, 1989, A5A; Lee Berton, "Andersen and Price Waterhouse Scrap Merger Talks Due to Incompatibility," ibid., September 27, 1989, A5; Lee Berton, "AA, PW Say They're in Formal Discussion on Merger," ibid., July 7, 1989, A3.

96. O'Malley, Daley, and Tarantino Interview; Alison Leigh Cowan, "A Wrenching Time for Accountants and Clients," *New York Times*, July 11, 1989, D2; "Mixed Marriage: Accountants' Merger Tests Idea of Meshing Partners World-Wide," *The Wall Street Journal*, April 22, 1987, 27, quoting John C. Burton, former SEC chief accountant; Emerson, *The Emerson Report*, 9.

97. Richard D. Fitzgerald, "International Accounting and Reporting: Where in the World Are We Headed?" *PW Review* 2 (1983): 16–24; "Accounting Firms Shift Direction," *CPA Journal* 57 (February 87): 8; John N. Turner, "International Harmonization, a Professional Goal," *Journal of Accountancy* 155 (January 1983): 58. See also "Current Complexities Cited in Audits of Multinationals," ibid. 157 (January 1984): 34; Jane Sasseen, "Take the Cash and Let the Standards Go," *Forbes* 134 (July 2, 1984): 180; Lane A. Daley and Gerhard G. Mueller, "Accounting in the Arena of World Politics," *Journal of Accountancy* 157 (February 1982): 40; O'Malley, Daley, Tarantino Interview.

98. Michael Coates, Interview (July 11, 1988); Connor Interview, Part I.

99. Peter Granger, Interview (August 23–25, 1988).

100. Price Waterhouse, Partnership Agreement, June 29, 1982; Granger Interview.

101. Connor Interview, Part I. See also James T. Areddy, "Price Waterhouse Chooses Connor as Its Chairman," *The Wall Street Journal*, September 16, 1988, 1.

102. See generally, *Global Strategy*; Connor Interview, Part II.

103. Tarantino Interview. See also O'Malley, Daley, Tarantino interview.

CHAPTER 8

1. Biographical Information [Shaun O'Malley], Price Waterhouse Public Relations Department; Lee Berton, "Price Waterhouse Picks Shaun O'Malley as Chairman, Surprising Many Partners," *The Wall Street Journal*, November 30, 1987, 26.

2. Interview, Dominic A. Tarantino (December 18, 1989).

3. Shaun F. O'Malley, Letter to Partners, February 19, 1988; Lee Berton, "'Gearing Up' to Run Price Waterhouse, Chairman-Elect Revamps Management," *The Wall Street Journal*, March 16, 1988.

4. Ibid.

5. Price Waterhouse, The Vision: General Information (November 21, 1991), 1. The authors are grateful to Gary R. Pell for providing this and other materials. Interview, Gary R. Pell (March 3, 1992).

6. O'Malley, Letter to Partners, February 19, 1988; Pell Interview. See also Interview, Peter J. Hart (November 29, 1989); Tarantino Interview.

7. Tarantino Interview.

8. Lee Berton, "Talk of Mergers Sweeps Through Accounting Field," *The Wall Street Journal*, June 19, 1989, A5A; "Arthur Andersen, Price Waterhouse Say They're in Formal Discussions on Merger," ibid., July 7, 1989, A3.

9. Shaun F. O'Malley, James E. Daley, and Dominic A. Tarantino, Interview (December 18, 1989). See also "Arthur Andersen, Price Waterhouse Extend Discussions," *The Wall Street Journal*, September 6, 1989; Alison Leigh Cowan, "Slow Talks by Andersen, Waterhouse," *New York Times*, September 5, 1989, D1, D6; Lee Berton, "Andersen-Price Merger May Be Scuttled by Differences over Retirement Funding," *The Wall Street Journal*, September 25, 1989, 36; "Andersen and Price Waterhouse Scrap Merger Talks Due to Incompatibilities," ibid., September 27, 1989.

10. O'Malley, Tarantino, Daley Interview.

11. Shaun F. O'Malley, "Closing Remarks," Annual Partners' Meeting, October 19–20, 1989; Shaun F. O'Malley, "Price Waterhouse Strategy: Sharpening Our Competitive Focus: A Commitment to Our Clients and Each Other," Annual Partners' Meeting, September 27–28, 1988; Pell Interview. As part of its effort to develop a commanding position in markets it chose to enter, Price Waterhouse merged with two companies in the information technology field in 1989. One was Errico Technologies, an information technology firm, and the

other was Actron Information Data Systems, a leading public utilities information services company.

12. Price Waterhouse, 1990 Retired Partners' Meeting, October 22–23, 1990, speech of Shaun O'Malley, 120–131, Office of the Firm Secretary, New York.

13. Ibid.

ACKNOWLEDGMENTS

Many people helped to turn the idea of a Price Waterhouse centennial history into a successful reality. The PW History Advisory Committee, chaired by Robert G. Nichols and composed of Albert H. Cohen, Burnell H. DeVos, Jr., Richard D. Fitzgerald, Roger G. Marcellin, and Harvard Business School professor Richard H.K. Vietor, played a key role. Over many days, and with good humor and courtesy, they helped to correct errors of fact and interpretation and to guide the book toward its completion. Others within PW who made valuable comments on the manuscript were James M. Coriston, James E. Daley, Eugene I. Krieger, Thomas M. McDonald, Shaun F. O'Malley, Deborah E. Rothschild, Ulric R. Sullivan, Dominic A. Tarantino, Frederick M. Werblow, and Allen I. Young.

Still others assisted by volunteering to be interviewed, furnishing historical materials in their possession, and providing leads to additional sources. Price Waterhouse partners gave their wholehearted backing to this project and never hesitated in their willingness to have the firm's history told by outsiders. Each of these current and retired partners gave generously of their time and support: Walter M. Baird, Herman W. Bevis, Thomas O. Beyer, John C. Biegler, Sheridan C. Biggs, Jr., Hugh M. Campbell, Michael Coates, Albert H. Cohen, Joseph E. Connor, Alphonsus T. Cummins, Maurice J. Dahlem, James E. Daley, Burnell H. DeVos, Jr., Francis C. Dykeman, Roscoe L. Egger, Jr., Robert E. Field, Richard D. Fitzgerald, Paul B. Goodstat, Peter Granger, Henry Gunders, Robert Hampton III, Peter J. Hart, Henry P. Hill, John B. Inglis, Benjamin F. Jackson, Lewis J. Krulwich, Mark D. Larkin,

Raymond C. Lauver, Brendan J. Meagher, William C. Miller, John B. O'Hara, Shaun F. O'Malley, Wyman G. Patten, Gary R. Pell, Thomas L. Raleigh, Jr., Weston Rankin, William A. Schan, Kenton J. Sicchitano, Dominic A. Tarantino, A. Carl Tietjen, Arthur B. Toan, Jr., George C. Watt, J. Robert White, John W. Zick, Russell A. Zimmermann. Partners Olaf M. Falkenhagen, Donald F. Markstein, and Eldon Olson also generously provided documents and reference material. In addition, the law firm of Cravath, Swaine & Moore allowed access to historical files on PW, a longtime client, and two of its partners, Steward R. Bross and John R. Hupper, agreed to be interviewed about the 1970s.

Others within Price Waterhouse assisted in the research process. Eleanor C. Mertsen, Secretary to the Firm, and Kathleen C. Gaffney, Isabel M. Nolan, and Judith H. Arnold from her staff provided a friendly working environment and ready access to official records. James R. Alexander, of the New York practice office Records Center, supplied numerous documents and moral support. Arden Eidell of the National Office Communications Department also gave steady encouragement. Harold Haddock, Jr. and his staff at the National Administrative Center in Tampa provided useful information for charts and exhibits. Marybeth Capron in National Human Resources quickly furnished data on firm personnel. Linda Terrasi and Nick Ullo of the Continuing Education Art Group, Michele Morgan of the Los Angeles office Entertainment Group, and Ann Paterra, of National Office Public Relations, all cheerfully helped with photographs. The librarians at the National Information Center, headed by Masha Zipper, were always unfailingly courteous and helpful. John Barrett allowed access to the U.K. firm archives and gave liberally of his time to help this project.

The manuscript was very much improved as a result of comments by outside readers, including Paul J. Miranti, Jr., Kenneth J. Lipartito, and Edgar Jones as well as two anonymous reviewers. Editors Carol Franco and Natalie Greenberg expertly shepherded the manuscript through the editorial and production processes at Harvard Business School Press.

Although much of the research involved sources proprietary to Price Waterhouse, extensive information about the firm and the accounting profession exists in the public record. The vast resources of the New York and Boston public libraries and the libraries of Harvard University proved invaluable. The AICPA's research library in New York under the direction of Karen A. Neloms also furnished data and photographs more specific to the accounting profession. The helpfulness of the librarians and staff of these institutions made the research process flow smoothly.

The Winthrop Group contributed to the project in many important ways. Davis Dyer served as general editor of the manuscript upon the departure of David Grayson Allen, and provided invaluable intellectual inspiration, practical counsel, and editorial advice. George D. Smith developed and organized the project and supplied critical information and assistance throughout its latter stages. Bettye H. Pruitt made helpful suggestions about particular points. Linda Edgerly carefully identified the research material available in PW's National Office and National Information Center. Paul Barnhill, Daniel Jacoby, Bill Story, and Mary Curry assisted with research and helped prepare the exhibits. Susan Surapine, Pamela Bracken, and Linda Tillman were speedy and accurate transcribers.

Finally, Ms. McDermott wishes to thank her husband, F. William Nigreen, whose cheerful support and steady encouragement made working on this long project a pleasure.

INDEX